Rebecca Harding Davis
and American Realism

Rebecca Harding Davis and American Realism

Sharon M. Harris

upp

University of Pennsylvania Press

Philadelphia

Library of Congress Cataloging-in-Publication Data

Harris, Sharon M.
   Rebecca Harding Davis and American realism / Sharon M. Harris.
     p.   cm.
   Includes bibliographical references and index.
   ISBN 0-8122-3080-9
    1. Davis, Rebecca Harding, 1831-1910—Criticism and interpretation.   2. Women and
literature—United States—History—19th century.   3. Realism in literature.   I. Title.
PS1517.Z5H37   1991
813′.4—dc20   91-7806
                                                    CIP

Some women write "because there is in them a message to be given, and they cannot die until they have spoken it. . . . distinctively American portraits and landscapes are the work of woman."

—Rebecca Harding Davis,
"Women in Literature" (1891)

[Davis] succeeds in giving a truer impression of American conditions than any writer we know except Mr. Howells, while there is a vast difference between his delicately illuminated preparations of our social absurdities and Mrs. Davis's grim and powerful etchings. Somehow she contrives to get the American atmosphere, its vague excitement, its strife of effort, its varying possibilities.

—The Nation (1878)

Contents

Acknowledgments

I WOULD LIKE TO THANK those institutions that so generously made available to me manuscripts and papers in their collections relating to Rebecca Harding Davis: Richard Harding Davis Collection (#6109), Clifton Waller Barrett Library, Manuscripts Division, Special Collections Department, University of Virginia Library; Overbury Collection, Barnard College Library; James Fraser Gluck and Charles Wells Moulton Collections, Buffalo and Erie County Public Library; Rare Books and Manuscripts Library, by courtesy of the Trustees of the Boston Public Library; The Connecticut Historical Society; Paul R. Reynolds Collection, General Manuscripts Collection, Theodore F. Wolfe Collection, Harper Bros. Collection, Rare Book and Manuscript Library, Columbia University; St. James Episcopal Church Papers, Manuscript Department, William R. Perkins Library, Duke University; The Huntington Library, San Marino, California; the Houghton Library, Harvard University; James R. Gilmore Collection, Ms. 37, Special Collections, Milton S. Eisenhower Library, The Johns Hopkins University; Alfred W. Anthony Collection, Century Company Records, William Conant Church Papers, and Josiah Gilbert Holland Papers, Rare Book and Manuscripts Division, The New York Public Library, Astor, Lenox and Tilden Foundations; Henry W. and Albert A. Berg Collection, The New York Public Library, Astor, Lenox and Tilden Foundations; The Pierpont Morgan Library, New York, MA 1950; Mary Mapes Dodge, St. Nicholas Correspondence, Donald and Robert M. Dodge Collection of Mary Mapes Dodge, and Wilkinson Collection of Mary Mapes Dodge published with permission of Princeton University Library; Special Collections and Manuscripts, The University of Iowa Libraries; Horace Howard Furness Memorial Library, Special Collections, Van Pelt Library, University of Pennsylvania; Archibald W. Campbell Papers, West Virginia and Regional History Collection, West Virginia University Libraries. References to quotes drawn from specific manuscripts are further acknowledged in the "Notes" to this book. Portions of Sharon M. Harris's article, "Rebecca Harding Davis: From Romanticism to Realism," are reprinted by permission of McFarland & Company, Inc., Publishers, Jefferson,

N.C., from Vol. 21, no. 2 of *American Literary Realism 1870–1910* © Mc-Farland & Company, Inc.

As with all scholars who begin a serious study of Davis, I am indebted to the early, meticulous work of Helen Woodward Shaeffer, whose unpublished dissertation (University of Pennsylvania, 1947) remains a significant source. As noted in the "Introduction," I am also indebted to Tillie Olsen's early work. Further, I wish to thank several scholars whose own pioneering work in American women's literature has made possible a reassessment of Davis's body of work—most notably, Nina Baym, Josephine Donovan, Judith Fetterley, and Jane Tompkins. My own contributions to Davis scholarship could not have been completed without the generous assistance of the numerous institutions which house Davis's materials. Specific data on collections are identified in the notes.

On a more personal level, I wish to thank several friends and colleagues who have generously supported my work for several years: Laverne Kawamoto, whose heartening encouragement has been there from the beginning; Janet Polk, whose support and abiding love of American literature is a continuing joy to me; Pat Mallory, Dean Penttila, Karen Kaivola, and Malcolm Griffith, all of whom reminded me of the healthfulness of laughter and relaxation during some difficult years—and still; Michael Hollister and Allan Emery, whose early encouragement was impetus to a career in academics; Harold Simonson, Ross Posnock, and William Streitberger, whose direction during my doctoral education was generous and challenging and acts as a continuing model; and my colleagues and friends Bill Hendricks, Don Kraemer, and Lyn Tribble, whose astute comments on the introductory portion of the manuscript were instrumental in helping me rethink this portion of the text (they are, of course, exempt from any responsibility for its content). Last, but most of all, I wish to thank the members of my family for their love and support, with special thanks to Kathleen Nicole Harris and James Joseph Harris—just for being who you are; I dearly love you.

Notes on the Text

THE VAST MAJORITY of Davis's works (eleven novels, sixteen serialized novels, more than 260 short stories and fifty essays, and an autobiography) are available only in periodical collections or in the rare book collections of university libraries. Davis was also a prolific letter writer. For this study I have read all of her letters that I have been able to locate; but again, these items are uncollected and, although the largest holding is at the University of Virginia, they are dispersed at more than twenty-five institutions. Therefore, to give scholars access to Davis's own words whenever possible rather than only to my interpretation of them I have quoted liberally from Davis's correspondence. In addition, and equally important, I have included quotations from Davis's correspondence wherever appropriate so the reader may garner a better sense of Davis's voice and personality. Emendations have been made only in the case of accidentals, such as missing closure to a quotation or end punctuation (and then only a period has been supplied without notation). Davis was adamant about the art of spelling, and I have honored her choices in this respect.

The more difficult aspect of working with Davis's correspondence evolved out of her failure to date most of her letters. After studying several hundred letters, I was able to discern three phases of Davis's penmanship: a tight, neat, highly legible handwriting of the 1860s; a looser, less controlled script of the late 1860s through the early 1880s; and a final and much more difficult hand to decipher that was the result of age and of decreasing eyesight. This last style tended to occur only from the late 1880s or early 1890s until her death. These phases have helped me to "date" some of Davis's letters, but to a large extent the process depends upon being able to place them in the context of her life and literature. I have carefully acknowledged in the notes accompanying this text any assumptions about dates which I have made. Thus, if I can be sure of a date because of a specific contextual reference, I have enclosed that date in brackets (e.g., "January 4, [1892]"); if I am relatively sure about a date but unable to verify it with complete accuracy, I have noted it as "circa" (e.g., "January 4, c. 1892"); if I have been unable to accurately date or assume a date for a letter, I note it simply as "undated" or with the appropriate detail from the letter that will make it in some way identifiable to other scholars wishing to locate the original (e.g., "dated only 'Thursday morning' ").

Rebecca Blaine Harding Davis: A Chronology

1831	Born June 24 in Washington, Pennsylvania; eldest daughter of Rachel Leet Wilson and Richard W. Harding. Within a few weeks, taken home to Big Spring, Alabama.
c. 1836	Harding family settles in Wheeling, Virginia.
1845–48	Attends Washington Female Seminary; graduates valedictorian.
late 1850s	Apprenticeship on Wheeling *Intelligencer*.
1861	"Life in the Iron Mills" published in *Atlantic Monthly*, to national acclaim; begins correspondence with Nathaniel Hawthorne; begins regular contributions to *Peterson's Magazine*.
1860s	Regular contributor to *Atlantic Monthly*, publishing numerous innovative short stories focusing on the consequences of industrial capitalism and the Civil War.
1862	First novel, *Margret Howth*, is published; travels to Boston (where she meets Hawthorne, Emerson, the Alcotts, the Fieldses), New York, Baltimore, and Philadelphia (to see L. Clarke Davis); also publishes second novel, *David Gaunt*.
1863	On March 5 marries L. Clarke Davis; the newlyweds move in with Clarke's sister, Carrie Cooper, at 1429 Girard Avenue, Philadelphia.
1863–64	Illness leads family to insist she adhere to a "rest cure," probably administered by Dr. S. Weir Mitchell.

1864   Father dies March 20. On April 18, gives birth to first child, Richard Harding Davis; in the fall, the Davises move to their first home, a rented row house at 1817 North Twelfth Street.

1866   Birth of second son, Charles Belmont Davis, on January 24; in the fall, the Davises move to 1816 North Camac Street, another rented row house.

1867   Publishes *Waiting for the Verdict*, her seminal study of the Civil War; becomes a contributing editor for the *New York Daily Tribune*.

1867–68   Dropped by the *Atlantic Monthly* as a regular contributor for serializing *Waiting* in the *Galaxy*. Begins writing for numerous other literary periodicals.

1868   Publishes *Dallas Galbraith*; with publication of " 'In the Market,' " beings to focus her writings on woman-centered issues.

1870   The Davises purchase their first home, at 230 South Twenty-first Street; Ralph Waldo Emerson is one of their first guests.

1871   Begins publishing children's literature, becoming a major contributor to *Youth's Companion*.

1872   Last child and only daughter, Nora, is born.

1874   Publishes *John Andross*, a political novel on the Tweed Ring.

1876   Publishes *Kitty's Choice*.

1878   Publishes *A Law Unto Herself*.

1879 to
early 1880s   "Retires" for a period of years, severely reducing her literary output; but travels through the South.

1882   Begins publishing in *The Independent*, a New York weekly.

1884   Mother dies.

1887   *Natasqua* published in book form; travels again through the South.

1889   In dispute over First Amendment issue, resigns position with the *New York Daily Tribune*; begins regular contributor status with *The Independent*, a position she retains until her death.

1892   Publishes *Kent Hampden*; selected short stories are collected in *Silhouettes of American Life*.

1893   Ends thirty-two-year association with *Peterson's*.

1895   With Nora, takes first trip to Europe.

1896   Publishes *Doctor Warrick's Daughters*.

1897   Publishes *Frances Waldeaux*, her last novel.

1904   Publishes autobiography, *Bits of Gossip*; Clarke dies on December 14.

1906   Travels with Nora to Europe.

1910   Dies on September 29.

Introduction

I. The Need for a Reassessment

In April 1862, Emily Dickinson wrote to her sister-in-law, Susan Gilbert Dickinson, "Will Sue please lend Emily 'Life in the Iron Mills'—and accept Blossom."[1] Dickinson's acquaintance with "Life in the Iron Mills" and her eagerness to read or possibly reread the short story reflects the literary impact of Rebecca Harding Davis's first major publication. Immediately recognized as a startlingly experimental story, "Life" was published as the second article in the April 1861 issue of the *Atlantic Monthly*. The remarkable depth and originality of vision in this short story has garnered it a place as one of the pioneering documents in American literature's transition from romanticism to realism, and the naturalistic plot leading to Hugh Wolfe's death challenges our traditional conceptions about the influences behind the movement from realism to naturalism in the United States. None of the standard studies of these genres—Charles Child Walcutt's *American Literary Naturalism, A Divided Stream* (1956), Lars Ahnebrink's *The Beginnings of Naturalism in American Fiction* (1961), Warner Berthoff's *The Ferment of Realism* (1965), and Donald Pizer's *Realism and Naturalism in Nineteenth-Century American Literature* (rev. 1984)—include analyses of Davis's fiction. Nor have recent studies of women's literary traditions—Josephine Donovan's *New England Local Colorists: A Women's Tradition* (1983), Judith Fetterley's *Provisions: A Reader from Nineteenth-Century American Women* (1985), and Sandra M. Gilbert and Susan Gubar's *Norton Anthology of Literature by Women* (1985)—afforded Davis more than passing commentary.

Two factors in Davis's personal life forever changed her vision of what the function and form of literature should be: first, being raised in a rapidly growing mill town, and second, experiencing at first hand the brutal realities of war. Out of these experiences she shaped her distinctive literature of the mid- to late-nineteenth century. My purpose in presenting this critical reassessment of Davis, then, is to place her in the context of the literary movements of that period, to challenge traditional assumptions about the rise of realism that exclude women's contributions, and to delineate Davis's artistic abilities and pivotal role in the development of American realism and naturalism.

When Perry Miller sought to reestablish Jonathan Edwards as a noteworthy literary figure, he observed that in large part scholars had failed to acknowledge Edwards because they believed he was "an anachronism," thereby relegating Edwards, "through failure of comprehension, even further into an unusable past."[2] There has been a similar "failure of comprehension" in the analysis of Davis's work and of her place in American literary history. This failure has been abetted in large part by the misattribution to Davis of a highly conservative tract concerning a woman's role in society; that tract was entitled *Pro Aris et Focis*. The confusion arose because both the author of *Pro Aris et Focis* and Davis had anonymously published books entitled *Waiting for the Verdict*. At the time *Pro Aris* appeared, Davis was contributing editor of the *New York Daily Tribune*, and the following disclaimer was immediately printed:

> A recent work entitled "*Pro Aris et Focis*, by the author of *Waiting for the Verdict*," has been absurdly attributed to Mrs. Rebecca Harding Davis. That admirable novelist and magazine writer had no more to do with it than she had with the Hindoo Vedas or the books of Confucius; and not wishing to wear unearned honors she desires to have the fact known.[3]

Unfortunately, the misattribution resurfaced in the twentieth century, beginning apparently in 1933 when Fairfax Downey lauded Davis's literary talents and contributions in an essay entitled "Portrait of a Pioneer" but attributed *Pro Aris* to her. In a 1947 dissertation that remains unpublished but has been a source for several Davis scholars, Helen Woodward Shaeffer erroneously included *Pro Aris* as part of the Davis bibliography, as did Gerald Langford, who had used Shaeffer's dissertation as a source for his 1961 biography of Davis and her son, Richard Harding Davis. Although Philip Eppard attempted to correct the error in 1975, Tillie Olsen unfortunately perpetuated the by-then entrenched misattribution in her interpretative bibliography that accompanied the Feminist Press's reissue of "Life." Olsen used both Shaeffer's and Langford's biographies as sources. The details of my own efforts to recall Philip Eppard's work and to correct this error are briefly reiterated here because of the tenacity of this bibliographical myth.[4] As this present study of Davis's literature will reveal, a major intent of her

realistic fiction and her nonfiction essays was to challenge precisely the sex-
ist rhetoric and ideas perpetuated in *Pro Aris*.

No one confronts Davis's work without immediately becoming aware
of a great indebtedness to Tillie Olsen for her reclamation of Davis's seminal study of the lives of iron-mill workers in mid-nineteenth century
America. That my own view of Davis's work diverges from Olsen's in several instances in no way diminishes that debt, which I wholeheartedly acknowledge. Where I do differ with Olsen is in the view of Davis as "Poor
Rebecca." Olsen's biographical reading of Davis's literature casts the nineteenth-century author into the role of a reclusive, discouraged artist whose
talent quickly faded. My emphases upon placing Davis in the context of
American literary history and upon "flushing out" several biographical details seek to challenge those perceptions. I do not see Davis as reclusive, I
certainly do not see her talents as fading after "Life in the Iron Mills," and
I do not agree with Olsen's claim that, "*Without intention*, [Davis] was a
social historian" (emphasis added). That intent was clearly set forth from
her earliest writings, and her creation of a literary theory of the commonplace in the practice of her craft incorporated a well-developed sociohis-
torical perspective, as this study will detail.

Thus I have found myself in the rather paradoxical position of more
fully establishing Davis's literary merit at the same time as I am reassessing
the embryonic critical commentary on her literature. But it is a necessary
reevaluation if Davis's contributions to literary theory and history are to be
understood. As serious as the perpetuation of the misattribution of *Pro Aris*
has been the failure on the part of some critics to return to the primary
sources. A few scholars—most notably, Jean Pfaelzer and James C. Austin—have begun the process. In extending it, I hope to encourage a flood
of newcomers to Davis's body of work, for there is much yet to be done.

From her first major publication, Davis sought to challenge the tenets
of romanticism by actualizing her theory of the commonplace. It is that
theory, as expressed in her literature and letters, that deserves special recognition in American literary history.[5] Too often we forget how flexible, in
some ways, the American canon has been. Only thirty years ago Edwin
Cady argued in his biography of William Dean Howells that Howells's
realistic fiction deserved to be considered as part of "the novels which the
public is gradually rescuing from neglect" and that the best way to do so
was to pay "close attention to Howells's principal writings as the true basis
of his right to fame."[6] I assert the same premise for Davis and in doing so
suggest, as have several other scholars of women's literary traditions, that

the rise of American realism was a much longer, more widely pursued process than traditionally assumed.

Before detailing how this reassessment places Davis in the context of both traditional and "other" realists of the middle to late nineteenth century, it is necessary to note that several misconceptions in addition to the misattribution of *Pro Aris* need to be eradicated. In terms of Davis's life prior to her emergence in the pages of the *Atlantic Monthly*, biographical details have been described repeatedly as sparse and Davis herself has been subject to charges of reclusiveness. The inaccuracies of this description seem to have emerged from Langford's early study. He asserts that because the family records include "no reference to any suitors . . . [or] close friends" Davis "must have seemed to everyone a clear case of the born spinster"![7] In fact, Langford's main source for these years is Davis's retrospective 1904 autobiography; more important, he ascribes some of her characters' ascerbic comments to her instead of to her fiction. As my study reveals throughout, Davis had a wide circle of female and male friends (in and out of the literary profession) with whom she maintained contact throughout her life. While Tillie Olsen carefully acknowledges that she used Langford's study "for biographical fact (not interpretation)," the inferences of her otherwise insightful biographical analysis have unfortunately been repeated by other Davis scholars.[8]

Another and more significant gap in Davis scholarship has been the belief that, like a phoenix, she somehow arose out of the (quite literal) ashes of Wheeling, West Virginia, and into the pages of America's most renowned literary journal of the period. It is a myth that carries a certain appeal, of course; but, as I detail in chapter 1, Davis had carefully apprenticed her literary skills for some time before she ventured to submit her fiction to the *Atlantic Monthly*.

Finally, the assertion that Davis was not a feminist needs an especially detailed response, which this study as a whole will set forth. Specifically, it has been asserted that Davis's focus in her fiction was on men's lives.[9] Several points need to be made in this context. First, Davis did write about men's lives, a fact that in no way negates her position as a feminist. Her concerns for the civil rights and well-being of *all* American citizens was not limited by gender any more than it was by race or ethnicity. Nor was it necessarily her *focus*; a study of her correspondence with her editor during the 1860s reveals that titling her works after a (white) male character was repeatedly James Fields's choice. Many such short stories and novels in fact focus upon a woman and/or a slave (an alignment of the oppressed that

Davis repeatedly made). Second, the condition of women in nineteenth-century America was, to Davis's mind, "a tragedy more real . . . than any other in life." A major shift in perspective came in the 1870s when she turned her attention specifically to women's lives. In her fiction, nonfiction, and autobiography, she suggested many feminist solutions to "Woman's Needs" and, perhaps most significant, forthrightly asserted women's strengths, intelligence, and capabilities. Third, Davis's feminism did have limitations. She is best understood in the tradition of conservative feminism. This tradition included, most notably, Catherine Maria Sedgwick and Harriet Beecher Stowe, who often presented a model of domesticity that characterized women as competent, educated, and self-sufficient but rarely depicted their power outside of the realm of domesticity. Although Davis veered away from the melodrama of some of the early feminists' fiction, extending both the concept of the domestic and the concept of women's capabilities, she was incapable of recognizing the importance of women joining forces in organized groups to demand their rights. She advocated woman's suffrage, but she often demeaned the "New Woman." The complexities of her stances are immense and they are explored at length throughout this reassessment.

In understanding Davis as a pioneer realist in conjunction with her significant demands for changes in women's lives, one must also discuss her place in the literary transition from romanticism to realism. That transition, of course, includes not only those two labels but other designations such as sentimentalism, local color, domestic feminism, documentary realism, naturalism, and undoubtedly many others. My perspective is that to insist that a writer fit only one of these labels, even within one work, is to limit our assessment of that author's work from the beginning and to limit our understanding of the development of realism itself. Certainly our assessment of Walt Whitman and Emily Dickinson, writers once relegated almost solely to the rubric of romantics, has been enhanced by a recognition that they are, in fact, transitional figures themselves. It is even more limiting to insist upon a single classification when a writer—such as Davis or Henry James or Elizabeth Stuart Phelps or Herman Melville—has a body of work spanning several decades.

Terminology, legitimately or not, also continues to dictate our assessments of a writer's work.[10] "Local colorist," for example, has far too often been a designation that belittles women's contributions to realism.[11] While local colorists may indeed have "forged the tradition of realism,"[12] so, too, did some sentimentalists (most notably Harriet Beecher Stowe). Further,

Alan Trachtenberg has noted that the term *realism*, even as late as the 1880s, designated "not so much a single consistent movement as a tendency among some painters and writers to depict contemporary life without moralistic condescension."[13] The best writers among the early realists did not employ "moralistic *condescension*," although they certainly had a moral perspective. While William Dean Howells has long been credited with the origins of American realism, in truth several writers of fiction and nonfiction (including Catherine Maria Sedgwick, Frederick Douglass, Davis, and many others) had been contributing to the development of this movement for more than thirty years before Hamlin Garland and William Dean Howells—and later Frank Norris, Stephen Crane, Kate Chopin, Jacob A. Riis, Edith Wharton, and Sarah Orne Jewett—extended these early literary techniques. My inclusion in the second list of several authors whom we typically designate as naturalists is intentional, since the literary and theoretical lines between realism and naturalism have also become less rather than more distinct in recent years. Thus we can have a collection of essays on American realism introduced, albeit with an acknowledgment of the disparity, by an analysis of Stephen Crane's *The Red Badge of Courage*, once a touchstone of American naturalism, and concluded with an essay asserting that *The House of Mirth* "is primarily a romance of identity."[14]

II. Reconceptualizing American Realism

Where, then, does Davis's canon fit in this mélange of labels? Perhaps it is best, in the limited space of an introduction, to identify how she is similar and dissimilar to certain other writers who have been, nominally at least, designated under one or more of these traditional headings. I do so with the cautionary note that this is not to encourage the separation of these literary styles but to demonstrate how many links there are between them, a process that is continued throughout the text. This study as a whole will explicitly align aspects of Davis's fiction with techniques and theories of various writers and movements during her fifty-year literary career (1859–1909).

Davis was a realist in that she insisted upon reporting quotidian American life, abandoning the "rose-tinted" and homogeneous perspective of that life and rendering her material so as to give her readers an illusion of actual experience; and further, she rejected many aspects of romanticism—characterizations that rely upon hero-villain or master-victim dichotomies, nature's organic processes as analogous to human experience, and the assertion of harmony between human and nature, a sublime transcendence into sacred selfhood, and the use of fantastic and occasionally melodramatic events in rendering those ideals in fiction. But, as Eric Sundquist has observed, "romance remained a persistent force in American realism" well into the late nineteenth century.[15] Davis synthesized many of these styles, most often using the techniques of both romanticism and sentimentalism (as traditionally defined) to draw readers into stories wherein the realities of quotidian life were of primary significance; and she often insisted upon a moral perspective, although not one defined by a particular religion. Certainly her own work was informed by earlier romantic, realistic, and sentimental styles. Davis was acutely interested in historical locales and in how the ideologies of the past informed the present, ideas that also interested writers as diverse as Catherine Maria Sedgwick and Nathaniel Hawthorne, whose literary explorations of these issues were undoubtedly influential to varying extents in Davis's own belief that to study American history and, as often necessary, to expose the myths of the past were requisite preliminary stages if one was concerned with artistically recording the "accurate history" of the present. In addition, the concerns of sentimentalists, such as Harriet Beecher Stowe, for social reform are at the heart of Davis's artistic vision, as it was for William Dean Howells. Unlike the sentimentalists, however, she did not always envision her women characters as heroines; even the women in her fiction who might be defined, however cautiously, as "heroines" are realistically characterized through both their "good" and their "bad" traits. She adamantly adhered to what has been traditionally deemed a sentimentalists' dictum: that the characterization of a "true woman" depended upon the trait of frugality. It was a philosophy that had been instilled in Davis from her earliest years through her mother's tales of early Southern life, and it is a trait that was incorporated into the fiction of most early women realists as well. Although she did not advocate a domestic life for her strongest female characters, she did believe that marriage and a home life were ideals; however, she realistically portrayed the inequities of marriage and especially the laws enforcing those inequities. She did not adhere to the utopian ideals of Stowe or Elizabeth Stuart Phelps or, later, of Edward Bellamy and Charlotte Perkins Gilman; but she did value the rural over the urban life—and thus was in the forefront of detailing the consequences of industrialization upon the American landscape.

Davis's work aligns itself best with that of writers we typically term regional realists (although I also use this term with caution since it is often employed not to celebrate but to denigrate women writers' realism; certainly Norris's New York and California settings, Crane's Civil War locales, and Dreiser's Chicago and New York settings also constituted "regionalism"). Davis is aligned with these regional authors—most notably from Sedgwick to Stowe and Cooke to Jewett and Freeman—through her attention to the realistic creation of a literature of place, in the richness of her descriptions and her use of symbolism indigenous to the region, and in the almost anthropological study of its people. This is especially true of Davis's New Jersey "wrackers" stories of the 1860s and 1870s. She distinguishes herself from the New England tradition with which we are most familiar by avoiding certain elements inherent in that tradition as it moves from romanticism to realism: nowhere in Davis, for instance, does one find the almost requisite "worship tableaux" that are to be found in Stowe, Sylvester Judd, and others;[16] what one does find in Davis that is absent in most of the regional realists of her era is an astute attention to urban settings and the consequences of the rise of industrialization. If she was influenced by several early writers (perhaps Sedgwick and certainly Stowe, Hawthorne, and Cooke, among others), she was also a highly influential writer, most notably in terms of Howells, Phelps, and probably Jewett, who faithfully read the *Atlantic Monthly* during the 1860s, when Davis published some of her most radical fiction.[17]

Davis's most significant contribution to American literary history, however, was her pioneering creation of naturalistic plots of decline in several of her early works and her contributions as a political novelist and essayist. Like later French and American naturalists, she depicted the brute-self as determined by the natural forces of heredity and environment and as compulsively instinctual (especially in terms of a comprehensive "hunger"), and subject to social and economic forces (especially those of class). She did not explore brutal sexual desires as explicitly as later naturalists such as Émile Zola and Frank Norris, but she did address the issue of prostitution as early as 1863. She also depicted the indifference of nature toward the individual and identified the naturalistic plot of decline as tragic in the sense of an individual's losing battle against circumstance. Although she deftly used the techniques of deterministic fiction for many years, she always yielded to the possibility of reform. Davis's contributions as a political novelist and essayist spanned her lifetime. Beginning with numerous short stories and essays and the novel *Margret Howth*, which discussed the abuse of workers by industrial capitalists, Davis also exposed the economic and political realities of the Civil War and the gulf between freeing slaves and making them an integral part of American life. After 1870, Davis turned her attention to such contemporary political issues as the Tweed Ring (*John Andross*, 1874), the abuse of mental patients in state institutions (*Put Out of the Way*, 1870), and other topical issues that she explored in the pages of the *New York Daily Tribune* and *The Independent*. A significant aspect of Davis's contributions in this genre is that she addressed these controversial issues while they were at the forefront of American thought rather than from hindsight. The "story of to-day" remained central to her literary voice throughout her life.

Most influential, however, was Davis's literary theory of the commonplace as practiced and defined in her fiction. In "Life in the Iron Mills," Davis found new avenues for her voice of social protest and for her insistence upon a literary rendering of the commonplace. Langford has asserted that Davis wrote "out of no literary theory but out of compassion."[18] Later Davis scholars have, for the most part, accepted this evaluation. However, theory and compassion need not be at odds,[19] nor were they for Davis. As this study will reveal, Davis had a well-developed literary theory of the "commonplace" nearly two decades before Howells shaped his own version of the concept; in her theory, Davis also exposed the quotidian realities of life and challenged contemporary literary modes and values.

Early twentieth-century critics, such as Fairfax Downey, Arthur H. Quinn, and Van Wyck Brooks, noted that Davis's realism as it was employed to urge the American public's exploration of "vulgar" American life was, as Brooks termed it, "to become a familiar note with the growth of American realism from the days of Howells and his contemporaries to the days of Dreiser, together with the analytical approach that supplanted the kind of heroic feeling one found in the earlier authors from Cooper to Whitman."[20] In spite of this, Brooks failed to recognize that this acknowledgment thus requires a reconsideration of the entire period of American realism/naturalism. Late-nineteenth-century American critics and authors were consciously striving to establish a national literature (a process already begun, of course, in the eighteenth century). Davis herself was well aware of these issues, with which we still struggle today. Late in her career, Davis published "The Temple of Fame," an article in which she dissected this process. The numerous newspaper and magazine polls to determine which writers were most popular had reached the height of incongruity with the establishment of a "Temple of Fame" for Americans who

a University of New York committee deemed worthy of national reverence. The system failed to distinguish between "fame" and "honor," Davis
asserted, noting that "Zola, for instance, has been pounding at the door of
the Academy for years in vain" though "the common people of all Europe
know him." She was aware that "fame" was transitory, and her acknowledgment of that reality is particularly ironic today in terms of her own
literary fate. But neglect is always rectifiable; we need not leave ourselves
ignorant of our own literary history. As one step in the process, it is time
to afford Davis the honor due her.

That honor is due not only for the quality of her fiction and the keen
insights of her essays on contemporary issues but, as noted above, for
Davis's early and far-reaching contributions to the theory of the commonplace, which is at the core of all facets of literary realism and which dates
back at least to Caroline Kirkland, who also used the term "commonplace"
and was, as early as the 1830s, concerned with mimetic fiction and capitalist
exploitation.[21] If we have forgotten Davis's contributions today, she was
not unrecognized in her own time. Even when younger critics were unaware of her earliest works in the field, her later fiction and commentaries
were well known. From 1861 until her death in 1910, every year except four
saw articles by Davis published in major American literary periodicals. Her
shorter works appeared in more than twenty-five American journals, and
she was known by all of the most influential editors of the era. Every major
American realist and naturalist of the nineteenth century (as we traditionally designate them)—Norris, Crane, Garland, Howells, Wharton, Chopin, Riis, Harold Frederic, James—published alongside Davis in these
periodicals. So, too, did Elizabeth Stuart Phelps, Rose Terry Cooke,
J. W. DeForest, Mary Wilkins Freeman, Louisa May Alcott, Kate Field,
Sarah Orne Jewett, and many other significant contributors to the evolving
literary styles.

Certainly Howells, as much as any other American realist, was influenced by Davis. He was assistant editor of the *Atlantic Monthly* in the late
1860s when Davis gained national recognition for her innovative fiction
and was publishing in that journal some of her finest realistic studies,
which detailed her theory of the commonplace. More important, every major point raised by Howells in his theoretical tract *Criticism and Fiction*
(1891) and by Garland in *Crumbling Idols* (1894) was shared by Davis. However, because she, like the majority of early nineteenth-century women realists, explicated the premises of her theory in her fiction rather than by
writing a separate theoretical tract, her contributions to the development

of these concepts have been virtually ignored by scholars. She anticipated Howells's insistence upon morality (on a "spiritual principle") in art that recognized the equality of all classes. She also anticipated his criteria that any work of the imagination be accurate in its representation of the impulses and principles that actually shape human existence, including the use of dialect and vernacular. Davis moved beyond Howells, albeit before him, by not limiting her theory to "the more smiling aspects of life"; whereas Howells criticized Norris's naturalistic novel *McTeague* (1899) as "not true, because it leaves out beauty," Davis understood that not all lives include beauty, or that when they do it may be a "strange beauty" unacknowledged by traditional definitions, thus new art forms must realistically convey such lives.[22] Whereas Howells rejected the need to study the past, Garland followed Davis's lead in acknowledging that we need to understand the past in order to understand the present and the future.

In her fiction, Davis anticipated Garland on several other theoretical points: a rejection of "provincialism" that depended upon European literary models, the need to "decentralize" the nation's literary perspective from Boston and New York to other regional influences, and an advocacy of the "border-life" of the West as a precursor of what Garland called the "mighty rush toward civilization."[23] While Davis embraced in her theory of the commonplace what Garland would later term "veritism," she did not adhere to the evolutionary idealism that Garland admired, especially in terms of his belief that, in the future, fiction would be able to celebrate a world in which all aspects of privilege between individuals had been abolished.[24] Perhaps because she had lived a border-life herself during the brutalizing years of Civil War, she was not as celebratory about the future as Garland. Her purpose in developing a fiction of the commonplace was to expose the harsh realities of life and to demand change: change that would require hard work and confrontation with those realities. Certainly Garland also believed that fiction would be instrumental in the evolution he foresaw. Perhaps the greatest distinction between the two realists was that Garland believed the future *would* be democratized while Davis asserted that it *could* be. There is an abiding despair in her fiction of the 1860s which, despite the reformer's inherent optimism, is never fully eradicated. When Garland proferred his vision of the future in 1894, Davis had already confronted such challenges for more than thirty years—and relatively little had changed since she had published "Life in the Iron Mills."

Davis also anticipated Garland's adherence to Impressionism, which he defined as "the statement of one's own individual perception of life and nature, guided by devotion to truth."[25] For Garland this included a complete but momentary "concept of the sense of sight" that was rendered through "the use of 'raw' colors . . . nature's colors,—red, blue, and yellow; and [the artist] places them fearlessly on the canvas side by side, leaving the eye to mix them, as in nature" (100–101). This technique had been used by Davis in her realistic novels of the early 1860s (see, for instance, *Margret Howth, David Gaunt*, and *Waiting for the Verdict*). But Garland, and later Jewett, saw the realist as "really an optimist, a dreamer" (43). The latter was a term that Davis adamantly rejected for the realist. Her reformer's optimism relied upon the belief that change could be implemented by rolling up one's sleeves and going down "into the thickest of the fog and mud and foul effluvia,"[26] but mere dreaming, even as part of an artistic endeavor, would never suffice. Where Garland did coincide with Davis's earlier theoretical propositions was in his rejection of romanticism; both authors constitute important transitional figures in this literary shift. Realism, Garland noted, is "segments, not circles; for nothing begins or ends in this world. All is ebb and flow. It is only in the romance that things are finished, rounded out, and smoothed down" (83). His reference to "circles" alludes, of course, to Ralph Waldo Emerson; Davis had challenged the transcendentalists' philosophical position for more than thirty years by the time Garland addressed the issue. (See below and section III for a discussion of Davis's anti-transcendentalist perspective.)

Furthermore, Garland's assertion that much of Ibsen's work could be identified as realistic because it was thematically sociological could as easily have been asserted about his compatriot Davis, since her complex theory of the commonplace enveloped her sociopolitical concerns. Yet Davis's theory was first and foremost a challenge to ensconced literary forms, a challenge that recast those forms through realistic and naturalistic techniques while at the same time incorporating a demand for "accurate history" of today and of the past. As an acute analyst of the sociopolitical tensions that had been developing in the nation since the 1830s, Davis recognized that increasingly stratified class distinctions were undermining the very concept of democracy in American life. By focusing on working-class citizens and everyday events, Davis sought to expose industrial capitalism's distortion of human lives as well as its ravagement of nature. She did not uphold the ideal of realists—complete objectivity—in her depiction of commonplace life;[27] in this she was more closely aligned with the sentimentalists. To her mind, the commonplace was as valuable and noteworthy as life in the mansions of Boston; yet her recognition that it was being crushed under the oppression of capitalistic concerns for profit was acutely realistic. Western lives were "rough, democratic, hardy," she asserted,[28] but the wheels of "progress" were rolling over the common folk, making life little more than a "drunken jest." The "smiling aspects of life" alone were only half-truths, for they ignored the hardships and deprivation inherent in many lives and the baser elements in all human beings. If acknowledging these baser elements "assembled the gloom" that oppressed many Americans, as her *Atlantic* editor James T. Fields asserted, it also challenged the accepted definitions of Beauty and of Art itself.

Davis's art form, wrenched from the "story of to-day" as she observed it, was consistent with her subject. Real life included plain women, oppressed workers, drunken and brutish men and women, prostitution, and miscegenation as much as it included the strong, hearty worker. "Vulgar" American life demanded characterizations that reflected the complexities of collective as well as individual human nature. For Davis, the prevalent "saints-and-sinners" juxtaposition of characters in most contemporary fiction denied the diversity of emotions and motives within each person. Like Stowe before her, she recognized that attention to the commonplace also required a realistic rendering of the language of the people; and like Twain, Davis developed the use of multi-dialect vernacular in her fiction, emphasizing such language as a means for more truthfully evoking the psychological effects of environmental conditions on human beings. Thus a character such as Lois Yare (*Margret Howth*) is created: compassionate and loving, but physically crippled by her years of hard labor, uneducated, and socially hindered by prevailing attitudes toward "mixed blood." Lois, like the Korl Woman, bears the "strange beauty" that reflects an inner hunger. With her first published short story in the *Atlantic Monthly*, Davis became a leading figure in the challenge to traditional literary modes that had limited an artist's freedom to capture the realities of quotidian experience. Romanticism, and especially transcendentalism, struck Davis as ultimately passive and outside the mainstream of life. Those theories too easily devolved into escapism, which Davis symbolized through the dream state.[29] Realism, as Davis defined it, demanded a synthesis of theory and application. Most specifically, she rejected passive responses to the commonplace. Pity aided only the observer; compassion armed with activism was Davis's banner.

We can best begin to understand Davis's life-long disdain of transcendentalism if we view its basic tenets from a literary perspective: the resistance to the idea of art as a commodity, the disparagement of "merely popular writing," and a belief that authorship incorporated prophecy.[30] Davis agreed with the first proposition, although she was equally concerned with depicting how art *could* be commodified in order to expose the increasing propensity toward commercialization. It was an issue with which she constantly struggled in her own literary career. So, too, did she agree that "popular" writing was of little or no value; she felt that the present-day "army of cheery story-tellers" was besetting young people with false images of life.[31] But her philosophical separation from transcendentalism occurs at the highly crucial point of the third tenet, for Davis did not envision the author as prophet, in spite of the fact that prophetic-didactic literature was highly marketable in the 1850s and 1860s. Instead, she viewed the author's role as that of a reformer, one who exposes the reality of present-day inequities. As she told her publisher, James T. Fields, she wanted prompt publication of her fiction because of its timeliness—"Am I at work for future ages?"[32] (Her own dilemma, of course, centered on reconciling her artistic ambitions of writing for future ages with her reformer's zeal for writing for the moment of crisis.) She also rejected the Emersonian assertion that it was the author's duty to create a mythology for his or her era.[33] Davis devoted her life to debunking mythologies, of the past and the present, recognizing them as the process of glossing over the harsh realities of life in favor of a romanticized vision.

Davis sought social reform specifically as an artist, and the literary themes and techniques that she developed in conjunction with her theory of the commonplace command a place at the forefront of American literary realism's early stages of development. Not only did she report the realities of everyday life in the language of the working class or the enslaved, but she also understood the implications of a deterministic philosophy in terms of human psychology and motivation. Thus she depicted the drifting masses as representative of human dislocation in an increasingly industrialized society. So, too, did she recognize the irony of that drifting movement, for while it seemed to evoke a kind of freedom, in fact it was a trap as surely as if it were the sullied canary's wire cage in the opening scene of "Life." Speculation and greed, encouraged by the seemingly easy access to wealth in a capitalistic society, brought forth the "brute self" in human nature, as Davis depicted it in "Life," *Margret Howth, Waiting for the Verdict*, and all of her major fiction of the 1860s and after. In later works, she also extended her awareness of the psychological costs of these inner tensions; the rendering of a split personality in "Anne" and stream-of-consciousness passages in *Frances Waldeaux* are precursory literary techniques to the modernist movement. Davis recognized that the sociopolitical tensions prevalent in late-nineteenth-century America contributed to the fragility of the human psyche.

Yet Davis's theory was not without its element of hope, and that hope lay in establishing what her mother had first impressed upon her as "accurate history." For Davis, essential history was the "story of to-day," but that story had meaning only when placed in the context of demythologized American history. She had ample reason to be concerned with the presentation of American history in her own time. From 1820 until 1850, historical writing had been at the height of its popularity, especially as produced by leading Brahmin historians William Hickling Prescott, George Bancroft, John Lothrop Motley, and Francis Parkman.[34] Probably most influential was Bancroft's *History of the United States* (1834–76), a highly romanticized rendition of an American past that laid the foundation for the future of America as a progressive destiny arising out of the embryonic New England republic; it is, indeed, little distanced from the Puritans' national typology. Since Davis was outside of the New England tradition, she was able to present her ardent anti-Calvinism with a more objective eye, discerning (as, to a degree, did the rare New Englander, such as Sedgwick, Hawthorne, and Dickinson) Calvinism's pervasiveness in nineteenth-century New England's collective consciousness. Realism itself is a recording of momentary human history, and Davis sought from the beginning to challenge the "quaint history" of America's past in order to educate her audience through the realities of past experience, especially the experiences of commonplace citizens. Thus she abhorred the chivalric view of war, whether in the context of the Civil War or in the policing of the Phillipines by the United States at the turn of the century. So, too, did she reject historians' tunnel-vision attitudes toward American history. New England's history, its people, and its literature were extraordinary and worthy of study, but no more so, she argued, than those of New Jersey, Delaware, Pennsylvania, West Virginia, or North Carolina. Davis not only wrote about those locales in her fiction and in nonfiction essays, but also encouraged her reading public to pursue the history and literature of those regions. It was the necessary counterpart to burgeoning realistic studies of "to-day." What Davis sought most of all was for history in conjunction with literature to "live and breathe." That, for Davis, was realism.

III. Literary Professionalization

No discussion of Davis as a mid- to late-nineteenth-century American woman writer can be complete without an understanding of the place of authorship in the collective consciousness of the time and of the socioeconomic pressures exerted on middle-class authors, especially women authors. Lawrence Buell's recent analysis of literary New England during this period, *New England Literary Culture: From Revolution through Renaissance* (1986), is a thorough assessment of these issues in terms of one American region, although I agree with Wendy Martin that his study has limited value in terms of women's literary traditions.[35] Buell's data is valuable; however, since his text is presented as revisionary, the interpretations of women authors' status need to be extended. Buell distinguishes "major" authors from "their lesser contemporaries" in socioeconomic terms—their social and educational advantages; their association with liberal, "gentry" churches; their literary ancestry (L. M. Alcott, Stowe, Emerson, Fuller, Holmes, Hawthorne);[36] and most significantly, their economic advantages through inheritance or through support of family and friends (Hawthorne, Emerson, DeForest, Longfellow, Lowell, Dickinson, Bronson Alcott).[37] This is an important acknowledgment of privilege, since we repeatedly discover in the biographies of most women writers of the period a forced entrance into what was formerly termed "hack-writing" and in recent years has been more accurately included in the term the "professionalization" or the "commercialization" of American letters. For some women, a moment of crisis led them to literature as a career, but our concern here is with the group of women writers who had literary ambitions—Buell includes New Englanders such as Lydia Sigourney, Ann Stephens, Elizabeth Stoddard, and Harriet Beecher Stowe—but who were forced through ongoing family financial circumstances to consider the economics of publication as dearly as they considered the artistry of their trade. Certainly Davis fits into this category. However, I would question Buell's designation of these women as writers "who had *previously* evinced literary aspirations" (382; my emphasis), suggesting a finite break between professionalization and artistry. For Davis, and certainly for the majority of writers in this group, the struggle to purchase time for writing literature of artistic value was a painful and life-long struggle against the economic rewards of the higher paying but less literary magazines.

So, too, must we question the assertion that women authors "seem especially to have gained from the professionalization of writing" (378).

Further explanation is needed. Gained in what way? As Buell acknowledges, publishing in antebellum America was a solidly patriarchal enterprise. How much did women gain when they had no power over journal content, editorial commentary, or publishing trends? Beginning her career directly before the onset of the Civil War, Davis is a pertinent example of the controls that an editor wielded over an author, not only in terms of acceptance of materials but also in the content of the author's fiction and in shaping (and sometimes denigrating) an individual's artistic vision. If the publisher-author relationship was paternalistic (as Mary Abigail Dodge ["Gail Hamilton"] pointed out in her 1870 exposé of her own professional relationship with James Fields), so, too, was the average marriage relationship of mid-nineteenth-century America; and, as Buell notes, marriage often limited a woman's literary production except in the rising number of "literary partnership[s] between spouses" (379). Yet here, too, we must consider this assertion with caution. Davis and her husband might conceivably fit this partnership status—both were writers, they shared concerns for many of the same causes (both, for instance, wrote on the issue of maltreatment of the mentally ill), and Davis's income was viewed as a requisite supplement to her husband's. But this is precisely what frustrated Davis's artistic development: her husband admired her profession and her economic contributions to the family, but he did not support her need to pursue the writing of serious fiction or understand her artistic vision. He identified her work as secondary to his own and secondary to her roles of wife, mother, and housekeeper. The tragedy is that while Davis's fiction and nonfiction often raged against these inequities in other women's lives, she was not always able to rise above them herself, personally or professionally.

One way in which we might begin to expand upon Buell's precepts is through a return to the issue of the transcendentalists' philosophy of creativity and Davis's rejection of that philosophy. In Buell's succinct explanation, transcendentalism substituted "a Romanticized version of the mystical idea that humankind is capable of direct experience of the holy" for the Unitarian belief that truths come only via "a process of empirical study and by rational inference from historical and natural evidence"; transcendentalists such as Emerson envisioned "the creative process (in Romantic terms) as originating in the experience of divine inspiration" (46–47). That is, "the Emersonian theory of creativity as divination furnished the strongest justification for serious literary effort that American criticism had yet seen . . . by placing the creative endeavor on the most exalted moral plane" (47). "Serious" literature is a term that Davis repeatedly used for her own endeavors for the *Atlantic Monthly* and other major literary periodicals, but she was at odds with the romantic concept of the origins of creativity. This difference is perhaps more fundamental even than financial need to women writers' movement into the professionalization of authorship: Emerson's vision of the creative process is dependent upon a patriarchal hierarchy that, importantly, has allowed one to participate in positions of power; to consider one's literary creativity as divinely inspired assumes an egocentrism unknown and unavailable to the suppressed. While women's literature of the period was also insistent upon the maintenance of a high moral plane, their own position as creator was one of disclaiming superiority except in the realm of observation. It is small wonder, then, that their romanticism or sentimentalism was so often a literature of place and so often ventured into the realms of realism. Davis was able to begin her career with a realistic vision only because so many women had paved the way—from Hannah Foster's epistolary realism to Sedgwick's and Stowe's blending of romanticism and realism to Cooke's refusal to idyllicize New England village life.

All of which signifies the necessity of rethinking the rise of American realism. I suggest this with a certain intentional edge in my voice. In 1978 Nina Baym asserted that "if critics ever permit the woman's novel to join the main body of 'American literature,' then all our theories about American fiction, from Richard Chase's 'romance' to Richard Poirier's 'world elsewhere' to Carolyn Heilburn's 'masculine wilderness' will have to be radically revised."[38] Yet in 1985 feminist scholars were still fighting old labels; as Judith Fetterley observed, "Another theory of American fiction that would require revision if the work of nineteenth-century women were admitted to the category of American literature is that which claims the 'rise of realism' as the significant event of post- Civil War American literary history. American women writers were realists well before the Civil War."[39]

It is 1989 and, as a male colleague once told me, the wheels of academe move slowly. Both Baym's and Fetterley's assertions, however, suggest that feminists must wait for someone else to "admit" these works into the canon; as Davis suggested, it is time to roll up our sleeves and head into the mire of reclassification ourselves. With recent studies by Josephine Donovan, Eric Sundquist, Nina Baym, and Lawrence Buell delineating the increasing difficulty of defining realism as distinguished from or growing out of local color or regional realism and from romanticism, sentimentalism, and naturalism, perhaps one way to begin is through analyses of these various prose styles in the works of individual authors, not only from New England, with its specific traditions, but from writers throughout nineteenth-century America. It is thus that I present the following reassessment of the life and literature of Rebecca Harding Davis—as a contribution toward establishing her own place in American letters and in the broader context of American literary realism studies.

"No genre," Eric Sundquist asserts, "is more difficult to define than realism, and this is particularly true of American realism."[40] But certainly that should not discourage scholars from beginning the process. In this study, I often designate early realists as "metarealists" in the attempt to capture the comprehensive nature of their movement into realism. Metarealists such as Davis typically synthesize several modes (romanticism, sentimentalism, regionalism), but realism remains their most explicit focus, and the incorporation of realism into their writings is a conscious effort to transform literature from the mystical or other-worldly realm of romanticism into an art form that represents quotidian experience. Thus when I refer in the body of the text to "romanticism," "realism," and so forth, I am assuming that readers will understand these terms as highly contested labels, as the context in which they are used will support. The terms "metarealists" and "new realists" are chronologically determined and are not intended to suggest a separation but, quite the opposite, to reveal the continuities in realistic techniques from the early nineteenth century through the 1880s and 1890s. These terms, like "romanticism" and "sentimentalism," can remain viable facets of our discussion only if we recognize that they apply to literary techniques and styles of an author rather than to an entire work itself. Even Hawthorne's insistence that he was writing a romance rather than a novel was for purposes of *inclusion*—"to claim a certain latitude"—rather than exclusion.[41] I see the metarealists as precursors of the later or "new realists" of the 1880s and 1890s who have traditionally been designated as the instigators of the "rise of realism." The present study of Davis's metarealism, when joined with the earlier studies by Donovan, Baym, Tompkins, Sundquist, and others and, hopefully, to be conjoined with future studies of many other women writers' contributions to the rise of American realism, may open the floodgates to a better understanding of the elusive field of American realism.

1. "Life in the Iron Mills"

REBECCA BLAINE HARDING was a strong-willed, highly intelligent young woman who would emerge at the age of thirty as an excitingly new and innovative writer. She was born in Washington, Pennsylvania, a small community located twenty-five miles south of Pittsburgh. The historic old family home in which she was born, at 73 South Main Street, was then the residence of her mother's eldest sister, Rebecca Wilson Blaine (1789–1866), and her brother-in-law, James Blaine (1787–1848).[1] As the eldest child and first daughter born to Rachel Leet Wilson (1808–84) and Richard W. Harding (1796–1864), Rebecca was named in honor of her maternal aunt. Her mother's family was one of the most prominent in Washington. Rachel's father, Hugh Wilson (1763–1832), was an eminent businessman and property owner, and her mother, Rachel Leet (1770–1818), had raised three older children and Rachel in accordance with their position in the community. When Rachel was ten years old, her mother died, and her sister Rebecca accepted the role of surrogate mother. Theirs was an especially close relationship, and thus Rebecca Wilson and the entire family were taken by surprise when Rachel eloped in 1830 with the thirty-four-year-old Richard Harding.

The adventurous if not young lovers were married at Uniontown, Pennsylvania, on August 12, and shortly thereafter settled in Big Spring (Huntsville), Alabama, where they would remain for almost six years. The area around Big Spring was populated with families of Protestant Irish and Catholic French ancestry and was supported by enormous cotton plantations. In spite of her elopement, Rachel's relations with her eldest sister remained quite close, and she sought the support and strength of her sister's presence during the birth of her first child. She returned to the family home in Washington shortly before Rebecca Blaine Harding was born on June 24, 1831.

Richard Harding, Rebecca's father, was an English immigrant of little business ability but strong community spirit. When the family finally settled in Wheeling, Virginia, he held many civic positions, including officer and director of the Fire and Marine Insurance Company and chairman of the city's sanitary committee; he was elected city treasurer continuously from 1850 until his death. Although he was a partner in McKee, Harding & Co. of Wheeling, Richard Harding was best remembered by his children as a talented storyteller; indeed, Rebecca inherited her father's natural talent and his acute social consciousness. Yet, as she grew older, she found her father to be a distant man, hard to know and impossible to fathom; she ultimately concluded that he had been a displaced Englishman who had never felt at ease on American soil.

Rebecca was five years old when the Harding family moved to Wheeling. Years later she would recall that, for a child, Wheeling presented a perfect world of security and enchantment: "There were no railways in it, no automobiles or trolleys, no telegraphs, no sky-scraping houses. Not a single man in the country was the possessor of huge accumulations of money such as are so common now. There was not, from sea to sea, a trust or a labor union."[2] Yet, located as it was on the Ohio River and constituting the central passageway for transportation between the North and the South, the town's activities afforded a child's imagination numerous opportunities for growth—the daily stagecoaches that clattered through the streets of town; the great steamboats filled with exotic passengers; and most of all, the romance of the Conestoga wagons that carried pioneers heading for the open plains of the West. Rebecca recalled her fascination with the Conestogas: "They came up with these strange people out of far-off lands of mystery, and took them into the wilderness, full of raging bears and panthers and painted warriors, all to be fought in turn" (3–4). Had the times been different, she may very well have been one of the great adventurers herself, writing of the West and its mythic mystery and wildness. But the once-agrarian community of Wheeling was rapidly moving toward industrialization in 1836, with its first steel mill symbolically hovering on the edge of town, and it was that site that would not only capture her imagination but would instill in her the need to expose the realities of American life.

Rebecca's eldest brother, Hugh Wilson ("Wilse"), had been born the year before the family moved to Wheeling, but her three remaining siblings—Richard Harris (b. 1838), Henry Grattan (b. 1840), and Emelie Berry (b. 1842)—were born in the Wheeling home where Rebecca would reside until her marriage. As a young child, she was full of gaiety and harbored an intellectual curiosity whetted by parents who encouraged both education and imagination. Rebecca's mother had been educated by Alexander Campbell, founder of Bethany College, and like many women of the period, she taught Rebecca and Wilse at home until they were old enough for the private tutoring that would prepare them for their respective advanced educations. Their father preferred the delights of storytelling. Most memorable was his creation of Monsieur Jean Crapeaud, the mysterious stranger who resided on the dark, unreachable top shelf of the locked closet near the dining-room chimney. M. Crapeaud traveled the world, fighting adventurously for all good causes, but returned at night to the comfort and security of his closet.

So, too, was Rachel Harding an avid storyteller. Although she gave her eight-year-old daughter a volume of Shakespeare's plays, suggesting Rebecca read *Julius Caeser* and *The Tempest*, Rachel's own tales were drawn from her early life experiences. She was especially prone to tell Rebecca stories of her early married life in Alabama, of "the mixed magnificence and squalor of the life on the plantations . . . the great one-storied wooden houses built on piles; the pits of mud below them in which the pigs wallowed; the masses of crimson roses heaped high on the roofs, a blaze of pure and splendid color; the bare floors, not too often scrubbed; the massive buffets covered with magnificent plate" (68–69). The juxtaposition of crimson roses and wallowing pigs, of beautiful tableware and dirty floors in Rachel's tales of her Southern home presented for young Rebecca the paradoxical nature of everyday life. A significant aspect of Rachel's retelling of her own history was to demythologize Southern life, especially Southern women's daily existence. Rebecca recalled her mother explaining, "The women of these families did not lead the picturesque idle life which their northern sisters imagined and envied. Much of the day was spent in weighing provisions or cutting out clothes for the field hands. They had few books—an odd volume of poems and their Bibles, which they read devoutly—and no amusements but an occasional hot supper, to which they went in faded gowns of ancient cut" (69). Rebecca learned her mother's lessons well: from her earliest publications, she reported in detail the complexity of women's existence in nineteenth-century America, an existence that was valued most for its Franklinesque "industry and frugality."

Rebecca's sense of indebtedness to her mother is evidenced in the dedication to her first novel: "To My Mother." So, too, was her interest in accurate history honed by family experiences. As a child, the American Revolution and the Indian wars had been "close and real" rather than just "misty legends" because many of her relatives who had participated in those events were still living; they shared the realities of soldiering at Valley Forge and presented a balance against the thriving mythic status of a Lafayette or a "Lady Washington" (6). Such a living heritage "made you feel that you had rocked the cradle of the new born nation in your own hand," Davis later commented (6–7). This last image captures what would become one of Rebecca Harding Davis's most prevalent metaphors for personal activism: a "grasp of the hand."

In 1845, at age fourteen, Rebecca was admitted to the Washington Female Seminary in Washington, Pennsylvania. She returned to her birthplace, residing with her "Aunt Blaine" and Uncle James. The community of Washington was still home to many of Rebecca's relatives, and her family's close contact with them over the years created the sense of a large, extended family for the young student. Although she studied French at the Seminary, it was her Aunt Harriet Preble[3] who taught her to read and speak French with fluency. Rebecca's close ties with her numerous Wilson cousins also afforded her a rapt audience with which to hone her own storytelling skills. Her cousin Clara Wilson, ten years Rebecca's junior, would remain a lifelong friend and ardent supporter of Rebecca's literary ambitions.

At the Seminary, Rebecca studied geometry, literature, music, and drawing, and took courses in Evidences of Christianity, Mental Philosophy, and Butler's Analogy—the standard courses for young women at the Seminary. She excelled in her studies, graduating in 1848 as valedictorian of her class. Then, like so many young women of potential in the nineteenth century, she returned home to assist her mother in running the family household. Yet Rebecca did not allow herself to succumb to the stifling fate that entrapped so many intelligent young women of the period. Much of the encouragement to choose another path came from her mother; through their long discussions, Rebecca inherited an avid interest in local history, and long after Rachel Harding had died Rebecca still recalled her as "the most accurate historian and grammarian I have ever known, and [she] had enough knowledge to fit out half a dozen modern college bred women."[4] This inherited admiration for *accurate* history would become an influential element in the development of her literary theory.

Rebecca fought against domestic duties that completely consumed her days. Even though the Hardings had household servants, Rebecca was required to assist her mother in the seemingly unending chores of sewing and cooking for a family of seven, and she took over the role of educating her younger siblings. It was only as Dick, Henry, and finally Emma followed Rebecca's own educational pattern and were transferred to private tutors that she gained additional time for her growing literary ambitions. She hoarded that time against all invasions, often preferring to stay at home rather than join in the social activities that many of her young women friends were enjoying. In these years, she also developed an especially close intellectual bond with her brother Wilse. As a man, he had the privilege of a college education, attending Washington College to study German, but in the summers he taught that language to his older sister. After graduating in 1854, Wilse was hired as a teacher at Wheeling's Classical Academy, where he remained for several years, becoming the principal in 1859. In those years of close proximity, Rebecca and Wilse read and discussed not only the classic literature of France, Germany, and England but also contemporary European and American literatures.[5]

At the same time Rebecca also honed her humor, her acute sense of human nature, and her political acumen; the latter, in these as in later years, was often exposed through the former two attributes. Early evidence of this combination appears in November 1860, when Rebecca learned that her uncle, Hugh Wilson, had severely sprained his knee; she wrote the bedbound uncle a letter to interest and amuse him:

> What do you do to amuse yourself? Read the World and abuse the South? You must want somebody to tease you terribly. Don't you wish I was back? The election here came off on Monday. Clemens and Hubbard, Union men were elected. There was more excitement than at any election I ever saw here. However, I breathe freely now, our liberties are safe. Sherrard said in his speech at the Athenaeum, "My spear has struck the leviathan of disunion. Virginia and I will save the Union." That's a fact.[6]

Letters to family and friends would remain an important avenue for political discussions throughout her life, sometimes acting as the impetus for her articles and short stories.

The most significant aspect of these years in terms of Rebecca's literary apprenticeship, however, was a much more formal training ground. Because of her father's public involvement with numerous civic organizations, Davis came in contact with many of Wheeling's leading citizens; but it was her own energetic intellect that captivated Archibald W. Campbell, editor of the Wheeling *Intelligencer*.[7]

At the time, Wheeling was one of the largest cities in the western region of Virginia, capable of supporting three newspapers, but the *Intelligencer* could boast of having the largest circulation in western Virginia.

The *Intelligencer*, under Campbell's leadership, reprinted the national news from the larger New York and Philadelphia papers; supplied local news and trade reports; published poetry in every Tuesday and Thursday edition; reprinted fiction (including E.D.E.N. Southworth's "The Hidden Hand" in February 1859); and commented on the major issues of the day. As it became evident that Virginia was considering secession, the newspaper recruited correspondents in Richmond and in other states to report more objectively on the proceedings for local subscribers, most of whom were anti-secessionists. Archibald Campbell was only eight years older than Rebecca, and they became close friends as well as colleagues on the newspaper. (Several years later, when Rebecca shyly announced her impending marriage, Annie Fields thought perhaps she would marry "the editor" of whom she had spoken so graciously and so often, but Rebecca insisted that they were only friends.[8]) Campbell, recognizing Rebecca's developing literary talents, engaged her as an editorial correspondent. In the late 1850s, she submitted reviews, editorials, and occasional poems to the paper, and in early 1859, when Campbell was away from Wheeling, Rebecca controlled the editorial column of the *Intelligencer*, if only for a matter of days.[9] Shortly before he departed, she sent him an article written "to order," which she insisted he publish as an editorial because, she admitted, "I have a most insane ambition in that way."[10] It was, indeed, an almost "insane" idea at the time, since, with the notable exception of Margaret Fuller, no woman held such editorial power in America during the mid-nineteenth century, even among the periodicals of the era, unless they were specifically designed for children (e.g., Mary Mapes Dodge's editing of *St. Nicholas*, beginning in 1873) or as "ladies' magazines" (most notably, Sarah Josepha Hale's editorships of *Ladies' Magazine* [1828–37], and *Godey's Lady's Book* [1837–77]). Later, Rebecca would follow in the footsteps of other American women such as Mary Abigail Dodge and Rose Terry Cooke, who harbored ambitions of becoming newspaper correspondents, by becoming a contributing editor to the *New York Daily Tribune* and *The Independent*. During her years in Wheeling, Rebecca was not only ambitious to have her say in an editorial capacity, but she declared that "like all new editors I am going to define my position" as distinct from her editor's.

The article she submitted to Campbell was, she admitted, toned down out of regard for him; as she amusingly noted, "If it had not been for a due regard for your prospects with your lady readers, I should have been unmerciful."[11] Although she had meant her comment humorously at the time, this willingness to shelter her true opinions for the sake of an editor was to become a self-disserving habit when she began publishing in the literary journals of Boston and Philadelphia. But for now, she was delighted to have the opportunity to express herself in the capacity of an editor.

Her item was titled "Women and Politics," and it appeared in the February 2, 1859, issue of the *Intelligencer*.[12] It was intended as a satiric assessment of women's complacency in their sidelined political roles and as a satire of prevailing attitudes toward women and their political abilities. The article acknowledges the ludicrousness of laws that "ignore the existence of women in the body politic, bar them from the bench, the rostrum, the ballot box, yet permit them to form a part, unaccredited but far from powerless, in the complex machinery of government," that is, a woman's power in her domestic setting to influence the man whose fingers "hold the pulse of the nation." Yet since time immemorial—from Rebecca and Jacob to Madame de Maintenon and "Louis Quatoize"—"woman has shown an irresistible proclivity to interfere with politics." But women too readily decide they are Whig or Democrat simply because their male relatives are; or on the contrary, they proclaim themselves Whigs precisely because their father and brother are Democrats. A woman decides issues from the heart, out of compassion, she asserts, and sooner or later the heart interferes with her reason and says, "hitherto shalt thou go, but no farther." Thus even the Lucy Stones and George Sands, while they lecture and write, "carry with them the elements of their own defeat . . . just when they think they have overcome, ["their own better nature"] will assert its divine power, and with a touch—cripple and bless them." Ultimately, the satire is almost too subtle; its intended ironic conclusion, "cripple and bless them," in fact creates an ambiguity that undermines her message. In the two years between this publication and the appearance of "Life in the Iron Mills" in the *Atlantic Monthly*, however, she would hone her ironic skills to a fine precision. By that time she had also become fully aware that this and earlier items for the *Intelligencer* were the work of an apprentice; after the publication of "Life," when James Fields questioned her about her previous literary publications, she brushed aside his query with the assertion, "Whatever I wrote before the Iron Mill story I would not care to see again—chiefly verses and reviews written under circumstances that made them unhealthful. I would rather they were forgotten."[13] Why the conditions were "unhealthful" is unclear, although Davis sarcastically admitted when she submitted the editorial item to Campbell that it had been written in "the intervals of that all important cooking." Domestic pressure against her literary ambitions would only increase in the coming years.

It was during these apprenticeship years, when she was exposed to the national and local intricacies of political life, that Rebecca began to recognize her own era as one of tremendous growth and equally rampant friction. Out of this knowledge, she shaped her literary theory of the "commonplace." She viewed as corrupted history the proclamations of unhindered progress—the "glory" of expansion and the "necessity" of slavery—that filled the pages of American newspapers and the after-dinner conversations of Northerners and Southerners alike. The core story of "Life in the Iron Mills" is set thirty years in the past, allowing her to debunk the historical myths of that era in order to write what she believed was the essential history: "the story of to-day."

Davis[14] scholarship has centered on "Life" as a landmark in American literary history. Gerald Langford identifies the novellla as "one of the revolutionary documents in American writing"; and Tillie Olsen acknowledges that the "commonplace" Davis chose as her topic "was nowhere in books" at the time.[15] Jay Martin classifies Davis as "one of the earliest and best of the American realists" and notes that, though she was writing in the wake of Whitman, she "helped to shape the patterns of the kind of national fiction that DeForest and Howells would perfect."[16] Perhaps most representative of the majority opinion is Sandra M. Gilbert and Susan Gubar's comment that "[s]ome six years before the French novelist Émile Zola began publishing what were called 'naturalistic' novels, a thirty-year-old Virginian had brilliantly dramatized the socioeconomic implications of environmental determinism."[17] Yet scholars have not known quite what to make of this early example of American realism and naturalism. All agree it is grimly realistic, that it is a pioneering work. But many question the passages that seem to offer religion as a panacea for Hugh Wolfe and the "lower" class, passages that use the language of romanticism and seem to deny the determinism of Hugh's fate. Coppelia Kahn, for instance, in a brief but insightful review of "Life," finds the story compellingly realistic but concludes, "The sole weakness of the book, I think, is that Davis hints vaguely at some doctrinal, probably Christian answer" for the meaning of such suffering.[18] Kahn's tentative prose ("I think . . . hints vaguely . . . probably Christian") indicates the tenuous discomfort many critics evoke in discussing "Life." John Conron, for instance, admires Davis's realism but feels the "gestures" of the characters are "elaborately sentimentalized," a term few other critics apply to this work.[19] In contrast, Josephine Donovan described "Life" in a 1980 study as "grimly realistic . . . a far cry from sentimental romance."[20] Yet, three years later, Donovan aligns Davis's work with the general nineteenth-century "tendency toward romantic hyperbole."[21]

These alternating analyses represent the typical critical conundrum surrounding "Life." The failure to align these difficulties is not, however, in the text; it is in our own failure to understand Davis's awareness of the changing literary modes she was advocating through her seminal realistic study of a mill town and her recognition of how difficult it would be for her readers to accept these changes in literary style. In this awareness, Davis extends earlier writers' attention to village life, most specifically Catherine Maria Sedgwick's novels of the 1820s: *New-England Tale*, which exposes the provinciality of village life, and *Redwood*, which more ambitiously assesses regionalism itself. Davis, however, avoids Sedgwick's "Cinderella plots" and melodrama in her desire to inculcate mimesis as a fictional device.

The analysis that follows will examine the complex narrative structure of "Life" in terms of its movement from romanticism to realism and will reveal that, at its core, "Life" is clearly naturalistic. Scholars have also often failed to recognize that element of Davis's fiction which is, in many ways, most important to her literary theory: a sense of the ironic. Therefore, this analysis will also illuminate the numerous levels of irony with which Davis undermines any sense of panacean solutions to the industrial ills being perpetrated upon American society and which constitutes the beginning of her particularly strong rejection of American transcendentalism.

I. Narrative Structure[22]

The three-tiered narrative structure of "Life" is a recreation of the hierarchical social strata of mid-nineteenth-century America.[23] The "upper" tier is the narrator's middle-class world, and her observations frame the inner stories. Critics often assume that the voices of Davis and her narrator are interchangeable. In the beginning of the story, Davis does often incorporate her own values and intentions into the narrator's assertions; but at significant junctures in the text, she separates herself from the narrator. At the story's conclusion, Davis radically deviates from this alliance to reveal the narrator as unreliable, the same technique that Henry James would later use in his fiction. The narrator is a necessary initial guide, one whose language and social status are familiar and comfortable to Davis's reading public. The middle stratum is Deborah's arena. Since most of the narrator's peers were oblivious to the realities of working-class life, Davis connects them with Deborah, who acts not only as a guide but as a translator, moving them from the narrator's frame down to Hugh's underworld. Deb is of both worlds: she resides in the lowest economic stratum certainly, but she has not yet been completely dehumanized. She bears no last name, signifying that she, unlike Hugh *Wolfe*, has not yet devolved into that last, animalistic stage, an aspect of characterization that would become prevalent in deterministic fiction of the 1880s and 1890s. Deborah retains both compassion and a humane sense of others. Finally, at the core of the narrative is Hugh Wolfe's story, one of the earliest renderings of naturalism in American literature.

After Hugh's plot of decline is detailed, the reader is led back out of the iron mill's pit, once again into Deborah's intermediary level, and finally back into the narrator's concluding frame. This closing frame will again draw on the narrator's language of romanticism but will contextually demand that Davis's readers evaluate the story's conclusion in decidedly realistic terms. Each level of the narrative structure addresses the issue of language as an instrument of power, and each challenges passive, traditional Christianity as a solution for the nation's ills. Each level also revolves around a particular question: for the narrator's frame, it is the question of an awareness of quotidian existence; for Deb's stratum, it is the question of compassion; and for Hugh's realm, it is appropriately that of art, since Davis herself is questioning the old forms and creating new.

Davis's purpose in the narrative frame is to lure readers into this new form of fiction without alienating them before they descend with the narrator into the lower realms. Thus the narrator begins with a conversational "exchange" with the reader that immediately addresses the realities of a mill town. It is a cloudy day, an everyday occurrence, but the narrator asks, "do you know what that is in a town of iron-works?" (430)[24] The sky is "muddy, flat, immovable. The air is thick, clammy with the breath of crowded human beings. It stifles me" (430). In this suffocating conjunction of nature and the human, Davis demonstrates how an economic system aborts human potential. At a time when optimism presupposed a transcendental divinity that shapes humanity through nature, Davis rejects such "heady" abstractions and recognizes a rapacious industrialization that corrupts nature and crushes the human spirit. This is reinforced by the image of a "dirty canary" that the narrator observes as it "chirps desolately in a cage beside me" (430). Similar caged-bird images will recur throughout Davis's early fiction and serve as a leitmotif throughout turn-of-the-century naturalism (e.g., in Frank Norris's *McTeague* and Kate Chopin's *The Awakening*). Davis invokes this image of the bird in order to debunk its traditional implications of transcendence: "Its dream of green fields and sunshine is a very old dream,—almost worn out, I think" (430). The "dream" that has outworn its usefulness becomes in Davis's literature the symbol of Emersonian transcendentalism, a philosophy she rebukes for its potentially corrupting influence on American life. Begun in "Life," this rebuke culminates in Davis's 1864 short story, "The Wife's Story" (see chapter 3), and recurs in subsequent novels and short fiction.

In "Life," the narrator refutes this "old dream" by recording the commonplace details of a mill town as she struggles to observe through the haze its idiosyncracies. No place in the town offers refuge from the soot. The merchant, the drunken immigrant, even the beasts of burden are connected by the profoundly "foul vapor" of the town that oppresses man and beast alike. Irishmen lounge on the grocer's porch. Davis's inclusion of immigrants in her depiction of the mill town, and especially Irish immigrants, is a significant element of her realism. Between 1815 and 1865, approximately five million immigrants had entered the United States. Two million of these immigrants were Irish, constituting the largest nationality. Of these five million new Americans, almost eighty percent settled in the industrial Northeast.[25] In "Life," even the beasts that once plowed the fertile earth now bear loads of pig iron and carve ruts only into muddy and barren streets. All movement and production is stifled, not encouraged, by the town's industry. In such a town, everything becomes distorted: the canary is no longer yellow, the river is "dull and tawny-colored . . . slavishly bearing its burden day after day" (430). Davis emphatically joins this distortion of nature with that of human life, now a "slow stream . . . creeping past, night and morning, to the great mills" (430). This image of drifting, of human dislocation, became central to the literary practice of American naturalists, most explicitly in Theodore Dreiser's *Sister Carrie* (1900), as did Davis's alignment of man as beast through the burdened laborers who are "laired by day in dens of drunkenness and infamy" (430). In the following century, Upton Sinclair explained that he had written *The Jungle* (1906) to expose "the inevitable and demonstrable consequence of an economic system."[26] In 1861, Davis also insisted that readers acknowledge this oppressed class existing within their midst, and her narrator asserts in a tone of indictment and challenge: "What do you make of a case like that, amateur psychologist? You call it an altogether serious thing to be alive: to these men it is a drunken jest, a joke,—horrible to angels perhaps, to them commonplace enough" (430). As Davis later demonstrates, the joke is becoming commonplace even among angels.

Yet Davis knows that her nineteenth-century readers, weaned on romanticism, will insist upon the comfort of a traditional happy ending, and the narrator teases them with a momentary suggestion of that resolution: "What if it be stagnant and slimy here? [The river] knows that beyond there waits for it odorous sunlight,—quaint old gardens, dusky with soft, green foliage of apple-trees, and flushing crimson with roses,—air, and fields, and mountains" (430). The vibrancy of these colors, juxtaposed against the "tawdry" effects of the mill, suggests an Edenic life beyond the mill's control. But Davis has her narrator immediately confront the reader with the conflicting reality: "The future of the Welsh puddler passing just now is not so pleasant. To be stowed away, after his grimy work is done, in a hole in the muddy graveyard, and after that,—*not* air, nor green fields, nor curious roses" (430). And certainly not transcendence. As Annette Kolodny's excellent study of American authors' responses to the landscape has revealed, the diverse response to the despoiling of the American landscape, epitomized through opposing emphases such as those of the romantics James Fenimore Cooper and William Gilmore Simms, were pastoral visions that, "in fact, mark the differing orientations of North and South that . . . foretold the inevitability of the clash of the 1860s."[27] Davis's study suggests that the "pastoral possibility," so valued by both Cooper and Simms, was rapidly becoming an impossibility.

Through her narrator, Davis further juxtaposes the transcendent images of romanticism against realistic details to awaken the reader's otherwise passive response. Three times in the first pages of "Life," however, the narrator refers to her "idle" thoughts and actions; these asides are the first significant clues that Davis and her narrator should not be considered one voice. The narrator is psychologically outside the disastrous cycle of the drifting laborers, just as her descriptive narrative acts as a frame around the stories of Deborah and of Hugh Wolfe. But in a deeper sense, Davis positions the narrator as a symbol of the idle lives of those who need not go down into the hell-fires of the mill. Mocking the reader's desire for "quaint old gardens," she denies the viability of romantic stories that, in their familiarity of style, can be read in a "lazy, *dilettante* way" (431). However, as her readers are being admonished, they are also lulled back into a sense of security by the narrator's assertion that "the fragments of an old story" are coming to her. Davis believed that only in this state of seeming comfort and distance would her readers shed their dilettantism and listen to a story

> as foggy as the day, sharpened by no sudden flashes of pain or pleasure.—I know: only the outline of a dull life, that long since, with thousands of dull lives like its own, was vainly lived and lost: thousands of them,—massed, vile, slimy lives, like those of the torpid lizards in yonder stagnant water-butt. (430–31)

That it is an "old story" allows readers the comfort of momentarily distancing themselves, but the readers are also being forced to see the truth of everyday, stagnant life. "I am going to be honest," the narrator asserts. "This is what I want you to do. I want you to hide your disgust, take no heed to your clean clothes, and come right down with me,—here, into the thickest of the fog and mud and foul effluvia. I want you to hear this story . . . I want to make it a real thing to you" (431). Those who have been trained to transcend the realities of everyday life—"You, Egoist, or Pantheist, or Arminian, busy in making straight paths for your feet on the hills"— are blind to truth: you "do not see it clearly" (431). Davis specifically evokes the image of "seeing" in order to challenge transcendentalism's "transparent eyeball" that, to her mind, avoided the grimy facts of existence for much of humanity. In her autobiography she recalled the working-class men and women who, ironically to her mind, made pilgrimages to Concord in order to hear the great Sage, but Emerson offered them only "theories [that] were like beautiful bubbles blown from a child's pipe, floating overhead, with queer reflections on them of sky and earth and human beings, all in a glow of fairy color and all a little distorted."[28] It is precisely the histories of these working-class pilgrims that Davis records, without the "fairy colors," in her literature of the commonplace.

In exposing these underground lives, Davis realizes that if her details exceed propriety or if she too rapidly forces her mid-nineteenth-century readers to descend the tiers of social strata, she will alienate them. Therefore, she presents Deborah as a transitional guide into the lowest realms. Deb is no less a victim of the system than Hugh, but she has not yet devolved into his realm and thus is not as threatening. Deb's position as the keeper of the middle realm is signified by her movements both above and below ground. As with her attention to the nationality of immigrants, Davis's specific choice of a cotton mill for Deb's place of employment also attests to her keen perception of recent economic history. The "cotton revolution" had been a central factor in the expansion of both the plantation South and the industrialized North, and Deborah's laboring in a cotton mill in a border state closely aligns her with her enslaved Southern counterparts. By 1831 nearly seventy percent of the fifty-eight thousand cotton-mill workers were women. These women were mostly white, but their existence was little better than that of slave women. In 1845, a Massachusetts woman laborer had testified before the state legislature about unhealthy mill conditions, yet five years later little if any change had occurred in working conditions, although cotton manufacturing then ranked first among industries in the United States.[29] On the street outside the cotton mill where Deborah works, she is with "a crowd of half-clothed women" who have just finished their twelve-hour shift at the cotton mill and who are now slowly heading home. As a transitional figure, Deb is not as morally debilitated as her companions who, like the men in the iron mills, assuage their weariness in carousing and in "lashin's o' drink" (432).[30] Yet Davis acknowledges Deb's potential for decline because of environmental influences: "Perhaps the weak, flaccid wretch had some stimulant in her pale life to keep her up,—some love or hope, it might be, or urgent need. When that stimulant was gone, she would take to whiskey" (432). The middle realm is always tenuous, and the slide is almost always downward.

An important element in Davis's linking of her readers' middle-class world and the workers' lower realm is the parallel between the narrator's home, described in both the opening and closing frames, and Deb's residence. The latter is merely the cellar of a house shared with several other families. The cellar is "low, damp,—the earthen floor covered with a green, slimy moss,—a fetid air smothering the breath" (432). Her area is shared with Hugh Wolfe, his father, and sometimes young Janey. At the end of "Life," Davis indelibly connects these two homes: this is the same house from which the narrator, thirty years later, retells Deb and Hugh's story. That the mill's grime permeates the house, even in its recovered state, suggests the capacity of the mill's filth to invade all social realms.

To delineate Deb's world as intermediary is not to deny her victimization. The debilitation of this life is physically symbolized in Deborah herself, who is "deformed, almost a hunchback" (432). There is no beauty in Deborah's life and none in her face, which is "ghastly" because of her blue lips and watery eyes (432). This "Zolaesque" description, preceding the French naturalist's work by half a dozen years, shatters the tradition of the blue-eyed, fair-haired heroines typical of the mid-nineteenth-century American romanticism of Cooper, Hawthorne, and Melville, among others. Instead, Deborah becomes one of American fiction's earliest realistic grotesques, a precursor to those depicted in Sherwood Anderson's *Winesburg, Ohio*. In Anderson's portrayals, a person's physical disabilities often represent a gentle human spirit caught in the webs of a particular obsession. For Deb, the obsession is Hugh, and she becomes the first in a series of "thwarted woman's forms" that Davis depicts in her fiction and nonfiction. The significance of Deb's "hunger" swells to overwhelming proportions in "Life." Like all the workers, Deb is physically hungry, but she is also sexually and emotionally deprived because of her deformity. Further, both Hugh and Deb are hungry "to know," to have that secret forever released from the silence of the upper classes which will allow the oppressed to rise socially and economically. Most importantly, both victims are spiritually hungry—Hugh for a means to express his creative voice and Deb for an unnamed fulfillment which she believes only Hugh can effectuate.

Yet in spite of the numerous parallels Davis establishes between Deb and Hugh, she identifies one significant difference that acts as the impetus for Deb's salvation at the story's conclusion: compassion is part of Deborah's innate nature. Whenever young Janey seeks refuge in the cellar because her father has abandoned her, Deb welcomes Janey and feeds her from her own sparse rations, even though she knows the girl is the object of Hugh's attention. But Deb's compassion extends especially to Hugh. Weary as she is after her own shift of hard labor, Deb carries Hugh's dinner to him every night. Her compassion is sacrificial, but as the story evolves so, too, does Deb's ability to discriminate between who is and is not worthy of her care. Hugh ranks first in her concerns, but she will not join him when he sacrifices his life. Nor does she condescend to acknowledge the visitors who come to the mill on this particular night. The visitors' greed and self-aggrandizement abolish their worthiness for Deb, who merely turns her back on them and goes to sleep.

That Deb carries Hugh's dinner to him each night at the mill is crucial to the narrative structure; this movement allows the reader to follow Deb along the streets of the town, passing the "skulking" mill hands as the shifts change and entering the furnace rooms of the mill. Since the "upper-tier" inhabitants of a mill town seldom "know the vast machinery of system by which the bodies of workmen are governed, that goes on unceasingly from year to year" (433), Davis's readers need Deb to guide their descent into that naturalistic core realm in which Hugh Wolfe dwells. In 1890, Jacob

Riis would again confront Americans with the realities of slum life in his exposé, *How the Other Half Lives*. But as Alan Trachtenberg has observed, Riis established in his writings about the impoverished "a pattern of spatial penetration that provided his readers with vicarious expeditions into mysterious quarters"; in fact, both Riis and Stephen Crane wrote from "a curiously asocial perspective."[31] Davis, however, achieves an adamantly social perspective by no longer allowing her nineteenth-century audience what at first had seemed to be the distance of a "vicarious" experience; and she further rejects an asocial perspective by denouncing the visitors precisely for their own distancing techniques (see section II, below). Deb takes us directly into that underground world so that we almost literally feel the stifling heat and oppressive air. In one of the earliest naturalistic depictions of the hellish power of the machine, Davis personifies this "vast machinery of system" that is Kirby & John's iron-producing mill: "the unsleeping engines groan and shriek, the fiery pools of metal boil and surge" (433). Deb herself admits, " 'T looks like t' Devil's place!"

Recognizing Deb's exhaustion on this particular evening, one of the men scrapes the ashes from the fire, after which Hugh tells her, "Lay down there on that heap of ash, and go to sleep" (434). The ashes provide the only warmth available to the mill workers, and, significantly, the ashes suggest a twentieth-century American literary motif that identifies the human detritus of society's "progress" with symbolic ashes. Here they still retain a barren element of warmth; later they will have devolved into the massive ash heap of F. Scott Fitzgerald's *The Great Gatsby*. Lying in the ashes and looking "like a limp, dirty rag," Deb appears as "not an unfitting figure to crown the scene of hopeless discomfort and veiled crime" (434). The narrator had warned us in her opening frame that we would enter a world "pregnant with death," and Deb's "thwarted woman's form" lying in the ashes exemplifies that world: there is no sense of fertility in her decrepit young body. The tragedy is that Deb, who still retains the capacity to love, can never find fulfillment—can never become "pregnant"—in this ash-filled environment.

While Hugh will struggle to understand what it is that confines his artistic genius to the iron pits, Deb is more pitiful because she understands the hopelessness of her desires:

> . . . no one had ever taken the trouble to read [her eyes'] faint signs: not the half-clothed furnace-tender, Wolfe, certainly. Yet he was kind to her: it was his nature to be kind, even to the very rats that swarmed in the cellar: kind to

her in just the same way. She knew that. And it might be that very knowledge had given to her face its apathy and vacancy more than her low, torpid life. (434)

Thus Davis distinguishes between Deb's genuine compassion for others and Hugh's eclectic kindness that carries no personal commitment. This passage also expresses Davis's lifelong concern for women deprived of love, of significant work, and of opportunities to express their intelligence in meaningful political and social ways—that is, to find power outside the "cult of domesticity." To Davis, this deprivation was one of the most significant social tragedies of nineteenth-century America. She describes its pervasiveness in every aspect of Deb's life: "There was no warmth, no brilliancy, no summer for this woman; so the stupor and vacancy had time to gnaw into her face perpetually" (434).

Yet there is another, equally important reason for Deb to lead us into Hugh's world. Environmentally induced, Hugh's decline is especially poignant because he is an artist. Scholars have typically insisted that Hugh is Davis's representation of herself and her own thwarted artistic endeavors. Nothing could be further from Davis's intention. Instead, she attributes the destruction of the true artistic spirit to Hugh's *acceptance* of the capitalists' vision of Beauty when they visit the mill. What has "gnawed" into Deb's face is precisely the realism that Hugh, the artist, has captured in the face of the Korl Woman. He uses the mill's refuse, korl, to shape "figures,—hideous, fantastic enough, but sometimes strangely beautiful" (435). His own vision of beauty is little Janey—"timid, helpless, clinging to Hugh as her only friend" (434)—that is, the most traditional of all images of woman: demure, helpless, completely dependent. Being limited to this vision is tragic since Hugh also, if unwittingly, "sees" the potential in the refuse to be remolded. It is the same technique Davis suggests for reshaping the lives of these victims who are the "refuse" of industry: whittle away their filth and their silence and they become "sometimes strangely beautiful." Hugh's passion is a resurrecting art; it is the Korl Woman and her lingering question that remain at the story's conclusion. Yet his potential is corrupted because he accepts the prevailing standard of Beauty. Deb knows, if Hugh does not, that this love of the Beautiful causes him to sicken "with disgust at her deformity, even when his words were kindest" (434). Davis acknowledges her debt to Hawthorne through this parallel disparagement of the "Artist of the Beautiful" and the allusions to "The

Birthmark," but does so from the perspective of a realist rather than of a romanticist.

It is when the capitalists' associate, Mitchell, enters the mill that Hugh is further drawn into this prevailing standard of Beauty. Mitchell's physicality and upper-class demeanor fascinate Hugh; he stares at the visitor's finely contoured hands and "the blood-glow of a red ring" (437). Mitchell uses this beringed hand to scrape away the ashes beside him, and Wolfe does "obeisance to it with his artist sense, unconscious that he did so" (437). Hugh is unconscious that the "blood-glow" symbolizes the "blood" drawn from workers like himself to support such accoutrements. More importantly, Wolfe's imitation of Mitchell in sweeping away the ashes repeats the visitors' dismissal of Hugh—and more specifically of Deb, who has come to be associated with the ashes. Ironically, this act of rejection thereby encompasses that other form of "refuse" as well—Hugh's Korl Woman. Through his own acceptance of Mitchell's values, then, Hugh prefigures the visitors' rejection of art (and artist) that is not of the Beautiful. Davis's valuing of "strange" beauty over the beauty of perfection gives preference to the realistic over the romantic—in all forms of art.

The Korl Woman has a face "like that of a starving wolf's"; as noted earlier, many scholars equate this with Hugh's own hunger. But that association does not occur until the end of the story, and the figure is more complex than such a direct analogy implies. Hugh does not understand his own work of art; the ravaged face of the Korl Woman is starving for Hugh *Wolfe's* affection, drawn as it is from Deb's "gnawed" face. When Doctor May questions Hugh about the meaning of the figure, Hugh explains, "She be hungry. . . . Not hungry for meat"; but when he is pressed to explain further, he can only respond in bewilderment, "I dunno" (438). Davis further denotes Hugh's acceptance of the popular definition of Beauty when he begins his downward spiral. He leaves the mill and walks the town's streets, above ground, only after accepting the visitors' valuation of himself and his art. He has been an abstainer, but suddenly his "artist-eye grew drunk with [the] color" of nature's artistry. This would seem a positive awareness for an artist, but it is immediately diminished by Hugh's belief that he is entering that promised Edenic world that will fulfill all of his dreams: "The gates of that other world! Fading, flashing before him now! What, in that world of Beauty, Content, and Right, were the petty laws, the mine and thine, of mill-owners and mill-hands? A consciousness of power stirred within him" (444). Hugh usurps not only the artistic philosophy of the powerbrokers but also their "consciousness," rooted in force. For Davis, dreams are always to be observed with skepticism: they are "old dreams" that blind one to the realities of existence and to one's potential. The passivity of dreaming is particularly offensive to Davis's advocacy of social reform. Thus as Hugh's "soul took in the mean temptation, lapped it in fancied rights, in dreams of improved existences," those existences are deemed "drifting and endless as the cloud-seas of color" (444). Hugh has no real power; he is drifting in a dream-world based upon myths perpetuated by the capitalists who, during their brief visit to the mill, held out to him the great American dream. But the attention to colors, to edenic visions, recalls the already debunked romantic vision from the opening narrative frame. It is as false in the underworld as above, and much more cruel. Hugh's acceptance of these capitalistic valuations lead him only into a prison cell (the naturalistic "trap") and to his death.

II. Language

Each segment of the narrative structure addresses the issue of language. Davis's ironic use of the language of romanticism in the narrator's frame is juxtaposed against the vernacular and the deterministic language of the inner stories. Just as the nineteenth-century audience needs a guide into the exigencies of the lower stratum, so too does it need a translator. Thus the narrator's frame incorporates the language of romanticism with which Davis's readers were familiar and comfortable, and this assumed language allows the readers to absorb glaringly realistic details almost unconsciously. It is then woven into the mid-level structure where the vernacular reigns. The vernacular had, in fact, found its way into American literature during the late eighteenth century, when the rustic new American was honored precisely for his or her "Yankee" traits.[32] But much of the antebellum romanticism (especially of Emerson, Thoreau, and Fuller) had been rooted in oratorical eloquence and aestheticism. It was the writers outside the pale, as it were (Melville in his seafaring romances and, most significantly, the great sentimentalists and early "regional" realists of antebellum New England), who reinstated the vernacular, not as heroic but as quotidian reality. Davis also edges the language of the iron-mill pits into the world of nineteenth-century aestheticism without condescending to her characters' language differences. She extends the process by beginning to assert pressure on the narrative structure at this point through the language of naturalism from Hugh's world. At the core, the language of determinism dominates as environmental and hereditary forces propel Hugh downward. When the narrator periodically reasserts herself and her language into the core narrative, she does so to insist upon the reader's personal alignment with this tragic figure, an alignment necessary to Davis's purpose when the reader is brought back up from Hugh's pit into the closing frame.

The narrator's language of romanticism is linked with Davis's position on traditional Christianity (see section III, below) and is always used ironically, as earlier, when she teased the reader into considering visions of an Edenic life beyond the iron mills. When the narrator announces that there is a "terrible question which men here have gone mad and died trying to answer," she expunges theories about Truth as the answer; rather, the answer is to be found in that reverberating silence that is the "voice" of oppressed, "dumb" humanity. The narrator's ironic language of comfort, when used in conjunction with Davis's shockingly realistic imagery and characterization, challenges readers to rouse themselves from dilettantism; they must hear that silenced voice—and discover who is silencing it. To achieve this, Davis delicately balances the narrator's language against the dangers of slipping into melodrama. For instance, when Deb feels a "fierce light of pain" after realizing that Hugh's vision of beauty is completely outside of herself, the narrator asserts herself into Deb's text by employing the language of the outer frame, yet counters it as well. "You laugh at [Deb's pain]?" she admonishes the reader. "Are pain and jealousy less savage realities down here in this place I am taking you to than in your own house or your own heart,—your heart, which they clutch at sometimes?" (434) This "clutching of the heart," however, is not allowed to devolve into mawkishness. The narrator immediately cautions the reader that she will not embellish "the outside outlines." The retelling of human history must be done realistically: "whatever muddy depth of soul-history lies beneath you can read according to the eyes God has given you" (435). Davis exerts pressure on her audience not to dream of an elusive Truth but to participate in the process of discovery. As part of this process, the reader is required to translate the wisdom of both Deb (compassion) and Hugh (resurrection). "[See] him just as he is," Davis has the narrator assert, ". . . look back, as he does every day, at his birth in vice, his starved infancy . . . the slow, heavy years of constant hot work" (435). Hugh is not recoverable, however. Too many years of deprivation have mutilated him. Davis will offer no easy solutions, no happy endings: "There is no hope that it will ever end. Think that God put into this man's soul a fierce thirst for beauty,—to know it, to create it; to *be*,— something, he knows not what . . . his nature starts up with a mad cry of rage against God, man, whoever it is that has forced this vile, slimy life upon him" (435). Davis requires her readers to confront this "slimy life" before they can know this man's history and, importantly, so they can begin to ask themselves: who *has* forced this tragic life upon him?

In the narrator's closing frame, Davis openly mocks her readers' desire for traditional endings. "You wish me to make a tragic story of it?" the narrator asks. Melodramatic tragedies are written every day of the week:

> Why, in the police-reports of the morning paper you can find a dozen such tragedies: hints of shipwrecks unlike any that ever befell on the high seas; hints that here a power was lost to heaven,—that there a soul went down where no tide can ebb or flow. Commonplace enough the hints are,—jocose sometimes, done up in rhyme. (445)

But they are not truthful renderings of the commonplace realities of life. The distortions inherent in such "reportage" are exposed when, a month after Doctor May had visited the mill and conversed with Hugh, he espies an item in his morning paper that recalls the visit to his mind. He exclaims to his wife:

> Oh, my dear! You remember that man I told you of, that we saw at Kirby's mill?—that was arrested for robbing Mitchell? Here he is; just listen:—'Circuit Court. Judge Day. Hugh Wolfe, operative in Kirby & John's Loudon Mills. Charge, grand larceny. Sentence, nineteen years hard labor in penitentiary.'—Scoundrel! Serves him right! After all our kindness that night! (445)

Ironies abound in this passage, and the reader is now required to translate Doctor May's telegraphic language. Since his language removes the details the reader has been forced to observe, Dr. May can no longer be viewed as presenting a version of "reality." Instead, the reader must discern that the only court Hugh warrants in Doctor May's world is a "circuitous" one, facing his Judge[ment] Day. Of course, as the good Doctor is so willing to point out, it is the only "right" that this tribunal will serve Hugh. And the sentence of nineteen years suggests a cruelly ironic repetition of Hugh's early life of hard labor. Thus, by the story's conclusion, the reader is engaged with the action as a first step toward the participation that Davis demands.

In the middle realm, Deb introduces the language of the common-place folk, the vernacular. Like Mark Twain, Davis employed a variety of dialects in her fiction: the Welsh immigrant, the slave and the educated black, the New England fishermen, and often the generic uneducated, such as Deb. In "Life," the vernacular is a language distinctly separate from that of the narrative frame and particularly from the language of the visitors who engage Hugh's attention. The visitors are part of Hugh's core story and will be discussed more fully in the section on his language, but Davis satirically attacks their distortion of the work ethic when the narrator comments on Deb's potential for decline: "Man cannot live by work alone" (432). Davis satirizes the implications of Franklin's maxim because it has been seized by the capitalists to encourage slave-like endurance and to codify the myth that every person may climb the social ladder. When Deb enters Hugh's hellish world, her representative nonentity status is contrasted with the "important" people in the upper realm. Hugh sees Deb as a "slavish" supplier of food and depersonalizes her simply as "woman." His fellow workers do the same by labeling her "t' hunchback" (433). It is a cruelty born of ignorance, depriving everyone of the language of affection; and, ironically, this negation of feelings is directed toward the character who is most concerned for others. That concern remains only rudimentary in the men of the pits. "Hout, woman!" they call out to Deb when she enters, "ye look like a drowned cat. Come near to the fire" (433). Unlike the Christian reformers who come to the mill and are repelled by such comments, the readers will be called upon to discern in this primitive language the humanity that lies beneath the grime and inarticulateness.

It is in Hugh's world, however, that Davis explicitly sets forth her theory that language is a tool that may be used for destruction or for change. Davis's movement into naturalism is most explicit in her revelation of the capitalists' abuse of the working class through control and manipulation of language. Using the image of the veil, Davis symbolizes the oppression of the workers by an act which, ironically, they must effectuate themselves: each Saturday evening, Hugh and his co-workers are required to veil the machinery, but the act of covering the raucous monsters requires the workers to shout as loudly as possible; yet their voices are never heard above ground. In fact, when the visitors enter the mill on the night of Hugh's crisis, their presence invokes a silence that acts as a veiling of the workers' voices, paralleling their symbolic act.

More important to Davis, however, is the capitalists' intentional use of language for control. Young Kirby's synecdochical phraseology—

referring to the workers as "*his* hands" while discussing the mill's net profits—impresses upon them their role of slave and his as master. That he acts to preserve the conditions of slavery is made explicit when the narrator remarks that this mill sits on "the borders of a Slave State." Nor is it only the mill workers who have been silenced. One of the visitors is a reporter, presumably skilled in observing the facts of his surroundings and of objectively rendering them for public consumption. This man, however, is writing praise of the manufactory. He only peers at his surroundings; he does not *see*. His own inarticulate "um" and his "mumbled" responses to the visitors' comments reveal that he, too, has been silenced by the "vast machinery" of industrial society. Industrial capitalists' control over reporters would become a recurrent theme in later naturalism, particularly for those novelists who had been initiated into fiction writing through journalism during the great upsurge in newspaper publishing of the 1880s and 1890s: Harold Frederic, Robert Herrick, and Frank Norris.[33]

Davis also introduces in this section another theme that became prevalent in later American realism and especially in naturalism: the extent to which capitalists control the "voices" of their "hands" through control of votes. Alan Trachtenberg, in discussing the metaphors of "wreckage and self-destruction" that were pervasive in the 1880s, suggests that the "[s]ubtle interweavings of destruction and creation formed the inner logic of the industrial capitalist system"; he notes that analysts in America and Europe were beginning to formulate the contradictory claim that the industrial capitalist system "possessed a baffling unconscious energy which resulted in recurrent cycles of expansion and contraction, inflation and deflation, confidence and depression."[34] In 1861, however, Davis denied the "unconscious" evolution of this system. Young Kirby admits how useful the idea of "the system" as an independent force is to the mill owner in the perpetuation of industrialist capitalism—there is nothing "unconscious" about his manipulation of his employees anymore than the industrialists' manipulation of the economy's "energy" is "unconscious." Rather than accept such conflict and change as inevitable (as the Social Darwinism of Herbert Spencer would project in the very near future), Davis was among the first of a small group of writers who sought to challenge those myths at the outset and to expose the ideology engendering such "inevitability." This theme is depicted more fully by Davis in *John Andross* (1874) and subsequently by Hamlin Garland, Elizabeth Stuart Phelps, Upton Sinclair, Sarah Orne Jewett, and Mary Wilkins Freeman.[35] In "Life," the theme is revealed by Kirby's gloating acknowledgment that his father controls workers' votes by enticements of alleged patriotism, equality, and the opportunity to rise in the economic structure of capitalism:

> my father brought seven hundred votes to the polls for his candidate last November. No force-work, you understand—only a speech or two, a hint to form themselves into a society, and a bit of red and blue bunting to make them a flag. The Invincible Roughs,—I believe that is their name. I forget the motto: 'Our country's hope,' I think. (436)

The most painful and ironic aspect of this manipulation is that the capitalist's control comes from a little speech, precisely what he is denying those who labor for him. Whereas Davis denies the system itself as an unconsciously evolving force, she does recognize that Kirby has inherited his lifestyle and his way of thinking, just as Hugh has and Hugh's father before him. Davis's insistence upon thus linking heredity and environment, not only in "Life" but subsequently in *Margret Howth* (1862) and *Waiting for the Verdict* (1867), confirms that these "scientific" elements at the heart of naturalism[36] appeared in American literature before Zola began to publish his experimental work.

Davis exposes another, even more ironic, manner in which the capitalists deny the rights so blatantly thrown before Hugh: denial through silence. Mitchell is especially guilty of this act of omission. It begins when Kirby ironically repeats "I do not think at all" (439) in response to his associates' assertion that he is responsible for his workers. Not thinking is, at best, "idle dilettantism," a solution that Davis refuses to allow her readers. When Doctor May sarcastically asserts, "That is true philosophy. Drift with the stream, because you cannot dive deep enough to find bottom, eh?" (439), Kirby fails to "catch the meaning." But he does not want to understand. "I wash my hands of all social problems . . . ," he exclaims. "My duty to my operatives has a narrow limit,—the pay-hour on Saturday night" (439). At this moment Mitchell has his best opportunity to intervene because he alone has truly recognized the anguish of the workers as depicted in the Korl Woman's face. Yet he abdicates through cynicism. "Money has spoken!" he declares and thereafter remains silent (439). His mannerisms take on a theatricality that allows him to distance himself from the truth: he seated "himself lightly on a stone with the air of an amused spectator at a play" (439).

Once again, Davis introduces a theme—theatricality—that will become pervasive in later American naturalism: the tableaux of Edith Wharton's

The House of Mirth (1905), the seductive role-playing of Laura in Frank Norris's *The Pit* (1903), and the ever-worsening theaters of *Maggie: A Girl of the Streets* (1893) versus the increasingly reputable ones of *Sister Carrie* (1900). Davis develops the theme of theatricality throughout her literary career, in *Waiting for the Verdict* (1867) and in numerous short stories such as "Across the Gulf" (1881), "A Wayside Episode" (1883), and "The End of the Vendetta" (1892). In exposing Mitchell's theatricality, Davis excoriates the manner in which he thereby distances himself from responsibility. He now dispassionately views Hugh as "a rare mosaic," much more "amusing" than the Korl Woman. " 'Yes, money,—that is it,' [he said] rising and drawing his furred coat about him. 'You've found the cure for all the world's diseases' " (440). But Mitchell's cynicism is merely another form of denial. The "furred coat" symbolizes his own animalistic devolution; William Dean Howells later repeats the image of the fur-lined coat in his own realistic fiction to represent upper class guilt. After Mitchell thus insulates himself from Hugh, he silently tips his hat and exits.

Davis also indicts the abuse of language when it intentionally seeks to thwart rather than abet communication. In "Life" and throughout her fiction, she satirizes certain characters through their pretentious uttering of foreign phrases.[37] The language of the educated visitors is already foreign to the workers ("Greek would not have been more unintelligible to the furnace-tenders"), but the visitors further emphasize their distance from the impoverished by interjecting phrases specifically meant to alienate: "*Ce n'est pas mon affaire*," young Kirby ironically asserts—as heir to his father's ways it is precisely his "business," in every sense. To reinforce his denial of responsibility, Kirby invokes the typical capitalist refuge: "I have heard you call our American system a ladder which any man can scale. Do you doubt it? Or perhaps you want to banish all social ladders, and put us all on a flat tableland,—eh, May?" (439). Such a proposition is completely beyond the comprehension of the "puzzled" Doctor May. Kirby continues to remonstrate upon the topic: " 'I tell you, there's something wrong that no talk of '*Liberté*' or *Égalité*' will do away. If I had the making of men, these men who do the lowest part of the world's work should be machines,—nothing more,—hands. It would be kindness. . . . What are taste, reason, to creatures who must live such lives as that?' He pointed to Deborah, sleeping on the ash-heap" (439).

This passage is worth exploring in some depth. Kirby's need to evoke concepts of liberty and equality in French rather than English is particularly ironic; he cannot, of course, "afford" to honor those concepts. For him to suggest that he does not have "the making of men" is also ironic, since it is he and his forefathers who have shaped the workers into "hands" for his profit. So, too, is it ironic that Kirby points to Deborah: in so doing, he identifies the one figure who most clearly understands the hunger for compassion and for freedom of expression that is rendered in the Korl Woman's face, qualities Kirby wishes to deny his workers. Even Mitchell partakes of such posturing. Once he has decided upon theatricality instead of compassion, he also assumes the distancing technique of using foreign phrases: "Why, May, look at him!" he exclaims, pointing to Hugh. " '*De profundis clamavi.*' Or, to quote in English, 'Hungry and thirsty, his soul faints in him' " (439). Davis's satiric depiction of Mitchell in this stance denies his credibility as a translator for her audience; Deb's inarticulateness is preferable because it is at least honest. If Davis thwarts the language of romanticism, she much more stridently indicts the visitors' elitist manipulation of language.

Davis also makes a radical connection between transcendentalism and the evolution of capitalism. Her compelling theory begins in "Life" and culminates in "The Wife's Story" (1864). In the latter story, Hester Manning has been weaned on Concord's prevailing philosophy. To Davis's mind, the insistence upon "Me" and the "Not Me," meant to be fused in the "Over-Soul," was too easily left distinct. Thus Hester finds no value in her commonplace husband and his "Western" family:

> There might be more in them than this, but I had not found it: I doubted much if it were worth the finding. I came from a town in Massachusetts, where, as in most New-England villages, there was more mental power than was needed for the work that was to be done, and which reacted constantly on itself in a way which my husband called unwholesome; it was no wonder, therefore, that these people seemed to me but clogs of flesh, the mere hands by which the manual work of the world's progress was to be accomplished.[38]

The language of capitalism is synthesized with Hester's New England philosophy; and the transitions from transcendental theories of the Self to New England pride to industrial devolutionary complications of the merely mechanistic value of "clogs" and "hands" is central to Davis's belief that Concord training, with its elevation of the Self "over" nature and others, could transmogrify into complete disregard for the humanity of others when it was coupled with the nation's onset of industrialization.

In "Life," this philosophy of the Self is most evidently fused with capitalistic values in her characterization of Mitchell. He is "*blasé*" about every aspect of life, "a man who sucked the essence out of a science or philosophy in an indifferent, gentlemanly way; who took Kant, Novalis, Humboldt, for what they were worth in his own scales; accepting all, despising nothing . . . but one-idead men; with a temper yielding and brilliant as summer water, until his Self was touched. . . . Such men are not rare in the States" (437). In that scathing final comment, Davis rejects a philosophy that she deemed could be converted too easily into an opportunistic, self-based attitude. Further, the "Self" that Mitchell values is "ice, hardened and uncaring"; the metaphor of ice/cold/coolness that begins in "Life" is developed more fully in Davis's next three novels, in which the metaphor represents people's responses to one another in an industrial society or in a world ravaged by war. It is, she declares caustically in *Margret Howth*, a "learned conservatism." When Mitchell has distanced himself through theatricality and cynicism, the ice-Self immediately returns: "Bright and deep and cold as Arctic air, the soul of the man lay tranquil beneath" (439). It is only then that he can deny Hugh the same "rights" he has so fluently advocated as every man's.

The tragedy lies in Hugh's acceptance of this man's creed, believing in Mitchell's self-portrayal as "a Man all-knowing, all-seeing, crowned by Nature, reigning,—the keen glance of his eye falling like a sceptre on other men" (441), a kind of debauched Emersonian prophet. Hugh's own instinct had "taught him that he too—He!" had value; but viewing himself in the light of Mitchell's values, his own self-worth diminishes: "He looked at himself with sudden loathing, sick, wrung his hands with a cry, and then was silent" (441). Numerous themes culminate in this moment: the power of language—theoretical or otherwise—to silence the oppressed; Hugh's acceptance of the popular concept of the "beautiful" renders his mirror-image concept of himself as a grotesque disfigurement of the Man "crowned by Nature"; and thus, he devalues his own "flawed" Self. The pathos of the moment is excruciating when Hugh unwittingly completes the scene with a symbolic gesture: "He got up and helped [Deborah] to rise" (441). Hugh had dreamed that he would be Mitchell's prophet who would help other oppressed people to rise. Instead, all hope fades: "He gave it up that moment, then and forever" (441).

Thereafter, Hugh is truly lost as he incorporates the language of the capitalists as well as their values. When he repeats their rhetoric ("His right! The word struck him. Doctor May had used the same. . . . Why did this chance word cling to him so obstinately?" [443]), he feels a surge of power and thinks he is clear-witted, but in truth it clogs his thinking: "His brain was clear to-night, keen, intent, *mastering*. . . . Therefore the great temptation of his life came to him *veiled* by no *sophistry*, but bold, defiant, *owning* its own *vile* name, trusting to one bold *blow* for victory" (443; emphases added). Hugh usurps not only the philosophy of the powerbrokers but their "consciousness," rooted in force, as well. Thus, while he wanders "aimlessly down the street," he does so believing he is strengthened by "his sense of possession" (444). By appropriating the language of the capitalists (ownership and possession), Hugh also begins to embrace their sense of class distinctions. With only a "half-consciousness," he determines to return to the back alleys, into "the filth and drunkenness, the pig-pens, the ash-heaps covered with potato-skins, the bloated, pimpled women at the doors" (444). But now he does not do so in order to help his fellow victims to "rise"; he does so "with a new disgust, a new sense of sudden triumph" (444). Ironically, pathetically, this disgust parallels Mitchell's farewell tipping of his hat.

Even imprisonment and impending death cannot sway Hugh from these values. In jail, he is bound in iron manacles. Davis's symbolic use of iron in "Life in the Iron Mills" is particularly significant in terms of her precursory role in naturalistic fiction. In studying the rise of naturalism in American literature, Donald Pizer notes that "the major characteristic of the form of the naturalistic novel is that it no longer reflects [a] certainty about the value of experience but rather expresses a profound doubt or perplexity about what happens in the course of time."[39] He observes that there are numerous narrative techniques that lead to this new form, especially the naturalistic symbol: each of America's major naturalistic works has "a pervasive and striking symbol which, in a sense, accompanies the protagonist on his adventures" (Pizer 35). Thus, in *McTeague* the naturalistic symbol Norris employs is that of gold; for Dreiser in *Sister Carrie* it is the rocking chair; and for Crane in *The Red Badge of Courage* it is Henry's wound (35). In "Life," the naturalistic symbol is iron. Pizer continues, "A major characteristic of each of these symbols is that it functions ironically within the structure of the novel" (35). For Davis the *ironic* symbol is iron itself. Hugh has completely assimilated the values of the iron-mill owners; he carries those values with him throughout the core narrative and literally employs iron to hone the piece of tin with which he kills himself.

Davis extends the irony still further: when Hugh is jailed, it is market day; as he mechanically scrapes his piece of tin across the iron bars, the only thing that awakens him from this activity is the distinct sound of "the clink of money as it changed hands" (446). Looking toward the sound, he sees a mulatto following her mistress and thinks, "It was good to see a face like that. He would try to-morrow, and cut one like it" (448). Just as he had failed to understand his recreation of Deb's hunger in the face of the Korl Woman, he now fails to see his own representation in the mulatto's face or to understand that it does not represent "good." They are both slaves to a system. He so unwittingly incorporates the values of his masters that he envisions the marketplace outside his window as if it were "a picture . . . the dark-green heaps of corn, and the crimson beets, and golden melons!" (447) Hugh longs to go back into the marketplace; he sees only the idealized version of it presented here in picturesque beauty. There had been no "clear light" in Hugh's marketplace world and certainly no lush corn or juicy beets among the flitch. This is perhaps Davis's most indicating scene in terms of Hugh's being truly lost. He has "bought" the marketplace's concept of hegemony, even though he has lived its realities. Unlike the Korl Woman's question ("What shall we *do* to be saved?"), Hugh's question is passive: "what had he done to bear this?" (447) He struggles to understand, "What was right? And who had ever taught him?" (447) It is the greatest difference between Hugh and Deb: "Hur knows" is Deb's most oft-repeated phrase. Tragic as Hugh's fate is, he is the emblem of expendability in an industrial society, and Davis will not allow her readers to recover this human "refuse." In their blindness, they accepted his expendability; it is not redeemable.

This loss is especially tragic because Hugh had the power of expression through art, the "language" that can effect change. When the visitors come unexpectedly upon the Korl Woman, they are silenced. Staring into her face, Mitchell is forced to admit, "I see." He could ignore the silenced workers around him, but he cannot ignore the question artfully carved into the Korl Woman's face. As Walter Hesford notes, the "local 'representative men' " who come upon this figure reveal "their individual natures as the men aboard the *Pequod* reveal their's interpreting the doubloon."[40] The realism depicted in the iron ore's refuse exchanges the language of the owners for that of the art form itself. Though Hugh is lost, the Korl Woman survives to reframe his question and to challenge both narrator and reader.

III. Traditional Christianity

The Korl Woman's question ("What shall we *do* to be saved?") is drawn from Scripture, which leads us to the final inclusive theme of Davis's realism: the denial of passive, traditional Christianity as a means for alleviating the nation's social ills. Prior to 1865, American literature, like American thought, was decidedly religiocentric, and the 1850s, as Jane Tompkins has pointed out, saw a tremendous upsurge in millenarianist revivalism; the sentimental fiction of the period by Stowe, Warner, and Cummins captured and edified those beliefs.[41] As one scholar of American millenarian movements has asserted, "a concern with the truth about power is a religious activity."[42] For Davis, that was certainly true, in the sense that she desired to make known the truth about industrial capitalists' usurpation of religion—not only through the romance of the machine but very literally through a corruption of religious language. This belief led her in a fictional direction that was different from both the pietism of the sentimentalists and the anti-pietism of Hawthorne and Emerson. As discussed earlier in this chapter, the issue of Christianity in this text has probably caused the most difficulty for Davis scholars. James C. Austin presents the critical consensus when he concludes that "Life" depicts "in realistic detail the lot of the mill workers, whose only hope is a pitying God."[43] Yet Davis wants her readers to draw an opposite conclusion, that one cannot sidestep the issue of oppression by relying upon "a pitying God." She repudiates any theory allowing for passivity or transcendence. This repudiation begins in the opening frame; on the mantel in the narrator's house is a "little broken figure of an angel." Its wings are broken and smoke-covered, "clotted," making flight (transcendence) impossible. Befouled, it is now earthbound.

Although she was a Christian raised in the Episcopalian faith, Davis had rejected organized worship at an early age and periodically struggled with her faith, especially during the Civil War years. When she came to terms with her beliefs, she aligned herself with a loving and merciful God (her attacks on Calvinists are strident).[44] But she believed that the Word was often converted into a means of oppression. Specifically, she insisted that one has to work for salvation, and that work requires a concern for others as for oneself, a notion personified in Deb and the Quaker. Thus, throughout "Life," Davis employs irony, as heavy as the desolate air that clings to everything in the mill town, to deny passive Christianity as a means to salvation. Yet Davis allows her readers to toy with this idea, luring them once again into her core story through the narrator's comforting language, verging on a Stowesque pietism, in order to facilitate their own discovery of the vapidity of a passive response. The narrator guides the reader into Deb's realm with just such a proclamation:

> I dare not put this secret [that lies in the mire] into words. I told you it was
> dumb. These men, going by with drunken faces and brains full of unawakened
> power, do not ask it of Society or of God. Their lives ask it; their deaths ask
> it. There is no reply. I will tell you plainly that I have a great hope; and I bring
> it to you to be tested. It is this: that this terrible dumb question is its own
> reply; that it is not the sentence of death we think it, but, from the very
> extremity of its darkness, the most solemn prophecy which the world has
> known of the Hope to come. (431)

This certainly seems to suggest a traditional Christian response, the reliance upon "a pitying God." Yet unraveling of the text's ironies draws this response into question. Davis challenges her readers' traditional securities: Egoism, Pantheism, passive Christianity. At the core of her theory of the commonplace is the demand for a clear vision that confronts reality in both its "strange beauty" and its grimy depths. The "extremity of . . . darkness" can never be conquered by ignoring its presence; it is precisely the romantic concept of a "perfume-tinted dawn" that must be tested.

If Davis is impatient with "idle dilettantism," she is even more impatient with Christian "reformers" who exhibit idle Christianity:

> [The Wolfes' lives] were like those of their class: incessant labor, sleeping in
> kennel-like rooms, eating rank pork and molasses, drinking—. . . . Is that all
> of their lives?—of the portion given to them . . . nothing beneath?—all? So
> many a political reformer will tell you,—and many a private reformer, too,
> who has gone among them with a heart tender with Christ's charity, and come
> out outraged, hardened. (431)

These missionaries, armed with "Christ's charity" but unprepared for society's darker side, come bearing maxims and a surreptitious pride in their own act of charity. Maxims never suffice in Davis's philosophy. Her disgust with pious "reformers" who cannot see human beings beneath the dirt and drunkenness is at the core of her ironic view of Christian "hope," and her later fiction often includes the traditional realistic figure of the fallen clergyman.

Of particular interest to Davis is the capitalists' exploitation of Christian ritual and rhetoric. This begins with their mock piety in veiling the machinery each Sunday; yet the evil never disappears, for "as soon as the clock strikes midnight, the great furnaces break forth with renewed fury, the clamor begins with fresh, breathless vigor, the engines sob and shriek like 'gods in pain' " (433). Not only are the engines the new, more powerful god-force, but they have also become the new nature-force, sounding "through the sleep and shadow of the city like far-off thunder" (433). Neither the natural nor the spiritual realm can stave off their encroachments. The irony deepens as the bells toll the dawning of Sunday morning immediately after Hugh determines that he and his kind will never be equal with Mitchell: "Whatever hidden message lay in the tolling bells floated past these men unknown. Yet it was there. Veiled in the solemn music ushering the risen Saviour was a key-note to solve the darkest secrets of a world gone wrong,—even this social riddle which the brain of the grimy puddler grappled with madly to-night" (437). In spite of its surface language, the passage's "hidden message" refutes the preacher's belief that Christian salvation is available to the workers. Not only is the message incomprehensible to the men, just as the capitalists' language had been, but it is also "veiled," simulating the owners' covering of the machines and the workers. The message of dawn depicted here, though not evil, is cruel because its phatic language of "ushering [in] the risen Saviour" recalls the empty promises the so-called reformers had proferred for this "social riddle." It is only a riddle because the capitalists wish to keep it so. They repeat this "risen Saviour" image of hope to Hugh but suggest that there is nothing *they* can do; only a "prophet" rising out of the refuse can save the poor.

For Davis, however, clarity of vision demands an activism that extends beyond what benefits oneself—the "ice" Self—to what benefits all human beings. Davis's satire is unmistakable when it is Mitchell who accepts this corrupted symbol of the "prophet" as a harbinger of awakening. When the machines are veiled, he observes, "I like this view of the works better than when the glare was fiercest" (437). Not surprisingly. When the glare is "fiercest," the flames of the hellish furnaces illuminate the reality of the workers' lives; but the veiled vision, as Mitchell himself acknowledges, makes "the amphitheatre of smothered fires . . . unreal" (437). Thus he asserts that the fires are like "wild beasts, and the spectral figures their victims in the den" (431). Instead of metaphoric "theorizing," a true clarity, a true "dawn," would reveal that the human beings are victims not of the fires but of those who stoke them for profit. In fact, when the owner's son is asked what he will do for an artistically endowed worker like Hugh, he passively relies upon Christian rhetoric to excuse his rejection of social responsibility: "The Lord will take care of his own; or else they can work out their own salvation" (438–39).

Mitchell also employs merely the rhetoric of Christianity to mock Kirby's response. The answer, he suggests, is "[v]ery clear . . . I think I remember reading the same words somewhere:—washing your hand in Eau de

Cologne, and saying, 'I am innocent of the blood of this man. See ye to it!' " (439) Unlike the Korl Woman, however, Mitchell perverts the language of Scripture, exposing what Davis viewed as the dangers of a Christian training in the words of Scripture without an emphasis upon intent and application. Thus Doctor May, whom Mitchell terms "a philanthropist, in a small way" (439), likes to envision himself as the Great Almsgiver. However, the Doctor's sense of philanthropy is small, indeed. He sympathizes with Hugh and believes that "much good was to be done here by a friendly word or two: a latent genius to be warmed into life by a waited-for sun-beam. Here it was: he had brought it" (439–40). Not only does his arrogance allow him to equate himself with God and yet do nothing, but the "sun-beam" image reinforces the irony of the Sunday dawn which was supposed to offer a swift solution for the social riddle. Afterward, the Doctor prays, morning and night, "that power might be given these degraded souls to rise"; in so doing, "he glowed at heart, recognizing an accomplished duty" (440). Doctor May has learned the rhetoric of Christianity well: light, heart, duty. But it is precisely this self-gratifying perversion of religion that Davis attacks; it falsely warms the heart with its passive sense of *accomplished* duty.

Davis naturalistically depicts the destructive influence of such attitudes through Hugh's fate. Once again he accepts the visitors' creed, for when he follows their advice and keeps the stolen money as his by "right," he attributes the act to God: he believes the money will "raise him out of the pit" because it is "straight from God's hand" (443). Ironically, Hugh believes he knows the Truth: "God made this money . . . for his children's use. . . . The Something who looked down on him that moment through the cool gray sky had a kindly face, he knew—loved his children alike. Oh, he knew that!" (443–44) Yet Hugh *knows* nothing. Now consumed by greed and educated to marketplace values, he converts everything to "use." In spite of his protestations, Hugh continues to feel a disquieting dread, relieved only once during his night of crisis when, ironically, he enters a church of wealthy parishioners. In this church, everything is corrupted—the "light," the words of the minister, the promises of Eden. The light that filters through the stained glass windows "lost itself in far-retreating arches; built to meet the requirements and sympathies of a far other class than Wolfe's" (444). That is, the "light" which is absorbed in gilding cannot enact an awakening. The preacher is "a Christian reformer," and he loves to preach to "Humanity in its grand total" with words he "painted" for his audience, "beautiful words" (444). However, Davis's satiric depiction of this reformer who uses the language of Beautiful Words reveals that such "words passed far over the furnace-tender's grasp, toned to suit another class of culture" (444), because the preacher delights in his own voice more than in his mission. Hugh had entered the church in the full flush of accepting that promised Edenic world as fulfilling all of his dreams; but with the minister's failure to save Hugh, those tenuously proffered promises are shattered: the "golden mists" created through the mill owners' mythology have vanished; all that remains is a sky that is "dull and ash-colored" (445). Instead of the reformer's version of Christianity saving Hugh, it recreates his smothering, ash-filled world and propels him into his decline: "The trial-day of this man's life was over, and he had lost the victory. What followed was mere drifting circumstance" (445). This is the language of determinism; Hugh's fate is sealed, and he dies in a prison cell.

Even at this final point, Davis refuses to allow her readers the comfort of an appeasing rapidity to the furnace-tender's death, which would allow them to distance themselves. Although readers may anticipate a comforting statement assuring them that Hugh has found peace at last, Davis denies the viability of such platitudes: "Whether, as the pure light crept up the stretched-out figure, it brought with it calm and peace, who shall say?" (449) And if no one can "say," language (the Word as corrupted by capitalists, reformers, and, ultimately, the narrator) has completely failed Hugh. Kirby, the coroner, and other curious onlookers come to view the furnace-tender's corpse as though he were once again a specimen laid out for their amusement; only a quiet Quaker woman acts with compassion. With the Quaker's entrance into the narrative, the reader begins the ascent of the structural ladder, moving out of the naturalistic inner core that has depicted Hugh's demise and into the realms of realism and romanticism. But both of these outer realms have now been drastically changed by the reader's new literary experience of the core story.

The middle realm is Deborah's. By noticing the Quaker and her concern for Hugh, Deborah is the link between the irreparable despair of Hugh and the possibility of change in that outer frame. It is a tenuous link; Deb, too, may be lost, because at this moment she no longer harbors her sense of compassion. No sorrow lines her face: "the stuff out of which murderers are made, instead" (449). Though Davis does not idealize the Quakers, they most often represent her alternative spiritual perspective. For decades, New England authors had employed Quaker characters in their writings as symbols of Puritan persecution, but Davis carried no New England guilt that needed to be thus expurgated. Rejecting the platitudes of so-called Christian reformers, she presents the Friends as those who know right from wrong and who actively pursue the rights of others in that context, not in the perverted sense of Doctor May's system. Exemplifying Davis's desired activism, the Quaker woman quietly tends to Deborah's needs, and when the last of the visitors have gone, she lays beside Hugh a bouquet formed of common, natural elements—"wood-leaves and berries." It is day, "dawn" in a realistic sense. Symbolically, the Quaker opens the window, instinctively knowing the scents and the fresh air for which Hugh had longed. Deb is astonished at the Quaker's insight: "Did hur know my boy wud like it? Did hur know Hugh?" she cries. "I know Hugh now," the Quaker responds, but her eyes bear "a heavy shadow" (449); she also knows that she, like the reader, came too late for Hugh.

Davis's theoretical movement from romanticism to realism and naturalism in "Life" also involves truly "seeing" reality and educating others to do the same. Thus when Deb cries that she does not want Hugh "smothered" under the mud and ash in the pauper's grave, the Quaker takes her to the window and helps her to "see" the far-off hills. The popular theorists, we recall, were "busy in making straight paths for [their own] feet on the hills." The Quaker, however, reaches out to Hugh in his death; more significantly, she also realizes that Deb is salvageable and offers her a new life. After Deb serves her sentence, the Quaker assures her, "thee shall begin thy life again,—there on the hills" in the Quaker woman's own community (450). Thus Davis moves the reader out of the middle ground via a prophecy of Deb's rebirth, rooted in the promise of action; without such assistance, Deb undoubtedly would have succumbed to the corruption of the mill world as well. Throughout her fifty-year writing career, Davis insisted upon this kind of personal activism. In the winter of 1877, the *New York Daily Tribune* reported an incident in which a woman and child were left to freeze to death on a busy New York street. Readers responded, condemning the incident in terms of the failure of charitable institutions to fulfill their duties. In a letter to the editor, Davis penned her strongest objection to such passive pity and misplaced blame, which concluded: "In a word . . . when a man shifts his personal responsibility for the poor wholly to legal action or organized associations, does he not rob his needy brother and himself of that reality of human brotherhood . . . ?"[45] She also educated her children in such activism. When her eldest son was away at school and felt dissatisfied with his advisor's suggestion that prayer was a sufficient antidote to melancholy, Davis counseled, "when you feel as if prayer was a burden, stop praying and go out and try to put your Christianity into real action."[46]

In "Life," as Davis moves the reader back into that comfortable outer frame, the narrator reenters the text by repeating the words of the Quaker woman: "Not too late." But Deb is "old, deformed"; her worn face still shows her struggles. She has come into the narrator's frame where, rooted in romanticism as it is, she can find the "happy ending" denied Hugh in his naturalistic world, but not without the scars from her own experiences. Yet what seems the end of the narrator's story is not the end of Davis's; her purpose has always been to challenge the reader's expectations. This is the significance of the narrator's closing frame. What has survived in the outer frame is not the broken angel figurine; it is the Korl Woman, intact. Her arm extends in a representative "gesture of warning," the legacy of this prehensile figure modeled on Deb. The narrator concludes that she has the gnarled figure "here in a corner of my library. I keep it hid behind a curtain,—it is such a rough, ungainly thing" (450). Davis's readers, nearly forgetting Hugh's demise, appeased with Deb's salvation and comfortable with the story's apparent conclusion, must be jolted from their apathy by this statement. Why is the narrator, their primary guide down into and out of the underworld, *veiling* this symbol of oppression? It is Davis's ultimate irony. Each reader, abruptly awakened from a regained "idle dilettantism," must now become his or her own guide.

The narrator looks at the imploring face of the Korl Woman through which Hugh's voice finally echoes—"Is this the End?"; that is, have I been forgotten so soon? The reader cannot accept the proffered sentimental "promise" at the story's conclusion, recognizing at last the ironic twist of Davis's narrative structure. The author's desire all along has been to place the reader in the role of one who "knows"; that is the only way to enact true reform, the kind effected by the Quaker. Davis signals this need for questioning the narrator now by having her intone a romantic soliloquy: "Aphrodite; a bough of forest-leaves; music; work; homely fragments, in which lie the secrets of all eternal truth and beauty. Prophetic all!" (451) Clearly, this is the rhetoric of the Veilers, capitalist or mock-Christian. The narrator, still clinging to her idle dilettantism of the opening frame, relies upon the presupposing language of passive Christianity for her conclusion: "a cool, gray light suddenly touches [the Korl Woman's] head like a blessing hand, and its groping arm points through the broken cloud to the far East, where, in the flickering, nebulous crimson, God has set the promise of Dawn" (451).

That this "promise of Dawn" is intended as an ironic posture is further reinforced by Davis's 1863 short story of that title, in which a prostitute is the central character (preceding Crane's Maggie by thirty years). In Davis's story, the prostitute is denied "dawn" by all of the self-proclaimed Christians with whom she comes in contact; therefore, the desperate woman concludes that it is only by committing suicide that she can free her brother from the downward cycle of poverty and debasement that she had inherited from her mother. Davis implies that the prostitute will fare better in God's Heaven than she did with hypocritical earthly Christians. It is the same emphasis Crane later made in his inscription of *Maggie* to Hamlin Garland: "It is inevitable that you will be greatly shocked by this book. . . . For it tries to show that environment is a tremendous thing in the world and frequently shapes lives regardless. If one proves that theory, one makes room in Heaven for all sorts of souls (notably an occasional street girl) who are not confidently expected to be there by many excellent people."[47] Reinforced by the scathing attacks against just such promises of "dawn" as are incorporated into the text of "Life," Davis seeks in the story's conclusion an adamant rejection by her audience of that false sense of dawn: "Why, you tell me," she has the narrator state at last. The reader must become the active participant who unveils the realities of life for the class represented by the Korl Woman. As Houston Baker, Jr., has detailed, in 1900 the great Afro-American historian and author W. E. B. DuBois used the veil as the governing metaphor of *The Souls of Black Folk*: "The Veil signifies a barrier of American racial segregation that keeps Afro-Americans always behind a color line—disoriented—prey to divided aims, dire economic circumstances, haphazard educational opportunities, and frustrated intellectual ambitions"; DuBois's "penultimate vision" occurs when the "Veil is rent."[48] Davis's governing metaphor and vision is the same—her concern is for a class of individuals who were kept perpetually behind the barrier by capitalist Veilers.

*   *   *

Davis was well aware that she had created a radical work of fiction. Although there was some attention to industrial working conditions at the time, Jacob Riis and the members of the women's movement in New York would not begin their assaults on the conditions of the working poor until the 1880s. Thus Davis sought to publish her story in a publication that would attract the appropriate audience and criticism: she submitted "Life" to the *Atlantic Monthly*, a journal that had led the way in publishing more realistic fiction since James Russell Lowell had taken over the editorship in 1857. She had followed the progress of the *Atlantic* since its inception, and the Wheeling *Intelligencer* had often included excerpts of the journal's pertinent articles and stories in its own pages during the years she was associated with the Virginia newspaper.

In January 1861, the *Atlantic*'s assistant editor (and soon to be editor), James T. Fields, responded to Davis's submission. Years later, when her eldest son had his first article accepted for publication, she recalled her mixed feelings of dread and excitement at receiving Fields's response: "I carried the letter half a day before opening it, being so sure it was a refusal."[49] It was, in fact, an enthusiastic acceptance and included payment of fifty dollars for "Life in the Iron Mills." As the manuscript was prepared for press, Fields questioned her choice of title. She replied, realizing he preferred a title that was "more 'taking' " but asserting, "I should like something suggestive of the subdued meaning of the story."[50] If not "Life in the Iron Mills," she continues, "how would 'The Korl Woman' do? *I* would be sure to read an article with that caption in the hope of discovering some new race of Hotentots perhaps. However, I shall be satisfied with your choice—whatever it may be."[51] Davis sought two things in this request: that her title signify the complexities of her narrative and, in spite of her playful reference to "Hotentots," that it illuminate the originality of her work. Yet she was a new author, excited about her first major acceptance and unwilling to be too difficult at this early stage; she allowed Fields the final say.

It was the beginning of a decision-making process that would haunt her throughout her decade-long association with Fields, beginning with the next story she submitted to him. But by March 13, her business sense was beginning to surface, although it would never be her strongest attribute. Fields had praised "Life" and requested another story. Her response begins with the typical courtesy and self-effacement of mid-nineteenth-century women's letters (one thinks of Emily Dickinson): "Your kindness touches me the more because it is so unexpected. I see that the novelty of the scene of the story has made you over-estimate it—another, most probably, would disappoint you. However, I will try."[52] After the amenities, however, Davis immediately takes control of the situation. Fields offered to advance her one hundred dollars for the next article, but she prefers artistic freedom in a world all too accustomed to commodifying art: "I receive the offer as frankly as you made it but you must pardon me if I decline it. Money is enough a 'needful commodity' with me to make me accept with a complacent style whatever you think the articles are worth. But if I were writing with a hundred dollar bill before me in order to write on it 'I have paid him' I am afraid the article would be broad and deep just $100 and no more."

Economic pressures would continue to force Davis to acquiesce to Fields's judgment about her work; but it is also evident in this early letter that Davis realized the artistic value of her work exceeded monetary compensation. What she preferred was access to criticism: "I will ask a favor of you instead of money. If any of your exchanges notice the story will you send them to me? That is a trouble, is it not? I would like to see them, partly from selfish notions and partly because it would please my father and mother—I trust to your kindness, to give me the pleasure—provided any one likes the article as you do—." It is a request that Davis often made of Fields, later dropping the notion of her parents' enjoyment and ardently seeking constructive analyses of her writing. Yet she rarely received a response from Fields to such requests; his replies to her desire to see critical reviews of her work and later to her desire for the freedom of publication in England were very selective. But in this instance Fields reciprocated, and from the critical success of "Life" Davis garnered the courage to write to the author who had most influenced her reading as a child. To Nathaniel Hawthorne she wrote:[53]

> I do not think for a moment you will care what partial glimpse of this To-day has come to a woman's eyes in her corner but I want to send you *something*— because, when the woman's eyes were child's eyes, your words used to bring the tears to them, often—bring them still—and I wish to thank you for the words—if you will allow me—in even this uncouth fashion.[54]

Davis's literary association with Hawthorne extended back to her early youth when, secure in her tree-house hideaway, she had discovered three short stories by Hawthorne in an otherwise "thin & cheap" collection of *Moral Tales*. These unique entries enlivened her imagination in direct proportion to the author's weaving into his tales the fabric of "the commonplace folk & things which I saw everyday"; and this new "fabric" had an immediate appeal for a young girl whose era considered appropriate reading to be highly romanticized moralism: "only Bunyan and Miss Edgeworth and Sir Walter."[55] Even at that early age, Davis had begun to realize that romanticized locales, of whatever creative quality, were unreal.

As she explained in 1892 to the Shakespearean scholar, Horace Howard Furness, who had sent her a copy of *The Tempest*, his gift reminded her of reading Shakespeare's tales as a child: "They were only accounts to me of the same world which I knew in Crusoe and Ivanhoe and the Pilgrims Progress—a place far outside of the dull Virginian village which I should see for myself some day. Well,—I haven't found it yet!"[56]

To Davis's amazement, Hawthorne responded to her literary gift. Nearly sixty years after reading those three tales, she recounted the episode of his reply with well-remembered excitement:

> Years afterward, when he was known as the greatest of living romancers, I opened his "Twice-Told Tales" and found there my old friends with a shock of delight as keen as if I had met one of my kinsfolk in the streets of a foreign city.
>
> In the first heat of my discovery I wrote to Mr. Hawthorne and told him about [the tree house] and of what he had done for the child who used to hide there. . . . I presently received a note from him saying he was then at Washington, and was coming on to Harper's Ferry, where John Brown had died, and still farther to see the cherry-trees and—me.
>
> *Me.*[57]

2. After "Life": A Savage Necessity[1]

THE APPEAL OF "the commonplace folk & things" was to become the commanding force behind Davis's fifty-year contribution to American literature and certainly constituted the impetus for her subsequent personal association with Hawthorne. But this was 1861, and the war invaded every aspect of American life. The new year began with an article in the Wheeling *Intelligencer* headlined "A Warning to the Secession Traitors in our Midst," and an editorial at the end of the week cautioned against the "dis-union conspiracy."[2] Almost every issue addressed secession in some manner. Two days before Richmond announced its decision to secede, the editorial column of the *Intelligencer* began not with the usual commentary but with a picture of the American flag and the words of the "Star-Spangled Banner" printed beneath the flag. Thereafter, the flag remained a staple of the column, with various poems, war news, and commentaries accompanying it. As a result of the Richmond convention, Virginia seceded from the Union on April 17, 1861.

It took the western region of the state nearly a month to organize itself, but on May 13 a convention was called to order in Wheeling with the specific purpose of countering Richmond's action. The Wheeling gathering drew delegates from twenty-four Virginia counties to discuss the secession of eastern Virginia and to rally support for nonsecession and the Union cause. The front page of the *Intelligencer* of May 21 carried the prepared statement of a designated committee of the convention; the statement, addressed "To the People of North Western Virginia," termed secession "a deed of darkness" that could only result in "bankruptcy, ruin, civil war . . . [and] military despotism."[3] The committee demanded that citizens participate in "the work of saving your country from becoming the theatre of a bloody war, brought upon you without your consent and against your will." No anti-slavery call is recorded; in fact, the only reference to slavery comes in the last sentence of the prepared statement and it converts the issue from the very real and present enslavement of blacks in the South to a potential enslavement of whites: "If you hesitate or falter all is lost, and you and your children to the latest posterity are destined to perpetual slavery" under the tyranny of the Richmond convention secessionists and President Jefferson Davis.

The Wheeling Conventions lasted through 1862, and West Virginia did not become a bonafide state until 1863, but the citizens now designated their region "New Virginia" and the separation process was begun. Wheeling became the capital of New Virginia, at which time, Davis observed, " 'New Virginia' and its capitol are in a state of panic and preparation not to be described."⁴ Wheeling also became headquarters of the Mountain Department of the Union Army, and in the early spring, the Confederates seized the furthest western section of the Baltimore and Ohio Railroad, an event that abruptly aborted Hawthorne's journey to Wheeling. Returning home, Hawthorne extended an invitation for Davis to visit him in Massachusetts; it would take more than a year to arrange safe passage and to engage the required male traveling companion before Davis could put her enthusiastic acceptance into effect. At the beginning of May, President Lincoln had announced the Union's need for volunteers, requiring forty thousand enlistees willing to serve the Union cause for three years.⁵ Davis's younger brothers, Richard and Henry, were in their early twenties and eagerly sought to volunteer. Nowhere are the political tensions of border life so evident as in Davis's letter to her cousin, Jim Wilson, in which she details the pressures exerted against the willingness of the young men of Wheeling to answer Lincoln's call: "the Mayor sent [Richard] and the other boys word that if they went it would ruin their families—spoke of Pa particularly."⁶

For the time being, Richard remained in Wheeling. The young men who withstood the local political pressures and enlisted in the Union army—approximately one hundred and sixty volunteers from Wheeling—were directed to Harper's Ferry.

In the meantime, Davis continued to write. In mid-April she notified Fields that she had a short story near completion with the working title, "The Deaf and The Dumb."⁷ No record of this manuscript remains, though it may have been an early form of her next major project, a full-length novel which she intended for serialization in the *Atlantic* under the title of "The Story of To-Day." As its title suggests, Davis adamantly sought to record the tumultuous events surrounding her in a manner that was in explicit opposition to the "army of cheery story-tellers who beset the young people to-day."⁸ Not surprisingly, considering the success of her literary innovations in "Life," she chose to extend her sharply realistic techniques in unveiling the continuing consequences of industrialization on American life, especially in terms of mill employees. The year after Davis's novel appeared, reformers in New York City organized the Working Women's Protective Union to assist poor women who worked in the city. The union emphasized the necessity of protecting their "less fortunate sisters" from exploitation by their employers.[9] Davis confronts this pattern of abuse in her characterization of Margret Howth, a strong-willed young woman who nevertheless remains vulnerable to her employer because of her financial situation. When she submitted this manuscript to Fields, however, he politely but pointedly refused it because it too readily "assembled the gloom" so rampant in the country. A subdued Davis wrote him on the tenth of May, apologizing for "the disappointment."[10]

Fields apparently saw no irony in his request to eliminate the "gloom" from a story that was intended to expose the causes of that mood. Not only did the idea that literature must propagate "the good" still prevail in American publishing but Fields himself was an admirer of that tenet; his highest praise of Nathaniel Hawthorne was that his writings "have never soiled the public mind with one unlovely image."[11] Davis attempted to explain to Fields that for her the "holier meaning of life or music" had been replaced by realities of war that were literally at her doorstep, and she sought to clarify the origins of her art: "When I began the story, I meant to make it end in full sunshine—to show how even 'Lois' was not dumb [mute], how even the meanest things in life, were 'voices in the world, and none of them without its signification.' Her life and death were to be the only dark thread. But 'Stephen Holmes' was drawn from life and in my eagerness to show the effects of a creed like his, I 'assembled the gloom' you complain of."[12] She cautiously asked if she might revise the story to meet Fields's requirements, but could not completely forego her artistic choices: "Let [Lois's] character and death (I cannot give up all, you see) remain, and the rest of the picture be steeped in warm healthy light. A 'perfect day in June'—Will you tell me if that is your only objection—the one you assign? Would the character of Holmes be distasteful to your readers? I mean—the development in common vulgar life of the Fichtian philosophy and its effect upon a self made man, as I view it?"[13] Then she must ask the question that has hovered between the lines: "If you do not think I could alter the story, shall I try again, or do you care to have me as a contributor?" The self-confidence gained from her initial success had been severely bruised by

Fields's rejection, but it had not been extirpated. She concludes her letter with a tentative request for more artistic freedom: "If I write for you again, would it be any difference if the story was longer than the last? I felt cramped, and we of the West like room, you know—."[14]

No manuscript survives of this first, gloomier version of "The Story of To-Day." The novel, serialized in the *Atlantic* under that title and published in book form as *Margret Howth: The Story of To-Day*, is ultimately a failure in artistic terms precisely because of the incongruous insertions of "full sunshine" into an otherwise stridently realistic work. Yet the novel is important to American literature for several reasons: it reveals the bitterness with which Davis added what Fields termed "cheerful" elements to her realistic text; it records significant historical revelations of mid-nineteenth-century American life; and its place in literary history is confirmed by the extension of the naturalistic techniques begun in "Life," which survive here in spite of her publisher's admonishments against them and her own acquiescence to his demands. Equally important, it exposes Fields's failure to understand the literary challenges and innovations in Davis's fiction, a fact which renders her epigraph ("My matter hath no voice to alien ears") painfully ironic.[15] The artist within Davis struggled not to despoil her own work; she hedged wherever possible on Fields's instructions.

The opening pages of *Howth* offer extraordinary insights into the devastating effects of life in an industrialized border-state community at the beginning of the Civil War. Out of this "gloom," Davis wrenches an art form consistent with her subject: "My story is very crude and homely . . . only a rough sketch of those you see every day, and call 'dregs.' "[16] Her writing is "a dull, plain bit of prose," she suggests, attuned to the warehouses and back alleys about to be exposed (6). Although this type of insistence upon realism was not yet commonplace, it harks back at least to Caroline Kirkland's *A New Home—Who'll Follow?* (1839); Kirkland also described her book as "very nearly—a veritable history; an unimpeachable transcript of reality; a rough picture . . . but pentagraphed from the life." Davis extends earlier realists' boundaries by insisting that the issue of class is part of American reality. Fully cognizant of prevailing literary tastes, she also knows that her radical departure will disturb many readers. She expects they will call it "stale and plebian" because that will allow them to ignore its message (6). They want "delicately tinted" visions of life and "passion-veined hearts," that is, romantic escapism; but the realist commands her readers "to dig into this commonplace, this vulgar American

life, and see what it is. Sometimes I think it has a new and awful significance that we do not see" (6). The war remains a backdrop in *Howth*, but
it acts as a metaphor for different aspects of American life—the working
class's daily battles for survival, and the struggle to find faith in the face of
impending devastation—and, for Davis as an artist, the effort to express
her own vision of "To-Day." She may have lost her war, but she claims
victory in many of the literary battles enacted in this novel.

As Houston Baker, Jr., has observed, when Kantian aesthetics ("bour-
geois" aesthetics) are employed to distinguish "Art" from " 'low taste,' "

> then one has effected a [Foucauldian] confinement that can be enforced
> merely by mentioning a word. Such distinctions . . . can be used to defend
> and preserve canons of literature and to protect "artistic" masterpieces from
> all criticism. Only "*men* of taste" are held to possess the developed "aesthetic
> sense" and sensibility requisite to identification and judgment of genuine
> works of ART. If such men declare that a product is *not* ART but a product of
> some other category, there is no escape from their authority of confinement—
> except subversion.[17]

What we have in *Howth*, then, is not the story Davis originally wrote, but
the one to which she acceded but subverted. The irony was not lost on her
that such indirect tactics forced her to subvert her own creation. Revisions
after Fields's initial rejection may be assumed in several instances by the
bitterness with which "full sunshine" is incongruously inserted into the
story.

The first problem with a realistic novel that has been "softened" is that
it prepares the reader to expect a traditional hero or heroine. Many critics
today still refer to Margret as an ambiguous heroine.[18] From the beginning,
however, Davis intended no such delineation for Margret, as she explained
to Fields when she sought to have the book's title remain "A Story of To-
Day": "I don't like 'Margret Howth' at all because she is the completest
failure in the story, beside *not* being the nucleus of it."[19] Davis was concerned with characterizations in *Howth* that extended far beyond the traditional heroine: "I wish I had some brilliant dyes . . . [to] take you back
to 'Once upon a time' in which the souls of our grandmothers delighted,—
the time which Dr. Johnson sat up all night to read about in 'Eveline.' . . .
None of your good-hearted, sorely-tempted villains then! . . . no trouble
then in seeing which were sheep and which were goats!" (101) Stories once
had morals, she acknowledges, and clearly defined characters, as do many
yet today. But such figurations are contrived and unrealistic: "I only mean

to say that I never was there . . . I am willing to do my best, but I live in the commonplace . . . [and] I never saw a full-blooded saint or sinner in my life" (102). The delightful tone and emphatic assertion of her theory in the last line is Davis at her best, and her complex characterizations exemplify her theory.

The introduction into the text of the title character exposes the organic element in Davis's theory of the commonplace. Margret is a ledger-keeper for Knowles & Co., wool manufacturers who supply the Indiana region. Her crisp, precise writing is perfectly suited to the occupation of "record-keeping." Margret does not succumb to the prevailing standards by "dramatizing her soul in her writing," nor by embellishing her "dress" (8). The extent to which Davis believed this stringency necessary to her own style is evident in her correspondence with Fields concerning revisions for both the serialization and the book form. The exchange focused on her desire to enhance the factual basis of her realism. *She* was now the one "disappointed" in the story because of the required revisions ("It was so much like giving people broken bits of apple rind to chew"[20]) and frustrated that she could not "touch forbidden subjects" in order to "write a true history of To-day."[21] She wrote Fields almost every week during the summer of 1861, requesting the opportunity to make revisions. On August 9, she suggested he return all but the first section of the manuscript for revision, but a week later she had to admit that the sporadic mail service caused by the War made it impossible to risk returning her manuscript: "If Gen. Lee can pass Rosecrans' force," Davis cautioned, "it is probable he will scatter our Wheeling government and our mails will be deranged. I do not think it likely, but it is well to be safe."[22]

Out of the author's frustration, however, comes for posterity a record of numerous points she sought to clarify. Davis had learned the technique of suggesting, often humorously, that Fields do as he please while at the same time couching her own preferences in her seeming acquiescence. For instance, when Fields questioned the weather in one part of the novel, Davis explained, "the weather is all right for our Indian summers," but she jokingly offers to "alter it if it affects your calmer New England temperaments."[23] It remained as she had written it. She also scrupulously requested the date at the top of Margret's ledger be changed from merely "Oct. 2" to "Oct. 2, 1860" in order to enhance its specificity.[24] But the system was imperfect, at best, and she was angered when the serialization appeared with the spelling "Margaret." "Is the proof reader *quite* killed?" she wrote Fields. "That's one good thing. I hope he has no ghost."[25] To her continual chagrin, George Nichols's unauthorized editing would haunt her through-out her years with the *Atlantic*.

By the end of summer, Davis had surrendered. She resignedly pro-fesses to no longer care about further changes, "What is *today* fifty years hence? . . . Am I at work for future ages?"[26] Since the story was highly topical, Davis asked for prompt publication. But when critical response warranted a book form of the novel, she again requested the opportunity to revise it thoroughly, intending to conclude with Dr. Knowles's death at Manassas.[27] But Fields asserted editorial control by indicating he was "con-tented" with its conclusion. Her resigned reply was that Knowles "may as well see the war out, I suppose."[28] Acquiescence was becoming more galling as Fields's victory became apparent.

Why did Davis acquiesce? Why didn't she demand her authorial vision be honored? No easy answers remain. She was inexperienced, certainly. Further, the acclaim she had received following the publication of "Life" was a heady experience that she longed to replicate, and Fields was a re-nowned Boston editor of the major literary journal of the decade. Such acquiescence is not a pattern limited to women writers, of course; at the turn of the century, Theodore Dreiser would allow his editor and his spouse to greatly alter his masterpiece and, like Davis, with seemingly little disdain for the process. In Davis's case, however, perhaps the most proba-ble cause for her response is revealed in her early education in the prevail-ing proprieties of male-female relationships, which she extended to the author-publisher relationship; and, as she once told Fields, she believed in standing by "the proprieties." She established with Fields, at his behest, a system whereby his opinion ruled: "Indeed I *will* leave all care of author-ship in your hands. You don't know how your kindness touches me."[29] Although her fiction would soon begin to challenge such "educated" re-sponses from other women, it would be several years before she would enact such reforms within her own author-publisher relationships.

For the time being, she chose subversion. In the passages concerning religion, Davis disavows most explicitly the revisions Fields sought in *Howth*. She cannot completely excise from her record the despair she reads daily on every face. "Hands wet with a brother's blood" are part of com-monplace life now, and she questions prophecies of "the great To-Morrow" through asides such as "if God lives" that challenge traditional answers (4). Certainly the novel is rife with prophecies of God's mercy in a future life, once the struggle is over—Lois Yare expresses in word and deed the truest faith—but the narrator's assertions are too insistent, too bitterly uttered to be accepted as heartfelt. Thus dawn is initially described as "giddily" revealing its "rosy blushes," but the author rapidly shifts to images of sunlight that are "like pointed swords . . . led by the conquering wind [to] Victory" (66). The violent imagery of the latter passage invokes the beginning of war and death rather than "the new life." Nor can churches offer refuge, since they too have been converted to a capitalist philosophy; they lift "their hard stone faces insolently, registering their yearly alms in the morning journals" (18). The only "House of Refuge" for the poor now is the communist facility envisioned by the reformer, Dr. Knowles; and the reaction to reformers explicated in "Life" is reinforced in *Howth* by Dr. Knowles's obsessive manipulation of and "mastery" over his converts.

Thus while Davis adds her message of "full sunshine," she also undermines it with repeated interpolations, because the story of tomorrow has lost its meaning for today. Americans' willingness to scramble toward the latest "ism" is exposed in *Howth* as futile, whether it be Margret's solidified Christianity or Knowles's communism or Holmes's Fichtian transformation of the Self. Davis offers what she believed was the redeeming philosophy—Lois Yare's living faith, which incorporates a triunal belief in God, others, and oneself. Yet it is Lois whom the author sacrifices through the lingering effects of the fire at the mill. Lois's death echoes little Eva's, acting as what Jane Tompkins has termed the epitome of Christian soteriology in *Uncle Tom's Cabin*,[30] but with a significant distinction: Eva's self-sacrifice is redemptive for others, but there is no redemptive aspect to Lois's death. As an impoverished mulatto, her life, like Hugh Wolfe's, is deemed expendable in the milieu of industrial capitalism. If Davis offered her readers the required placebic happy ending, it was ironically accomplished at the expense of the single potentially redeeming figure in the novel.

What Davis salvaged in *Howth* were her pioneering naturalistic techniques. Although after the war she would begin to embrace in her fiction a more positive sense of God's mercy, she would also continue to incorporate into her artistry the symbols and themes of naturalism whereby the possibility for Hugh Wolfe's plot of decline remains preeminent in every brute life. There is no promise that God's mercy *will* prevail. In this novel, Davis expands the startlingly naturalistic descriptions of the working conditions under industrial capitalism begun in "Life." Knowles & Co.

constitutes seven floors of monstrous, thundering looms and the oppressive, stagnating fumes of copperas. As a factory clerk, Margret warrants a slightly better environment than the mill hands: her office is a converted closet with one window that overlooks the acrid dyeing vats. Little sunlight can seep through the dust and cobwebs that shade the window. More than the physical condition, however, Davis's concern is for the psychological effects of these conditions. Stephen chooses to live in the factory, and Davis succinctly expresses its pervasive control over the young man: "In the mill he was of the mill" (117). The use of iron as a metaphor for constricted lives is also extended. The factory's interior is a "maze of iron cylinders and black swinging bars and wheels" (116). In an attempt to stifle his natural desires, Stephen recreates that atmosphere in his room at the mill: the bedstead, the chairs, all fixtures are of iron. Even his step becomes "an iron tread" (87). In Margret's actions, Davis manifests the rapidity with which workers incorporate the mechanistic rhythms of the machines: after her first day of work in the factory, Margret wipes the ink from her pens "in a quaint, mechanical fashion" (10). Within days her step becomes "mechanical" and her eyes become "schooled" to gaze straight ahead, "indifferently" (224).

Also continued from "Life" is Davis's naturalistic motif of the caged bird as a symbol of imprisoned souls. In *Howth*'s version of this symbol, however, Davis incorporates the black humor that she usually reserved for her personal correspondence. Here is no delicate albeit befouled canary; in the wire cage is a "miserable pecking chicken" (11). The cage is hung in Margret's office; when she wants to take it home with her to the country, Knowles laughs, "You take it for a type of yourself, eh?" He insists it remain in the dimly lit, suffocating atmosphere of the closet-office, because it has work to accomplish. Its "master" is Stephen Holmes, who ironically is about to entrap himself by marrying a woman he does not love but whose dowry is co-partnership in the mill.

Further outlining the dangers of accepting the marketplace philosophy, Davis depicts how it has wended its way into the countryside in an attempt to conquer the environment itself. Though Margret escapes to her country home each evening, the time is near when this region will no longer be a "House of Refuge" either; the ashy clouds from the mill are drifting further and further into that Edenic territory, powdering the greenery with its gray cloak and choking the life from any new growth. While "an eternal quiet" remains in the country for now, the landscape bordering the city has become a dumping ground for the mud and filth of the mills. The Wabash writhes and curdles as it laps against the banks.[31] Prefiguring Hamlin Garland's exposure of the demise of the countryside's purity and strength, Davis castigates the "torpor" that now pervades the distant prairie as well. These polluted scenes are becoming, she laments, "thoroughly American" landscapes.

In conjunction with industry's despoiling of the American landscape, Davis offers another perspective on nature that will become a requisite theme in late-nineteenth-century naturalism: the indifference with which nature confronts human struggles. As Dr. Knowles surveys the countryside's peaceful silence, he chafes under its "unfeeling mockery [of] a sick and hungry world" (46). Even the catastrophies of war are met by nature's indifferent pouring forth of "an unknown fulness of life and beauty" (197). Touched upon in *Howth*, this will become a predominant theme in Davis's Civil War novel, *Waiting for the Verdict* (1867). She, like the later naturalists, suggests that man may choose to envision this beauty as prophecy, but, in fact, it entails nature's complete indifference to his petty rantings.

That insistence upon honest expression is the core of Davis's realism and encompasses her opposition to the period's popular forms of art. Through the figure of Mr. Kitts, the city artist, she satirizes modern art's failure to see the "strange beauty" of Lois and her cart. Every day Kitts watches the young entrepreneur pass his room, and he thinks seriously about the figure that Lois and her cart make. "But he had his grand battle-piece onhand then," Davis explains, "—and after that he went the way of all geniuses, and died down into colourer for a photographer!" (75)

What is not humorous to Davis, however, is the suppression of an artist's voice. As "Life" had its broken-winged angel, *Howth* has a marble figure on the mantel as well: it is one of the Dancing Graces; the other two have, ironically, been pawned, much as Davis's own art had been "pawned" in this novel. She certainly felt that Fields did not understand it. Though not as evil in intent, Fields's failure parallels Dr. Knowles's wielding of an almost demonic "kingly power" over Margret. He has been watching her, studying her, reading every move she has made for years; now he envisions himself as holding "the master-key" to her nature. In mutedly rapacious terminology, he imagines that he will "break [her] silence into electric shivers of laughter and tears,—terrible subtle pain, or joy as terrible. . . . Meanwhile she sat there, unread" (45). That is the sentence with which Davis chooses to end the first chapter of *Howth*; it recaptures the essence

of her epigraph and of her own literary experiences. She reveals that compelling artistic desire to name oneself, to find one's voice, in the segment
of the novel concerning "P. Teagarden." When Margret begins her first
day's work, she discovers on the broken plaster walls "sketches burnt with
coal, showing that her predecessor had been an artist in his way,—his
name, P. Teagarden, emblazoned on the ceiling" (10). Even a discarded
raisin box has "P. Teagarden" scratched on its lid. If, in the stifling environment of the factory, P. Teagarden struggled to maintain his identity and
to give voice to his artistic sense, so, too, did Davis attempt to maintain a
realistic vision in her fiction. Perhaps the deepest irony is that one of
Fields's requested changes was Teagarden's name.[32]

Such demands upon an artist to gild her fiction also reflect what Davis
perceived as a pervasive trend toward theatricality in society. If Margret
shields her true emotions by cementing the expression on her face in the
manner of "a slave putting on a mask, fearing to meet her master" (17), it
is a technique condoned by society. Davis's exposure of this theatricality is
conjoined with the decadence of "Art" as defined by high society. Stephen's self-styled "artist's sense" includes the need to "weigh" and to "cal-
culate" the extent to which his bride, Miss Herne, will be a hindrance; yet
the only portrait of this lady that he can call to mind is "as he had seen her
once in some masquerade or *tableau vivant*. June, I think it was, she chose
to represent that evening,—and with her usual success; for no woman ever
knew more thoroughly her material of shape or colour, or how to work it
up" (125). Later naturalists, such as Frank Norris in *The Pit* (1903) and
Edith Wharton in *The House of Mirth* (1905), also disclose the sexual allurement that is inherent in society's admiration for *tableaux vivants*. In *Howth*,
Davis presents this underlying seduction while extending her ridicule of
Mr. Kitts, the city artist:

> Could June become incarnate with higher poetic meaning than that which
> this woman gave it? Mr. Kitts, the artist I told you of, thought not, and fell
> in love with June and her on the spot, which passion became quite unbearable
> after she had graciously permitted him to sketch her,—for the benefit of Art.
> Three medical students and one attorney, Miss Herne numbered as having
> been driven into a state of dogged despair on that triumphal occasion.
> (125–26)

As humorous as this portrayal of popular tastes is, there is pathos as well
when such stylized art becomes the only acceptable form. Mr. Kitts "fell in
love with June"; so, too, apparently, had the publishing world, for Fields

had explicitly requested that *Howth* convey the mood of a "perfect day in June."[33]

*   *   *

In spite of their differences, Davis and Fields remained friends throughout her seven-year association with the *Atlantic* and after. Though many of his comments seem patronizing, she most often judged him kind and concerned for her welfare as well as for that of the periodical. It was in many ways an unfortunate beginning author-editor association, however; had she started with someone like William Conant Church, for whom she wrote in the late 1860s when he established *Galaxy Magazine*, she may have more quickly developed the spirit of adamant assertion concerning her artistry that she later demonstrated in her relationships with other publishers. But with Fields, her usual response was the ironically passive agreement with the editor's opinion, tempered only by "I suppose." Another aspect of Davis's acquiescence, however, is revealed in an incident that occurred at this time. She was approached by Charles Godfrey Leland, editor of the newly established *Continental Monthly*, who asked her to become one of "his corps."[34] Anxious to expand her opportunities for publication, Davis wrote Fields immediately, asking if the *Continental* was "to be a friend or a rival of '*ours*?' " If friend, she would like to write for this strongly pro-Union publication. The spirit of family that she felt in relationship to the *Atlantic*, its authors, and its editors—"*ours*"—compelled her into a self-limiting loyalty. Fields, well aware of Davis's artistic talents and knowing she would soon be courted by all of the editors of the major literary journals, had sought acknowledgment from Davis a few months earlier that she would write exclusively for the *Atlantic* in the coming year;[35] she had agreed, but it would become a point of contention between them in the not too distant future.

In truth, Davis had begun writing for another journal only months after "Life in the Iron Mills" had appeared in the *Atlantic*. Her association with the popular Philadelphia "ladies' magazine," *Peterson's Magazine*, was precipitated through a Philadelphia correspondent, Lemuel Clarke Davis. Clarke had read Davis's fiction in the *Atlantic*, and his admiration had blossomed into a steady correspondence with the Virginia author. At the time, Clarke was still a law student and supporting himself by editing two highly respected Philadelphia publications, *Law Reports* and the *Legal Intelligencer*. When Clarke, not unlike Davis, found the economic rewards of these journals inadequate, he turned to his friend Charles J. Peterson for the more lucrative editing of *Peterson's*. Copying the style of *Godey's Lady's Book*, *Peterson's* had moved into the forefront with the largest circulation among ladies' magazines in the nation. Thus his praise for her *Atlantic* work was conjoined with soliciting her contributions to the Philadelphia magazine. Davis believed that writing for a popular magazine did not breach her agreement with Fields, an agreement that she deemed limited to the major literary periodicals, yet there is an element of unconscious subterfuge in this decision, too. For now, she told herself, as family illnesses and economic crises seemed to increase almost monthly, writing for *Peterson's* was to earn money; the *Atlantic* was for artistry.

Her first submission to *Peterson's* was a two-part murder mystery, "The Murder in the Glen Ross," which appeared at the same time the *Atlantic* was serializing "A Story of To-Day"; she was identified in *Peterson's* simply as "a New Contributor." "Glen Ross" is a well-written mystery, narrated by a gray-haired, "crusty hermit" lawyer from Virginia who now practices in Philadelphia. John Page's age differs from Clarke Davis's, but the other details of his life are amusingly similar. Although many of Davis's later contributions to *Petersons's Magazine*, for which she would write for more than thirty years, were trite and melodramatic, some of her submissions are well-written tales that incorporate her artistic strengths. Contributions to popular magazines are often deemed "hack work," sometimes legitimately so; but in Davis's case (and in those of many other women writers of the period), these works should not be overlooked because of traditional assessments of such publications. Several of Davis's contributions to *Peterson's* are of as high literary quality as her *Atlantic* submissions. Although Davis recognized that she was writing for a different audience in *Peterson's*, she sought from the beginning to emphasize in this magazine as well as in the literary journals the mimeticism of her fiction: "All the facts . . . came within my own personal knowledge," John Page, the narrator of "Glen Ross," asserts, noting that he is relating the facts that remain "untold in the technical record of the murder case."[36]

Davis continued the use of John Page as narrator through several subsequent stories. In the December 1861 issue carrying the second installment of "Glen Ross," the editor notes that the author of this story will become a regular contributor in the forthcoming year. Davis did not allow her name to be used in any of these early contributions, preferring "by the author of 'The Murder in the Glen Ross.' " In 1863, however, when she published her first serialized novel, "The Second Life," in *Peterson's*, the editor identified her by name as part of a small group of serial novelists (Davis, Ann S. Stephens,[37] and Frank Lee Benedict) who were to become regular contributors. Whether or not this was with Davis's permission is unknown; she had not yet allowed her name to appear as a by-line in any of her short stories or serializations for the *Atlantic* and, until 1867, would adamantly insist that it not be given.[38]

Her subsequent fiction in *Peterson's* reverted to identifying her only as the author of "The Second Life." She published twenty-nine short stories and five serial novels in *Peterson's Magazine* during the 1860s. In April 1865, however, she published another short mystery, "The Haunted Manor-House"; this time she was acknowledged as the author of "Margret Howth." The editor happily announced, "We give in this number, a story by the author of 'Margret Howth,' one of the most powerful novels which has appeared for many years. We hope, often, in future, to have the aid of the same forcible and original writer."[39] Thereafter, she published short stories under both pseudonyms, the author of "Margret Howth" and the author of "The Second Life," the latter occurring as late as 1893, long after her own name had become a regular by-line. She seems not to have distinguished between the types of submissions she was making under each pseudonym; more likely, she did not wish the quantity of items she was publishing with the popular magazine to be known. Her reasons for writing for *Peterson's Magazine* from the beginning had been financial, and they remained so. Peterson paid her as much as one thousand dollars for a serialized novel in the early 1860s, several times the amount she could receive from Fields at the *Atlantic*, and even after her marriage, money remained a scarce commodity necessitating her continued authorship for *Peterson's*. Her association with *Peterson's* was apparently known to Fields from the beginning; however, it would soon lead her into an embarrassing episode of alleged plagiarism.

For the time being, however, she maintained her allegiance to Fields in all correspondence with him, refused to write for the *Continental Monthly*, and submitted the manuscript of "John Lamar" to Fields in November 1861. Davis breathed a sigh of relief when Fields accepted the story without admonishing its dark vision: "Perhaps," she doggedly remarked, "I need not have written it 'with one hand tied behind my back' as Artemus Ward says—after all."[40] She postscripted her letter with what would become one of her most common requests during this decade: "won't you publish John Lamar as soon as you can? I have a fancy for writing of *today* you see." In his acceptance letter, Fields had invited Davis to visit him and his wife, Annie, in Boston. Davis was still trying to arrange her visit to Hawthorne and other friends on the East Coast, but she knew that it would be impossible to leave Wheeling during the winter; thus she reluctantly declined his offer.

With the new year, she turned her attentions toward the book publication of *Howth*, seeking to make whatever changes she could. Both Fields and his wife sent praise for the novel, from themselves and friends. Davis thanked them kindly but continued her requests for an opportunity to revise the manuscript. She would agree to the title *Margret Howth*, she wrote, if the first name were spelled correctly; but she once again warred with the *Atlantic's* proofreader. She directed her comments to Nichols through Fields, thereby allowing herself to express to the invisible proofreader the dismay she suppressed when directing her comments to Fields personally, "My spelling calls out most adamantly to your proofreader to be let alone. Some 'slang' I will restore *right*—he cannot be expected to understand slang. As for the rest I abide by your judgment."[41] As usual, however, she continued in spite of having "abided": "Out here we never open Webster— swear by English dictionaries and as I am a native of out here *mayn't* I spell honour with a u? Childish you think?—well spelling is my hobby." The philosophy behind that "hobby" was continued in her comments about a new story she was writing ("David Gaunt"): "It is a desperate tragical concern . . . but I *hope* you'll publish it. *I* like it being written honestly—."[42]

The publication of "The Story of To-Day" was still having national repercussions as William Davis Ticknor and Fields readied the book form of the novel. A clergyman had used the story as the topic of his sermon, encouraging his parishioners to awaken themselves to the impoverished in their own community. Davis jokingly, though with a hint of reprisal, wrote Fields that, obviously, the minister had been "a man of taste."[43] Pleased as she was that her story would have such consequences, she also knew the other side of criticism. Another religious critic published an article in which he denounced her as "a Fourierite," concluding that the only hope for the author, whom he assumed was a man, was to offer him "an engraving of 'The Light of the World' so that [he] might know who Christ was!"[44] Such misreadings would plague Davis throughout her career. Yet overall the publication of *Howth* in book form was pleasing. She thought the appearance satisfactory, but she was most interested in receiving intelligent criticism of her work. Her repeated requests to Fields for notices produced only what she termed "sugary" reviews; always concerned with strengthening her literary skills, she especially wanted reviews "finding fault."[45] The novel went into three printings in 1862, totaling two thousand five hundred copies. As with the serialization, Davis had insisted that her name not appear on the book and that it be kept completely out of the newspapers. Criticism she sought openly; recognition was to be private.

Although she had refused to write for the newly founded *Continental Monthly*, her novel received a balanced assessment of its quality by the *Continental*'s literary editor.[46] The *Continental Monthly* carried the banner, "Devoted to Literature and National Policy," and its fiercely abolitionist editorial stance drew many writers of renown; its "Literary Notices" section was also especially favorable to the burgeoning realism in American fiction. The literary editor attacked Harriet Beecher Stowe's *Agnes of Sorrento* as "a second-rate romance inspired by rococo sentimentalism," but the next month highly praised her *Pearl of Orr's Island* for its realistic portrayal of "the social life [of] America at the present day."[47] The reviewer also designated Gail Hamilton as one of "the most promising" American essayists (although he wished she were not so bound "by Puritanical chains," the release of which would allow her writing and ideas to "fly far and fast"[48]). Several years later, Henry James would have his first short story published in the *Continental Monthly*. One of their earliest reviews, however, was of *Howth*, which began by praising the author's "strength of genius" and continued:

> One may believe, in reading it, that the author, wearied of the old cry that the literature of our country is only a continuation of that of Europe, had resolved to prove, by vigorous effort, that it *is* possible to set forth, not merely the incidents of our industrial life in many grades, in its purely idiomatic force, but to make the world realize that in it vibrate and struggle outward those aspirations, germs of culture and reforms which we seldom reflect on as forming a part of the inner-being of our very practical fellow-citizens.[49]

The reviewer especially appreciated the author's "strong intellect and fine descriptive power" and noted that she was exploring "a new field, right into the rough of real life, bringing out fresher and more varied forms than had been done before, and in doing this makes us understand, with strange ability, how the thinkers among our people *think*" (467). The reviewer's attention to Davis's ability to escape the Brahmin style must have caused her great pleasure: "few, especially in the Atlantic cities, know what becomes of culture among men and women who 'work and weave in endless motion' in the counting-house, or factory, or through daily drudgery and the reverses from wealth to poverty" (467). He asserted, "no one American has dared such intricacies of thought and character in individuals . . . without falling into conventionalism or improbability. Unlike most novels, its 'plot,' though excellent, is its least attraction" (467). He understood that she was not attempting to "spin" a romantic tale; yet he noted that the novel had become extremely popular and "the general praise awarded it by the press, proves that it has gone right to the hearts of the people—whence it came" (468). Recognizing that there had also been a great deal of criticism of *Howth*'s "harshness," the reviewer reminds his audience:

> The pioneers of every great natural school (and every indication shows that one is now dawning) have quite other than lute sounding tasks in hand, however they may hunger and thirst for beauty, love, and rose-gardens. Under the current of this book runs the keenest, painfulest craving to give free to life these very elements. (468)

The *Continental Monthly*'s recognition of the rising school of realism, and Davis's pioneering contributions to it, is one of the most astute comments on the burgeoning movement from romanticism to realism in mid-nineteenth-century American literature. The reviewer's recognition of the love of beauty that underlies Davis's fiction detects the ideals of the romantics that she had not completely abandoned, even in her most realistic works. However, as in "Life," she was concerned with an "other" beauty that defies traditional aesthetics. Further, her reformer's goals also bound her to other early realists and to many of the great sentimentalists of the 1850s and 1860s. Like Stowe, and unlike later realists and naturalists, Davis ultimately was not willing to abandon human beings to forces outside themselves. If the potential for their loss was prevalent in nineteenth-century American culture—as she had suggested in her characterizations of Hugh Wolfe and Lois Yare and would soon capture in the slave Ben and the prostitute Charlotte Tyndal—that fact only emphasized for Davis the necessity of reform and activism to counter the prevailing forces.

*   *   *

In April 1862 the *Atlantic* anonymously published "John Lamar," for which Davis was paid seventy-five dollars. Tillie Olsen describes this story as "chilling and perfectly executed,"[50] and indeed it is. As with most of Davis's fiction in the 1860s, the title character is not the true focus of her story. Fields preferred titles that invoked the names of male characters, and he often designated titles that he believed would have popular appeal; but in this instance Davis also preferred its published title. Yet John Lamar, the slave owner, is secondary to the psychological study of Ben, the slave who is exposed to Northern ideas but denied their realization. Ben knifes his master after being inflamed by an abolitionist who mouths the words of freedom but whose only answer to Ben's "What shall I do?" is to have the slave join him in a hymn to freedom.

The depths of Davis's psychological awareness in "Lamar" are staggering for the time: not only does she analyze the strange bond of hate and affection between slave and master, but she also captures the prevalence of prejudice in all races through Ben's own denigration of "white trash" like Dave Hall. In "Lamar," there is also an openly acknowledged thematic influence from Harriet Beecher Stowe, but the story challenges Stowe's premises by offering a devastatingly realistic depiction of slavery: Dave Hall is the Christian abolitionist who "had enlisted to free the Uncle Toms, and carry God's vengeance to the Legrees."[51] Davis and Stowe would correspond in later years, but at this time Davis implies an irony in Dave Hall's adherence to the admonitions of *Uncle Tom's Cabin*. While the extraordinary influence of Stowe's novel acts as impetus to Hall's actions, he remains ignorant of what true freedom is. Ben finds Dave's oratorical promises of freedom inspiring and he stands up, asking, "What shall I do?" (an echo of the Korl Woman's plaintive cry), but Dave offers him no answers, only "unutterable pity" (420). Ironically, as the slave finds his voice, the abolitionist loses his.

Commentaries on vengeance or prophetic songs would never suffice for Davis. There are no heroes in "Lamar." She ardently sought fair treatment and freedom for slaves, but for Davis they were neither "saints nor sinners" any more than other human beings. Like Frederick Douglass in his 1845 *Narrative*, Davis is chiefly interested in designating how much these enslaved people are like her readers—they have feelings, dreams, and they know how to seek revenge when they are oppressed for generation after generation. This understanding of human nature came from Davis's own life experiences. Her earliest memory was that of her mother carrying her to safety when their home in Big Spring was set afire during a slave revolt, an event that undoubtedly affected the family's decision to move to Wheeling.[52] There is no sense that Davis was taught to believe the slaves' revolt was unwarranted, but neither is any reason for the revolt ever defined in the family legends about the event. Her childhood experience helped her as an adult to detect whites' fears of black insurrection and to demand that they open their eyes to "what is." It is only when a man is treated like an animal, teased with ideas of freedom but lashed with inequities, that he strikes out physically (the killing of Lamar) and sexually (Ben's lustful thoughts of returning South and "claiming" his former mistress for his own). In this latter point, Davis records the common paranoia of whites in the North and South; although she undoubtedly believed she was detailing the fears of others, the repeated reference to Ben's lust for his white mistress may reveal a twinge in her own unconscious that aligned her more closely with prevailing attitudes than she would have cared to admit.

She did believe in the abolitionist movement, however. Davis, as an adult living in Wheeling, which was perfectly situated on the Ohio River to effect quick movement of escaped slaves into the safety of the northern United States and Canada, had been well aware that the involvement of some townspeople in the Underground Railroad was resented by other citizens of Wheeling, creating a highly volatile environment. Yet that did not inhibit her own involvement in aiding the northern abolitionists. She also recognized the ignorance of some white abolitionists who thought they were helping the cause. As early as 1845, Frederick Douglass had recorded his own disdain for people who sought personal attention and gratification by blatantly professing their involvement in the underground, thereby exposing its existence and endangering everyone involved. It was only the details of this abuse of knowledge that she would record; even into the next century, she discussed only those abolitionists who had themselves publicly revealed their involvement in the movement.

In 1862, a leader of the abolitionist movement in Boston contacted Davis, explaining that a French scientist who was a friend of his wished to help the American abolitionists: "I have sent him directly to you, hoping that your brothers will use their influence with some of the southern leaders to enable him to travel safely through the seceded states. If this is not practicable, will you assist him to creep through the lines in disguise?"[53] Davis did not object to assisting the movement of slaves out of the slave-holding South, but she was unwilling to jeopardize those efforts for the passage of one white man into the South. The naiveté of the Boston abolitionist's ideas of what was "practicable" in a war zone amazed Davis. She ignored the fact that his recording of the request in itself endangered both her life and that of the Frenchman. Of more concern was how to convince the well-intended "M. d'A." that, in spite of his letters of recommendation from Horace Greeley, Charles Sumner, and others, there was no such thing as safe travel between border states. The Frenchman's refusal to recognize the necessity of discretion and secrecy deeply angered Davis. New Virginia was under martial law at the time, but M. d'A. would not listen; he eventually attempted to cross into the South via St. Louis and was immediately arrested and imprisoned.

Davis also knew many of the nation's leading abolitionists of the 1850s and 1860s. When she recorded her memoirs years later, she lauded their concern for the freedom of all slaves. She also recognized their personal eccentricities and, as always, sought to record "a truthful picture of them."[54] They, too, were neither saints nor sinners. Her own subjectivity, however, pervades her depictions. A Southerner at heart but a Northerner in her abolitionist beliefs, Davis's portrayals often reveal as much about herself as about her friends and associates. To her mind, the two extremes of abolitionists were represented in the "noble" (and Southern-born) John Charles Frémont[55] and the exasperating but "sincere" Horace Greeley. She praised Wendell Phillips for his efforts to engage the Philadelphia Quakers in the Underground Railroad, but she was careful to acknowledge equally the black man, William Still, who was the agent of the Philadelphia underground. So, too, was Frances Harper a prominent, capable figure whom Davis admired, recalling her "strange, bitter eloquence."[56] F. Julius Le-Moyne had been a family friend during her childhood, and she delegated to him the honor of being "the truest representative of the radical Abolitionist in this country," while Henry Ward Beecher was deemed, not surprisingly, the most aggressive (188–89).

Two other groups of abolitionists warranted Davis's attention—the poets, and those Quakers who perhaps have not gained as significant national fame but who were, to Davis's mind, the heart of the movement. As to the poets, she knew both John Greenleaf Whittier and James Russell Lowell; the latter's "politics and poetry were, as a rule, kept inside his books," yet his sincerity was impressive in its simplicity. Whittier was more complex. While he never separated his artistry from his abolitionist mission, he rendered his views of slavery, Davis asserted, with the mild aestheticism of "a Presbyterian country minister . . . with a gentle, unwearied obstinacy"; yet Davis was exasperated with his refusal to acknowledge the Southern side of the question (188–89). If she hated slavery, she hated regional prejudices as well, sometimes with a blind defiance.

But it was the Quakers who garnered Davis's deepest respect for their quiet perseverance: Eliza Randolph Turner, who also founded the Children's Week, a relief organization, and later established "an immense guild of working women in Philadelphia" (190–91); and Mary Grew and Margaret Burleigh, housemates of Turner, also warrant Davis's special commendation. She was with Grew and Burleigh in 1870 when word came that the Fifteenth Amendment, guaranteeing the voting rights of citizens against federal or state infringement based on race, color, or "previous condition of servitude," had been passed. No one, however, stood as high in Davis's estimation as Lucretia Mott, "one of the most remarkable women that this country has ever produced" (192). Anyone in need of assistance found refuge and assistance from Mott. Her intelligence was unparalleled: "No man in the Abolition party," Davis asserted, "had a more vigorous brain or ready intelligence"; and Davis especially enjoyed that "her power came from the fact that she was one of the most womanly of women" (192–95). After her marriage and subsequent move to Philadelphia, Davis had an opportunity to know Mott personally and she visited the Mott home on several occasions. From their first meeting, Davis was enraptured by Mott's "grand caring" and a natural demeanor that immediately put Davis at ease.[57] As she told Annie Fields, Lucretia Mott may not be their blood relative, but she was kin "as a woman and a sister."[58]

In 1862, however, Davis remained unconvinced that the American public would ultimately embrace abolition, and some of her most stringent naturalistic passages occur in "John Lamar." As Ben struggles with the idea of his slavery and potential escape, he clings to the familiar face of his master, "like a man drifting out into an unknown sea, clutching, clutching some relic of the shore" (419). Once he believes he has killed Lamar, he becomes completely crazed, clutching the bloodied knife in the "iron muscles of his fingers . . . [and] chuckling at the strange smell it bore" (421). In political terms, this depiction of Ben represents Davis's most explicit alignment with authors who radically opposed slavery. She does not, like Stowe, find a solution in the proffering of a (distant) spiritual salvation and advocacy of slaves' passivity, but instead aligns herself with authors such as Martin Delany and Frederick Douglass, who believed, as Douglass asserted in the 1855 edition of his autobiography, that a slave master is "every hour silently whetting the knife of vengeance for his own throat." Davis, like Delany and Douglass, knew that slaves had the capacity—and incentive—to foment a bloody revolution.[59]

Throughout the story, Davis questions the reader: Who can blame Ben for his actions? To what end is Ben's "awakening" if there is no place in which he can be truly free? The North as well as the South is indicted in "Lamar." Davis concludes the story with the chilling admonition that war has become "a daily business" that has "doomed" the nation. The final, ironic question remains: "The day of the Lord is nigh . . . and who can abide it?" (423). "Lamar" undoubtedly influenced Louisa May Alcott's short story, "The Brothers" (1863), in which the themes of lunacy in the heat of revenge and the sexual appropriation of women also occur. But Alcott opts for a narrative closure that Davis avoided in her realistic fiction: in Alcott's story, an abolitionist nurse heals the slave's tortured soul with prophecies of a better life in the next world. Several other women writers also wrote Civil War stories, such as Rose Terry Cooke's "A Woman" (1862) and Constance Fenimore Woolson's notable "Crowder's Cove" (1880); however, few created the realistic depictions of war that Davis offered, and even fewer published them while the war was in progress.[60]

*   *   *

As the spring wore on, Davis focused her thoughts on two upcoming events: the completion of what she termed "a very abolition story" entitled "David Gaunt,"[61] and her impending trip to Boston, New York, Baltimore, and Philadelphia. The Boston segment of the journey was planned so she could meet Hawthorne and stay with her friends, Jessie Benton and John Charles Frémont. General Frémont had been commander of the Mountain Department of the Union Army at Wheeling during the beginning of the war, with his headquarters directly across the street from the Harding family home. She remained a steadfast friend to the Frémonts throughout their perpetually turbulent lives. No reality of war was spared Davis at that time, as she told Annie Fields: "My secession proclivities (if I had any) are oozing out at my elbows, like Bob Acres' images—."[62] In fact, it was the abolition novel, "David Gaunt," to which these scenes gave birth.

After visiting the Frémonts in New York, Davis intended to stop in Baltimore to visit an unidentified woman friend of several years' acquaintance and to visit with the Reverend Cyrus Dickson[63] and his family. More important, however, was the Philadelphia leg of her journey, for it was there that she would meet the man with whom she had been corresponding since the publication of "Life" and who would become her husband by the next spring: L. Clarke Davis.

Delays in beginning her trip seemed preeminent, however, as Richard Harding became seriously ill. Davis had nursed both of her parents through illnesses the previous year, and her father was declining rapidly. In addition, when she submitted "David Gaunt" to Fields on May 14, she indicated that if the story did not receive "cordial welcome" she would have to remain in Wheeling "and write something else."[64] For the last two years the family had relied on Davis's financial as well as moral support; her father's debilitation had weakened an already unstable financial contributor to their family. Thus, in the same letter, Davis postscripted to Fields that another publisher had approached her for an article on the rebellion, offering liberal payment if she would have it ready by June. She wrote Fields: "What do you think? Had I better still abide by the old flag? meaning T&F?"[65] Within days Fields sent a two-hundred-dollar payment for "David Gaunt"; the crisis was once again temporarily abated.

With her acknowledgment of payment, Davis inserted one of her recurrent requests for artistic freedom: "Don't leave any thing out of it in publishing it," she instructed Fields, "deformity is better than a scar you know."[66] So, too, did she repeatedly ask Fields about the status of *Howth*— she had read in a newspaper that it was in the third printing and wondered if that were true. The consequences of Fields's "kindness" in taking on the business aspects of her submissions now surfaced, but she failed to understand her publishing rights. In spite of the pressures of her financial situation, she was still unsure of the percentage she was to receive from the sale of *Howth*. It was not until May 1862 that she was informed the sales to date totaled two thousand copies and that she would receive one-half of one percent; having already received fifty dollars in advance, she could expect to receive only fifty dollars more for sales to date. *Howth* eventually sold an additional five hundred copies, earning for Davis a total of $125 for the book form of her novel. Even in 1862, this was a ludicrous arrangement. Since the 1840s, the standard royalty for an author had been ten percent; between 1850 and 1857, royalties had increased to fifteen percent, and occasionally went as high as twenty-five percent. The financial panic of 1857 had instilled a sense of caution in the publishing field, but the *norm* in the 1860s was ten to fifteen percent, and, in fact, rates stayed at that level until the 1890s.[67] Thus, even for a relatively new author, a one-half percent royalty was unheard of.

Although sales of five thousand texts were necessary before a novel could be considered a success,[68] Fields had indicated pleasure with *Howth*'s sales. The cost books of Ticknor and Fields end in 1858, so it is impossible to establish the publisher's printing costs since aspects of an edition such as tokens, forms, and quires as well as how the gatherings were printed varied greatly. Nor do we know how many copies were printed. But we can observe that in 1857, the year that the economic panic was tempering royalty payments by publishers, Charles Reade and Nathaniel Hawthorne were authorized ten-percent royalties for *White Lies* and *Snow Image*, respectively; so, too, did lesser-known authors' works such as Mary T. Mann's *Christianity in the Kitchen: A Physiological Cook Book* and Eliza B. Lee's *Parthenia: or, the Last Days of Paganism* warrant ten-percent royalties.[69] Davis should have received, at a minimum, five times the amount paid to her by Ticknor and Fields. She remained ignorant of this abuse, although she was very unhappy with what she perceived as the public's lack of interest in her novel. At the end of the decade, when Gail Hamilton (Mary Abigail Dodge) published her exposé on similar business aberrations she had encountered during her author-publisher relationship with Fields, she confided to a friend that even though Fields had been "rather mean" to her, there was a lesson to be learned: "If I had been wiser he would have been juster, so the fault is partly mine."[70]

Hamilton's book did not come soon enough to be a cautionary tale for Davis, who decided, with the future of "David Gaunt" secure and her father's health finally improved, to let the matter slide as she eagerly prepared for her journey to Boston, New York, Baltimore, and Philadelphia. There remained only one final hurdle to overcome: the problem of an escort. An unmarried woman could not travel alone in wartime (as her short story "Ellen" would soon evidence). "How good it must be to be a man when you want to travel!" she lamented.[71] At the beginning of June, however, Davis was finally able to confirm her plans; her brother Wilse needed to travel to New York on business and agreed that she could accompany him.

In Boston Davis forged her friendships with Annie and James Fields. In May she had told James, "I *must* say it—I do hope you will all like me."[72] Indeed, they did. Prior to the visit, Davis and Annie Fields had exchanged polite notes, but in Boston their friendship was solidified. Nearly the same age, Annie and Rebecca shared confidences and developed an intellectual intimacy during those few short weeks in Boston that would last through the difficulties of the coming years. Annie also introduced Davis to several other women writers, including Celia Thaxter and Kate Field. Few women in the nineteenth century were as influential in literary circles as Annie Adams Fields. But Annie's influence was much more than personal support. As she had for Louisa May Alcott, Harriet Beecher Stowe, Sarah Orne Jewett, Elizabeth Stuart Phelps, Celia Thaxter, and later, Mary Noailles Murfree, Mary Wilkins Freeman, Edith Wharton, and Willa Cather, Annie ardently supported Davis's literary endeavors, becoming a sensitive critic and at times a persuasive intermediary between the Virginia author and James Fields. Covering nearly six decades of involvement—during which she supported women writers, edited selected letters by Harriet Beecher Stowe and Sarah Orne Jewett, and published her own poetry and essays— Annie Adams Fields's legacy to American literature is an impressive one.[73]

But for a new author, the real excitement lay in traveling to the "modern Athens" where the American "Aeropagites" reigned.[74] There is more than a little irony in this pioneering realist's trek to the throne of the great romantics, but the experience solidified her ironclad convictions about the importance of telling "the story of to-day." Davis stayed with Sophia and Nathaniel Hawthorne at Wayside. It was Hawthorne's custom to introduce writers he admired to his Concord compatriot, Ralph Waldo Emerson. When James Russell Lowell introduced the young William Dean Howells to Hawthorne, the great romance writer in turn introduced Howells, via a note on the back of his calling card, to Emerson.[75] As with Davis, in March 1862 Hawthorne had extended a similar invitation to visit Concord to Mary Abigail Dodge with the enticement that he would escort her to Emerson's.[76] Thus, during one memorable evening of Davis's visit to Wayside, Hawthorne continued the tradition by gathering together in his parlor some of his famous neighbors to meet the writer from Virginia.[77]

Among the local guests were Emerson and Bronson Alcott. When the latter began to expostulate on his philosophical propositions, Davis discovered in his words "a stale, familiar ring as if often repeated before," but she noticed that Emerson listened to Alcott with rapt attention (33–34). That evening, however, Hawthorne was in apparent agreement with her, revealing his disdain for Alcott through "his laughing, sagacious eyes . . . full of mockery" (33–34). Alcott chose that moment to lecture about the war to their guest from Virginia. Davis's response to this "would-be seer" who knew less of the war in reality than when, as a child, she had "dreamed of bannered legions of crusaders debouching in the misty fields" represented Davis's growing disdain for theoretical posturing that lacked any basis in fact or, particularly, in experience:

> I had just come up from the border where I had seen the actual war; the filthy spewings of it; the political jobbery in Union and Confederate camps; the malignant personal hatreds wearing patriotic masks, and glutted by burning homes and outraged women; the chances in it, well improved on both sides, for brutish men to grow more brutish, and for honorable gentlemen to degenerate into thieves and sots. War may be an armed angel with a mission, but she has the personal habits of the slums. (33–34)

The irony, as Davis came to see it, was that while these members of "the 'Atlantic' coterie . . . thought they were guiding the real world, they stood quite outside of it, and never would see it as it was"; in fact, Davis concluded, they were "always apart from humanity" (32–33). Hawthorne is otherwise exempted; she did not feel that he was truly part of that coterie other than in his place of publication. Her isolation of Hawthorne from the other romantics is rooted in what she had earlier discerned as his interest in the commonplace. "Hawthorne was in the Boston fraternity but not of it," she deduced. "Even in his own house he was like Banquo's ghost among the thanes at the banquet" (55, 56). Whereas Emerson presented the poet-author as a hero, Hawthorne always shied away from such pretensions, preferring to define himself simply as a storyteller. For Davis, the difference between the two romantics was as minor as pretension versus modesty and as major as the rhetorical extremes within romanticism itself—that is, between the visionary and the ironic.

In spite of her early concerns about transcendentalism, Davis had begun her journey to Concord firmly believing that Emerson was "the first of living men . . . the modern Moses" (42). In private conversation with him, the usually reticent Davis found herself almost immediately divulging her personal impressions of the war, freely expressing her opinions because she was convinced that there was nothing the Concord Sage wanted more to hear. But she quickly learned, as so many before and after her had, that Emerson's interest was completely apersonal. It was not the value of the individual or the extraordinary events in commonplace war-zone life that interested Emerson but "the abnormal freaks among human souls";[78] what particularly disturbed her about Emerson's manner was that he "took from each man his drop of stored honey, and after that the man counted for no more to him than any other robbed bee" (43, 45). Perhaps Davis would have more readily excused becoming one of the many "robbed bees" if the issue had not been that of the war—or if Emerson's actions had not joined so immediately with the Alcott incident.

Thus it was during this visit to the seat of transcendentalism that Davis confirmed her growing discomfort with the doctrines of its proponents. She had felt their tenets to be facile at best; but observing the scores of followers who flocked to Boston, Davis discerned a disturbing trend:

> never were the eternal verities so dissected and pawed over and turned inside out. . . . But the discussion left you with a vague, uneasy sense that something was lacking, some back-bone of fact. Their theories were like beautiful

> bubbles blown from a child's pipe, floating overhead, with queer reflections
> on them of sky and earth and human beings, all in a glow of fairy color and
> all a little distorted. (36)

Davis certainly could appreciate nature as a source of wisdom. A few years
later she would describe to Annie her favorite seaside retreat where "Nature looks at you with so sad abstracted a face through all the changes of
bright skies and cool driving winds that you fancy you have come upon
her in one of her melancholy unreticent moods and that presently you will
learn her secrets as never before."[79] The difference, of course, is that nature
is not merely "bright skies" but a moody, melancholy force that at times
abets and at times thwarts one's search for truth. Davis's fiction had long
focused upon the potential indifference of nature to man's folly, and she
would always recognize the whimsical, arbitrary power of nature. She was
not one to seek to build a "kingdom of man *over* nature."[80]

Still, these were seemingly harmless differences in philosophy. It was
not until Davis discerned the underlying perils to those who absorbed transcendentalism's doctrines that she rejected any acquiescence toward its
harmlessness. She knew the irony of Emerson's fame as an American
"prophet": he had fueled the desire to claim a national literature, and he
had warranted unprecedented nationwide praise; yet few people outside of
Concord had actually read his works. Most of his followers, and those of
the other transcendentalists, including Margaret Fuller, only knew that
they were distinctively American, and therein lay their dangerously blind
allegiance:

> New England then swarmed with weak-brained, imitative folk who had stud-
> ied books with more or less zeal, and who knew nothing of actual life. . . . To
> them came this new prophet with his discovery of the God within them-
> selves. . . . The new dialect of the Transcendentalist was easily learned. . . . Up
> to the old gray house among the pines in Concord they went—hordes of wild-
> eyed Harvard undergraduates and lean, underpaid working women, each
> with a disease of soul to be cured by the new Healer. (45–46)

This poor, "diseased" soul, however, did not gain insight into his or her
own means of renewal; he or she had merely transferred dependence to the
prophet-healer. Instead of fidelity to the dictum "Never imitate," rote adherence to "easily learned" mottos took precedence. They had broken away
from the restraints of Calvinist Puritanism but had found no place to reat-
tach their allegiance—until Emersonian transcendentalism. Later realists

responded to transcendentalism in much the same way as Davis. In 1868, William Dean Howells wrote Charles Eliot Norton, his good friend and editor at the time of the *North American Review* and the *Nation*, "The Emerson lectures came to an end one week ago. I heard the last: how little wisdom it takes to lecture the world!"[81] There remained areas in which Davis, like Howells, could agree with Emerson—their support of free states, their abhorrence of the United States policy of Manifest Destiny, and, especially, the importance of self-sufficiency—but her rejection of transcendentalism per se was adamant and remained so.

Other aspects of Davis's Boston visit boded more favorable for her later memories of the place and the people she met there. One of the genuine marvels was her meeting with Louisa May Alcott. Alcott had published a few short stories and poems during the late 1850s and in 1860 had published "Love and Self-Love" in the *Atlantic*, but she was as yet little known outside her own circle. Davis's appreciation of Louisa made her feelings toward Bronson even more disdainful. Though the father was a "kindly old man," Davis abhorred the poverty that he forced upon his family; his wife supported him and their children while he filled his library with unpublished folios of his own writings. "The homelier virtues were not, apparently, in vogue in Concord," Davis scoffed (38–39). In Louisa, however, she recognized "that watchful, defiant air with which the woman whose youth is slipping away is apt to face the world which has offered no place to her" (38). Echoes of this attitude recur throughout Davis's fiction of the 1860s; she portrays numerous women whose lives are wasted because they cannot find means to fulfill their hunger for expression. She saw the potential in Louisa May Alcott, so "generous in soul" and so talented even then as an oral storyteller.[82]

Louisa had also seen the potential in Davis; she traveled to Boston specifically to join one of the gatherings that Annie and James Fields were hosting for Davis. Louisa wanted to meet the author whose work she, like Hawthorne, so greatly admired. Davis recalled Louisa's comments: "These people may say pleasant things to you but not one of them would have gone to Concord and back to see you, as I did today. I went for this gown. It's the only decent one I have. I'm very poor" (39). Louisa's affinity with Davis undoubtedly grew out of the Virginian's concern for the impoverished; Davis was deeply moved that this young woman, who with her mother struggled daily to keep the family fed and clothed, had sacrificed such precious time in order to honor her. To Davis, it was an act indicative of who Louisa May Alcott was, and Louisa's life story echoed the old stories of women's lives that Davis's mother had told her as a young child.

Oliver Wendell Holmes was a renowned figure of the time whom Davis also came to admire during her stay in Boston. "Autocrat" that he was, he took Davis to the Mount Auburn graveyard—not to show her the famous gravestones but several newly covered mounds. He could relate the details of each unrecognized life, acknowledging the significance of such commonplace lives in a way that Davis especially appreciated. Holmes explained to her: "I search out the histories of these forgotten folks in records and traditions. . . . When I have found out all about them they seem like my own friends" (52–53). This graveyard conversation was the kind of memorial to commonplace folk that Davis would create years later in her own autobiography. Holmes was not, she concluded, an impractical dreamer "like his friends in Concord. He was far in advance of his time in certain shrewd, practical plans for the bettering of the conditions of American life" (53). As was Davis herself.

So, too, had the young Kate Field impressed Davis during her Boston visit: "When I think of Boston her face with its true beauty comes up surely among the first. I have a fancy she and I are to be fellow pilgrims on good road somewhere again—and my presentiments are *always* true."[83] Davis felt that there was "such earnest power . . . cased up" in Field, a power that needed a creative outlet.[84] Kate Field was an ardent supporter of the Union at the time; she would later turn to journalism as a career. She also became a popular lyceum-circuit lecturer and tried her hand at a theatrical career. Her most important contribution to American letters, however, was the publication of *Kate Field's Washington*, a weekly newspaper that she published from 1890 to 1895. Undoubtedly, Davis was drawn to this young woman's intelligence, her satirical sense of humor—and her activism. Although their pilgrims' paths took them in different directions, they continued to keep track of one another through sporadic correspondence or, most often, through mutual friends such as Annie Fields.

But it was Hawthorne who remained Davis's most cherished acquaintance from her Boston sojourn. She revealed her heartfelt admiration for the renowned author in the distinction she drew between the "diseased" people who sought out Emerson and the "healthy, commonplace people" who had a "natural feeling" toward Hawthorne (59).

One of Davis's tenderest moments with Hawthorne occurred during a joyful walk that he, Sophia, and Davis took to the Old Manse and through the wooded hills of Sleepy Hollow Valley that had been converted into a burying ground. Hawthorne was relaxed and witty. When they stopped to rest, he laughingly told her that, contrary to popular belief, New Englanders do enjoy themselves—"when we are dead!" (63) But as the day passed and the sky overhead darkened, so did Hawthorne's mood, and they returned home. As she was leaving Concord, he extended his hand in farewell. Davis would always cherish his last words to her: "I am sorry you are going away. It seems as if we had known you always"(64). Though Davis would receive a letter from Sophia within weeks, this was the last time she saw the great romancer; he died before they could renew their acquaintance.

Davis also admired Sophia Hawthorne. She was, in Davis's experience, a gracious hostess and the perfect mate for Hawthorne. During this visit, Davis garnered evidence of Sophia's protectiveness of her husband through an episode instigated by Elizabeth Peabody. Peabody was Sophia's sister and a vital member of the Transcendental Club; Davis admired Peabody as "a woman of wide research and a really fine intelligence" (59). If they disagreed on transcendentalism, they shared an advocacy of social reform, and they continued their association over the coming years. But Davis was aghast at Peabody's lack of discretion and failure to understand her famous brother-in-law. A highly energetic woman, Peabody apparently refused to accept Hawthorne's desire for solitude, a desire with which Davis empathized: "I happened to be present at [Elizabeth Peabody's] grand and last *coup* to this end" (60). While Davis was staying at Wayside, Peabody organized a group of neighbors to visit—without informing the Hawthornes. Peabody also felt it was time Sophia, who had been reclusive, met her neighbors; Davis's visit afforded her the opportunity to achieve both goals. The guest list included, to Sophia and Nathaniel's dismay, a figure whom Davis satirized as the local "Intelligent Questioner who cows you into idiocy by her fluent cleverness" (62). The woman immediately besieged Nathaniel with her admiration for his romances, wanting to discuss them in detail. Sophia interceded, telling Nathaniel he was wanted elsewhere and giving him the opportunity to escape, though she herself remained to endure the evening's events.

For a brief period Davis and Sophia Hawthorne engaged the thought of corresponding, but each let the acquaintance fade, even as they remained aware of the other's activities through Annie Fields. In August, back in Wheeling and corresponding regularly with Annie, Davis commented in passing that "I have never had time to reply to [Sophia's] letter."[85] In part the breach was probably due to Sophia's distaste for Davis's graphic realism. Sophia's confessions of this opinion to Annie Fields are often quite humorous in their zealous nature. She told Annie in May of 1863 that James Fields should forbid Davis's "unpardonable" use of " 'pulsing' and 'pulses' and 'pulsated' " as verbs.[86] Then Sophia admonished herself for her criticism of Davis's realism. "Alas that I should say so. I always read what she writes because of the ability she shows, but I also tire of the moldiness, her east wind and grime which she will mix in with her pictures of life."[87] Three years later Sophia still professed a dislike of Davis's "moldy style." She wishes "Mrs. Davis would cease to write about disgustful, flabby men and dried up old women and present truth in a rather more Greek style. She makes me sea-sick. Why will she be so 'moldy' as my husband said to her she was. Why does she have squalor? Oh, why? There is mire enough in the streets without smearing the pages of books with it. Tell me, do not you hate this meanness of the gifted Rebecca?"[88] Sophia was never able to forgive Davis's realism or her refusal to employ a "more Greek style."

If Nathaniel had actually commented negatively on Davis's realistic style, Davis never mentioned it; but Sophia's comments perfectly distinguish the tastes of the romantics and the realists. It is sad that Davis and Sophia did not rise above their literary differences to maintain the friendship begun so propitiously. Davis's first letter to Annie after she left Boston avowed her affection for Sophia. "I never shall cease being glad that I knew her *well*."[89] Even then, however, the tone suggested that their friendship was in the past.

*   *   *

Even as she traveled through the Atlantic states that summer, Davis did not stop working. In Baltimore, while she was proofing pages of "David Gaunt," she also gathered facts about a black, imbecilic pianist which she would develop into her moving account of "Blind Tom."[90] Once again the *Atlantic* proofreader stalked her: "Where is that wretched proofreader?" she queried Fields. "Couldn't a situation be got for him to guard bridges down here? He and *we*—inaccurate essayists—would be safe then."[91]

But she was enjoying her travels too much to be long hindered by the perpetual frustrations of publishing. She had promised Annie when she left Boston that she would have a photograph taken in Baltimore and send it to her. But Davis abhorred having her picture taken, and she humorously explained her failure to meet her promise: "I meant 'honour bright' Annie to send you the photograph from Baltimore and had thrice taken different ones which every one pronounced to be me without a trace of *any* expression—so I destroyed them. I am sorry. But seriously—I did my best. I console myself by the fact that a '*thorough* beauty never is photographed' vide London paper."[92] One sober-faced picture of her in her youth does remain; she would not have another photograph taken for nearly thirty years. Baltimore, however, she declared to Annie, was beautiful, especially compared with "the barred windows of New York."[93] Baltimore homes are

> very stately sometimes (I *couldnt* say that of 5th Avenue you know "the mark of the bank note is over it all") but these houses grew up slowly you fancy, taking in air and light, knowing their master's whim and growing out from that. . . . Another peculiarity is . . . that in the evening every family sits out on the balcony or porticos. So different from the jail-living in New York & Philadelphia! It looks as if human nature cared or trusted and did trust itself . . . there was a bright cheerfulness, a buoyancy in the air of Baltimore that those cities want—.[94]

Lest she think New York the only city of unrest, however, Baltimore "offered me her specialité in the shape of a mob, which detained our carriage in Mt Vernon place one day. Otherwise it is a beautiful city."[95]

From Baltimore, Davis traveled to her final destination, but the trip into Philadelphia to meet Clarke remains almost a complete blank. Later comments suggest that they fell in love during that "happy week," if they were not already so from their year-long correspondence and apparently earlier visits she had made to the city. Morning boat rides on a lake and long walks that offered time to talk and to know one another ended in an understanding. But Davis remained silent with all of her correspondents about the love affair, only mentioning it when her wedding day approached. As she later told Annie, she preferred to write about other women's lives, not her own.

Back in Wheeling in early August, Davis lamented the dust and smoke of the old mill town that made her longings for her Eastern friends even more emphatic.[96] In some ways, it is unfortunate that Davis did not have an opportunity to remain in Boston. As she matured, life in Wheeling was becoming more lonely and intellectual stimulation was limited; but as the eldest daughter, and one who abided by proprieties, she felt it her duty to remain at home and help care for her family. On her journey home, she already hungered for details about Boston's literary activities: "*Do* write," she commands Annie, "—tell me everything . . . all the news—new ideas—spirits—books—people—scandal—who and what will be in the next Atlantic? If anybody speaks of me—water their memory—dip under it keep it alive. I want to be remembered by somebody in Boston for I *love* Boston."[97] As the cool Virginia fall of 1862 settled around her, she lamented to Annie, "Do you know sometimes I reproach myself so much for my visit to Boston. I think why did I not show more how happy I was? Make them love me more? At times, looking back over all the wasted years I feel as if I could say I have lost not a day—but a life—."[98] But her life was soon to follow a path that would lead her even further from the possibilities of returning to her beloved Boston.

*   *   *

The publication of part one of "David Gaunt" as the lead item in the August issue of the *Atlantic* helped abate her remorse over the smog and the soot and the stifling atmosphere of Wheeling. "Gaunt" is the story of a young Calvinist minister whose stringent teachings force him to reject passion and to corrupt his morals when he is confronted by the realities of war. More than Gaunt's story, however, it is the history of Theodora (Dode) Scofield's stifled life in the hill country of Virginia, a history representative of "the drift of most women's lives."[99] As in "Lamar," the war is no longer a backdrop; its center-stage position forces both Gaunt and Dode to question their beliefs and to redefine themselves through their war experiences. Davis believed that woman's role in American life had been as radically reconstructed by the war as had the soldier's, a theme which Constance Fenimore Woolson also projected in "Crowder's Cove." Further, "Gaunt" confronts the issue of families torn apart by differing views on slavery and secession. It is the surreptitious actions of Dode's father for the Rebel cause that cost him his life and nearly kill her lover, Douglas Palmer. It was a story Davis saw reenacted throughout the war years. In her 1904 autobiography, she deplored the fact that the standard histories of the Civil War in no way captured "the general wretchedness, the squalid misery, which entered into every life in the region given up to the war. Where the armies camped the destruction was absolute."[100]

Davis's theme in "Gaunt," as in "Lamar," is that while farsighted politicians may have seen the war in the offing, it came to the average citizen as unexpectedly as an earthquake and left as much destruction in its wake. One way in which the common man and woman reacted to this rampage was to adhere blindly to the rhetoric of patriotism and faith without understanding the implications of their actions. It was not a *cause* to which they adhered; it was fear. Davis was confronted every day with her compatriots' fervent clutching to the symbols of peace. She recalled one neighbor who suggested that the Declaration of Independence be read daily in every American home. Another neighbor advocated that schoolboys be required to memorize the Constitution. Women were urged to sing "The Star-Spangled Banner" at all gatherings; and in many Virginia communities, "bands of young girls marched through the streets singing it in a kind of holy zeal, believing, poor children, as they were told, that they would soon 'bring again peace unto Israel.' "[101] This is precisely the blind Calvinistic patriotism that Gaunt brings to the war. Davis explicitly juxtaposes the image of Christian's battle as portrayed by Bunyan against the realities of the war as she lived it. Bunyan's is "quaint history"; Davis has "a modern story" to tell that will not deny the meetings with Evil or Humiliation but will detail the everyday suffering and disillusionment that American soldiers and civilians faced. Americans do not know "what kind of sword old Christian used, or where it is, or whether its edge is rusted," Davis asserts, but those details are available about their own war (257).

In divulging David Gaunt's distortion of Christianity for the purposes of warfare, Davis was identifying a complex psychological aspect of the Civil War applicable to most wars. If, as Gaunt insists, the Federal cause was "God's cause" because the war is an impetus to the millennium, how, when the war is over, does that believer reconcile the atrocities he has had to commit? How does the Southerner, as ardent as the Northerner in his belief that God was on his side, find solace in his faith when he is defeated? And, most importantly, Davis asks, why, in all their zeal, is the issue of slavery nearly forgotten? Their cause is rooted in forging a way for oneself, while trampling down those who are most needy. In this, Davis revealed how her concern for self-sufficiency differs from her interpretation of Emersonian self-reliance. For Davis, independence is self-sufficiency but it never places self over others. Like most women writers of the nineteenth century, from Sedgwick to Stowe to Jewett, the self and the other cannot be separated.

Davis's themes in "Gaunt" echo those of "Life" and *Howth*, but the battlefield has become a literal rather than figurative scene. She depicts how the business of war *incorporates* Christianity. Since Gaunt is the itinerant preacher for the area, his allegiance with the Union persuades others to join. Those debating the issue are reminded that with victories come raises in their salary. One observer of the debate is Nabbes, a reporter for a New York newspaper, who explains that it has all been mapped out by the government:

> Was a fellow . . . that set me easy about my soul, and the thing. A chaplain in Congress: after we took down that bitter Mason-and-Slidell pill, it was. Prayed to Jesus to keep us safe until our vengeance on England was ripe,—to "aid us through the patient watch and vigil long of him who treasures up a wrong." Old boy, thinks I, if that's Christianity, it's cheap. I'll take stock in it. Going at half-price, I think. (405)

That is the "Judas-cause" that Davis rejects in "Gaunt." Davis, like Sedgwick, was careful to separate her Virginia realism from the regional realism of New Englanders such as Stowe and Phelps, whose works synthesized realism and evangelicalism.

Some of Davis's most original tropic language comes into play in this novel. As in all of her fiction, she insists upon aligning the oppressed, the oppressors, and the passive observers in their humanness. We are all "like a cuttle-fish sucking to an inch of rock," she insists, whether we are slave or master, Northerner or Southerner (258). More important in terms of literary history, Davis's 1862 novel prefigures Stephen Crane's realistic depiction of war and its psychological effects in *The Red Badge of Courage*, published in 1895. As Joe Scofield slips into the Rebel camp under cover of darkness, the enemy takes on the monsterish persona that Crane will also render: "[Joe] could not see the Federal troops, but he heard the dull march of their regiments,—like some giant's tread, slow, muffled in snow. Closer,—closer every minute" (409). It is even more monstrous for Gaunt, as he wends his way toward the enemy camped at the Gap, because the troops behind him sound "like the breathing of some great animal" (410). Finally the "column, sweeping up on the double-quick, carried the young disciple of Jesus with them. The jaws of the Gap were before them—the enemy" (410). Gaunt has become part of a "blue demonstration."[102] But Gaunt, like Henry Fleming, learns that unity is fractured once the rage of the moment is squelched: after the Rebels are slaughtered, the "Federal column did not return in an unbroken mass as they went. There were wounded and dying among them; some vacant places" as they individually staggered back down the hill (411).

Crane does not approach one aspect of war that Davis revealed in "Gaunt," perhaps because it had never been written into history books: the pillaging in which soldiers on both sides participated. Thus, when the Union soldiers leave the Gap, "every homestead but two from Romney to the Gap was laid in ashes," while women and children fled in fear. The bounty that soldiers brought home always repelled Davis:

> I knew, for instance, of a company made up of the sons and grandsons of old Scotch Covenanters. They were educated, gallant young fellows. They fought bravely, and . . . were kind and humane to their foes. But they came home, when disbanded, with their pockets full of spoons and jewelry which they had found in farmhouses looted and burned on Sherman's march to the sea; and they gayly gave them around to their sweethearts as souvenirs of the war.[103]

In later years Davis asserted that it had been politicians and leaders who had recorded the history of the war from their "elevated" positions (110); "David Gaunt" is a history of the Civil War as Davis and "commonplace" people experienced it. She knew the pathos of "farmers, clerks, dentists, and shopkeepers to-day—presto! to-morrow, soldiers!" (118); and she proffered the idea that would be popularized during America's involvement in Vietnam: "When we hear of thousands of men killed in battle it means nothing to us," Davis observed; but the dead body of one you love, "*That is war!*" (120).

Davis revealed the personal heartache of living in a border state to Annie in late August, just before "Gaunt" appeared in the *Atlantic*. Her letter is an important document not only for the revelations of Davis's personal views but for its historical realism as well:

> These are sad lonesome days for us here—the war is surging up close about us. O Annie if I could put into your and my true woman's hurt the ever present loathing and hate for it! If you could only see the other side enough to see the wrong, the tyranny in both! God rules—Yes I know—But God in His inscrutable wisdom suffered great wrong to work out His ends—and this is one of them. . . . I could tell you things *I know* that would make you really sick. Yet it is not because of these apparent horrors that I think the war unjust. You will say, I know, that my judgment is warped by sympathy. From the first I upheld the right of revolution. Granted to the South what Garibaldi Emmet Washington claimed, though I never would—never *could* have lived in a slave confederacy.[104]

She abruptly breaks off, asks Annie to forgive her outburst, and turns to "pleasanter thoughts." Out of these wretched emotions, Davis carved her literary theory.

*   *   *

George Nichols, the *Atlantic*'s proofreader, once again haunted Davis when "Gaunt" appeared: "I do wish Mr. George Nichols would learn to spell before he corrects mine. *Papaws!* Is that Webster? It looks like him— Did you know I have a terrible temper?" she asked Fields.[105] Otherwise, she was pleased with "Gaunt" and had subsequently completed her nonfiction study of "Blind Tom," which she submitted to Fields at the same time. In the letter that accompanied this submission, Davis praises a recent item in the *Atlantic*, "A Complaint of Friends" by Gail Hamilton (Mary Abigail Dodge). Davis had been following Dodge's work for several months. Dodge was an early contributor to several journals with which Davis would also become associated in coming years (most notably, the *Independent* and the *Congregationalist*), and her rising concern for women's economic independence, especially through writing careers, had immense appeal for Davis. Still, in the publishing battle that was about to erupt between Dodge and James T. Fields—she charged him with underpaying her in terms of royalties and published an account of her experiences with Fields, *Battle of the Books* (1870)—Davis ironically (considering her royalties from *Howth*) remained faithful to her friend Fields during the controversy, as her letters to Annie and James attest, although she would soon feel that Fields had not reciprocated that support.

For over a year, Davis had sought publication of her work in England, where she felt she could have the political freedom to write as realistically as she desired; for an American audience she feared to "touch forbidden subjects."[106] She told Fields that she wanted "to obtain a place in one of the best English magazines and write *only* for that and *ours*."[107] But Fields remained mute on the issue in spite of her numerous urgings and the interest of at least two English publications. Macmillan had shown interest in reprinting both *Margret Howth* and *David Gaunt* (the latter had been published in book form by Ticknor and Fields), and the *Cornhill* had shown a similar interest in publishing some of her short stories. Fields did, rather ironically, send a later story, "The Promise of Dawn," to the *Cornhill*; it was the one short story of hers that he balked at publishing (see below).

Copyright laws made simultaneous English and American publication tedious, but Harriet Beecher Stowe had managed an excellent arrangement with English publishers. As William Charvat has discerned, an American publisher's willingness to pursue preliminary arrangements was often sufficient to overcome British copyright laws.[108] For whatever reasons, Fields did not achieve English publication for any of Davis's works other than "Blind Tom." As late as 1877, she was still seeking an avenue into English publication, this time from her friend Kate Field, the young journalist whom she had met on her trip to Boston years earlier and who was residing in England at the time. After apologizing for asking favors, Davis details her questions:

> To plunge in *medias res* at once I want to write for an English magazine—one of the best class, of course. How shall I go about it? I do not find the editors of our magazines disposed to help me in the matter. What magazine or what editor would be most likely to consider *mss.* sent fairly? Secondly, I am going to begin a novel (running about six months) in July in *Lippincott's Magazine*. Do you think it likely I could arrange to have it published simultaneously there as *Black's*, *Macdonald's* etc. are here? And, thirdly, how do the rates of compensation there compare with our own? You see I am absolutely ignorant of the whole matter and I know that in all probability you have the *carte du pays* of the literary world in your hand, and can advise me what to do. I have been heartily glad to hear of your great success in England.[109]

The novel to be published by Lippincott's, *A Law Unto Herself*, was never published in England.

This time, however, Davis did not acquiesce to Fields's silence. In early September 1862, disappointed that the English deal had apparently fallen through and that *Howth* would not go into a fourth printing, she told Fields that she had decided to write only short articles for the *Atlantic* in the future; serials seemed out of favor with the public, she testily observed, and if she had a full-length project she would publish it only in book form.[110] But she had devised a plan to see that "Blind Tom" was published in England. Aware of Fields's acquaintance with Charles Dickens, Davis suggested "Blind Tom" as an appropriate article for Dickens's magazine, *All the Year Round*. Fields and Dickens had wanted to begin simultaneous publication of articles in their respective journals. When Fields agreed with Davis's suggestion and submitted "Blind Tom" to Dickens, the Englishman responded, "I have read that affecting paper . . . with strong interest and emotion. You may readily suppose that I have been most glad and ready to avail myself of your permission to print it."[111] With such an enthusiastic response, one is left to wonder why Fields did not continue to seek avenues of publication for Davis's work in England. Dickens's version of the article altered the title to "Blind Black Tom" and eliminated the poetic epigraph that Davis had selected, substituting his own brief commentary on the origins of the extraordinary account of this "idiot-savant": "We have received the following remarkable account from a valued friend in Boston, Massachusetts. It will be published in that city, within a few days after its present publication in these pages."[112]

It is not surprising that Dickens was drawn to Davis's painful account of the abuse of this child genius. Tom, a blind slave, mentally incapacitated, possessed musical abilities so extraordinary that his master realized immediately there was profit to be made from this oddity; Tom was put on an exhausting whirlwind tour of major American cities to demonstrate his classical piano-playing abilities. Davis had gone to see the child's performance when she was visiting Baltimore; her account insists on a realistic appraisal of the slave's abilities in preference to the aggrandizing advertisements of his talents, but his abilities were undeniable. Yet the real story, to Davis's mind, was "Tom's own caged soul within. . . . Some beautiful caged spirit struggled for breath under that brutal form and idiotic brain"; but the bars were solidified for Tom.[113] Davis then turned to her readers. If Tom's life is lost, it need not be so for the thousands of caged souls in their own backyards, who are more to be pitied because they have no such means of releasing their despair. In September of 1865, Davis noted that Tom was still on the circuit tour. She declined viewing him again.

In its startling pathos, "Blind Tom" is one of Davis's most vivid indictments of slavery. The article received an extraordinary response from both its American and English audiences. Davis received an influx of clippings from journals that had reviewed her article and letters from individuals who wanted to comment on "Blind Tom." She was amazed by the public outcry and observed that "those who have heard Tom believe the story—those who never did disbelieve it at which I am not surprised."[114] Davis's literary contributions to the cause of freeing all slaves are significant, heartfelt, and often far advanced of other authors' positions; but she was also part of her culture, and in the midst of her reformer's zeal she sometimes slipped into rhetoric that reveals how far she was from escaping the prejudices of her own time (for example, she refers to black children as "pickaninnies" or describes black features as "blubber lips"). Her love of the South, its people, and its culture was deeply imbedded; and in spite of her abhorrence of slavery, she, like Harriet Beecher Stowe and Theodore

Parker, did not always rise above the nation's racism, even when she was, as in "Blind Tom," "Lamar," and *Waiting for the Verdict*, at her abolitionist best.

At this time, the realities of Davis's own world were brought forth in a manner she could no longer avoid. Payment for "Blind Tom" had been surprisingly low; with both her mother and her sister Emelie ill with diphtheria, financial pressures loomed before Rebecca, who was still living at home and remained a major contributor to the household income. She wrote to Fields that she must rectify the situation. "You know I would like to write *only* for you," she explained, "partly because we are friends, and partly because I am *in earnest* when I write and I find the audience I like in the Atlantic readers."[115] But *Peterson's* had offered her three hundred dollars for a short story equivalent in length to "David Gaunt." Writing for the ladies' magazine was not to her liking, she admitted: "It does me no good and for others is neither harmful nor helpful. Yet as times are I am not justified in refusing the higher price."[116] If Fields could convince Mr. Ticknor to agree to higher rates, she would remain exclusively their contributor. Fields promptly wrote back, acknowledging that the *Atlantic* would pay Davis eight dollars per page for her work, making her one of their highest-paid contributors.[117] In her acceptance, she agreed to write for the *Atlantic* "exclusively," if exclusive was understood to mean *American* publications; she still hungered for the freedom of English journals. In spite of her agreement with Fields, she also continued to write for *Peterson's*; in the next year she published a six-part serialized novel and three short stories in the Philadelphia magazine.

Davis at the same time began what would become an annual process: the publication of a Christmas story. In subsequent years, the stories would be written to please Clarke. Her future husband's tastes in literature were never as studied as her own, and throughout their marriage he vocally asserted his preference for romance rather than realism. Typically, the Christmas gifts written for Clarke were trite and bespoke the popular tastes of the day. But this year, before Clarke's influence had been felt to any great extent, Davis published the ironically titled "The Promise of Dawn" in the *Atlantic*; she was paid $120 for the short story.

Before it could be published, however, she had to gain Annie's assistance. The depiction of a prostitute, driven to her decline not by her own sinfulness but by societal hypocrisies, was not "realistic" in James Fields's opinion. As Davis confided to Annie, however: " 'Lot' [the prostitute] is from life. You know, here in a town like this it is easy to come into direct contact with every class and the longer I live—the more *practical* my observation is—the more I am convinced that the two natives remain in the mss. degraded souls until the last—and struggle until the end for victory."[118] If practical observation was not enough, Davis's years of working for the Wheeling *Intelligencer* had supplied ample exposure to such realities. One case reported in that newspaper during the period when Davis was one of their editorial correspondents, for instance, involved "the low den of Mrs. Harris, on Clay Street, in East Wheeling. It was the common resort of the most abandoned characters of both sexes, and the place presented a daily scene of debauchery, degradation and prostitution."[119] A six-year-old child, abandoned by his drunken mother, was found "lying in a writing desk, upon a pile of rags, almost dead from cold and neglect."[120] In spite of attempts by the police to resuscitate the child, he died that same evening. The women and "one or two worthies" who were in the Clay Street house at the time of the raid were jailed. As always, Davis's fiction was drawn from life. She knew that the topic would offend some readers; she admitted to Annie, "I never wrote anything so hard or repugnant to my feelings to write"; yet once it was completed, "I was [never] more indifferent to censure or praise. I *knew* I was right."[121]

The prevalent attitude at the time, as revealed in the New York Female Reform Society's journal *The Advocate*, was that prostitution was a pollutant destroying the major cities in America and one that drew upon the "lascivious and predatory nature" of the male participant.[122] Davis was more concerned with the environmental forces that led women into prostitution, and she sought in "Promise" to synthesize those forces with the idea that prostitution was often an inherited "career." As in her earlier work, she focuses upon the economic conditions that support the necessity of women turning to prostitution. A survey that was conducted in New York City in 1858 suggests that Davis was again working with the materials of "to-day." Officials surveyed two thousand prostitutes who had served time in the city's jails; they discovered that seventy-five percent of the women had occupations as servants or seamstresses, positions that typically paid less than living wages. The same percentage of those who were incarcerated were under the age of twenty-five, and the majority were teenagers. Davis's prostitute, Charlotte Tyndal, and Charlotte's younger brother, Benny, are both illegitimate and the prostitute must support both of them, a fact also validated by the survey: half of the prostitutes surveyed had children, 50 percent of whom were illegitimate.[123] Economics, as Davis knew, was a major factor in the victimization of women and children.

Annie's admiration for "The Promise of Dawn" prevailed over her husband's reluctance, and it was published in the January 1863 issue of the *Atlantic*. A precursor of Stephen Crane's *Maggie: A Girl of the Streets* (1893), Davis's short story employs both the war and the Bible as metaphoric influences, and it represents a synthesis of sentimentalism and realism. This metaliterary synthesis, like that of romanticism and realism, was prevalent in many of the early realists' works of fiction, most notably Harriet Beecher Stowe's *Pearl of Orr's Island*. Davis not only synthesizes sentimentalism (Adam's interior monologues) and realism (the facts of Charlotte's life and the prevalence of prostitution in New York) but also continues her interest in naturalistic techniques. The combination of these styles is not as incongruous as once thought. As observed in the *Continental Monthly* review of *Howth*, realism was beginning to receive some attention in American letters, although realism, and especially naturalism, were not yet fully accepted literary styles. More importantly, the combination of styles and theories allowed Davis to bridge her insistence upon realistic bases for fiction and her reformer's concern for educating her audience. She increasingly felt the need to depict the brute self as a consequence not of innate human nature but of social failings. Charlotte's death, unlike Lois Yare's, is redemptive.

The rhetorical style of "Promise" echoes that of "Life," with its abhorrence of the smoke-filled clouds that stifle dawn and the indifference of nature to this season's "crop" of dead soldiers. The character in "Promise" who will have an awakening is *Adam* Craig, but his spiritual discoveries will come too late for Charlotte ("Lot") Tyndal.[124] Born to a mother who "drank herself to death in the Bowery dens," Charlotte admits, "I learned my trade there, slow and sure."[125] She has remained in the trade because of societal attitudes and because she must support herself and Benny. Charlotte had no chance to rise—the men who used her have a place in society, Davis notes, but "when a woman's once down, there's no raising her up" (19); this recognition of society's differing treatment of men and women would become increasingly central to Davis's fiction.

Though Charlotte has a talented voice which could serve as a means of support, Davis refuses to designate her as distinguishable from the fifteen thousand other prostitutes in New York City at the time. Charlotte is raucous, often drunk, and finds escape in opium. Prostitution was a problem of the times, one which Davis believed could be eased only by personal activism. She again mocks the traditional systems—not only charitable institutions, but people like Adam and his wife Jinny, Christians who take special interest in the distant Indian missions but refuse to help the poverty-stricken young woman who comes to their door. The opening pages of the story are rife with Adam's pietistic thoughts, but he is oblivious to the conditions that abet Charlotte's fate. Throughout the story, Charlotte yearns to end her struggles by quietly slipping into the nearby river; if it were not for Benny, she would do so. When she realizes that Benny's only chance to escape this hereditary cycle is her own demise, she arranges for Adam to take him in, and kills herself. To Davis's mind, the crime was society's.

3. Other Women's Stories

SOME OF THE DARKEST DAYS of the Civil War were yet to come, but for Davis a new life was beginning. In January 1863, she shyly wrote Annie that she would be leaving for Philadelphia in a few weeks. She and Clarke were to be married in early March: "It isn't easy for me to tell you this. I don't know why. I would rather tell other women's stories than my own."[1] Illnesses in both families had already caused the couple to postpone their marriage, and Davis's uncle was near death at this time. Rather than delay their plans again, she and Clarke decided to have a small, private wedding, a decision that pleased Davis. She squirmed through the few requisite premarital customs that she could not avoid, longing to be at her desk writing instead of being "fitted and inspected and looked at by women with mouths full of pins and one eye shut."[2] She and Clarke were married in Philadelphia on March 5, 1863. One unintentionally ironic note to their marriage was the Fieldses' wedding gift, which reflected Annie's preferences: a seven-volume collection of the works of Emerson and a portrait of the Concord Sage for the living-room wall. Davis graciously thanked the Fieldses, slyly avoiding any comment on Emerson by insisting that the picture would be a pleasant reminder of the friends who had given it to her.

The Davises' first home in Philadelphia was with Clarke's sister, Carrie Cooper, and her family at 1429 Girard Avenue. Davis had not wanted "the 'wedding trip' ordained by rule"; she was anxious to meet her in-laws and to settle into her new home.[3] By the time of their marriage Clarke had finished his schooling and was a practicing if not highly profitable lawyer. To supplement their income, he also worked as a postal clerk and continued his editorial work for the prestigious *Legal Intelligencer*, a position that afforded him acquaintance with many of Philadelphia's most prominent businessmen and political leaders. Davis was pleased with Clarke's public involvement, but she sought a more reserved lifestyle for herself, carefully guarding the quiet and isolation necessary for writing. From the beginning of her marriage, she clarified her intention to continue writing; as she told

Annie, "I must have leave to say my word in the Atlantic as before, when the spirit moves me. It is a necessity for me to write—well or ill—you know every animal has speech and that is mine."[4] It was a demand to which Clarke readily adhered, although, in spite of his own literary career, he would never understand Rebecca's need to write for a reputable journal regardless of the pay. Even before their marriage, Clarke regarded her writing as a financially based career. Though he was proud of his wife's talents, he did not understand her artistic vision.

Life in someone else's busy home was not an easy adjustment, but Davis grew very fond of Carrie. And she continued to write. Shortly before her wedding, she had completed a three-part story for the *Atlantic* originally called "The Gurneys" but retitled "Paul Blecker" by James Fields for publication. She wrote the story in a period of exhaustion and felt that the "pages read 'fagged.' "[5] Davis also had to confront editorial tampering with this text, which greatly angered her:

> Mr. Davis says to tell you [Annie] that if you were the one who took a sentence out of Paul Blecker alluding to (your demigod) Gen. Butler—he thanks you—and applauds it highly. *I* want to know who did it—Mr. Nichols or Mrs. Fields? Because—

> _____

> What abysms of wrath lie in that blank, you may imagine.[6]

She immediately recovered her equanimity and thereafter was often able to tease Annie about her questionable literary tastes, since Annie had liked this story; but the issue of editorial control, even in minor instances, was becoming more galling. It is interesting to note, too, that however reticent she was with James Fields, Davis did not have any difficulty in voicing her opinions with Annie. Davis's assessment of the quality of writing in "Blecker" is accurate to an extent; some passages in the story are not on the same level as her earlier fiction. However, "Blecker" is a fascinating study that continues the commonplace history of the Civil War and, perhaps not unusual for a newlywed, moves Davis into another major theme that she would reshape throughout the 1860s and 1870s: the inequities of marriage for women.

"Blecker" is more highly steeped in the Civil War than any of Davis's previous writings on that subject. Harper's Ferry, Richmond, and Fredericksburg are frequent locales, and John Brown's prison figures as an ironic symbol of the life of Grey Gurney, a young woman sold into marriage.

Paul Blecker is a surgeon whose work is to tend to the wounded from the Ohio Valley battles. The story centers on his renunciation of the New England moral training he received, and of Grey Gurney's "taint" for having been sold into marriage; each is a "slave" to his or her past.

As Davis recrafted her tales of border-state life in this turbulent period, she carefully shaped her characterizations. These mid-1860s stories reveal the depth of human nature she was able to draw forth, a depth that would be replicated thirty years later by Hamlin Garland in his Border stories of another generation. As in her later novel, *Waiting for the Verdict*, Davis denounces martyrdom in this realistic tale; rejecting Calvinistic evangelicalism as a solution, she depicts both Paul and Grey as having to learn that earthly renunciation of love for a loosely held ideal merely destroys lives and offers little reward, here or hereafter. As James C. Austin has noted, the advocacy of instincts over second-hand ideals in "Blecker" "anticipated Howells' attacks on the dogma of sentimental duty for duty's sake."[7] In Davis's philosophy, the sensuous love that Grey and Paul achieve after they have faced their "days of trial" is more worthy of God's approval than the aberrant Christianity advocated by those who would keep Christ from the world "by shutting him up in formula or church."[8]

"Blecker" is also significant for Davis's refusal to condemn a woman who chooses to support herself by going on the stage rather than live in poverty, unfulfilled, as society would prefer. Lizzy Gurney's decision does not transform her into a happy-ever-after heroine; she is rejected by her church, family, and friends—everyone except Grey and, grudgingly, Paul. Yet the author insists that it is Lizzy who has learned "the truths of life,—to love, to succor, to renounce" (69). The latter infinitive is especially ironic: social norms would require Lizzy to renounce her livelihood; Davis suggests she renounce the artificial criteria that would deny her "voice."

Although Davis had continued to insist upon anonymity with the *Atlantic* audience, her work spoke for her, as Elizabeth Stuart Phelps acknowledged in a tribute to Davis, which subsequently appeared in the opening of Phelps's short story, "At Bay" (1867). The narrator of "At Bay" is a young woman who has been raised on a farm:

> I often think when I have finished a novel, or a story in a magazine or newspaper . . . that it is strange why the people who make them up can not find something *real* to say. It seems to me as if I knew a good many lives that I could put right into a book, if I only had the words . . . I read a story once—it was a good while ago—called 'Paul Blecker.' I saw in a paper that it was

written by a lady who had written something called 'Life in the Iron Mills.'
. . . I don't know who she is. I wish I could find her out and thank her for
having written that story. It made you feel as if she knew all about you, and
were sorry for you, and as if she thought nobody was too poor, or too uneducated, or too worn-out with washing-days, and all the things that do not
sound a bit grand in books, to be written about. I think of it often now, since
I have had the care and worry of the children here at home. It makes me love
her.[9]

Davis and Phelps would soon become acquainted. In this tribute Phelps
pinpointed, through the voice of an impoverished young woman, the class
to whom Davis wanted to give voice.

*   *   *

The early months of Davis's marriage were filled with romance. A
woman friend had once told Rebecca that "You—every woman has a right
to summer days in her life—," and Davis reported to Annie, "*My* summer
days are coming now."[10] She loved the afternoons that she and Clarke spent
with the Petersons in the Wissahickon hills, searching for mosses and trail-
ing arbutus to bring home for planting. She was also learning, however, to
accommodate herself to the ways of Philadelphia life. She was not comfortable with Clarke's church, which she noted was restricted to " '*Christians* and *patriots*' "; but, for the time, she attended with him.[11] One of her
less pleasant duties during that period was returning bridal calls. It was
pure "conventionalism," she told Annie, so she spiritedly converted it into
a lark: "But you see, I have such a cloak—'Literary women always affect
eccentricity' with a slight curl of the lip and you are forgiven. Only write
for a magazine Annie—and come live in the West and you can wear feath-
ers in July or pin your shawl behind with impunity if you like—." In passing, she jokingly reported that the head librarian of the Philadelphia library
had "laid himself and his books with 'a cosy corner and pen and paper' at
my feet in the Persian fashion. I knew a friend of mine had been there
telling him he *ought* to 'have read Margret' and 'greatly admired' etc etc.
But I only looked gracious and unconscious." (The "friend" was probably
Clarke, who sought thus to encourage her writing; Davis herself rarely
alluded to her national reputation, but she was now known to all of the
major editors and authors of the day.) She loved the privacy of the ancient
old library: "It's a splendid dark dingy place with little off shoots of
rooms."[12] A "room of her own" in the library not only afforded her the

perfect setting for writing but was also a necessary refuge from the demands on her time at home. After the birth of her first child, she would have to revert to writing at home.

Her first spring as a resident of Philadelphia, however, was spent tending to both Carrie and Clarke, who were ill periodically; by May, Davis could report, "The invalids are well—comparatively, but *I* still breathe 'Bay-rum' and sick room nausea—it hangs about my lungs somehow."[13] It was not until June that everyone was once again healthy. As soon as she could, she returned to her writing. The Philadelphia area seemed a rich source for material. In the early summer, Davis began outlining sketches of some of the more remarkable people she had observed, with her usual delight in cryptic portraits that satirized any act of pretense: "philanthropists, liturateurs—people with missions and cotton umbrellas."[14]

In September she had escorted her younger sister "Emma" around Philadelphia, and in mid-October her cousin, Clara Wilson, visited with her for a week, but Davis was not feeling well. She was highly fatigued and tried several patent medicines, but nothing seemed to help. She finally resolved to trust her "old Western habit of a long *fatiguing* walk every day and now I have old healthy cheerful days and dreamless nights."[15] She was in the early weeks of pregnancy. But her healthful regimen was not to last; only one submission ("The Great Air-Engine") was made in the autumn months. Then a great quiet descended upon the Philadelphia home. For several months, no letters from Davis reached the Fieldses, her family, or any other of her acquaintances. Clarke notified Annie that Rebecca was severely ill, diagnosed as suffering from nervous exhaustion. Her pregnancy is not mentioned; but in late 1863, Davis sent her "dear, *dear* Annie" a letter that reveals the spiritual turmoil wrought in her by the extended illness that intruded upon her pregnancy. Still bedridden, she tells Annie: "I wanted to write before only to say I loved you—God knows how dear and tender—all love has grown to me now but at first I was not able and now the doctor forbids the least reading or writing for fear of bringing back the trouble in my head. . . . Ma is with me and sends her *heart's-love* to Mrs. Fields."[16]

It is probable that S. Weir Mitchell, in later years a close friend and the family physician for the Davises, was Rebecca's physician during this siege also,[17] and the advocacy of the rest cure for women was Mitchell's standard prescription, as other women writers of the nineteenth century— most notably, Charlotte Perkins Gilman and Edith Wharton—painfully learned. Although years later Davis asserted that she owed her life to Dr.

Mitchell,[18] she did not forget the personal cost of being ordered to forego her writing. As late as 1886 she used the theme in her fiction; in that year she published a short story in the *Atlantic* in which the narrator has been ordered to abandon old associations and rest for one or two years: "My chief business," the narrator laments, "was to think of nothing, and to sleep. I lived [in St. Robideaux], if you choose to call it living, for a year."[19] In fact, the narrator laments that St. Robideaux was conducive to "[n]othing more active than dreams."[20] The devastating effects of Davis's illness, and perhaps of her "cure," still lingered through the fall, as she explained to Annie: "these days have been so like the valley of the shadow of death, that I grow afraid of the end—but I ought to have trust I know. I don't think God would take me from him. I wish you would pray for us."[21] The one note of hope in her letter is Clarke's promise that they will move to their own home upon her recovery; and through her illness and recovery, she asserts, Annie's letters were always received "like a loving grasp of her hand."[22]

Davis recovered sufficiently to travel to her family home for Christmas that year. Out of her illness and recovery, Davis experienced a resurgent faith in God, yet the unnamed terror of her illness had not dissipated: "God has held *me* in such a quiet blessing hand but I could tell you a story which I cannot write sadder and stranger than any fiction—which has made the days and nights very feverish for a long time. Some day I will tell you but maybe *now* I ought not to have even said this much. . . . There's a happy ending coming at last I hope—all through, the one Hand has been so strangely visible—I am glad of that—"[23] Months later, when Annie hinted that Rebecca could tell her of this horrifying period if it would help, Davis denied there had been any problem, having indelibly absorbed her pain through a renewed faith. As with so many things in her life that she could not alter or conquer, she never again spoke of her illness. Davis continued throughout her life to attack passive Christianity and its usurpation by industrial capitalists, but she now embraced a living faith which deepened through the coming years. It was, for Davis, the most significant aspect of her recovery, and from the security of her family home in Wheeling, with Christmas at hand, she could at last feel the "old life and the new coming together in this time of tender memories and first hopes."[24] She celebrated the coming year by informing the Fieldses that she was ready once again to become the *Atlantic*'s "favorite" contributor.[25]

The first story Davis wrote after her illness was "The Wife's Story," a story that combines autobiography with an impressive comment on literary philosophies; it is one of her most significant critiques of Emersonian transcendentalism. Recent Davis scholars, most notably Tillie Olsen and Margaret M. Culley, have emphasized this story's biographical overtones, suggesting that Hetty is representative of Davis herself.[26] Certainly, Davis's collapse is echoed in the darkest passages of "The Wife's Story," and letters she wrote to Annie prior to and after its publication reveal that her "problem" had not yet completely abated. She felt both a desire for escape (a "most amiable . . . [and] stupid desire to be quiet and forgotten"[27]) and a fear of escape: "I never felt before how hard it was to justify my right to love as since I was sick. . . . Sometimes I have a terror Annie that it will all disappear like a dream—that I will become suddenly indifferent to you all."[28] "The Wife's Story" is Davis's most autobiographical work of fiction, but the focus remains on "other women," and it embraces her growing concern with women's "thwarted lives."

Since her visit to Concord, Davis had grown more concerned about the effects of transcendentalism's philosophic "bubbles" on the minds of young Americans. She recalled that Bronson Alcott had built Emerson an arbor in which to "do his thinking," but the arbor had no door: "You could look at it and admire it, but nobody could go in or use it. It seemed to me a fitting symbol for this guild of prophets and their scheme of life."[29] Davis had begun her challenge of transcendental idealism in *Howth* with the depiction of Stephen Holmes, and "The Wife's Story" parody of the consequences of American transcendentalism is a cautionary tale for those New Englanders who blindly followed its teachings. *Hester* Manning is not branded with a scarlet letter, but her experience is evoked to make her—and Davis's readers—aware of the dangers of such a romanticized view of "reality." Davis had studied the imitative nature that, ironically, transcendentalism ultimately encouraged when she had visited Concord two years earlier. This is the "education" that Hetty had received prior to her marriage, and her dependence upon the teachings of such a dream world nearly destroys her potential for survival in the real world. The story at once critiques transcendentalism and acts as a sign of Davis's own struggle both to accept the limitations of marriage to a "Western" man and to value its benefits. While it is a painful assessment of women's lives in mid-nineteenth-century America, it is an enlightening extension of Davis's fiction techniques.

Since she had begun her writing career, Davis had been developing an anti-"dream" stance as part of her theory of the commonplace. When Hetty explains, after her recovery, that the details of this story are hers alone, "the history of one day," though anyone may learn from them, it reflects Davis's emphasis upon the quotidian and upon the unique perspective of reality that defines individuality. It is a creative philosophy that manifests what Hamlin Garland would later term "veritism." In *Crumbling Idols* (1894), Garland articulates in theory what Davis renders here, thirty years earlier, in her fiction: the demand that American fiction break with tradition and imitation of European models in order to explore the underlying meaning of truth and of reality. Such exploration requires fiction writers to confront the unpleasant as well as the "pure" aspects of life; Davis and later realists believed that transcendentalism ignored and sometimes consciously attempted to escape the wretched aspects of life.

"The Wife's Story" begins with Hetty's commentary after she has survived her moment of crisis. This use of an individual whose experience allows her to be the omniscient narrator of her own history is important in the development of American literary realism. As Mark Seltzer notes in his excellent study of the antirealism in Henry James's *Princess Casamassima* (1886), "Perhaps the most powerful tactic of supervision achieved by the traditional realist novel inheres in its dominant technique of narration—the style of 'omniscient narration' . . . gives to the narrator a providential vision of the characters and action."[30] Upon reflection, Hetty discerns that "on that day when the face of my fate changed, I myself was conscious of no inward master-struggle . . . it was by no giddy, blear-sighted free-will of my own that I arrived where I stand to-day."[31] Prior to her crisis, she was ignorant of her own capabilities; after, she bears an omniscient understanding of the events and their cause. Now she is aware that she had been "drifting" toward this crisis all of her life; indeed, she had been educated to it—born in Concord, where man learned "to stand self-poised and found *himself* God" (191; emphasis added). Nor is it merely from listening to the Concord Sages that Hetty has come to believe in the complete power of the Self; she was weaned on that philosophy from birth: " 'The only object in life is to grow.' It was my father's—Margaret Fuller's motto. I had been nursed on it. . . . There had been a time when I had dreamed of attaining Margaret's stature" (192).

Davis's reference to Fuller incorporates a double-edged irony. Hetty's father drew on Fuller's writings, and Hetty herself wanted to attain "Margaret's stature"—but that stature was limited in a very masculine-oriented school of philosophy, one that failed to give its strongest feminine voice its due. To Davis's mind, as she rejects the assertion of Self that Fuller advocated, Hetty has the ability to "say" more through her quotidian existence than Fuller ever attained; when trapped in the rhetoric of the Self, she cannot envision the value of her commonplace life. Even more important, under these educational influences, Hetty is incapable of original thinking. All of her grand ideas are simply echoes of the patterns established by her father, who himself had selected his ideas from Margaret Fuller's work. In Hetty's "dream" for her own child, Davis exposes the extent to which this philosophy in fact denigrates a woman's potential. Since Hetty's own life had been such a disappointment to her, she had long planned her child's future as a means of fulfilling her own dreams: "I had intended my child should be reared in New England: what I had lacked in gifts and opportunities he should possess. . . . But the child was a girl, a weazen-faced little mortal, crying night and day like any other animal. It was an animal, wearing out in me the strength needed by-and-by for its mental training. I sent it to a nursery in the country" (192). Hetty's neglect of her child's emotional development in preference for mental training and her complete devaluation of the child because it is female exemplify the dangers Davis envisioned in the unrealistic training of transcendentalism: no sense of reality, nor valuing of realism. Thus life, and the people in one's life, must always be a disappointment.

The rapid decline that Hetty confronts in the remainder of the story, similar to the core story of "Life in the Iron Mills" in its naturalistic techniques, is revealed at the conclusion to have been only a "dream"—this time. The realist's narrative style of omniscience as set forth from the story's beginning necessitates not a plot of decline for Hetty but one that is providential. Thus, as Henry Adams asserted, history is valueless if it is not a form of experimental learning, and its use should be measured by its usefulness to the evolutionary intelligence of the race. Davis presents through Hetty's narration of her personal history a microcosm of experience that must be learned by others to push forward the evolution of the intelligence of the human race, a narration that denies transcendentalism as part of that progression. The precise moment of inception of Hetty's "dream," Davis's recurrent symbol for transcendentalism, is merely "some latent, unconscious jar of thought" that reminds Hetty of a trip to Paris she had taken years ago, when she had entered Rosa Bonheur's studio to view her painting, *Horse Fair*. Hetty was deeply moved by "the peculiar life that seemed to impregnate the place itself . . . the sharply managed lights, the skins, trappings, [Bonheur's] disguises on the walls" (193). This recollection immediately follows Hester's rejection of her own pregnant creation—her female child; as a substitute, she is drawn into this "impregnated" atmosphere where everything is controlled and artificially arranged. As Davis presents it, this life is a false labor, as it were, one that embraces only the "trappings" and "disguises"—the artifice—of nature.

If, as Myra Jehlen suggests in her scrupulous study of Emerson, the Concord Sage played a key role in the distinction of man's move "not from nature to civilization but from history to nature, and himself evolves in the same direction; in history, he is encompassed all around by conventions, traditions, and other men, but his coming dominion over nature will seal his absolute independence,"[32] Davis rejected a vision of "progress" that, in its assumptions of "absolute independence," denied history, even with its ideological biases, as integral to the process from beginning to end. The exposure of ideologies in order to establish more accurate records of history was requisite to Davis's theory of the commonplace; more importantly, even if absolute independence could be achieved (something she questioned), Hetty's dream reveals Davis's assessment of the very weighty price of such "independence." Davis was much more likely to agree with Thomas Carlyle that Emerson ought to come down from his lofty heights.[33]

Davis did not reject a woman's work outside the home, as her previous writings have already revealed. But she always rejected artifice as a substitute for art, and that is what Hetty attempts to do when she goes on the stage. Lizzy Gurney in "Paul Blecker" had genuine talent, and Davis praised her decision to escape a stifling life and find her own means of expression. But Hetty is blinded to the limitations of her singing talents; her decision is rooted in a desire for fame, not for expression. She had the talent to compose music, but that was no longer enough. Thus she creates a myth about her talents, "I *had* been called, then,—set apart to a mission; it was a true atom of the creative power that had powered my brain; my birth had placed me on a fitting place of self-development" (193). This blind allegiance to her own artifice forces Hetty to reject her husband as well as her child. Instead of giving birth to herself and to her talents, Hetty's act disconnects her from others and from an ability to acknowledge her limitations as well as her potential.[34] The theater in which she is to perform, for what she defines as its "uncultured caste of hearers," is little better than the grotesque theaters to which Stephen Crane's Maggie will descend. Monsieur Vaux, the manager, is depicted as a brute animal, "pawing his chin with one hand" as he leers at her "with the eye of a stock-raiser buying a new mule" (198). Thus, in a scene that will have increasingly painful autobiographic correlations, Davis depicts Hetty as an artist who commodifies her own talents. If the cause of the commodifying was different for the author and her character, for each it was a matter of "education."

Zola later observed that the experimental novelist's goal "is to study phenomena in order to control them."[35] The control that Davis seeks through her providential narrator, her naturalistic depiction of M. Vaux, and Hetty's dream-fate is to argue, in fact, that the real danger to Hetty is her inability to accept marriage as a potentially unifying experience. Unlike many writers of the era, Davis does not suggest that her character should unduly restrict her sexual passions; instead she depicts Hetty as limited precisely because she tries to deny the "fever of the flesh" in her marriage. On the night of Hetty's ordeal, when she must decide to accept or reject M. Vaux's proposition, she lies beside her sleeping husband and struggles, on the one hand, against the knowledge that Vaux's scheme is "vulgar, degrading" and yet, on the other, her sense of having "been dumb and choking [for] so long" (205). At that moment, a beam of light crosses her husband's face, making him appear blue around the mouth—like a cadaver. "There was passion and power of love under my stiff-muscled fingers and hard calculating brain," Hetty admits, but to quiet her rising passions, she draws the sheet up over herself, thus refusing to use her "passion and power of love" to bring her husband back to life and unwittingly replicating the figure of a cadaver herself. On stage, she is jeered by the crowd as she stands "with my white gauze and bony body" revealed to the world—and to her husband, who is in the audience and who will subsequently die from heart failure. She realizes that, having rejected both her husband and her female child, her fate is that "I—I had my Self" (213). The ideal Self for Davis was not Emerson's separated Self, which Hetty achieves, but a self-sufficient Self that embraces others.

Prefiguring Dreiser's Hurstwood in the wintry Chicago streets, Hetty, knowing she has lost husband and home, leaves the theater and descends into a naturalistic scene of street activity and personal isolation: "The street was thronged with streetcars stopping for the play-goers, hacks, and omnibuses; the gas flamed in red and green letters over the house-fronts; the crowd laughed and swayed and hummed snatches of songs, as they went by. . . . I wondered if my child would ever know it had a mother" (213). Hetty is "saved" by awakening from this prophetic dream to discover that she has suffered from "brain-fever" (216–17). Thus, with the sense that "God had let me be born again," Hetty rejects the transcendental Self for a now loving and repentant husband. But, of course, Hetty's life is thereby rooted in a highly patriarchal world, which Davis, perhaps unwittingly, admits by allowing a male character, Hetty's step-son, to utter the very male-centered moral: "a woman has no better work in life than . . . to make herself a visible Providence to her husband and child" (222). It is a sentimentalist's conclusion, one which establishes the woman as spiritual authority; but it is a very dissatisfying ending for twentieth-century audiences.

Davis's purpose, however, was to expose the dangers of transcendentalist ideology to her audience. Whereas one school of New England writers (from Sedgwick to Hawthorne to Freeman) relied upon the requisite theme of Calvinist Puritanism as "inherently grotesque,"[36] Davis converts the theme to present-day transcendentalism, which harbored the same potential grotesqueness that she felt had the power to distort an entire community. This is the precise danger Davis perceived in transcendental theory: It was interpreted by its adherents as evidence that they were divine in and of themselves, that they were "set apart." Thus, they need not be *of* this world and may reject the opportunities for attainment within everyday life. Her concern centered upon the perception that transcendentalism was preached and absorbed as a distortion of commonplace reality. But if in "The Wife's Story" she rejected transcendentalism and Calvinism, she embraced a very limited role for women, one against which she would struggle for the remainder of her life—sometimes advocating the limitations, sometimes rising above them in her fiction of other women's lives, if not in her own.

*   *   *

On April 18, 1864, Davis gave birth to her first son, Richard Harding Davis, who would become a New York bon vivant and later a serious war reporter, covering many of the same battles as his acquaintance Stephen Crane. Richard was not a healthy child in his first few months of life; Davis told Annie that she did not want to show him off yet, not "until he has a chance to learn how to grow fat and to look better pleased with the new world he has found. Just now he is the smallest tiredest little thing, and homely too only with big dark eyes—"[37] She promised that in a year or two she would be proud of him; and, of course, within months she was proclaiming him the smartest, cleverest child ever. But his emergence into the world was not an easy one, and it is of little surprise that he was not healthy. On March 20, Davis's father, Richard Harding, had died, but her family chose not to tell her because of her pregnancy and her barely recov-

ered health. The decision was rooted in heartfelt concern, but its consequences were harsh. Not only did it deny Davis an opportunity to attend
her father's funeral and burial, but, ultimately, the decision backfired:
when Rachel Harding appeared at the Davis home three weeks later, her
daughter immediately discerned the cause of her visit. The shock induced
delivery, and Davis remained seriously ill for more than a month after
Richard's birth.

When she was well enough to correspond with Annie, she declared,
"I feel as if I had been in some foreign country and could not be enough
welcomed home again."[38] Even less surprising, she now found balancing
her marriage and a career even more exhausting with the addition of motherhood, as she lamented to Annie, "But talk of running three periodicals
like steam engines? Why a baby uses up twice the motive power! Think
what a woman is worth by night when all day she has been in momentary
expectation of seeing that infant hope of the world brought in choked by
a pin or strangled on a coal or whatever else its fingers can lay hands
on—."[39] Nor was Davis quiet about the inequity of responsibilities: "A
woman too who has a husband that has taken to fancy work at tools for
exercise and whittles and files away all regard for wife or family—Look
upon us as virtually divorced by means of this last hobby—My place is *quite*
filled by 'bits of wood with a beau-ti-ful grain' etc. etc.—If I can bring my
ears back from the din of the saw and sand paper I will be glad to hear the
music you promised us.—"[40] She asserts that she is only joking and is quite
proud of Clarke's "pretty little brackets," but even with a nurse to help her
with the baby the tension of her days is evident.

In May, Davis and Clarke decided that the best remedy for their health
would be a couple of months at the seashore during late summer. With the
house in the confusion of preparing to move to the shore, she reported to
Annie, "I am too weak yet to trust myself even with the particulars of war
news—Faint rumors of the Fair excitement come into our rooms, but I
know little about it."[41] The turmoil of Davis's inner world replicated that
of the outside world. Philadelphia was threatened with invasion as Lee's
troops advanced. Within a month the newly appointed commander of the
region, Major-General Napoleon Jackson Tecumseh Dana, would order
the mayor to supply two thousand men to dig entrenchments around the
city. Preparations were also beginning in May for the great "Central Fair"
to which Davis refers. Held in Philadelphia's Logan Square, the Fair con-
sisted of enormous rotundas that housed restaurants, horticultural and
commercial exhibitions, and works of art. Its purpose was to stand as

public testimony of support for the Union army.⁴² But while caring for her newborn child and her ailing sister-in-law, attempting to provide entertainment for Maggie, an old friend from Wheeling,⁴³ and preparing for the move to the seashore, Davis had little time for celebrations and none to think of her own career.

Nor were these her only concerns at this time. The issue she and Clarke had known would come now raised its specter: the draft. Clarke was an outspoken Federalist and had long been active in the abolitionist movement, but at this juncture he preferred to render his patriotism through his pen. Davis's explanation to Annie is one of the rare critical comments about her husband that she ever recorded: "As for the draft, I don't fast myself with it, as our Scotch cousins would say. Clarke was drafted and says very heroically $300 is very little service for him to offer his country, which is all very well for patriots of his and your persuasion to say. I notice however that he is nursing the rheumatism . . . [in] one foot very assiduously ever since Saturday. Of course I don't guess for what."⁴⁴

At this time, too, the widowed Rachel Harding decided to move back to her family home in Washington, Pennsylvania, where she could reside with her widowed sister. In the early fall, barely settled again in Philadelphia, Davis and her six-month-old baby traveled to Washington to console her mother. Davis had barely recovered from her own illness and was tending to her infant and two elderly women, but Clarke chose this moment to ask his "dearest Pet" to help her "old Boy" by writing an item for the *Legal Intelligencer*. He cautions, "Don't, dear Love, think I am hard on you for asking this, but I am so pushed I could not help it. Will you send it as soon as possible."⁴⁵ Clarke was handling a real-estate venture that required several legal documents to be drawn up immediately; therefore, he wanted Rebecca to produce "a first rate notice" about the *Atlantic*, which he had promised James Fields he would push in the *Legal Intelligencer*. Clarke cautioned his wife not to "refer [the notice] back to me to do, for indeed I have not the time—."⁴⁶ Davis records no comment on Clarke's insensitivity. Her notice appeared in the December 23, 1864, issue of the *Intelligencer*. It would be nearly a year after Richard's birth before she would again publish her fiction in the *Atlantic*.

Perhaps as compensation, though they had long planned to move, the Davises finally left Carrie Cooper's home later in the fall of 1864 and settled at least temporarily into a three-story brick row house at 1817 North Twelfth Street. Davis was thrilled to finally have her own home, and she jubilantly looked forward to their first Christmas at home as a family. During this period, too, she was contacted by Charles Eliot Norton, who became co-editor of the *North American Review* in 1864 and founded *The Nation* in 1865. He introduced himself to her by enclosing a letter he had received from a friend in Indiana highly praising Davis's fiction. In thanking Norton for his thoughtfulness, Davis revealed how distanced she had felt from her career for the past year: "an honest word of praise is a thoroughly healthful and helpful thing. . . . More people than the poor circus clown have met a fatal fall for lack of a little judicious clapping of hands. So I thank you—not exactly for the applause—as that you were thoughtful enough to be its medium."[47] She was well acquainted with Norton's reputation, and she invited him to call on her and Clarke if he ever visited Philadelphia; but once again she maintained her loyalty to the *Atlantic*. She did not publish in the *North American Review* until 1889, when the journal had moved to New York and severed its ties with the Brahmins. She never found a voice in *The Nation*, a periodical known to be hostile to women writers.[48]

Though she was not yet writing fiction again, Davis fine-tuned her critical skills in the last half of the year, as she had ever since her visit to Boston, by exchanging with Annie analyses of various articles in recent issues of the *Atlantic* and elsewhere. These exchanges are worth detailing for the glimpse they offer of Davis's critical assessments during her early career and of women's awareness of their sex's contributions to American literature. Davis appreciated the reprinting of some of Hawthorne's works and was especially pleased to see that Louisa May Alcott was garnering critical attention. Ever since meeting Alcott in Boston, Davis had followed her life through Annie, typically asking, "Tell me about Miss Alcott if ever she does any thing or finds rest—poor girl—how many hungry women with empty hands I know!"[49] Now she was pleased to acknowledge Alcott's burgeoning success. She had been deeply moved to the point of lingering fright, she claimed, by a mystery story Alcott had written. But she was critical of Alcott's departure from realms of life she knew personally, as she explained to Annie:

> I met her—don't you remember?—in Concord and Boston and felt so much pity and interest in her. The more perhaps because she is one of so large a class of women. But it seems to me this story of Debby's Debut falls far below her Hospital sketches—she knows hospitals perhaps is the reason—and fashionable society she evidently don't know. It is so long since it was thought necessary for a girl of untainted nature to make hay and eat bread and milk out of a bow.[50]

"Debby's Debut" was trite; but the hospital sketches that had so impressed Davis were drawn from Alcott's experiences as a nurse in the Union hospital at Georgetown, and their fact-based details measured up to Davis's literary criteria.

One author whose work Davis did not appreciate was Harriet Elizabeth Prescott (later Spofford). There were strengths to Prescott's writing—her graphic descriptions and her well-developed characterizations—that should have appealed to Davis. But Prescott was a writer of romances; her women characters were often of the saint-or-sinner school, though one wonders that Davis did not detect the complexities of characterization even within those tightly drawn lines. At one point in her correspondence with Annie, Davis charged Prescott with "usury of the buried intent"; Annie chided her for the harshness of her criticism, and Davis apologized, "I had no thought of saying a harsh thing of her God knows."[51] Thereafter, she mentions Prescott only in personal terms: How is she? Yes, they had heard she was now married, and so forth.

Elizabeth Stuart Phelps, on the other hand, garnered Davis's praise, both personally and professionally, although the latter was often praise tinged with restrictions. It is unclear who initiated the friendship, although it may have been Davis after Phelps's praise of her appeared in "At Bay." The two writers did not meet until years later, but they exchanged letters and followed one another's careers for several years. In 1866, Davis wrote Annie asking if she knew "a Miss Phelps of Andover?"[52] She admitted, "We like her thoroughly—and some things she has written—too."[53] The emphasis on *some* of Phelps's writing is not surprising: Phelps's early interest in realism, her use of an industrial milieu, and her concern for laborers and especially women was, as she later acknowledged, influenced by Davis's early fiction. But Phelps's insistent hyperbolic language and her sometimes too overt sentimentalism did not appeal to Davis; Phelps's later shift from realism to an antifeminist belief in "the inevitability of male dominion" would lead the two writers in opposite directions, but Phelps would never forget Davis's influence.[54]

Another writer in whose work Davis detected potential was Elizabeth Haven Appleton (1815–90), who published some short stories in the *Atlantic* at the time under the name "E. H. Appleton." Davis informed James Fields that he was to be commended for including Miss Appleton's fiction because she so accurately captured "Western manners."[55] Rather amusingly, Davis is willing to forgive some of Appleton's overt sentimentality because it is presented in "Western" garb. An earlier story that Davis would have read and admired was Appleton's depiction of a self-supporting woman teacher. The teacher's characterization is not feminist—she regrets not marrying and terms being single only "half a life"—but Appleton also presents the young woman's discovery that single life has its rewards as well: "how much there is to live for in my mind . . . ,"[56] asserts the protagonist, and she determines that she shall not be unhappy because she can thrive on an intellectual life.

Davis also followed with interest the career of Mary Abigail Dodge, or "Gail Hamilton." She at one time objected to a Hamilton novel that she was reviewing for Fields as both "unmanly" and "unwomanly," but she was drawn to some of Dodge's writing for much the same reason she was attracted to Alcott's hospital sketches: "Miss Dodge though is herself again in this number," she tells Annie a few months later. "What a thoroughly Western woman she is!"[57] "Western" was always Davis's highest compliment. She laughingly adds, "I don't know how she made the mistake to be born in New England." On a more serious note, Davis observes that Dodge would have received more acclaim in the West than she had in her native region: "Rough, democratic, hardy, common sense is the strength of western people and if she had belonged out there we'd have crowned her the genius of it—."[58]

Davis's conception of "Western" in no way propagates the Teddy Roosevelt mysticism of frontiers and conquest, a particularly masculine vision that Roosevelt popularized in the late 1880s but that was also prevalent in the westward expansion of the early 1860s. Whether or not Davis recognized the link between the 1862 Homestead Act and industrial expansionism, she had identified the encroachment of the eastern industrialists in "Life" the year before the act was established, and that encroachment remained a lifelong concern. Her most vociferously voiced complaint against the westward movement, however, was its effects on the young women left behind to eke out existences and to see their potential mates disappear. Her usage of the term "Western" was to suggest the healthy capabilities of the individual (most often referring to women) to carve their own paths—not necessarily to a particular region but beyond their assumed limitations. She liked "womanly women," certainly meaning femininity in a traditional sense but, more fully, embracing activism as part of womanliness.

Davis's inclusion of the concept of "Western" in her theory of the commonplace aligns her with a long tradition of early metarealism, most notably Caroline Kirkland's studies of Western life (*A New Home—Who'll*

Follow [1839] and its sequel, *Forest Life* [1842]). Although Kirkland and Davis's writings differed in many ways, metarealism in both writers' works does not exclude an appreciation of beauty; they recognize the possibility of more than one set of criteria to define beauty, as Davis suggested through her phrase, "strange beauty." Judith Fetterley has recognized Kirkland's realism as a synthesis of the "beautiful" and occasionally the "sentimental"; such realism, Fetterley discerns, offers a "sense of proportion, balance, and complexity," establishing "a realism that is not itself a distortion."[59]

Ultimately, "Western" became synonymous with "American" for Davis. As she told Annie in December 1862 after returning from Boston, her local friends now deemed her a "convert to New England" and uttered the phrase "with a mixture of awe and amaze[ment]."[60] But that was not the point, she insisted: "Why *dont* Americans know each other? When I see you in the spring I mean to argue this point with you—a regular debating club 'Europe or the West.' Mr. D'Orcay agreed with me that you (the literary people of Boston) knew *his* country better than your own."[61] Thus, the concept of "Western" is part of Davis's theoretical movement away from European models and toward the acknowledgment of the diversity of American regions; as she noted in the same letter, "Our Pennsylvania homelands are as curious and representative as those in New England." The term "Western" also incorporates her ideal of personal activism as an alternative to charitable institutions. In this vein, she is following the tradition begun by Kirkland, who noted that, in the West, necessities of life eliminate class differences: "In cities we bestow charity—in the country we can only exchange kind offices. . . . It is the true republican spirit."[62] Although Kirkland at first rebelled against her initiation into Western ways, Davis was born to them and maintained them as ideals throughout her life.

When Annie began to publish her own poetry, she cautiously asked Rebecca to read her first published ode "tenderly." Davis not only eagerly read the lyric but extended Annie the courtesy of taking it seriously enough to send her a critique. What she admired most was that the poem captured Annie's own "full and sacred tone" and earnestness,[63] an assessment that captures the elements of sentimentalism that Davis admired and often incorporated into her metarealistic fiction of the mid to late 1860s. But she encouraged Annie to extend herself, to "elaborate the idea more. It is so fine—when carried into detail—or would have been—that of making the organ the tone and exponent of not only the nation's victory but its trial—pain—prophecy—I wish you had not been afraid of holding the public ear too long and had done yourself more justice."[64] She suggests, in other words, that Annie view her own writing as artistry, an artistry that warrants public attention. It was the kind of encouragement few women writers of the time received.

When Davis had acknowledged Louisa May Alcott as representative of the "many hungry women with empty hands I know," she alluded to another, little-known aspect of her concern for other women's lives. Davis's metaphor for personal activism was "a grasp of the hand," and if she had advocated activism in her fiction from the beginning, she had pursued it in reality as well. She was never able to bring herself to join the public marches for women's rights, but she privately sought extended rights, especially in terms of careers, for many needy women friends.

Representative of Davis's involvement were her efforts on behalf of another Philadelphian, Sarah Wallace. Wallace's husband had been editor of the *Presbyterian Quarterly*, but when he died, Sarah discovered that she was left penniless with three children to support. Davis immediately offered assistance, but the proud widow did not want charity. Davis described Wallace as "a western woman—energetic, common sensible with a considerable talent for writing or acting."[65] But she was no longer young enough to begin a stage career nor did she feel she could rely upon the precarious income from writing if she were to give her children any sense of security. Instead, she told Davis of her plan: she would move to New Brighton, a village in western Pennsylvania, where her children's poverty would not hinder them in the way it would in status-conscious Philadelphia. The children's grandfather, George Cochran, lived in New Brighton and there, where clans were more important than money, they could live with dignity. As for herself, she intended to open a circulating library in New Brighton; she owned a good many books already, although she would need to supplement her personal holdings if the circulating library was to succeed.

In this manner, Davis was allowed to extend her grasp of the hand. Sarah asked Davis to contact James Fields for her, but Davis wisely chose to go through Annie, whom she knew would have a concern for this woman's situation. Doubting that Ticknor and Fields appointed agents for the sale of their books in small communities, Clarke had tried to deter Davis's efforts, but she pursued the possibility on Sarah's behalf. Although Ticknor and Fields did not appoint agents, Annie saw to it that a large supply of books was sent to Sarah Wallace within a week, a gift whose kindness brought Sarah to tears as she struggled for her independence. Davis did not stop there, however; in thanking the Fieldses, she suggested that James continue to send Sarah the latest books published by Ticknor and Fields, if not for an agent then as a courtesy. And she cautioned him to be sure that he sent books that "will *'circulate'* best,"[66] which he did for several years. By the end of the month, Sarah was settled in New Brighton and had begun her business. Davis, joyful over her friend's brightened future, was able to remark upon what "happy pine days" were in the air.[67]

*   *   *

That rough, commonsensical nature, aligned with the regionalism that Davis admired in other women writers, was about to burst forth in her own writings. The Davises began to escape city life by spending summer vacations at Point Pleasant on the New Jersey coast. The Manasquan River region then was vast, primitive farmland that edged within one-half mile of the seashore. The Davises stayed in a two-story cottage at Point Pleasant which they eventually bought and added rooms to as their family grew. "Vagabond's Rest," as they called this summer home, had an enormous stone fireplace, "patch-quilted cots," and a large porch where Davis could sit and write as Clarke went off to fish and her children explored the nearby "Treasure Island" that Robert Louis Stevenson later made famous.[68]

The area, like a siren, lured Davis in those early years: "These marshes on a dull gray day, it is a new feature in scenery to me—and has an indescribably weird and dreary effect—they look like gigantic ghosts passing on their way to some council in Hades—"[69] She loved the area's hard, seafaring life, its superstitious folklore, and its unique natural history, including the legend "of a certain bird which stands on the shore on dark nights and shows a phosphoric light under one wing to tempt fish of deep waters inland. Isn't that an appropriate story for 'wrackers'—for we are not far from the land of the 'Barnegat-pirates.' "[70]

The lives of the "wrackers" absorbed her writing, both in the *Atlantic* and *Peterson's*, for the next several years, and as her children grew up enjoying the freedom of summers at Point Pleasant, she would refer to them as her Barnegat pirates. The Davises savored their summers in this natural setting, and Rebecca lamented that residents talked of " 'a railroad to open the country and of a good site for large hotels'—on the very places which now the fishhawk and blue heron hold and own alone."[71] Before such damage could erase the region's rugged beauty, she began to write a series of stories about the Manasquans. The best of these New Jersey seashore stories, "Out of the Sea," appeared in the May 1865 issue of the *Atlantic*.

In subsequent years, Bret Harte, Helen Hunt Jackson, George Washington Cable, Mary Wilkins Freeman, and Sarah Orne Jewett, among others, would define specific locales through astute renderings of a particular environment and its people.[72] Catherine Maria Sedgwick and Sarah J. Hale, however, had preceded Davis in analyzing specific regions in conjunction with the theme of a native resident's move away from the region and the necessity of reacculturing himself or herself.[73] But, in addition to Davis's exposure to the Manasquan region itself, the most probable influence on her writings about this area was Harriet Beecher Stowe's *The Pearl of Orr's Island: A Story of the Maine Coast*, published two years before "Out of the Sea." In *A New-England Tale*, Sedgwick presents an orphan whose goodness acts as a model for others. In Stowe's novel, however, young Moses, who is orphaned in a shipwreck, at first lives a wayward life but ultimately repents his ways while Mara, orphaned in the same manner, is the figure of spiritual triumph. In Davis's story, the characterizations are less stereotypic, especially for the female characters, and the shipwreck at the story's end acts as a metaphor for the inner struggles that the three main characters undergo. It is a story of death and of lives saved yet still in need of rebuilding.

Although the locale is far from the war zone, the themes were undoubtedly shaped by the horrors of assassination and the hopes of Reconstruction that besieged the country during the spring of 1865. Davis recorded the personal trauma felt by every American when Lincoln was assassinated in April. She wrote Annie:

> All subjects but one were impertinences and upon that I felt no words were fitting.
>
> For the last month I have thought—God was dealing with us as with his chosen people of old—by such great visible judgments that we almost heard His voice and saw His arm, a present God even to the dullest.
>
> For selfish reasons I shall be glad when this present pain is in a measure past. The continuous excitement and nervous tension is more than one can bear—Mr. Davis has been ill. You know how deeper—than his life, I almost had said—is his love of his country and honor—Our little boy's face is the only bright, cheerful spot I can turn my eyes to—God grant his life may be from some day to us as great and holy a cause as that for which Abraham Lincoln died.[74]

Davis's greatest hope was that her infant would never know the smell of gunpowder. She rued the attitude of many young men who viewed war as "part of the daily business of life and not a savage necessity."[75]

In turning away from the sorrows of war to the New Jersey lee-coast life, Davis unleashed some of her most powerful descriptive talents. The rough seas and craggy shores of New Jersey become living landscapes under her renewed artistic force: "the air grew livid, as though death were coming through it; solid masses of gray, wet mist moved, slower than the wind, from point to point, like gigantic ghosts gathering to the call of the murderous sea."[76] As noted, "Out of the Sea" is a study of shipwrecked lives: Derrick, who masquerades as Dr. Birkenshead in order to hide his illegitimate birth; Mother Phoebe, Derrick's mother, who faithfully believes—for twenty years—that her son will return to her; and Mary Defourchet, who first appeared in Davis's *Atlantic* serial "The Great Air-Engine."

Defourchet has been a political activist all her life and is now engaged to Birkenshead. While the story suggests that Mary must give up some of her independence just as Birkenshead must come to terms with his illegitimacy, the story is most concerned with self-discovery, not through theories but through confrontation with one's abilities to survive "unmasked." "Out of the Sea" is important, too, for Davis's direct confrontation with the issue of illegitimacy. She remains nonjudgmental of Mother Phoebe, whose ignorance as a young woman had led her into an affair with a gentleman visitor to the seacoast. He had left her to deal with her pregnancy and the difficulties of raising an illegitimate child. Nor is Mother Phoebe contrite, ashamed, or "tainted," as such figures were typically depicted at the time.

During the recuperative period following her illness in the fall of 1864, when Davis had begun to move away from the purely naturalistic tenet of the brute self toward a belief in human nature as innately "great and beautiful" and guided by God's will rather than the forces of nature, she began to seek in her realism a balance between the vulgarity of commonplace life and the potential for redemption in even the most brutish life. Like the sentimentalists, she did not believe that this facet of human nature was readily exposed—"It needs some supreme torch of suffering to show us that in the image of God created He the very lowest & most degraded"[77]— but she insisted that these theoretical issues be presented realistically. She lost interest in a serial in the *Atlantic* when she discovered it was "not a bona-fide narrative" and insisted when she submitted some sketches she was writing for Fields that he be aware "the sketches I send are *true*—in all essential points."[78] Thus, in her characterization of Mother Phoebe, Davis depicts the woman's love for her son, her struggle to provide for him as best she could, and her faith in him. Having first approached the subject of illegitimacy in "The Promise of Dawn," Davis reshaped this subject through several short stories over subsequent years; still Mother Phoebe remains in many ways the strongest figure of this type.

The high literary quality she produced in the writing of "Sea" was very satisfying to Davis, as was the inclusion at this time of "Life in the Iron Mills" in a collection of short stories, *Atlantic Tales*, designed to present the best fiction published in the *Atlantic Monthly* in recent years.[79] The *Atlantic Tales* represented a diverse selection of authors and literary styles. In addition to "Life in the Iron Mills," there were stories by: Edward Everett Hale (two selections, including "The Man Without a Country"); Fitz James O'Brien, the Irish author who had settled in America in the early 1850s and whose Poesque short stories had established his reputation in his adopted country; Gail Hamilton, who contributed "The Pursuit of Knowledge Under Difficulties"; Robert T. S. Lowell, James Russell Lowell's elder brother, whose fiction reflected his experiences as an Episcopal clergyman and headmaster; George Arnold, the humorist; Caroline Chesebro, the talented sentimentalist; Charles Nordhoff, the Prussian-born author of sea adventures; Lucretia Peabody Hale, Edward Everett Hale's sister and a feminist advocate of women's education whose later writings satirized cultural Boston's self-absorption; Rose Terry (Cook), who submitted "Miss Lucinda"; J. D. Whelpley; Bayard Taylor, author of romantic adventures; and E. H. Appleton, who contributed "A Half-Life and Half a Life." These two events—the publication of "Out of the Sea" and of the *Atlantic Tales*—coupled with her renewed health, enabled Davis to declare shortly before her second wedding anniversary that she was living a "good happy life."[80]

Unfortunately, she could not foresee that she was on the threshold of what would be a very difficult period since, as she prophetically admitted, the "good life" that she was living "flies so fast."[81] If her personal life was fulfilling, her professional life was becoming even more strained than before. She was publishing prolifically in *Peterson's*—several short stories (of little merit) and a serialized novel within a six-month period—and she lamented that her work for the *Atlantic* was suffering from "hasty and incomplete" writing.[82] She had also been writing reviews for the *Atlantic* since early 1863, and the consequences of trying to bridge the two journals for so many years finally collapsed around her. In the July 1865 issue of the *Atlantic*, an article entitled "Ellen" was published under Davis's *Atlantic* pseudonym, the author of "Life in the Iron Mills." She had published a story of the same title in *Peterson's* two years earlier, using as its basis the same true-life experiences of Ellen Carroll and her search for her brother, Joseph, amidst the battlefields of the Civil War. Immediately after the *Atlantic* issue appeared, Fields was informed by a reader of the likenesses between the two stories and what appeared to be a case of plagiarism in the *Atlantic*, since the *Peterson's* story had been written by the author of "A Second Life."

Fields, of course, had known about Davis's work for *Peterson's*, but the use of the same story for two publications demanded an explanation. A formal letter—not, as usual, from her friend and editor "Jamie," but ominously from Mr. Ticknor as well—sought an explanation. Davis hurriedly replied to their queries, acknowledging she had used the material earlier for the *Peterson's* story, but she attempted to brush aside the embarrassment by noting that the *Peterson's* story was fiction drawn from the facts of Ellen Carroll's search while the *Atlantic* article was nonfiction and had been submitted in response to Fields's own request for "a series of sketches of real places or events which had fallen under my notice."[83] She asserted that it was the same thing Edward Everett Hale had done in one instance for the *Atlantic*, but she offered "to make an explanation public if you think it necessary" and added that if they felt the journal had been "wronged in a pecuniary sense" they should deduct payment for the article from her account.[84] No response from the publishers survives, but in early August Davis wrote Annie, "Ask J.T.F. the Silent *how* was that to be 'made right tomorrow.' Ticknor & Fields must not work themselves and a poor woman into such a fervor without some clearing up to her."[85] No public explanation appeared, and Davis continued to be one of the *Atlantic*'s contributors.

When she had submitted "Ellen" to the *Atlantic*, she was three months pregnant with her second child, exhausted, and overworked. Many explanations for the dual submission are possible—she did not remember using the material earlier; or she felt so pressured to supply both journals with manuscripts that she simply hoped the coincidence would go unnoticed; or she truly did not believe there was a problem with the duplication of materials between a short story and a nonfiction article.[86] None of these potential explanations, however, offers a satisfying answer.

*   *   *

In the fall, as Davis awaited the birth of her second child, her thoughts turned to marriage and the different views that men and women held about the institution of marriage. With her feminist proclivities rising again, if momentarily, she confided to Annie that she loved Harriet Beecher Stowe's "Chimney Corner" column in the *Atlantic*; the column, rather ironically written under the pseudonym of Christopher Crowfield, advocated women's rights. As Davis noted, "[Stowe's] sound vigorous sense comes to me once a month—a real 'time of refreshing' for which if I knew her I would send her the strongest word of thanks I know."[87] Davis had admired Stowe's writing for some time, and the housebound mother-to-be now especially valued those items that dealt with women's freedom. She had given Stowe's articles "to a young cousin to read who was on the verge of matrimony—and if I could would make it my bridal gift to all the newly married people in the country."[88] She pointedly compared Stowe's knowledge of her subject to another serial, "Needle and Garden," which had run in the *Atlantic* since January. She discovered that the series, subtitled "The Story of a Seamstress Who Laid Down Her Needle and Became a Strawberry-Girl. Written by Herself," had in fact been written by a man. Both it and Stowe's column used gender reversals from author to first-person narrator, but Davis's disdain for the "Needle and Garden" series was due to the author's lack of factual experience in representing his "Strawberry-Girl." She adamantly doubted that anyone could still "find refreshment" from such an overblown serial: "Insatiate monster! Is not 'Ten acres' of paper enough to cover with his prose? The story would have been effective in three pages—maybe."[89] If she could not agree with Stowe's strict evangelicalism, she found a bond with her in the New Englander's then-feminist views on domestic life.

On January 24, 1866, Davis gave birth to her second son, Charles Belmont Davis. Charley was named for Clarke's brother Charles, who had died in an early battle of the Civil War.[90] This year, like the one before, was to be an especially difficult one for Davis, beginning with her disappointment (registered in literary metaphors) over the anticlimactic reactions others had to her second child: "Nobody was enthusiastic about Charley—his brother had carried off all the Plaudits—as first child and first grand child and this boy was a sequel to the story."[91] As with Richard's birth, the new life was linked with a death that dampened the joy. Davis's beloved "Aunt Blaine," for whom she had been named, died on February 28. In her will, Rebecca Blaine left the old family home to Rachel Harding, who resided there for the next eighteen years until her own death, upon which Davis inherited the house that came to be the legacy of the Wilson-Harding women.

During the period following Charley's birth, Clarke was often away from home, traveling between Philadelphia and New York on business, and he was also sick several times during the early months of the year. Not surprisingly, Davis herself was stricken with neuralgia, which made writing very painful. In the spring, Davis wrote Annie, apologizing for not writing sooner: "But between sickness actual and sickness dreaded—(Mr. Davis and the baby both being ill—and the scarlet fever next door—) my brain is in a swirl as me Scotch cousins would say." She proclaimed that the "beautiful deceitful month" of March had deceptively hidden "one of its Judas-beams" in its beauty: "Clarke had a severe attack of what threatened to be pneumonia and is yet weak and nerveless from it, and poor Charley who has been fighting with trouble ever since he came—with the stillest gravest of baby faces—has been in my arms literally for many days back."[92]

As with the birth of her first child and the troubled months that immediately followed, Davis again longed for escape, away from the city and into her beloved Manasquan life: "Oh! just to sweep this mass of dull brick houses and patch of sky away—And sit to day watching the harvest wind ruffling great sweeps of yellow cornfield and the sun go down behind far lines of purple hills I know! . . . for the warm pure air that would bring healing on its wings and most of all the hills—they seem more beautiful to me now—*to remember* than the mountains of Beulah—unknown."[93] If Reconstruction was supposed to be a healing period for the country, Davis questioned it in personal terms. She asked Annie what had happened to Elizabeth Peabody and Louisa May Alcott: "Peace must have put a sudden barrier in the way of many women's new found careers." Certainly she felt little sense of healing in her own life.

For the time, she continued to write for the *Atlantic*. After the "Ellen" brouhaha had subsided, Davis wrote a rather formal letter to James Fields reminding him that more than a year earlier she had submitted to him "a sketch of Economy—the Rappite settlement." Was he still interested in publishing the story in the *Atlantic*? If not, "and if so dont hesitate in saying so and sending it back," she did not "want the material wasted for I always thought that place and people would make an effusive background for a story and if you dont want the sketch will use it in that way. If you would like the *story*—of course it is at your disposal." She did not avoid the issue of "Ellen," noting that she had recently heard through the colonel of Joseph Carroll's regiment that Ellen was still missing and that Joseph had procured leave to search for her—"his only clue being that which we gave"; she also reminds him that it was "a true story . . . despite your correspondent's letter."[94] Fields responded, without commenting on "Ellen," but indicating that he would be interested in the fictionalized story on the Rappite community. "The Harmonists" was the lead article in the May 1866 issue of the *Atlantic*. Davis's story is rooted, as always, in fact. George Rapp (1757–1847) had founded the Rappites, or Harmony Society, which advocated a decidedly utopian vision. Doctor Knowles, who first appeared in *Margret Howth*, reappears in "Harmonists"; it is the communist ideology of Knowles with which Davis is now concerned. Marx and Engels had published their *Communist Manifesto* in 1848, and the increasing popularity of communist philosophy in nineteenth-century America undoubtedly interested Davis as a writer.[95] Knowles is now older and separated from his wife, and although his four-year-old child is with him, as part of his philosophy he refuses to extend affection to the child. Wanting to escape a world that has become "a great property-exchanging machine," Knowles envisions the Rappites' Pennsylvania community as his salvation.[96] What he finds in this supposed utopian community, ironically, but in fact appropriately, called Economy, is a system as stridently structured as any big-city corporation. As much as Davis abhorred the ruthlessness of industrial capitalism, she knew that no one could any longer live outside the marketplace ideology, a painful lesson that Knowles learns during his stay at Economy. In spite of the fact that the "Ellen" incident seemed to subside and "The Harmonists" had been given the honor of lead item in its issue,[97] only one more story by Davis would appear in the *Atlantic* during the 1860s.

In the midst of her recovery from a lingering fatigue after Charley's birth, the "Ellen" incident, and the upsurge she felt in completing the story of the Rappites, Davis made a hurried trip home to Wheeling. It was no longer the wondrous playground of her childhood. The soot and smoke were more cumbersome than ever, seeping, she insisted, "into the brain as well as the skin,"[98] and even the security of her family home had been shattered by the departure of her brothers for the war and subsequently by one brother's removal to Kentucky. On her return to Philadelphia, she was supposed to meet Clarke in Pittsburgh but their train connections did not meet, and she and the children returned to Philadelphia alone. To her surprise, she no longer had the same home to return to:

> The babies and I . . . came to the door—rang & rang in vain, till a strange face appeared next door—"Nobody lives *there*." I looked up—Philadelphia houses are all twins, but this was certainly ours—I then . . . inquired if I did not live there & was told I had moved to the next street. Going round—to 1816 Camac a square off—I rang again & this time the open sesame opened home. There was the old carpet on the floor, the old curtains, Dante's face with the shadow of immortal sorrow looking out of the room & Annie's, red and shining, at the door—We had to move sometime this fall & Clarke had had it done to surprise me—So we are here—.[99]

Davis apparently found this odd episode quite delightful, perhaps because it constituted the third household move they had made in less than four years and she was more than willing to have it completed without her assistance. She quickly settled into her new home at 1816 North Camac Street, which she and Clarke dubbed, as they did each of their homes, the "Centre of the Universe."

She relaxed at Thanksgiving and wrote a long, friendly letter to her cousin Clara Wilson, who had married Andrew Todd Baird the previous summer. Davis obviously delighted in having a correspondent who appreciated details about young Richard, or "Hardy" as he was nicknamed: "Hardy has reformed in his general character, out of constant consideration as to what 'Santa Caus' will think of him, and he goes to the heater every day and calls up, 'How-do Santa Caus?' It rather destroys the poetry of Christmas to imagine Saint Nicholas getting in through a hole in the wall—doesn't it?"[100] Davis was so pleased with her new home, a rented row house, that she immediately forgot the discomfort of her visit to Wheeling and almost purred her contentment to Annie,

> It is enough to be alive in days like this—when the earth sits quiet-thinking, before she lies down for her winter's sleep. It was so good and resting to go West. Nature there is prodigal of life. There is such absence of struggle, or straining, such excess of beauty—of vigor,—such quiet strength in absolute repose. I wish you could go to the West—New England may be the brain—of the country—but I think its heart, the centre of its warm strong, life-giving blood is out yonder—I'm *glad* it is my home—.[101]

She breathes deeply in her contentment, and then laughs at herself, "I wonder what called out that effort of patriotism—." She had set aside "life's endeavors," which now, under increasingly burdensome financial pressures, included her writing, to enjoy herself and, wisely, to gather her strength for the coming months.

In June 1866, Davis had received a letter from F. P. Church, co-editor with his brother, William Conant Church, of the newly founded *Galaxy Magazine*. The literary journal was proposed as an alternative to what they depicted as the provincialism of the *Atlantic*. The editors sought Davis as a regular contributor, offering her the freedom to publish a long story which they had heard she was currently writing. After her frustrations in serializing *Margret Howth*, Davis had promised herself she would publish her serious work only as short stories and books, not as long serializations. She was still considered—and certainly considered herself—a regular contributor for the *Atlantic*, and she was writing regularly for *Peterson's* at this time to provide necessary financial support for the Davises' growing family. A serialized novel, "The Stolen Bond," had just finished running in *Peterson's* and four more short stories would appear in the pages of the Philadelphia magazine before the year's end. She felt it necessary, therefore, to decline the regular-contributor status the Church brothers offered, but she agreed to submit one or two short stories during the summer, since she believed the *Galaxy* would "fill a vacuum in our literature more apparent every year—a national magazine—in which the current of thought in every section could find expression as thoroughly as that of New England does in the *Atlantic*."[102]

She no longer felt it necessary to seek James Fields's approval before agreeing to publish elsewhere. It was her first act of professional independence, her first venture outside the familial-like halls of the *Atlantic*, and it came about without discussion. There is little wonder that Davis sought to publish with the *Galaxy*; with her submissions and those of the other writers whom the Church brothers had been able to draw to their pages, the new periodical was immediately recognized as a highly respectable literary journal—and Davis would earn $3,600 for her serialization, approximately six times what she would typically receive from the *Atlantic* for an item of similar length.[103]

Meanwhile, the Churches had accepted Davis's decision to submit several short stories, and apparently James Fields had no objection when "The Captain's Story" appeared in the December issue of *Galaxy*. But throughout the year the Church brothers had continued to discuss with

Davis the idea of publishing her novel-length story. During the summer, Davis mentioned to Fields that she wished to discuss with him a novel that she was formulating, but he did not pursue the subject. Therefore, in November she acknowledged the Churches' interest, explaining that she had completed the manuscript several months earlier, "but afterwards destroyed that copy having determined to entirely remodel and extend it. The subject is one which has interested me more than any other and I wish to put whatever strength I have into that book and make it, if possible, different from anything which I have yet been able to do."[104] Davis accomplished that goal. *Waiting for the Verdict* is one of her best novels and, as an epic of the Civil War and its aftermath, an important literary document of the period. Having spent nearly twenty-five years in Wheeling, she understood the attitudes of both the North and the South and sought to create in her novel a realistic and unbiased representation of both regions.

Writing for a new publication, however, brought unprecedented problems for Davis. When she was two-thirds through the novel, rewriting as it was being published, the editors of the new journal decided to change type and page sizes, which altered her space requirements; more detrimental, they contracted for another serial and, finding themselves in financial difficulties, sought to limit the length of Davis's novel in the last chapters. She fought for every line in order to do justice to her creation. She was no longer the newcomer who had allowed *Howth* to be battered by editorial demands. *Waiting* was her most significant work to date, and she intended to do battle with the *Galaxy* editors who, from her perspective, seemed intent upon destroying it.

At first she tried to compromise. Although she was not a cliff-hanger novelist, she agreed to end certain segments with a crisis situation; but when the editors insisted that she cut, unbelievably, thirty-four pages, she responded to William and F. P. Church on June 4, 1867, agreeing only because she knew that she had no choice but recording her disdain with the comment that the reduction "mutilates the story."[105] She detailed her anger and despair over their unprofessional treatment of her and sought to correct errors she felt had been made in their comments to her:

> And first, as to your impression that I intended forcing you to expense and loss by sending a longer story than you engaged from me. *No* such agreement as that on which you based your very peremptory demand the other day ever was made between us—oral or written.
> I never offered myself—no writer other than the merest penny-a-liner could bind himself—to write a story of exactly 279—or any given number of pages.

She reminds them that they had originally suggested the story's length to be about three hundred pages but that they had repeatedly assured her that she would not be limited by length. Their format changes and their decision to run another serial were the causes of the problems, she asserts: "If you find it necessary (unless I comply [with the cuts in length]) *for these reasons* to add extra pages to the magazine, am *I* fairly chargeable with the blame or loss? I too might have had complaints if I had wished to be captious—that you delayed the issue of the book from October until December by your altering from a fortnightly to a monthly issue, making it too late for the fall leads—."

She is equally outraged at their inferences that the financial success of the new publication was her responsibility as well: "I feel that while I have made every effort to fulfil my part of the contract, I have most unjustly been held chargeable—pecuniarily and morally, with difficulties brought on by your frequent changes of type, mode of publication etc—and with the success or non-success of The Galaxy. No money could pay me for the annoyance to which I have been subjected."[106] Their dealings were concluded in accordance with Davis's wishes—her contract was transferred to Sheldon & Co., which negotiated publication of the book form of *Waiting*. At the end of the experience, she vowed she would never again write for the *Galaxy*. Ironically, the unanticipated consequences of publishing *Waiting* in the *Galaxy* would soon force her to reconsider. Yet in spite of the frustrations caused by this conflict, the quality of the novel remains amazingly above the publishing fray.

Historical novels were a long-standing tradition in American letters, from Lydia Maria Child's *Hobomok* (1824) and Catherine Maria Sedgwick's *Hope Leslie* (1827) to Nathaniel Hawthorne's *The Scarlet Letter* (1850), but romantic novelists tended to depict the past as foreign and to select distant eras as their topics. Davis was always a writer of "to-day." She wrote *Waiting* during the period of Reconstruction in the South, and the novel explicitly addresses the major issue of the day: How was America going to deal with the slaves who had been freed? Her impression of events to date is revealed in the ironic epigraph to the novel:

"How will you be tried?"
"By God and the Country."
"God send you a good deliverance."

Waiting is a psychological study of miscegenation, an issue most Americans wished to ignore at the time. Chronicling the lives of three couples,

Waiting exposes the prejudices of the period as well as the potential Davis envisioned in all people. She insists here, as always, upon realistic characterizations; there are no clear-cut heroes or villains; each character is developed in the fullness of their biases and their tendernesses, and the histories of those characters whose lives have been corrupted expose the abuse necessary to create such brute existences. Nor are the good and bad drawn against lines of color; her purpose is to identify the value and potential in the freed slaves, but she will not romanticize them as purely noble and refuses to depict them as educated in speech or action, since that would have been impossible after their subjection to years of oppression that specifically sought to keep them uneducated.

As opposed to the slave system as she was, Davis did not fail to recognize the North's complicity in the status of slavery. In the relationship between Dr. Broderip and Margaret Conrad, she exposes the prejudice still inherent in Northerners and delineates just how deeply ingrained racism had become. As a child, Broderip had been a Southern slave until he was bought out of slavery by Ann Yates, a Quaker woman. Friend Yates reared Broderip as her son in Europe and educated him in the medical profession; when he returned to America, however, he passed as white. That ability to pass gains him access to social status and admiration but, as Davis demonstrates, it also forces him to forfeit his belief in himself. Broderip's fractured personality represents, on the one hand, the contributions that blacks can make to American society when they are educated and have an acknowledged place in that society; on the other hand, it represents the price that is paid (Broderip's isolation, dark moods, and ultimate martyrdom) when blacks are forced outside mainstream American life.

Broderip's decision no longer to "pass" is precipitated by a reunion with his brother, a situation Louisa May Alcott also employed in her short story of the Civil War, "The Brothers" (1863). In Alcott's story, the brothers' hatred for one another reflects the brother-against-brother realities of the Civil War; in Davis's novel, however, Broderip's acceptance of his black brother depends upon Davis's belief that the only way in which union could be restored in the United States was for brothers of all colors to begin to accept one another as they were. No easy answers are offered in her characterization of Broderip, however; he is forced to live a false life in white society and dies even though he attempts to rejoin his own people. As in all of Davis's fiction, martyrdom is a poor solution at best; she delineates how much change is still needed in the country before America would be ready to accept blacks as equals—and the extraordinary losses that such ignorance perpetuates.

Margaret Conrad is one of Davis's most interesting characterizations. A strong, plain-looking woman of keen intelligence, she cares for her father not in the traditional spinsterly fashion but in defiance of those standards. Her astute ability to detect hypocrisy threatens the Methodists who want to welcome her and her father back into their fold after Mr. Conrad has lost all of their money through speculation. Margaret notices that the Methodist leaders prefer her father now because his blindness and poverty act as assurances of his indebtedness to them; they castigate Margaret when she refuses to let her father be further impoverished by joining them as a poorly paid preacher. She would rather accept Broderip's offer of low rent for a neighboring farm and work the land for their livelihood than have to live with the burden of the Methodists' self-gratifying charity. Yet Margaret cannot conquer her own prejudice. She advocates the Northern cause but cannot bear to touch black skin. Davis does not openly endorse interracial marriage, as had Catherine Maria Sedgwick and Lydia Maria Child. Instead, she presents Margaret's ingrained prejudice as tragic precisely because the young woman cannot overcome her biases when she learns that Dr. Broderip is a mulatto. She has known him for years and deeply loves him; but when the truth is revealed to her, she turns a stony face toward her lover and declares, "the gulf between us is one which God never intended to be crossed."[107] Her voice now carries the tone of one speaking to an inferior. Margaret's decision leaves her thereafter in complete isolation.

A gulf to be crossed was Davis's metaphor for artificial barriers established by society. She used the term throughout her fiction to symbolize this concept, and in 1881 published a short story in *Lippincott's* entitled "Across the Gulf," in which society's denigration of actresses is once again challenged. In *Waiting*, it is the sexual fears of Americans toward freed blacks that she questions, as she had in her earliest Civil War story, "John Lamar"; but now she is able to present the issue without the traces of her former discomfort. Broderip dies honorably, but Margaret faces a lingering, self-inflicted death of the spirit.

In the coupling of Rosslyn Burley and Garrick Randolph, Davis challenges a rampant Southern prejudice of the time, closely related to that of racism but more encompassing: the purity of "blood." Randolph is a Southerner whose entire sense of self-worth is based upon the purity of his inherited blood. In his love for Ross, he is challenged by the discovery of her illegitimate birth. His own self-discovery comes through the painful awareness that his blood is also "tainted." It is the lesson that Davis felt all Southerners needed to learn. She knew that the gulf presented by inter-racial marriage would not soon be crossed, but the first step was to eradi-cate the myths of "blood."

Another pioneer realist whom Davis admired and who may have in-fluenced her own early realism,[108] J. W. DeForest, had also published a novel of the Civil War in 1867. But *Miss Ravenel's Conversion from Secession to Loyalty* is a decidedly pro-North, anti-South depiction of events. Davis believed that both regions needed to examine their philosophies, and in *Waiting* she offers, through the freed slaves Nathan and Anny, examples of what may be gained by such efforts. Of particular significance is Davis's depiction of the black woman's role during the Civil War. The history of Nathan and Anny's search for each other after their master sold them sepa-rately is an indictment of slave owners' callous treatment of families and a challenge to their traditional views of black people in general as animals who mate without commitment and feeling. Davis's chronicle of Anny's arduous, physically debilitating search for her husband as she carries her young child in tow offers some of the novel's most graphic realism and is obviously indebted to Stowe's depiction of Eliza Harris. Davis's ending, however, in which Anny and Nathan are rejoined, is not sentimentalized. Offered a small home by the Randolphs and an opportunity to work the land for their own profit, Nathan and Anny constitute Davis's hope for change in American attitudes. But when Ross tries to tell Anny that their sons will now have the same opportunities, Anny knows better: "Freedom and clo's, and a home of our own, is much. But it's not all. Forgive me. A mudder kerries her chile's life on her heart when he's a man, jes as before he was born; you know dat. I wondered what was my boy's birthright in his country" (354). This is the unanswered question of *Waiting for the Ver-dict*, a question, Davis reminds her readers, which only the American pub-lic can answer.

A review of *Waiting* that appeared in *The Nation* suggested that the answer was still in the future. The reviewer was Henry James, Jr. He and Davis had crossed paths in the pages of several literary journals, although there is no evidence that they ever met. James's distaste at the time for the "gloomier" examples of realism are well known, and in the review they lead to James's failure to understand the connection between the Margaret-Broderip and Ross-Garrick relationships in *Waiting* (and he completely ignores their most important link—to Anny and Nathan). In fact, James reveals more about his own disdain for realism than about Davis's novel:

The unfortunate people whom [Davis] transfers into her stories are as good material for the story-teller's art as any other class of beings, but not a bit better. They come no nearer doing the work for themselves and leaving the writer to amuse himself than the best-housed and best-fed and the best-clad classes in the community. They are worth reading about only so long as they are studied with a keen eye versed in the romance of human life, and described in the same rational English which we exact from writers on other subjects. Mrs. Davis's manner is in direct oppugnancy to this truth.[109]

If this was to be the verdict for realism and for the black race, it was indeed as yet a literary and political Reconstruction of little reward. But the negative review had an unexpectedly pleasant result. Davis's renown had long brought her correspondence from a wide variety of authors, but none so pleased her as now to make the acquaintance, albeit through the mail, of Harriet Beecher Stowe. Stowe had been so appalled by James's review that she wrote to offer solace to Davis. "The Nation," Stowe explained, "has no sympathy with any deep and high moral movement—no pity for human infirmity. It is a sneering respectable middle aged sceptic who says I take my two glasses & my cigar daily . . . But dont mind them & dont hope for a sympathetic word from them *ever* in any attempt to help the weak & sinning & suffering."[110]

Nor were all reviewers and readers of *Waiting* as negative as the young Henry James. In fact, James's review smacks of what a spirited Mary Abigail Dodge called his attitude "that woman must be kept away from the tree of knowledge."[111] The literary editor of the new journal *Lippincott's*, on the other hand, was especially astute in his analysis of the novel and equally revealing of the difficulty even appreciative readers of realism had with the new literary movement: "The festering spots of society, from which so many writers shrink, [Davis] probes with the unerring blade."[112] While the reviewer admits to wishing for more "geniality" in fiction, he also admits: "In this age of novel-reading—and in truth in every age—one is prone to look for hero or heroine as a little above the commonplace, as distinguished by some trait, but Mrs. Davis has very successfully tried the task of making her characters very like the 'vast herd' from which they are taken." He would have preferred more action and less detailed characterization and scenery, but in spite of these faults, "Mrs. Davis is a powerful writer. . . . Her field is that realism wherein authors of less talent would fail utterly." Years later Davis told her friend, the poet Paul Hamilton Hayne, that *Waiting* had been "thought radical among Radicals; so much so that the publishers carefully avoided sending it to the South lest they should hurt their trade there."[113] It was a policy that authors, such as Sara Jane Clarke Lippincott ("Grace Greenwood"), and publishers, such as Putnam's and Ticknor and Fields, alike had learned; the Southern literary market was dispensable, and several antislavery texts were published without benefit of Southern markets. The sentiments of the Northern reading populace more than compensated for the geographically smaller market.[114]

In her autobiography, written toward the end of her life, Davis reiterated her concerns regarding the prevailing depictions of the Civil War, especially those depictions that glossed over the complexity of the causes and the events in order to create a mythic sense of war as "a kind of beneficent deity."[115] In fact, war could "debate and befoul a people," and that aspect of violent confrontation needed to be recorded as well. For instance, Davis recalled, nowhere in the "painted" versions of the war are there details of the regiments that were recruited from prisons and jails and "raged like wild beasts through the mountains of the border States."[116] Nor did the history books admit that not all men, from the North or the South, volunteered from a sense of patriotism or from a concern for abolishing or preserving slavery; rather, it was a way to earn a living. Further, soldiering was in many respects an issue of class. Many of those who participated in the war were drafted and could not afford to pay for a substitute, in spite of the fact that the influx of immigrants prior to the war had made the purchase price of a substitute relatively inexpensive. So, too, did Davis recognize the psychological consequences of war upon the individual, which many Americans had ignored (and which they continued to ignore, even into the late twentieth century): "When Johnny came marching home again," Davis acknowledged, "he was a very disorganized member of society."[117]

If the positive consequences of serializing *Waiting* in the *Galaxy* had been its equitable monetary compensation, its critical reception, and the subsequent contact with Harriet Beecher Stowe, the penalty was severe. The serialized version had run from February through December 1867; Davis's last short story to be published in the *Atlantic* during the 1860s was "George Bedillion's Knight," a two-part serial also appearing in February and March of that year; ironically, it was the first item in which Davis agreed to have "Mrs. R. Harding Davis" denoted as the author. Davis had mentioned her Civil War novel to Fields first, but because of the "Ellen" episode or simply as an oversight, he had not pursued the suggestion. Her decision to accept the Churches' offer broke her exclusive contract with the *Atlantic*, which had hindered her from accepting numerous other literary journals' offers; but she had not anticipated being excluded thereafter from the pages of the most reputable New England literary periodical. Yet that is precisely what happened. In November, she wrote to Fields:

> I must tell you frankly that I did not understand the manner in which I was dismissed from your list of contributors for the coming year.
>
> It would have been more business-like—(not to say friendly) in T&F—if they wished one's relation to end to let me know before any engagements were made for next year. I made them with reference to writing for you—declining to write for other Boston magazines which I supposed were unfriendly to the A—
>
> I was the more surprised at it as I have been writing for the Atlantic for a year and a half at half the price per page paid and offered me by all the other magazines—I did not intend to speak of this to you, as I preferred to write for the Atlantic at even a pecuniary loss because it was my oldest friend and because too there were so many among its readers whom I liked and whom I think liked me.[118]

It was the most forthright statement she had ever made to Fields, but it came too late. Her astonishment and sense of betrayal were not without warrant. She had been one of the *Atlantic*'s major contributors for more than six years. She would publish only one other short story in the *Atlantic*—and that would not occur until 1873 when Fields was no longer the editor. She now began to publish in *Lippincott's, Hearth and Home, Putnam's,* and, in spite of her avowal, the *Galaxy*; and she continued to churn out short stories and serial novels for *Peterson's*. But the most painful consequence of the dispute between Davis and the *Atlantic* was the breach that it caused between herself and Annie Fields. No letters discussing the situation were exchanged. Their correspondence simply dwindled to near silence.

* * *

At the end of 1867, American authors from all regions of the country, as well as all readers of the novel, were discussing only one fact: the American tour of Charles Dickens, who was to offer public readings from his novels. The correspondence of authors of the era is rife with critiques of Dickens. Mary Abigail Dodge attended one reading, noting that both as a reader and as a writer he was "absorbing," and that her eyes "ached all next day from the intensity of my gazing."[119] His voice was not impressive in itself, she observed, but he knew how to use it "with great effect. He has wonderful dramatic power—a command over his face which recalls the old stories of Garrick. He reproduces, recreates almost the characters with whom his pen has made you familiar. I like him better than any public reader I have ever before heard."[120]

The realists of the day were equally excited to hear Dickens, but ultimately were somewhat less sympathetic. Davis appreciated his humor and his ability to effect an emotional response in his audience: "There is a certain emotion which I do believe never was wakened in anybody since the world was made until Dickens got hold of the key and let it out, a sense— a mixture of the comic and pathetic at once which brings a tear and a laugh at the same time."[121] But without humor, his pathos of "voice and manner had no effect upon me—one was metallic and the other artificial."[122] The young William Dean Howells, who, as the *Atlantic*'s new assistant editor, was invited to join gatherings honoring Dickens at the Fieldses' home and at Longfellow's, was less critical, but assessed Dickens in terms of his performance: "It was the perfection of acting . . . better than any theatre I ever saw. It was rather sad, however, for an American, who had naturalized Dickens's characters, to find that after all they were English."[123] Undoubtedly, no writer endowed with Dickens's reputation could live up to his public's expectations.

Davis herself was becoming less and less enamored of her chosen career. The toll of constantly having to write against publishing and financial deadlines was enormous. In early March, before her separation with the *Atlantic*, she had confided in Annie that she was coming to "dislike pen and ink" so much that even letter writing was becoming cumbersome.[124] Somehow, in the midst of the trials of seeing *Waiting* into serialization and book publication, Davis wrote her first full-length work set on the Manasquan coast, *Dallas Galbraith*; it is dedicated "To my friends at Manasquan." The newly founded *Lippincott's Magazine* published the novel as its lead item beginning in January 1868, the same issue in which the review of *Waiting* appeared and which included creative works by Julia Ward Howe, Harriet Prescott Spofford, and L. Clarke Davis, who had begun to write fiction as well. *Lippincott's* was a literary magazine published in Philadelphia which sought a broader national audience than the *Atlantic*, although the editors selected many of the same contributors as that New England journal, including Davis, Henry James, Sidney Lanier, William Gilmore Simms, Constance Fenimore Woolson, and Rose Terry Cooke, among others. Desiring to begin their publication with a strong drawing card, the editors ran *Dallas Galbraith* from January until October of 1868. But for

Davis it was an arduous process, once again; in spite of having promised herself after *Howth* and after *Waiting* that she would not begin to publish another novel until it was completely written, she had no alternative but to undertake serialization. With two small children to care for as well, her thoughts turned to her own mother residing in the old family home; she concluded that being apart from her mother created in herself a feeling she could only define as a "cypher."[125]

Davis's descriptive abilities are especially keen in *Galbraith*, especially as she establishes her locale:

> On shore, the mellow October sunset was shining pleasantly on the white beach, up to which the yellow, fishy little schooner was hauled close, and on the men in their red shirts: the raw wind was tempered to a bracing breeze, and the waves lapped the sand and the keel of the vessel, with a tamed, sleepy purr. The marshes, because of the heavy rains that year, still held their summer coloring, and unrolled from the strip of beach up to the pine woods a great boundary belt of that curious, clear emerald that belongs only to the sea and seashore growths. Beyond this belt, two or three comfortable brown cows were grazing at the edge of the forest, and here and there, in the forest, a whiff of smoke wavering to the sky, or a good-bye red glimmer of the sun on a low window, told where the houses of the village were scattered.[126]

In "Life in the Iron Mills," Davis had described the mill as "pregnant with death" and here again she juxtaposes birth and death imagery with the deterministic forces that seem to rule the sea: the sea, regardless of how calm it seems, is a "womb of death." The novel also juxtaposes two philosophies: that of the gentle, loving, and scholarly Manasquan, Dallas Galbraith, and that of George Laddoun, the boastful outsider who becomes a community leader. Laddoun depicts himself as a maker of men, professing to have made Dallas Galbraith just as the other fishermen make decoys. The only person in the town George cannot control is his fiancée, Elizabeth Byrne, the one-time love of another fisherman, Jim Van Zeldt.

A concurrent plot, that of Dallas Galbraith's mysterious past, which is as dark and forboding as the wailing sea, allows for a similar juxtaposition of the women characters: Honoria Dundas, whose love for Dallas reestablishes his self-confidence, even when his past is revealed, and Madam Galbraith who, like George Laddoun, seeks personal power in her desire to create a community whose members "owed their advance in well-being entirely to me. To me." It is an obvious romantic plot, but the particularities of the locale raise it above the stereotypic. It is not, however, a realistic novel. In *Galbraith* we have one of Davis's few works that truly constitutes a romance, in terms of its plot, although the environment and the "locals" are realistically rendered. *Galbraith* is sometimes slow-paced, but overall it is a very readable romance and one that continues to display Davis's strengths of description and characterization.

Literary reviews of *Galbraith* were highly favorable, with the notable, and not unexpected, exception of *The Nation*. Most reviewers remarked that it was a "story of unusual power," and one reviewer termed it "a noble romance."[127] *The Nation*'s review was once again penned by Henry James, who went so far as to deem Dallas Galbraith a "woman's boy."[128] It is a review that reflects James's disdain, at this point in his life, for what he termed American authors' preference for "aesthetic heroes" as opposed to the English novelists' selection of "a brilliant young man of affairs—a rising young statesman or a prospective commander-in-chief . . . ,"[129] hardly the class with which Davis was concerned. Nor does James appreciate Davis's depiction of Madam Galbraith; such a "monster" of a woman is against nature, he asserts, preferring the demure and self-sacrificing Mrs. Duffield, Galbraith's mother, in whom "Nature . . . is represented and not travestied."[130] It is a three-column review, and although James admits he likes *Galbraith* better than *Waiting*, the review is patronizing in tone ("Mrs. Davis, in her way, is an artist") and rarely insightful. Even when James praises Davis, he does so slightingly, through the use of double negatives and qualifying adverbs: "it would be unjust not to admit [that she confronts] nature and truth . . . she displays no inconsiderable energy and skill. . . . She may probably be congratulated on a success."[131] Indeed, he devotes an entire paragraph to an attack on Harriet Beecher Stowe as a reviewer. James synthesizes the literary styles of Stowe and Davis, and he concludes with extraordinary arrogance by giving "a word of counsel for the various clever writers of Mrs. Davis's school," whom he classifies as ultra-sentimentalists. They should read the works of Alexandre Dumas:

> In him they will find their antipodes—and their model. We say their model, because we believe they have enough intellectual resistance to hold their own against him, when their own is worth holding, and that when it is not, he, from the munificence of his genius, will substitute for it an impression of the manner in which a story may be told without being a discredit to what is agreeable in art, and various and natural in life.[132]

At the other extreme was the *Philadelphia Press*, whose reviewer noted that the novel concluded with a power, passion, and pathos which assure us that Mrs. Rebecca Davis may become ere long one of the very best of American novelists. Judging of her only by the present story, very many would declare that even now she is in the first rank of native writers. In the concluding chapters of this story she has put forth her strength, and has allowed her genius, for *that* is her dower from liberal Nature, to work out its own purpose. There are, we will not say passages, but whole pages, of superb and picturesque writing here; and few things in modern fiction are equal in truth and quiet force to the return of Dallas Galbraith.[133]

*　*　*

In addition to *Waiting for the Verdict* and *Dallas Galbraith*, which appeared during 1867–68, Davis also published one of her finest short stories in January 1868. " 'In the Market' " appeared in *Peterson's*—under the authorial designation of "By the Author of 'Margret Howth' "—and it signals a shift in Davis's professional career: first, in that she chose *Peterson's*, undoubtedly for financial reasons, for a story that is of the highest quality; second, and most important, in that it begins her literary shift to a much greater focus upon the lives of American women, a focus she would extend for the remaining thirty-five years of her literary career.

The theme of marriage-marketing was not new; as Josephine Donovan has determined, the tradition of critiquing marriage-marketing goes back, at least in some degree, to Maria Edgeworth and Catherine Maria Sedgwick.[134] Although Davis does not completely avoid the Cinderella plot in "Market," she does offer in her synthesis of self-sufficiency and marriage a liberal depiction of what a woman's role in marriage could be. It is a much more advanced perspective than she had proffered four years earlier in "The Wife's Story." Even in more conservative approaches of the day, such as the series on cooperative housekeeping that was published in the *Atlantic* at the end of the year, acknowledgments of the changing roles for women were offered as a starting place in the discussion.[135] The question was how to accommodate these changes, especially as they moved more and more outside the confines of the home. Melusina Fay Peirce, the author of the *Atlantic* series, suggested cooperative housekeeping for the woman who no longer chose to be a traditional housekeeper. (It would be thirty years before *Women and Economics*, Charlotte Perkins Gilman's radical vision for reshaping divisions of labor, appeared.) Peirce could not envision household chores as anything other than the woman's duty, but she did suggest ways for a woman to combine her new ambitions with the needs of the home. It was an idea that was receiving more and more attention from female authors and readers. For Davis, the issues were more complex.

Whereas her previous literature had centered upon the perils of living in a border state during the Civil War, " 'In the Market' " turns its attention to another kind of hinterland, "that miserable border-land between wealth and poverty, whose citizens struggle to meet the demands of the one state out of the necessities of the other."[136] In all her themes—of war, seashore life, or women's lives—Davis was concerned with the issues of class. In this short story, the tensions created between the demands and the necessities of life take center stage, because so many young women were, in the late 1860s. when numerous men were gaining vast fortunes through trade and speculation, consciously marketing themselves for a prominent marriage. The story uses the metaphorical richness of the process of courtship and marriage through two opposing strains: one is satirical and mocks the commodifying of marriage; the other is aesthetic and symbolizes the disparity between marriages for financial security and those for love.

These two metaphoric patterns structure the choices made in the story by the two sisters, Clara and Margaret Porter. Thus in the case of Clara, who will market herself to the highest, albeit sleazy bidder, the narrator "dowers" her, as her family has, with beauty but little sense of herself. The story begins with Clara's first beau pronouncing, "Check, and—mate!" John Bohme, however, will not be Clara's mate, as his triumphant victory in the chess game suggests. For those who view marriage as a game to be won, the stakes are invariably high; at the "trial-moment of their lives," as John waits for a signal from Clara, she stands at the piano and strikes only "a single note . . . struck it again, and went on mechanically to the window, while it vibrated through the room" (49). Clara and Margaret's interest in marriage is not just the healthy response of young women; it is enforced under the economic pressures of a family "burdened" by two older single sisters who, in their father and brother's eyes, missed their "chance." Thus, the family depends upon the next two sisters to marry well and lessen the burden both by leaving home but also by marrying well enough to help support the others. While Clara's *single*-note obsession with marrying is satirized, it is done so in terms of the pressures placed upon her to marry well. Her education, which comes from her mother as well as from the male members of the family, has instilled within her a belief that she cannot work outside the home; such a decision would demean her social standing and hence lessen her chances to marry above her present economic station. While Bohme decides whether or not to propose, he twirls the knight in his hand; but he will be only a knight-errant, as his name suggests,[137] continuing on his quest for a wife, because he cannot accept Clara's working-class family. The extent to which the Porters are working class, although they live in near-poverty because of their struggle to appear middle class, is told not only through the father's appearance, "a squat, pallid, over-worked man, with a stench of onions and strong tobacco hanging about him" but also in his son's very name, Mason Porter, which invokes two working-class careers. Bohme realizes that "[t]here was no divorcing [Clara] from her surroundings" (50). Thus in the opening pages of the story, the narrative has moved from the courtship and the unuttered proposal to the divorce, and John Bohme departs.

The second metaphoric pattern encompasses both Clara and Margaret. While Clara has participated in this mock courtship-proposal-divorce, she has been "nipping the dead leaves carefully from a fuchsia" (50). When Bohme declares he shall not be returning, Clara breaks "a branch of pendant drops of color—purple, and scarlet, and gleaming white," colors that ambiguously suggest the loss of virginity, and, indeed, it is a kind of "de-flowering" that will bear no fruit because thereafter Clara forsakes all sense of herself and gathers "the dead leaves in her hand and let[s] them fall on the open window, watching the wind whirl them away"; she chooses thereafter to market herself into a marriage that is "barren," figuratively if not literally (50–51).

Margaret, on the other hand, has the advantage of seeing her sister's choices, and the repugnance with which she views Clara's marriage partner aids her in determining to seek another "prospect" for herself. While Margaret has a fine young man who wishes to marry her, he, too, is without the means to marry; he supports an ailing mother and a single sister who would become even more impoverished if he were to attempt to support a wife as well. Davis does not adhere to the sentimental ideal that love assuages poverty; thus, although George Goddard is willing to take the risk, Margaret is not. If her brothers have their trade, she intends to have hers, and it will not be the trade that Clara chose. Nor will it be a traditional, woman's occupation—she knows that there are more single women than teaching or governess positions available.[138] While Margaret explains to George that she cannot marry him under their present circumstances, she stands near a currant-bush and "pluck[s] a handful of the fruit. The juice stained her white hand like wine; Goddard took it in his own, looked at it with flushed face and quickened breath" (52). In contrast to Clara's dead leaves and broken branches, Margaret's sweet "fruit" suggests a consummation, but it is she, not George, who will implement the means to a true consummation.

Margaret studies her own environment, determines what commodity suitable to that environment is needed in the large eastern marketplaces, and then goes into business for herself to produce and market the product: medicinal herbs. She is mocked unbearably, called "unwomanly," and told that she is an embarrassment to her family, but she perseveres. Her business is not an overnight success; she must learn by her mistakes the first year, when she makes no profit, and perfect her skills so that by the third year she does, indeed, turn a profit. In fact, Margaret becomes the leading businessperson in her community, builds a home for her family, and cares for all of her siblings and her parents, who now find her business quite to their liking. It is the happy ending we might expect of a cautionary tale, but it has distinguishing features that raise it above the field of many marriage-marketing stories.

Davis seeks to educate her audience, which she specifically designates as marriage-aged young women, in several ways: to the consequences of marketing themselves, certainly, but also to recognize that "fate" is often culturally defined and need not be personally limiting; to the necessity of knowing more than domestic skills, extending one's knowledge to the practicalities of business as well as art, literature, and "the great under schemes of politics"—in other words, to the realities and diversities of life outside a small mill town; and, perhaps most significant, to challenge the age-old definitions of what is and is not "feminine." Margaret Porter is Davis's ultimate depiction of self-sufficiency. She does marry George Goddard, after he accustoms himself to her new, dynamic personality; but she does not give up her business for marriage. George has his political career; Margaret has her manufactory: "Her household is better managed, and her cooking and sewing more thoroughly done, because she can afford to employ skillful-brained servants, and does not spend her strength in the desperate, incomplete endeavors of a maid-of-all-work" (57). Importantly, her daughters are being educated in Margaret's new school of thought: they will have a trade or profession, and they will always know that "there is no prison from which there is not a means of escape" (57). The only burden in Margaret's life is Clara, whose husband died, leaving her and her children impoverished. " 'In the Market' " constitutes Davis's most feminist depiction of woman's potential in the 1860s.

*   *   *

As she became fully ensconced in the American literary publishing world, Davis was able to publish her works in a wider variety of publications that allowed her to address a broad spectrum of issues. She continued to seek new outlets for her fiction, sketches, and essays; and she began to explore the possibility of writing children's literature. One new outlet was *Hearth and Home*, a weekly journal founded in 1868, which began as a supplier of agricultural information and later came to publish literature. During the weekly's existence (1868–75), its editors included Harriet Beecher Stowe and Mary Mapes Dodge. As it evolved into a full-fledged literary journal, its contributors included Edward Everett Hale, Louisa May Alcott, and Edward Eggleston. It was in 1869 that Stowe published a series of women's rights essays in *Hearth and Home*.

When Davis began her first serial for the periodical, Stowe wrote to her, noting that she was "beginning with intense and painful interest your story of the Tembroke Legacy,"[139] a story that reveals the dangers of alcoholism and the hereditary nature of alcoholic addiction (the ironic "legacy"). In Stowe's typically effusive assessment, Davis's subject was "one that admits all the pathos and power of the old Greek tragedy" and warranted God's guidance in the writing so "as to arouse the fears and quicken the cautions of mothers & fathers to meet this fateful evil ere it be too late—." Stowe cited several cases of inherited alcohol abuse that she had observed personally and, with little subtlety, insisted that she could foresee where Davis's plot would lead—she then sketched out her ideas of how she was sure it *would* proceed, ending with the assertive request, "So dear, *do* save Malbro." In spite of some literary and religious differences, Davis had long felt an affinity with Stowe. Here, at last, was the renowned Harriet Beecher Stowe addressing her as "dear," commenting that though she had never seen Davis she felt "well acquainted" with her; she even thought to add, "hope you will excuse my suggestions," and touchingly signed herself, "Your affectionate friend, H B Stowe."

In early 1869, Davis also began writing for *Putnam's Magazine*. After it had suspended publication in 1857, *Putnam's* resumed operation in 1868, declaring itself to be a thoroughly American literary periodical (in contrast to *Harper's*, which relied heavily upon established English authors for its contributors). This reborn *Putnam's* only flourished until 1870, but in that time it published the works of American writers as diverse as James Fenimore Cooper, Charlotte F. Bates, John Burroughs, Frank Stockton, Elizabeth Stoddard, and William Dean Howells. In the January 1869 issue, the editors had published an article entitled "The Woman Question," which was rapidly becoming *the* topic of the day. The article had strongly supported women's equality. Davis's responding article is ironically titled "Men's Rights."[140] She begins with the humorous assertion that "I have always had a perverse inclination to the other side of the question, especially if there was little to be said for it" (212). Yet the male perspective overrides Davis's own assertions to the contrary in this essay. She asserts that she prefers the term "Woman's Needs" to "Woman's Wrongs," a reference to Gail Hamilton's book by the latter title, which had appeared in 1868. Unlike Hamilton, Davis supported suffrage; the question of need is so evident, Davis asserts, "it is too late for argument about it"; one need only look at the increasing numbers of impoverished women, of prostitutes, and young women who market themselves for a husband to dispute any need for further argument. Their wretched lives, Davis insisted, was "a tragedy more real to me than any other in life" (212).

To relieve the bleakness of this picture for a moment, and perhaps in an attempt to replicate the pervasive wit of Hamilton's book, Davis seeks comic relief and turns to men "who are accused of all this misery, to find if they have not a word to plead on their side" (212). Aligning herself with women's rights advocates, she admonishes men who "flatter and sneer at us" and warns women against the "moderate and cool men" who, in fact, fear that the gaining of rights by women will somehow incorporate a loss of rights for men. Yet Davis cannot truly align herself with the New Woman, and her essay descends into a confrontation with young American women who refuse to recognize their grandmothers, the early "workwomen," as a potential source of wisdom for the movement.

This is an important point in understanding Davis's position on feminism, and it is an issue that reveals long-harbored resentment and sensitivities that Davis rarely confronted in herself and was consequently unable to overcome. "Men's Rights," juxtaposed against " 'In the Market,' " gives us a sense of Davis's inner struggle to overcome her own training into the proprieties of womanhood. As Mary Kelley has observed, this phenomenon was a distinctive characteristic of the fiction by women in this era[141] and, one might add, in much of the nonfiction as well. To criticize woman's oppression was to condemn oneself; thus, though many women authors of the period address women's issues and women's lives, the sense of their oppression is often sidestepped or couched in secondary aspects of their writings.

For Davis a novel that she would write in the next decade, *A Law Unto Herself*, came closest to approaching the subject directly. Instead of being able to advocate for the next generation what she and her mother had not been afforded, Davis resented the present generation's belief that they alone were the originators of ideas for liberalizing women's lives. In spite of her own accomplishments, Davis's resentment seems to have centered upon her lack of a higher education. She often diverted the issue from herself by referring to her mother, as when she noted that Rachel Harding "had enough knowledge to fit out half a dozen modern college bred women."[142] Thus in "Men's Rights," she suggests that while the ambitious young women of today can join their male counterparts in discussing "Bismarck's policy, or Herbert Spencer, or Renan," they have no intimate women friends. While they think they are being innovative and rebellious, they in fact form cliques that require them to dress and act alike; her bitterness is evident in what is intended as scathing: "They are girls who do not marry early, as a rule" (214), a rather ironic comment since Davis herself was in her thirties when she married.

Davis attempted to establish the value of the artistry and ideas that their grandmothers created, and she especially challenged young women's denial that these elder women had any "mental hunger." There is an integrity to Davis's position (established lovingly instead of spitefully a century later by Alice Walker in her tribute to our grandmothers). Davis asserts, "Suffrage, or work, any of the popular cries among us, are but so many expressions of this same mental hunger or unused power" (214); but her inability to embrace the younger generation, in spite of the rhetoric of "us" and "our," undoubtedly acted, in this instance, only to alienate those whom she wished to educate. Her cautionary note is that women are not moving in a better direction; they are simply falling into the decadence of men's patterns—again, a valid assertion. Yet while her explicitness about sexuality is also important, she loses both arguments by reverting to a discussion of today's "fast girl" and the fact that men will only want a "pure" woman for a wife.

Davis entitled her essay "Men's Rights" in order to suggest that women were diverting blame to men; but, she asserts, "I do not think that the guilt of man has anything to do with the responsibility of women"; like Margaret Fuller, she believed, "To our own master we stand or fall" (216).

After suffrage, Davis asserts that women's return to spiritual purity is the most important reform confronting American women. In this, she means a return to the values of industry and frugality that she had been taught as a child. If the "Domestic Woman," man's ideal, is a stumbling block for the New Woman, Davis suggests that the way to overcome this is to understand that "there is place and need and welcome in [the world] not only for this great path of progress, but for the quiet ground that is fruitful, and for the still, well-ordered homes" that men love to recall (219). Citing wrongs only gains women "valueless sympathy," she asserts; in order to take their rightful places on "the man's preempted ground, we must prove our right . . . by the hard logic of work well done" (216).

As her argument shifts back and forth between what men expect and what women need, Davis reveals a great deal about her own acculturation: she cannot rise above a concern for men's discomfort in the whole process of transition that women were undergoing, and she claims that it is the "noisy vehemence and unwise boasts of the leading [women] reformers" that caused the prevailing prejudice against women in the work place (219). Even before suffrage and property rights, Davis finally insists, we must confront the issue of women's inability to earn their own support; we must insist upon more work and better wages. Although she conservatively denies women access to the pulpit, because, she insists, there are too many poorly qualified candidates in that profession already, she acknowledges the contributions of Caroline Dall's "powerful downright logic" and Lucretia Mott's "great triumph" in her life's work (220). Her concern, she concludes, is not with upper-class women, but with the under-represented: seamstresses and the unemployed and especially young, middle-class women whose brothers receive all advantages while their minds are allowed to stagnate (222).

In this conclusion, no one's life is more representative than Davis's own; although she did not allow her mind to dwindle at all, nearly twenty years of suppressed bitterness over the unequal educations she and her brothers received is detectable to a twentieth-century audience. It was not to Davis. She sincerely believed she was presenting a logical position, an advanced position, on the woman question. In her view, the commonplace trades that middle-class women should and could learn were as valuable socioeconomically as the (relatively) advanced educations of the younger generation of women: "Art may be as truly worshipped in a carpenter's shop or a laundry-room as in the sculptor's *atelier*" (223).

In that assertion, we have both Davis's excellent contributions to the literary history of America and the limitations of her vision of herself as artist. Her theory of the commonplace greatly extended the contributions of early realists, and she would yet write several excellent short stories and novels, and numerous insightful essays, especially on "the woman question." Additionally, she had begun a new facet of her career in 1867 when she became a contributing editor of the *New York Daily Tribune*,[143] following a tradition begun by Margaret Fuller and joined in the 1870s by Sara Jane Clarke Lippincott ("Grace Greenwood") and other literary women. But the young woman whose literary career had begun so gloriously in 1861 would thereafter view a portion of her life's work only as a trade. Davis gave utterance to the burdens that forced her into such a position: "some time ago I mounted a certain 'family horse' which goes on, trot, trot, day after day—giving me precious little time for greetings by the way or meditations on the prospect—."[144] We might expect Davis thereafter to recede into that plodding life, but a second artistic wind was about to burst forth.

4. Women of Confidence and Confidence-Men

THE EARLY 1870S constituted a period of major artistic transitions for Davis and was certainly her most productive decade. She published two novels and one novella and serialized four others; extended her journalistic endeavors to include both the *New York Daily Tribune* and *The Independent*; and published more than 140 articles and short stories in sixteen periodicals, including literary journals (*Putnam's*, the *Galaxy*, *Lippincott's*, *Scribner's Monthly*, *Harper's*, the *Atlantic*, *Peterson's*, *Appleton's*, *Hearth and Home*, and *Wood's Household Magazine*), children's periodicals (*Riverside Magazine*, *Youth's Companion*, and *St. Nicholas*), and religious magazines (*Sunday Afternoon* and *Golden Rule*). The 1870s was a decade in which she wrote some of her most courageous political and social fiction, not only challenging Whiskey Rings and exposing confidence men but also continuing to delineate archaic legal and social attitudes toward marriage, women's right to work, and other inequities. Her association with the *New York Daily Tribune* became an impetus to her political fiction.

Little attention has been given to women writers' contributions to political literature other than the abolition and suffrage movements; studied in the context of American literary history, Davis stands out as a significant political novelist and social historian. In a decade that saw the birth of some of America's best-known realists and naturalists (Frank Norris, Stephen Crane, Theodore Dreiser, Willa Cather, Sherwood Anderson, and Jack London), Davis continued her metarealism of the previous decade. If she personally felt the sting of abandonment by the *Atlantic*, she was not stymied artistically by the forced change in publishers. Both she and Clarke were interested in several political issues of the day, and she immediately turned her attention to those problems.

Clarke decided in early 1870 to forego his legal practice, which demanded much time but afforded him little compensation, and turned his energies to journalism. He accepted the position of managing editor for the *Philadelphia Inquirer* and continued to write popular fiction. Rebecca and Clarke were now occasionally contributors to the same periodicals; Rebecca's association with various journals (such as *Lippincott's* and *Galaxy*) was often followed by Clarke's submission of fiction. His main artistic interest, however, was the theater, and he wrote several theatrical reviews for *Lippincott's* and other magazines. As Clarke developed his interest in drama and gained attention for his reviews, he began to form acquaintances among acting troupes. Philadelphia had a resident theater company at the Arch Street Theatre under the management of Louisa Drew, and in the mid-1870s the Walnut Street Theatre presented performances by Augustin Daly's company and the renowned Edwin Booth in a variety of Shakespeare productions. The Chestnut Street Theatre was noted for its musicals as well as drama, and Charlotte Thompson performed there several times during the 1870s. Soon, Clarke and Rebecca numbered among their friends some of the greatest actors and celebrities of the American stage, including the Drews, the Barrymores, and the great American comedic actor, Joseph Jefferson. After they bought their home on South Twenty-first Street, they often held breakfasts for the actors and interested patrons on the mornings of matinees, and their guests included Edwin Forrest, Ellen Terry, Augustin Daly, Ada Rehan, and many others. As a long-time supporter of women and men who chose the theater as a career, Davis extended her old Virginian "grasp of the hand" to these new friends.

As the decade began, Davis also renewed her acquaintance with Ralph Waldo Emerson. Though she rejected the philosophy of transcendentalism, she was always able to separate the person and his theory, and she harbored no personal ill will toward the great Concord Sage. He stayed with her and Clarke several times when he was in Philadelphia, the first time in 1870. She and Clarke had just purchased their first home, at 230 South Twenty-first Street, where they would reside for the remainder of their lives. When Davis learned that Emerson was scheduled to present a lecture in Philadelphia, she sought an opportunity to return the courtesy that he had afforded her in 1862. She invited him to make their home his, in the manner which she knew would be most appealing to an author: "I mean a home, literally. You shall have the quietest of rooms and come in and go out as you will."[1] Recalling the days she had spent in Concord, and willing to pander tongue-in-cheek to Emerson's "oracle" status, she wrote him:

It was such a relief to see you eat and drink! My oracle's voice came so much closer home to me when I saw he was human as we others. For, as you doubtless have noticed, to us downright commonsensible Western people the gods are intelligible just in proportion as their bones ache or their clothes are cut like our own. Sincerely, I shall not soon forget how kind and gracious you were to me, a raw Western girl then and I hope you will be as unselfishly kind now and give us this great pleasure.[2]

Not surprisingly, Emerson accepted.

In these early months of the decade, Davis was also preparing a novel that she intended as an eye-opening exposé on abuses perpetrated by administrators of insane asylums and abetted by the law. Rebecca and Clarke were in complete agreement on this issue and they both sought the public domain to highlight the abuses of the system. With the Civil War past and industrial capitalism entrenched, the treatment of the mentally ill became Davis's next major cause for reform. Two years before Davis published *Put Out of the Way*, her novel on the condition of insane asylums in the United States, Clarke had published an essay on the topic as it related to conditions in Pennsylvania. "A Modern Lettre de Cachet" takes a historical perspective, denoting the horrendous treatment of the insane during William Penn's era, and points out that little has changed in this respect in Philadelphia of the 1870s: criminals receive better treatment and are afforded the due processes of law. Clarke included a sample certificate of commitment in his text which, in its simplicity and nonspecificity, is little better than the ancient *lettre de cachet* that was used to imprison criminals and political adversaries in the Bastille. Clarke then cites several contemporary cases of questionable commitments to Philadelphia institutions, including the Pennsylvania Hospital for the Insane. His essay ends with a call for "official notice and reform."[3]

It was an important beginning to their mutual assault on the system, but the legal tone and nature of Clarke's presentation inevitably suffers in comparison to the fictionalized call for reform that Rebecca presented in her novel. Publication of Davis's novel was delayed in part because of what she termed "a bitter battle" that ensued after Clarke's essay was published.[4] Davis proudly asserted to a friend that Clarke had fought the battle "singlehanded through press and legislature" in spite of "virulent opposition."[5] That political fracas, in fact, afforded Davis the rare gift of time in which to craft her novel, which in turn acted as support for Clarke's legal efforts; it was probably also instrumental in her decision to set the novel in New York rather than Philadelphia. Her decision to publish *Put Out of the Way* in *Peterson's Magazine* was twofold: certainly the payment rate at *Peterson's* was an influence, but more important for this novel was the degree of public exposure that *Peterson's* would afford her subject, since the magazine's readership numbered more than 150,000 in the 1870s. The editorial column of the June 1870 issue in which part 2 of *Put Out of the Way* appeared carries a message that Davis insisted be included: "every leading incident has substantially happened."[6] The author's purpose, the editor continues, "is not to assail any particular asylum, but rather to assist in awakening public sentiment to the necessity of a reform in the manner in which patients can be committed to such hospitals."[7]

Interwoven into the story of Richard Wortley's institutionalization on fradulent charges are extensions of the legal premises Clarke had addressed in his essay. Colonel Leeds has agreed to care for his ward, Charlotte (Lotty) Hubbard, after her father, who was an old friend of his, dies. However, in desparate need of money, the colonel schemes to claim Lotty's inheritance by marrying her to his son. When the colonel realizes that Wortley threatens the enactment of this plan, he does not need to act outside the law to accomplish his goal of having Dick "put out of the way." He and his son simply find a physician who is willing to sign the certificate of commitment without examining the patient. It is not a difficult task; as gentlemen, their word is taken as fact, and the liberality of their pocketbook seals Dick's fate. Thereafter, the law supports the Leedses' claim *in toto*. Although a criminal would be afforded a lawyer and the right to a trial, no such rights were due an individual who was charged with insanity. Only the word of two "respectable" men was necessary to institutionalize an individual for life. Nor is Wortley, as a "patient," allowed any contact with the outside world; his whereabouts are confidential and his letters are read and then destroyed by the administrators.

It is, as Dick soon realizes, nothing less than being buried alive. This is not a tale of the grotesque from Edgar Allan Poe, however; it was the reality of asylum incarceration in New York, Philadelphia, and elsewhere in the United States during the 1870s, and Davis renders the inanities of the law with precision. But she is equally concerned with Americans' attitudes toward the insane. Having been told that he is under arrest on criminal charges, Dick is duped into taking the train ride to the asylum; but he sits quietly, assuming that when they reach their destination he will be allowed access to counsel. The Leedses, however, simply drop a hint or two to the other passengers that Dick is insane, and the passengers immediately discern in him the traits of the mentally ill: suddenly the spark of frustration in his eyes is deemed the look of a fiend, and his every word is ascertained to be irrational and threatening. When he arrives at the station and realizes that he is being kidnapped, he turns to his fellow passengers for assistance. One man does step forward, but when he sees the certificate of commitment, he assures Dick, "You are an American citizen. Your liberty is secure. The law is your defence. Go . . . quietly."[8] Similar scenes are rendered throughout the novel: secure in their belief in the law's protection of civil rights, the passengers forego aiding the wronged man, even when he is beaten and forced into a carriage.

The outer story of Lotty and Dick's romance and the diabolical intentions of the Leedses is unexceptional. In fact, the subplot of Fred Leeds's secret marriage to a blowsy foreign woman which he tries to hide in order to marry Charlotte Hubbard is a reworking of the plot of Davis's first story for *Peterson's*, "The Murder in the Glen Ross," from more than a dozen years earlier, and one that she will repeat again in *Kitty's Choice* (1876). It is also similar to the plot machinations of Mary Wilkins Freeman's "A Humble Romance," published in 1887; in Freeman's story, the first wife conveniently dies so the new wife may remain with her husband; in an era that did not socially condone divorce, it was apparently an effective way—in fiction, at least—to eliminate unwanted spouses! Lotty's characterization is enriched by the rendering of her transformation from a naive young woman who is easily seduced by the "glamour of romance" into a sentimental heroine who is the moral archetype of the novel, but she is for the most part peripheral to the central story.

The inner narrative of *Put Out of the Way*, however, is structured to complement the novel's theme of Dick's unjust incarceration; it is excellent, both in terms of the specificity of Davis's depiction of the asylum's environment and in the psychological breakdown of a once-sane man under extraordinary conditions. Dick's mental collapse is not depicted in the other-worldly, Poesque tradition of horror; the precisely "everyday" sense of his life, sudden imprisonment, and consequent breakdown constitutes the horror of Davis's novel. This process begins with her exposure of the American public's willingness to accept any new system if it is presented under the guise of being "scientific." Thus the administrators of the asylum need simply assert that they are using the very latest scientific advances in treating the mentally ill and the public is not only satisfied but pleased with this efficient model of American progress.

The theme also afforded Davis an opportunity to continue her assault on Americans who preferred to leave charity to the administration of large institutions. She begins with the ironically named Dr. Harte, who is assistant superintendent of the asylum:

> Dr. Harte . . . spoke as though his body were a machine wound up to talk, while the real man were asleep, or gone on a journey. The unutterable eye, and voice, and wooden manner, is too often common to men whose daily routine brings them into contact with suffering. One wonders whether the indifference, assumed at first for prudence, has not penetrated deeper and deeper, till the whole man is actually hardened into a wooden puppet, only to be set in motion by duty, or what he thinks duty. Whatever the explanation be, it is a sad fact, that almost the last place to look for genial temper, or quick sympathies, is in the actual manager of any charitable institution. (441)

The alternative—individual activism—comes at the end of the novel in the figure of an obscure young girl, Jessy Lawrence, who finds Dick's unstamped letter to his friend, Judge Cathcart. Jessy simply mails the letter. All of Dick's attempts to reach someone outside the walls of the asylum, as well as the endeavors of his family and friends to locate him, have failed; but this one act by a stranger literally saves Dick's life. In this seemingly minor event in the novel's plot, we have a clear definition of Davis's meta-realism as it had developed to this point and as it would remain: she no longer adheres to the "scientific" approach to realism and ultimately naturalism (with the exception of *John Andross*); instead, she notes the irony of Mr. Lawrence's insistence that Jessy discard the letter because her desire to send it is simply one more instance of her "absurd sentimentality" (113). If Davis did not adhere to the sentimentalists' representation of a matriarchal utopian society or to women as saints, she did adhere to the moral activism of sentimentalism and synthesized it with her quotidian realism.

Davis's depiction of Dr. Harte as a metaphorically "wooden" figure establishes not only his personality but quite literally his methods of punishment for any patient who attempts to defend himself. Dick is healthy and strong-willed when he enters the asylum, but he is also hot-tempered. The only other sane man he encounters during his year of incarceration is the elderly George Inman, who had been confined because of "mild melancholia" after the death of his wife. Mr. Inman has been imprisoned for ten years; his son has died and his grandson is enjoying his inheritance while his grandfather slowly dies inside the stone walls of the asylum. Inman attempts to warn Dick that insurrection will lead to worse punishment than mere incarceration. Two of the sixteen men's wards are modernized, clean and comfortable; these are the wards that relatives and visitors are shown. The next level of wards, where Dick is first placed, is horrible but, Inman cautions him, there are yet lower wards. Dick, however, in his youthful abrasiveness, refuses to listen.

As Inman had predicted, Dick's insubordination soon casts him into the foul stench and darkness of the eighth ward with Mike Brady as his keeper; Brady is a former boxer who was known as a "foul hitter." Dick's temper ultimately forces him into a brawl with Brady; he then learns what brute strength and complete brutality really are:

> Brady's great carcass of muscle was cool and slow. When the time seemed to him to be ripe, he gave a sniff, and leveled Dick with a foul blow, jumping on his chest with his knees. Dick remained quite quiet there. It did not need any blows, the weight was enough.
> Dick Wortley's head dropped to one side, grew sickly and livid as when he was a jaundiced baby; then the blood slowly rose to his mouth, and dripped, dripped on the floor. (35)

Nor is this beating the end. Dr. Harte wants Dick to fully realize that any act of resistance will not be countenanced; he prescribes "the hose":

> The hose was a wooden machine, on which Dick was tightly strapped on his back—head, legs, and arms, hanging down. He remained there as long as Messrs. Minch [another keeper] and Brady judged best, for the blood to be driven to his brain. Then they took him out, and finding that his head was heated, they fastened him under the shower-bath, suffering the slow drop of water to fall upon one spot in the brain, until from the frenzied eyes, and unconscious moans of agony, it seemed as though the tortured soul within was seeking, at eyes and mouth, some means of escape. (35)

This punishment leads to brain fever, and Dick is placed in the dormitory for recovery; because he is a well-subsidized patient, his keepers do not want him to die. "Brain fever" was the mental illness ascribed to Hester Manning during her dream in "The Wife's Story," the short story written after Davis's own confrontation with "mental exhaustion" in late 1863. In Dick Wortley's recovery, we may see a horrifying recreation of Davis's personal knowledge of psychological breakdown and recovery: it is June before Dick "was himself enough to know that the claw-like fingers, picking at his sheet, were his own" (35).

Dick's attempt at escape from the asylum—the months of cunningly planning escape and the treacherous events of the night during which he executes his plan—is tautly written, leaving the reader to agonize when Dick is ultimately foiled. This is not a "great escape" adventure story, however; it is a painful acknowledgment that no one escapes incarceration without outside assistance. When Dick is finally released, after Judge Cathcart receives the letter posted by Jessy Lawrence, his reunion with Lotty suggests a sentimental resolution, but Davis never fully aligns herself with sentimentalism. As with her use of naturalistic techniques, she employs aspects of sentimentalism to enhance her realistic vision. Thus Dick is freed and he in turn insists that George Inman have an opportunity for a trial. Both men are astonished, however, to learn that Inman "must prove his sanity, not his keepers' madness" (117). The result is a decision by the courts that no illegality was committed; the "massive respectability of the Asylum" cannot be scaled. The fact that Inman had been consigned to an asylum acts as *prima facie* evidence against him, and he is reincarcerated. Judge Cathcart convinces Dick that his case would differ little from Inman's; Dick must realize he can accomplish no retributive punishment against the Leedses.

Yet Davis wants to instill in her audience a sense that they *can* do something about such injustices; thus Lotty accomplishes through personal activism what the men and the courts could not. She goes to see Stacy Inman, George's grandson, and describes for him his grandfather's situation. Young Stacy had assumed from the institution's reports that his grandfather was perfectly happy and well cared for. When Stacy asks how he can rectify matters when the courts cannot, Lotty has the solution, one which Davis wants to explicate for her audience: stop paying, Lotty suggests, for the administrators have only a profit motive. When the funds are halted, George Inman is immediately deemed "cured," and he is released.

Lotty and Dick marry and settle in the hills near a small village on the Hudson, where they raise their family. They bring both George Inman and Dick's mother to live with them, echoing the actions of the Quaker in "Life in the Iron Mills." "Uncle" George regains his health as much as possible, is full of laughter, and becomes a great fisherman. Davis's sense of humor and her own brand of sentimental realism is rendered through the elder Mrs. Wortley, who has been the quietly suffering, "dying saint." Davis humorously depicts how readily Mrs. Wortley foregoes her stereotypic "duty" and thrives in her new role as an "everyday, loveable . . . grandmother." The Wortleys do not escape the "trials and storms" of everyday life, Davis assures her audience, but they embrace "that mellowed splendor . . . which belongs to the Indian Summer of our lives; to the season when the sap of the most shaded tree has had time to know its chance to leaf and blossom; when, however stormy the weather, there has been summer enough to teach us, that, behind the clouds, the sun is warm, and God is good" (118).

At only thirty-nine years of age, and with a prolific decade before her, Davis was not yet ready for her own "Indian Summer," though the sense of longing is evident in her tone. The woman who had accepted marriage and a family life as her "summer days" in 1863 knew the realities of variable weather, but she faced her future resolutely. The Davises and their supporters in the cause had the satisfaction of seeing their literature and legislative efforts take effect in the new laws that were established to protect the civil liberties of the mentally ill. Clarke had continued the assault in his editorial column of the *Inquirer* and was appointed by the governor to the state commission established to revise the laws in Pennsylvania.

* * *

In spite of Davis's earlier protestations that she would never again write for the *Galaxy* because of the publishing fiasco that had surrounded the serialization of *Waiting for the Verdict*, she had reached an agreement with the Church brothers in 1870 to submit occasional short stories. Some of these submissions are trite, though they demonstrate Davis's knowledge of newspaper-office types and include embryonic depictions of confidence-men which she developed more fully in her major political novels of the decade. However, her short story entitled "Two Women," published in the *Galaxy*, deserves close attention; it stands on its own literary merit and is important in the growing Davis canon that includes fictional and factual accounts of women who are like caged animals, trapped by social customs that restrict their conduct and self-expression.[9] The title also signifies the character juxtapositions that will run throughout Davis's fiction concerning women's lives: the domestic woman and the woman who seeks work outside her home.

In "Two Women," Charlotte Vane is described as a typical woman who is a victim of "hysteria"; Davis, however, depicts her as a capable, intelligent woman whose stifled existence leaves her no outlet for those capabilities. She is a natural woman who "had a mortal dread of being 'stagey,'" unlike Alice McIntyre, who, in the social seasons, "markets" herself before eligible young bachelors (803). Charlotte has money enough to live in comfort, but she finds "women's work" unfulfilling. "Two Women" outlines Charlotte's struggle against the social stigma of work which society claims "desexes" a woman. Part of her strength has come from her years as a Confederate spy during the Civil War: "Then I lived! Like a man" (805). Now in her attempt to join her lover, James Vogdes, in the potentially fatal work of attending yellow fever victims, Charlotte dons men's clothing in order to pass as one who is qualified to render such services. Vogdes has especially admired Charlotte for not being like other women, for being herself. Yet when he discovers it is she who is working beside him, he is aghast at her behavior: "Fate had struck the decisive hour for this mannish girl, as for the all-womanly Ophelia. But have these men-women hearts to break, or brains that the want of love will drive mad? Mr. Vogdes thought not. 'I will go now,' [Charlotte] said, letting her glove fall" (814). Thereafter, Vogdes defines her as "a nondescript, ridiculous creature, neither man nor woman" (814), and he marries Alice McIntyre.

The story concludes with the requisite scene that sums up the characters' individual fates. The Vogdes attend an evening at the theater several years later only to discover that Charlotte is playing the role of a page in *Hamlet*, replicating her earlier work in which she was disguised as a man. As silly as Alice still seems, she now appears to Charlotte to be too good for Vogdes. Charlotte feels sorry for herself, but not without cause; as the narrator observes, "the others have quite forgotten her in watching the sorrows of the gentle Ophelia." Once again, Charlotte has been upstaged by the "womanly woman." Davis remains confined by the concepts of "womanly women" and "mannish women," but through the story's conclusion she suggests that the oppression of women desexes them in a way that fulfillment of their ambitions never could.

*   *   *

In July, an event that saddened Davis and the entire literary community acted as impetus for a letter to Annie: the death of Charles Dickens. James Fields had written for the *Atlantic* an essay that Clarke termed "the noblest tribute to Dickens which has ever been paid."[10] Davis agreed, adding only that Clarke's sentiment "had not said half enough." She admired Fields's tact and "the genial feeling" with which he described his English friend: "it is the power by which in these simple facts he places Dickens before us who did not know him—genial and loveable—*as strongly as any of the great master's own work could do*." Davis made no direct comment to

James, but, in addition to this letter, she published in the *Tribune* a short item praising his article.

In the letter to Annie, Davis momentarily approaches the former personal level of their correspondence when she comments, "I feel a long way from you, and every body—I have had a great sorrow since I wrote you last—of which I cannot yet brave to speak." Not since her illness preceding Richard's birth had Davis expressed such feelings, but, as always, she is not wont to explicate her sorrow, and in the sparse correspondence between the two women during the early seventies, the subject was not raised again. Davis tried to mend the friendship with the Fieldses by inviting them to stay with her and Clarke and the boys when Annie and James visited Philadelphia in early 1871, but the Fieldses chose to stay at a hotel rather than have to select from among the several friends they had in Philadelphia. The decision was meant to be diplomatic, but it must have been a painful rebuff for Davis, even if she understood their reasoning. The following year, Annie invited the Davises to visit them in Boston; Rebecca replied, "I *would* like to see Boston again as I would like to go to a thousand places, but I am firmly rooted in Philadelphia and likely to remain so for years to come, as if I were a sponge or oyster on a rock."[11] She then turns to more pleasant topics, such as Annie's inclusion of Elizabeth Stuart Phelps in her Boston "coffee houses." Annie and she would not be able to bridge the rift in their relationship until the end of the decade.

*   *   *

By September of 1870, Davis was actively engaged with several social and political issues of her day. One of her rare letters to Annie recommends "A Physician's Problems" by Dr. Elam, and Davis included a little proselytizing for the book: "It is a book which has had a curious fascination for me and which I believe would accomplish great good by its mode of meeting the problem of constitutional inebriety. . . . I have written two or three articles for the Tribune trying to have it republished and would push it in that paper any other way I could. The subject is one that troubles me constantly, it seems so general a disease and the remedy at hand and yet unknown. Ask Mr. Fields to think of it."[12]

Although the Women's Christian Temperance Union would be formed in a few years, their method was not Davis's. She had begun her interest in this issue with the publication of the serial "The Tembroke Legacy." In addition to her own observations of friends and strangers on the street, her position with the *Tribune* afforded her daily perusal of articles on the effects of alcohol addiction. A typical daily entry in the *Tribune* records the consequences of alcohol abuse in mid-nineteenth-century American society: "A man named John Lawrence to-day shot Mrs. Atwood four times with a revolver. The shots entered her body in various places, and will probably prove fatal. Lawrence afterward cut his throat in a shocking manner, but the wounds are not considered dangerous. Rum and jealousy were the cause."[13] Quotidian exposure to such realities convinced Davis that an addicted person's abstinence would never be achieved without medical intervention. Out of this concern and from her exposure as a journalist to the corrupt Whiskey Ring, Davis shaped one of the nineteenth century's most uncompromising political novels, *John Andross*.

While Davis was beginning to gather the materials for *Andross*, she published a serialized novella in *Scribner's Monthly* entitled, *Natasqua*. *Scribner's* at the time was under the editorship of Josiah G. Holland, who had sought out Davis as a contributor. In the 1870s, *Scribner's* published novels by Edward Everett Hale, Frank Stockton, Bret Harte, and George Washington Cable; short stories by Julian Hawthorne, Constance Fenimore Woolson, Helen Hunt Jackson; and essays by John Burroughs and Edmund Clarence Stedman.

In *Natasqua*, Davis returns to one of her favorite topics—the capitalist. She parodies American businessmen whose success has garnered them a place of power in society but whose taste flagrantly exposes their lack of refinement. Yet the novel is a disappointing reentry into that theme. The plot is predictable, characterization—usually her strong point—is shallow, and both the tone and pace of the novel are plodding. It is of little literary significance, except for one interesting feature—its Impressionistic descriptions of her beloved Manasquan coastal region. Davis had crafted her art of description over the last quarter-century, and in the coming years it remained one of her finest literary assets. In *Natasqua*, she refined her typically realistic imagery with an early form of the Impressionist style that Henry James was developing in his psychological realism and which Hamlin Garland would define in *Crumbling Idols* (1894). Davis surely knew, however, that this novel was an artistic failure. The brief review it received in the *Nation* noted its "laconic" tone and correctly observed that its chief quality was its brevity.[14] Even *The Independent*, to which Davis often contributed, was only able to observe that "*Natasqua* . . . [is] a simple story with a good deal of dramatic force toward its conclusion."[15] While writing this novella, Davis's attention had been focused on the preparation of the background materials for *Andross*, and the hurried manner in which *Natasqua* was written is evident.

In January 1871, when the last segment of *Natasqua* appeared in *Scribner's Monthly*, Davis had also begun to write for *Youth's Companion*, a Boston children's magazine that assumed an audience of intelligent, interested children and young adults. In the 1870s its contributors included Elizabeth Stuart Phelps, Louisa May Alcott, Edward Eggleston, Samuel Woodworth Cozzens, and, in later years, Rose Terry Cooke, Harriet Beecher Stowe, Mary Wilkins Freeman, Kate Chopin, Celia Thaxter, Theodore Roosevelt, and Hamlin Garland. Davis wrote most of her items for *Youth's Companion* during the 1870s; she published more than forty stories in the magazine during that decade, becoming one of its major contributors. The *Companion's* editor, Daniel S. Ford, insisted on using a pseudonym at the time—a decision representative of Ford's self-effacing style which Davis admired; she was drawn to the publication because "he sincerely believed that the paper was a lever which would uplift the minds and souls of American children."[16] Although *Youth's Companion* used many reprints, Davis wrote only original stories for the magazine. The *Companion* also published serials, but Davis would not undertake such a commitment, preferring to write short children's stories and retain the novel and novella forms for her adult audiences.

Another journal to which Davis again contributed at this time was *Putnam's Magazine*, whose literary critic, Edmund Clarence Stedman, agreed with Davis's opinion of Emersonian philosophy. While Stedman concluded that his readers should read Emerson's latest work because it is "delightful reading," he cautioned that

> it has not fixed itself in our memories, either because we demand more *purpose* in what we read than is apparent here, or beause we have become so accustomed to Mr. Emerson's peculiarities, or excellences, if his admirers prefer, that we are no longer affected by them. . . . He never seeks to make proselytes—as, indeed, how should he, when he never seems to quite know what he believes, nor where he stands, except that it is somewhere in the region of abstract Thought.[17]

Stedman notes that Emerson "is everything to those who are prepared to receive him, and nothing to those who are not; it depends entirely upon the barrenness or the richness of the soil whether the seed of his thought falls dead, or blossoms into the ripe, consummate flower."[18] Stedman's conclusion was the same as the one Davis had drawn in 1862, when she observed the people who came to pay homage to Emerson in Concord. Davis would reinstate her anti-transcendentalism stance again in only a few years with the publication of *Earthen Pitchers* and *John Andross*, but for the present, *Putnam's* interest in French, German, and American realism that blended itself with "moral beauty" made it an apt publication for her work. In the same issue in which Stedman reviewed Emerson's book, he printed a long essay praising George Sand's "genius," her excellent "comprehension of the primitive elements of mankind," her ability to describe the "abuses of marriage," as Sand termed it, and the "unconquerable strength of womanhood," which will overcome man's brutishness.[19] Though Davis never achieved the status of Sand as a writer, these themes would pervade her own writings in the coming years.

At this time, too, an event of great significance to the literary publishing world occurred. James Fields resigned as editor of the *Atlantic Monthly*, and William Dean Howells became the doyen of the publication—one of New England's, and indeed the country's, major literary journals. Davis and Annie were corresponding sporadically, but the fact that Davis was not informed of Fields's impending retirement is evidence of how distant their relationship had become. She learned of it, as she put it, "with all the rest of the world" when it was announced publicly in December 1870.[20] Davis did not publish another article in the *Atlantic* until 1873. In the meantime, she continued to gather materials for her novel on the Tweed Ring, and in the interim she paid for her research time by publishing prolifically in *Peterson's, Youth's Companion*, and occasionally elsewhere.

It took Davis nearly three years to gather the materials for her novel on the Tweed Ring. In the midst of this process she became pregnant with her third and last child. Nora Davis was born in 1872. With Davis's prolific writing stint of this decade and her meticulous gathering of facts out of which she would weave her political exposé, little record remains of Nora's early months. The most significant reason for this lapse is not Davis's lack of interest in her daughter but the estrangement between Davis and Annie Fields, to whom she had detailed the birth and early years of her first two children. Two of the rare comments by Davis on Nora's infancy are shared with Mary Mapes Dodge. The first occurred in late 1873, when Davis responded to Dodge's letter seeking Davis as a contributor to *St. Nicholas*. Davis replied, apologizing for not sending congratulations sooner on Dodge's editorship of the magazine, but noting that the delay was due to "the baby for whom you ask. She keeps me busy and has brought me . . . such terrible arrearages of sleep that I write, walk and talk with my eyes half shut."[21] The next spring Davis is forced to write a hasty response to a query from Dodge because "my poor little girl is sick and scarcely leaves my arms."[22] Her particular concerns for her female child are painfully asserted when she adds, "Maybe *you* are the fortunate woman to have no daughter—you don't have so many heartaches—."[23]

Davis maintained a Book of Days for each child and encouraged their early development, but like so many aspects of Davis's personal life, her daughter's childhood blends into the background of her literary life. The bond between the mother and daughter, however, was as indelible as the one between Davis and her own mother. Nora never had to experience the sense of physical distance between herself and her mother, as Rebecca had when she observed that such a distance between herself and her own mother was like a "cypher" in her life. Nora remained at home until her mother's death in 1910; as Nora became an adult, she and Rebecca evolved into mutually admiring friends and amiable traveling companions.

Scribner's Monthly had sought Davis as a contributor when it was established in 1870, and its publishers continued the tradition in November 1873 when they announced their new magazine for children, *St. Nicholas*, under the editorship of Mary Mapes Dodge, author of *Hans Brinker; or, The Silver Skates* (1865). Dodge's editorship of *St. Nicholas*, which lasted until her death in 1905, made her the major force in shaping America's literature for children. The publishers of *Scribner's* noted that, in presenting this companion magazine to their publication for adults, they intended to make *St. Nicholas* "the best juvenile [magazine] that lives" and thus were seeking "the best writers" as their contributors.[24] They did not want the magazine to be a pseudo-adult venture; nor did they want it to descend into "sermonizing" or "wearisome spinning out of facts."[25] Davis's first piece for *St. Nicholas*, "Naylor o' the Bowl," appeared in the December 1873 issue; other writers for the magazine included Louisa May Alcott, Edward Eggleston, Samuel Clemens, Robert Louis Stevenson, Rudyard Kipling, George Washington Cable, Bret Harte, and William Dean Howells. At the turn of the century, *St. Nicholas* began to include stories written by children, and the magazine published first works by Edna St. Vincent Millay, William Faulkner, and F. Scott Fitzgerald, among others. Although most of Davis's contributions to *St. Nicholas* occurred during the 1870s, she continued to contribute to the children's magazine for more than thirty years; her last submission appeared shortly before her death.

The year spanning from the spring of 1873 until the spring of 1874 constitutes an amazingly energetic artistic surge in Davis's literary career.

During that period, Davis published her excellent short story, "A Faded Leaf of History," in the *Altantic* and numerous items in *Peterson's*, *Youth's Companion*, and the *Galaxy*, in addition to joining the contributor's list at *St. Nicholas*. But, most significantly, in that year she serialized two novellas and one novel: "Berrytown," which appeared in *Lippincott's* from April to July 1873 and was published later that year as *Kitty's Choice: A Story of Berrytown, and Other Stories*; *Earthen Pitchers* (in *Scribner's Monthly* from November 1873 until April 1874), her best novella and undoubtedly her best study of women's lives both in terms of its artistry and her ability to rise above her conservatism; and *John Andross*, the novel which was serialized in *Hearth and Home* from January until May of 1874 and immediately published in book form. If in "Berrytown" we see Davis continuing to struggle with the issue of women's changing role in society, as she had in "Men's Rights" and "Two Women," in *Earthen Pitchers* she conquers her doubts and finds the honesty and artistic integrity to present her opinions without the plot and characterization manipulations of the earlier works; she extends that same integrity to *John Andross*. It was a year of extraordinary artistic achievement, the best she had had since the publication of *Waiting for the Verdict*.

There is no record of Davis's correspondence concerning her submission of "A Faded Leaf of History" to the *Atlantic Monthly*, for which William Dean Howells had assumed the editorship. Important, if unannounced, changes in editorial policies had occurred in the years since Davis had submitted her work directly to James Fields. Howells has a reputation today as an editor who encouraged and published women writers, especially those in the realist school. But a survey of the last two years of James Fields's editorship of the *Atlantic Monthly* and of William Dean Howells's first two years in that capacity offers some interesting insights. Under Fields, one-quarter of the contributions were by women authors; when the gauntlet was passed to Howells, women's contributions actually increased slightly, to 27 percent. However, if we study the periodical's published works over this four-year period from a generic perspective, a quite different breakdown appears. Of the fiction and essays published when Fields was completing his editorship, 23 percent were by women authors and 77 percent by men. When Howells began his editorship, the percentage for women dropped to 17 percent, leaving 83 percent of the fiction and essays to be produced by the journal's male contributors. Thus, while each editor included approximately one-quarter of their selections from women writers, women's contributions were much more significantly relegated to poetry under Howells's early editorship, with less than one-fifth of the *At-lantic*'s essays and fiction being written by women. For an author such as Davis, who did not publish poetry, this represented a significant decline in publishing opportunities.[26] And, in Davis's particular situation, this fact simply added new difficulties to an already awkward situation. It undoubtedly took courage for Davis to submit a story to the *Atlantic* once again, but she also knew that she had an extraordinary short story, equal in artistry to her submissions of the early sixties.

Not only was the story accepted, but when the publishing firm of Houghton, Mifflin decided two years later to prepare a collection entitled *Little Classics: Childhood*, they sought permission to reprint "A Faded Leaf of History" in their collection.[27] The collection assembled previously published works that revolved around a child character; the other contributors included Louise de la Ramée (Ouida),[28] John Ruskin, Elizabeth Stuart Phelps, and Charles Dickens. *Little Classics* is aptly titled; "A Faded Leaf" is a classic short story in American fiction. The tale conveys Davis's insistence upon genuine history; it is beautifully written, uniquely combining grim realism with Christian allegory. In this story and, subsequently, in her centennial pieces, Davis blends the earlier historical romance tradition begun by Catherine Maria Sedgwick and continued by Nathaniel Hawthorne with a documentary realism similar to that employed by John Greenleaf Whittier in *Margaret Smith's Journal*.

During a quiet winter afternoon, the narrator of "A Faded Leaf" discovers in an obscure corner of an old library "a curious pamphlet" from William Penn's era. The narrator notes that, in spite of its formal beginning, it is not some dry government report but a personal testimony, almost too commonplace for standard historical interest. "I have left the facts of the history unaltered," she assures the reader, "even in the names; and I believe them to be, in every particular true."[29] Davis thereby once again explicates her theoretical valuing of the commonplace and genuine history. Her astute knowledge of Pennsylvania history, which would be revealed even more fully in America's centennial year, is here interwoven with the personal histories of her characters.

"A Faded Leaf" is the story of early colonists seeking financial and spiritual profit in the New World. John Dickenson was a real-life figure in Pennsylvania history. His story, as detailed by Davis, represents the abuse of Native Americans by some of the early colonists. When the colonists are shipwrecked off the Florida coast, Dickenson attributes their "fate" and, indeed, all their hardships, to a judgment of God rather than to his own mismanagement. Yet the colonists' decisions, especially as Davis depicts their negotiations with the Native Americans on shore, is always mismanaged by Dickenson, whose sense of superiority alienates the Native Americans at the same time that he needs their assistance if he and his family are to survive. Davis was, like her contemporary, Lydia Maria Child, a defender of Native American rights. She bitingly remarks upon the colonists' actions: "It is instructive to observe how these early Christians met the Indians with the same weapons of distrust and fraud which have proved so effective in civilizing them since" (223–24).

Yet, as with any other of her exposés on mistreatment of human beings, Davis refuses to depict all Native Americans as "noble savages." They, like members of all other races, are neither "saints nor sinners" but mixtures of both. The tribal chief, Cassekey, treats the colonists with hospitality, although Florida had been plagued in recent months by a deadly famine. To the Native Americans, Davis observes, the food and clothing they confiscated probably seemed like a gift from *their* God: "There is a good deal of kinship among us in circumstances after all, as well as in blood" (224). This summarizes the theory of democracy behind all of Davis's fiction, but it is a lesson John Dickenson refuses to learn. His distrust of Cassekey's advice leads him and his family into the hands of ruthless Native Americans who strip the travelers naked and stuff sand into his baby's mouth. It is only through the intervention of the chief's wife that Mary Dickenson is given something with which to cover herself and the child's mouth is cleared before it suffocates. A few of the Native American women nurse the white baby, saving its life and restoring its health.

The actions of Dickenson's wife and child offer alternative histories of colonists' settlement in the New World. It is the baby who occasions the colonists' final salvation after they have been forced to higher ground by a flood that covers the coastal region. Word of a white woman and child wandering through the wilderness spreads among the tribes and the Spanish fort at St. Augustine. The soldiers send out a rescue party, bring the nearly starved colonists back to their fort, and eventually convey them into the Carolinas. That spring the Dickenson entourage journeys on into Pennsylvania, where John Dickenson "became a power in the new principality" (237). The narrator, however, refuses to trace the child's history: "He will always be to us simply a baby . . . sent by his Master to the desolate places of the earth with the old message of love and universal brotherhood to His children" (237–38). The journey into the wilderness, Mary and the child, the flood, and St. Augustine all are allegories overlaid upon

Davis's genuine history to unite the brotherhood of man—and sisterhood of woman, she notes, for it is when the "savage foster-mothers" nursed the child that Christ chose to bless the pilgrims (238).

*   *   *

In April 1873, four months after the original publication of "A Faded Leaf," *Lippincott's* ran the first segment of Davis's serial, "Berrytown," which was subsequently published by Lippincott's press under the title *Kitty's Choice: A Story of Berrytown, and Other Stories*. At that time *Lippincott's* could count among its more frequent contributors Ivan Turgenev, Henry James, Sarah B. Wister, Sidney Lanier, Constance Fenimore Woolson, and Octave Thanet, and it had demonstrated that it was especially interested in publishing local-history stories. Davis's novella, appropriately, depicts the rise of "progressivism" in formerly rural areas. Berrytown is satirized as

> the Utopia in actual laths, orchards and bushel-measures of the advance-guard of the reform party of the United States. It was the capital of Progress, where social systems and raspberries grew miraculously together. Thither hied every man who had any indictment against the age, or who had invented an inch-rule of a theory which was to bring the staggering old world into shape. Woman-Suffrage, Free-Love, Spiritualism, off-shoots from Orthodoxy in every sect . . . Radical New England held the new enterprise dear as the apple of her eye.[30]

With "row after row of cottages" imitating the "row after row of prolific raspberry bushes" that supply "the great Improved Canning-houses," Berrytown is a prototype of the city of the Utopian future that Edward Bellamy would embrace in the next decade. But Davis does not embrace this vision of progress because it stifles imagination and creates a system in which humans become mere "dead weight [that] clogs the wheel of the machine" (5).

The novella fails artistically in several ways, but the work is important in Davis's canon, for it constitutes a continuation of the process she had begun in "Men's Rights": her struggle to find a balance between the Domestic Woman and the New Woman in her fictional representations of women. In *Kitty's Choice*, Davis delineates the negative aspects of each type of woman and also attempts to suggest strengths in each. But her discomfort with both types is apparent; her ambivalence may well come from the issue of "types" itself. As an artist, one of her greatest strengths had always been to avoid stereotypic characterizations, to assemble the complexities of human nature in each individual. But in this attempt to address what was a very topical issue of her day, Davis's narrative lurches from one side to the other and often leaves the reader bewildered as to a character's motives. Yet, from a late twentieth-century critical perspective, the novella affords us an opportunity to study one woman author's struggle with these issues and the resultant evolution of her position.

The two opposite types are Catherine (Kitty) Vogdes, the daughter of Fanny Vogdes Guinness and stepdaughter of Peter Guinness; and Maria Muller, the sister of the gentleman to whom Kitty's mother arranges marriage for her daughter. Maria's parents are not part of the story; she is an independent woman who participates in the business of the world on her own. Kitty, however, is a childlike eighteen-year-old who has never been more than walking distance from her home and has been discouraged from participating in the social activities of her small community by her mother, whose Calvinist Presbyterianism sees corruption in every aspect of Berrytown's progressive attitudes. If Davis attacks the questionable progressivism of Berrytown, she also critiques the other extreme—people like Fanny Guinness who fear any kind of progress. Fanny, "[l]ike the mass of women . . . viewed the matter of love from the sentimental L.E.L. standpoint. It had been a forbidden subject to Kitty" (7). Thus Kitty is raised to be a woman with no ideas and no opinions of her own. Davis does not admire Kitty or her self-definition, "I am Peter Guinness's daughter"; and she demonstrates how this debilitating education makes Kitty a complacent dupe in her mother's scheme to marry her to a socially prominent and religious middle-aged man for whom Kitty has no affection.

Mr. Muller desires Kitty precisely because she is so maleable and thinks her well-developed maternal instincts make her the perfect partner to assist him in running his reformatory school, which houses three hundred young boys. Kitty accepts the entire proposition because she has been raised to do "what's right" and to do her "duty." She convinces herself that the pending marriage and her work in the reformatory will be "working for Christ," the only explanation that aids her in understanding how this in fact *is* her duty. If Davis does not admire Kitty, she understands the process by which Kitty is forced into her role, "the closing-in process by which society, expediency, propinquity, even moral obligations hedge many a man and woman and drive them into marriage" (14). Kitty believes that working for Christ as a wife and mother is the only path open to her, although her mother insists that she is a "free agent" and may make up her own mind about Mr. Muller's proposal. Kitty's "choice" is ironic, of course, because it has been completely mapped out for her.

When Dr. John McCall, alias Hugh Guinness, enters her life, he provides the "mystery" that has been missing from her dull, unimaginative life, but he is about to become engaged to Maria Muller. Even with the changes that this state of affairs brings in Kitty, Davis observes that it is the "homeness" about such women, who are like "tame dog[s]," that attracts men; Kitty is repeatedly depicted as dropping to her knees to rest her head on her father's knees, and one imagines that will be her posture throughout life if she marries Mr. Muller. However, Kitty is bright enough to observe the differences between her relationship and Maria's relationship with John McCall: she is fascinated by the "alive, suggestive, brilliant" conversation the two activists and philosophers share "in a language she had never learned. . . . They were drinking life and love with full cups" (24). This discovery acts as impetus for the courage Kitty gathers to tell Mr. Muller that she cannot marry him. Davis is careful to depict the way in which men's attitudes toward women not only help to shape such women but to maintain them as an ideal: "Women like Kitty, to whom Nature has denied the governing power of ideas or great personal beauty or magnetism . . . [have] a certain impalpable force to their most petty actions and words, to which men yield"; they are the women for whom men die, and "whom the world yet keeps sacred in pathetic memory" (28).

Kitty's belief that the only path open to her is marriage also causes her to view other women as competition, and she finds Maria's intelligence and self-assurance especially threatening. Thus, when Maria and John separate, Kitty sees the way open for her and, in her least flattering moment, remarks with snide triumph, "Poor Maria." Yet suddenly, and without narrative support, Kitty finds the strength not only to pursue John McCall, but to leave her home and travel to Philadelphia to bring him back on the pretext that it is for her father's sake. Davis does denote Kitty's lack of sense in packing a huge trunk for a night's travel her failure to realize that she would need money in the city, and her complete ignorance of people and urban life, but the instant Kitty sees John's wife, an opium-eater and drunk, lying in a prison cell near death, she is transformed into a self-sufficient woman with compassion for the pathetic soul before her. She then takes command of her relationship with John and pronounces that, regardless of his present feelings, he must stand by this woman because that was an obligation he undertook when he married her. Davis seems to admire

Kitty's combined self-sufficiency and self-sacrificing nobility at this moment; and, of course, Louise McCall conveniently dies so that Kitty and John may marry.

Davis's characterization of Maria is even more variable, however, and in it we see the author's personal struggle with certain aspects of the New Woman she admired, others that she despised, and still others that she seems to have admired but to which her own lifelong education would not let her rise. Thus when Maria is first introduced into the novella, she is a refreshing opposite to Kitty, even if she is condescending to her brother's fiancée. When Kitty can only define herself as her father's daughter, Maria turns to her brother and asserts, "see how our social system works." Most women, she observes, with her own brand of competition, are content "to be the fool or slave of a lover or a husband or a son" (10). Yet when she witnesses Kitty's discomfort upon first seeing the young ruffians whom she is supposed to nurture at the reformatory, Maria takes her hand and gently tells her that there is work to be done other than just marrying. She quietly counsels Kitty to discuss her future life with Mr. Muller before she decides to marry; of course, this is an idea so foreign to Kitty that she cannot accept it and Maria never again attempts to assist or advise her young companion. In fact, when she finishes giving Kitty a tour of the reformatory, she "nodded down on Catherine from the heights of brusque sincerity of the Women's Rights people" (12). This supposed aspect of nineteenth-century feminists' behavior riled Davis, but in thus condemning feminists, Davis more readily revealed a defensiveness about her own lack of overt participation in the movement. Years later, she was reported to have proudly exclaimed to a friend, "I never belonged to a club nor to any kind of society; never made a speech and never wanted to do it."[31] Her assertion has a delightful sense of independence to it, unless we read it in the context of her life's struggle with her decision not to participate. She tried to engage women's rights issues through her artistry and sometimes she succeeded, but she was never comfortable with her own position.

Thus, as Davis shifts back and forth in her portrayal of Maria, the independent woman is seen as correctly identifying Kitty's lack of opinions and her "fine eyes and pink cheeks" as precisely what her brother wants in a wife, but, conversely, she is depicted as insincere in her own desires to live without a husband. When Maria enters the room which John McCall has just occupied, she becomes pale and is defined as suffering from "the hysterical clairvoyant moods and trances familiar to so many lean, bilious American women" and protests that a husband and children are "obstructions to a woman" who is a "free soul" like herself (22–23). In the next breath, however, she admits that "when I meet a kindred soul, higher, purer than mine, I give allegiance to it. . . . And then—Ah, there is something terrible in being alone—*alone!*" (23) Even Kitty discerns that what Maria defines as "spiritual affinity . . . looks very like love" (23). It is not until the tenth chapter of the novella that we are informed that Maria is *Doctor* Maria Muller; once she realizes that John is not going to marry her, she is described first with her title, then more fully as Doctor Maria Haynes Muller. Artistically, this progression is appropriate; in each step of her decision to recapture her sense of herself, she recaptures more and more of her own name, her own identity. But when a patient refers to her as Miss Muller, she rebukes him with self-revealing bitterness, " 'I earned my right to the title of physician too hardly to give it up for that which belongs to every simpering school-girl. . . . Besides,' with a queer pitiful smile, 'the sooner we doctors sink the fact that we are women the better for the cause—and for us' " (34). Davis ends the chapter with an ugly depiction of Maria collapsing in tears and knocking her medical books on the floor: " 'And I was willing to give him up for that—that trash! . . . He would have married me! And I must be kept from him by a law of society . . . a damnable law.' For Miss Muller had taught herself to think and talk like a man" (34).

Thereafter, Maria lacks self-confidence and must ask her brother to intercede in her relationship. She does not go after John, but sends her brother to bring back her lover. In spite of her declaration that their future lives depends upon John's remaining with them, her brother does not take her seriously, dawdles along the way, stops to see Kitty, and thereafter completely forgets his errand. Maria believes that John will not marry her because of his secret wife, so she determines to erase that difficulty. She struggles with her decision but is depicted as foregoing morality for her own personal satisfaction: she insists that John attend with her a meeting of the Inner Light Club because the discussion concerns the possibility of men and women living together without the bonds of wedlock when Berrytown's vision of the great new republic is fully developed.

The Inner Light Club is introduced as a woman's organization, and suddenly, although the reader expects Davis to continue her attack on Maria, she instead changes course to satirize men's expectations of a woman's club. John cannot believe that any great thinkers are among these women; he expects to see Advanced-Woman types, women who wear loose sacques and trousers and have short hair, a "sharp nose and sharper voice" (39); but although this gathering is held in a dirty and decrepit building, it is attended by no such stereotypic women. In fact, one-third of the audience are Quakers, women who fought slavery and have since "taken up arms against the oppressors of women with devout and faithful purpose" (39). Davis's admiration for the Quakers had been well established through her earlier fiction, and the satire of conservative men's expectations now leads us to expect support for Maria as a character. However, when John insists that Maria leave with him, asserting that if he had a sister she would never hear such things as these women were proposing—women have to be "pure and spotless" but the women inside are just "shallow girls" (40)—Maria does not protest, nor does she return to her meeting. Although she suddenly thinks to herself that John is "small brained" in his attitudes, she returns home and that evening has an "attack of syncope"; it is "about that time that the long and painful [affliction] of the ulnar nerve began which almost destroyed her usefulness as a surgeon" (41). This attack is not unlike the neuralgia that Davis contracted in the early years of her marriage which sometimes made her own career very painful to pursue. We are left at this point with the sense of Maria as a bitter spinster whose life's work depended upon the approval of her conservative lover.

But this is not the end of Davis's story. Kitty's choice, ultimately, is to marry John McCall. All the straggling ends of the story's plots are resolved: Fanny Guinness conveniently dies, but only after reassessing her attitudes toward John and deciding *he* is the perfect husband for Kitty; Peter Muller no longer runs his bookshop but lives with the McCalls in Delaware and travels to Berrytown a few times a year to check on the store; Kitty still has no opinions of her own, is too fond of dress, but is a "neighborly, lovable creature" (48). And we expect the novella to end thusly. But Davis herself cannot accept this portrait; she brings Maria back into the text. Maria is now a prominent and successful lecturer. The Guinness men are "hopelessly conservative," but Maria stays with Kitty and her family when she is in the area. After her visit, Peter and John discuss Maria's strengths in front of Kitty: Maria is a "fine woman . . . [with a] fine mind," better mind than many men have. Their discussion only reignites Kitty's jealousy and forces her to criticize Maria for the attention she pays to her dog (satirically named Hero). But when Kitty leaves the room, Peter tells John that, as men, they have the perfect world—an old-fashioned woman with no "ruling" notions such as they would have to put up with from Maria. John agrees and tells his young son that when he grows up his business in life will be to take care of his mother.

Davis ends the novella with the information that Kitty, in fact, rules her husband and her house with "little regard for justice"; John does not realize it and Kitty herself hardly does. It is a detailed indictment of the Domestic Woman, both from the perspective of men's manipulations to keep women in such a role and of the ineffectuality of domestic "power." Thus, although Maria has already faded into the background again, Doctor Maria Haynes Muller ultimately fares best in Davis's depiction. This conclusion is so tacitly asserted, however, that it tells us more about Davis's discomfort with her decision than it does about Maria herself. Yet Davis did make the assertion, and she would continue to try to find avenues through which she could argue for women's strengths, capabilities, and rights—without having to confront outright the decisions she had made in her own life. In the interim months between the completion of *Kitty's Choice* and the serialization of her next novella, Davis reshaped her thoughts, conquered her own fears, and finally wrote the story that she had been unable to achieve in *Kitty's Choice*.

*   *   *

The announcement of the founding of *St. Nicholas* coincided with the publication of the first segment of Davis's serialized novella *Earthen Pitchers*, published in *Scribner's* from November 1873 through April 1874. A perusal of the other contributions to the volume in which this serialized novella appeared reveals the blending of romanticism and realism in editorial policies of the time: James T. Fields's poem "Agassiz"; George Washington Cable's "Belles Demoiselles Plantation"; poetry by Celia Thaxter; Gail Hamilton's "Captain Millicent"; a poem and a short story by Bret Harte, "Luke. (In the Colorado Park—1873)" and "A Monte Flat Pastoral" respectively; Jules Verne's "The Mysterious Island"; and two essays that reflect the continuing assessment of women's positions in society—Mary E. Beedy's "The Health and Physical Habits of English and American Women" and William S. Tyler's "The Higher Education of Women." The latter advocated advanced education for women, but on the premise that women could thereafter use their education to keep men on the straight-and-narrow; in other words, we are little removed from previous decades' attitudes about women and education. That failure by women to find personal freedom is the central theme of *Earthen Pitchers*. It is Davis's best extended study of women's lives; for one sustained moment, she is able to bring her artistry and her honesty together to bear testament to the pervasiveness of the tragedy of women's stifled lives.

Earthen Pitchers is set in Philadelphia and on the Atlantic coast, Davis's two favorite locales. The introduction of Jane or "Jenny" Derby into the text through her family history recalls in many ways the early years of Louisa May Alcott's life—a father who is a truth-seeker, patriot, and reformer, renowned for his humanitarian views but with little capacity for earning money, and the daughter who shares in his exploration of the ideas and people of their time.[32] Jenny now lives alone in Philadelphia, writes for several newspapers, including reviews and "a woman's column," and she is renowned for the Bohemian Saturday evenings that she holds. She barely survives financially, but her ability to draw people to her has become an economic boon to artists' agents: they commission the walls of her room to display the latest European paintings, knowing that the right people will have an opportunity to view them there. Jenny is known for her forthright expressiveness, but cautions the English visitor who wants to stereotype her that she is not a typical American woman: "I am outside of all orthodox lines. But women can go on to man's ground with safety further here than in England."[33] Jenny puts that opportunity to use whenever possible; she knows that these people do not care about her personally, but she also realizes that the townspeople "talk of me as a sharp woman pushing into a man's place. People come here and they know me afterwards as Jenny Derby: a genial, warm-hearted little thing that needs help. And they're all ready to help" (77). She writes because she must support herself and her life-style of personal freedom, although if she had money her preference would be to write poetry. But Jenny's economic situation has forced her to learn to use others, including the women acquaintances that she makes; if they need assistance finding work, she supplies it, but she expects homage or some favor in return. She has entered the world of men, and she manipulates it as well as they and better than most. But Jenny's characterization does not make her unlikable; her strength and honesty have great appeal, although they are very disconcerting to her cousin, Kit Graff. When he tries to patronize her with compliments of her "genius," she denies that attribute: "I have covered up my real character in a reputation for wit and fancy just as I hid the bare walls with those pictures, which don't belong to me. It is shop-work with me" (79).

Earthen Pitchers is the story of two women who are trapped within the wrong realms: Jenny, who has her freedom and works outside the home, longs for the domestic life, for marriage to Niel Goddard, the up-and-coming artist of the day in Philadelphia; Audrey Swenson, on the other hand, appears to be an inane, domestic woman, one whom all the men assume needs to be protected, but she harbors within herself an assurance of seemingly unbreakable strength—she has a talent and she intends to pursue it at all costs. Audrey cares nothing for the ways of society or the literary world; she is at heart a musician and a singer, and she intends to escape the stifling life of marriage in order to pursue her art. Yet each woman has been taught that self-sacrifice is the duty of women. Jenny seems to have risen above that ideal; however, it is she who sacrifices her way of life, her property rights, her complete sense of self in order to marry Niel Goddard. Audrey, on the other hand, has been taught the legend of the coast—that selfishness will be punished; it can never be escaped. Thus she finally sacrifices her life and her talent to care for Kit. At the novella's conclusion, eight years after the events of the story, Jenny has her marriage to Niel and three sons; she manages their farm very successfully, but she and her sons live in near rags so that Niel might wear the finest linen. He winters in Philadelphia so he can be near the literary sources and people of the day, and Jenny sells part of their property to finance a trip for Niel to Venice so he may work on his great treatise (which still remains unwritten). Jenny, who wanted a love that "could be touched, tasted, handled" (204) has had to stifle her natural passion, and she has to ignore the periodic affairs in which her husband indulges. Her only satisfaction is knowing that he will always return to her. Jenny's life is a tragedy, as Davis depicts it, not so much because of these events but because Jenny accepts them as all that she warrants.

Audrey is no more domestic eight years later than she ever was, but her life centers on her husband and her child. During Kit's illness, which was the impetus to Audrey's decision to marry, she worked long hours providing music lessons for the children in the community and thereby destroyed her voice. Kit suggests that Audrey's talent served its purpose by helping them survive. Audrey loves her husband and refuses to lament having marketed her talent, but "unconsciously, she gives you the impression that she has her own home and her own people elsewhere, and will be gone to them presently" (720). Nor can she find the mystical element in nature that had acted as the muse for her own musical expressions. In the final scene, after the baby is put to bed and Kit has walked down to the beach, a flock of kingbirds fly up from the bushes: "Old meanings, old voices came close to [Audrey] as ghosts in the sunlight" (721). She seems to be "at home" once again and begins to sing in response; but her voice is cracked and tremulous: "Then she knew that whatever power she might have had was quite wasted and gone" (721). When Kit returns, he sees that she is troubled and asks in surprise if she is sorry that her "little song" has found no audience other than her immediate family, that her little song is all she leaves for posterity. Audrey replies, "I leave my child," and repeats it again momentarily. The novella concludes: "Her husband, at least, was sure that she made no moon over that which might have been and was not" (721). The pathos of the phrase "at least" is the lasting impact of *Earthen Pitchers*. This time there is no question as to which woman Davis sympathizes with or her belief that Audrey's life, like Jenny's, was tragically wasted. It is impossible not to read some sense of Davis herself in that portrayal.

Two other themes that the novella presents are of significance as well: the role of publishers in commercializing literature and the way in which American male authors are coddled, catered to, and supported whether they produce or not. Davis's satirical depiction of John Shively, the publisher, is superb. He is new to the field, having "advertised himself into a fortune, and now he's trying to advertise himself into society" (75). Shively especially denigrates sentimentalism, but he thrives on name-dropping European royalty as his "dear" friends. He loves to boast of his "errand boy" beginnings and of how he rose from his former class; he insists that he wants to raise his former class to the level he has attained, but in the next breath also insists he would not bring his daughter to Miss Derby's, though she is "very nice."

Shively has come to Jenny's party for a purpose: his social contact with artists here garners their work for his journals at a much cheaper rate. He currently wants a series of "half scientific, half popular" articles written by the well-known young writer, Niel Goddard. It requires the cynical philosopher and musical critic, Sturm, to delineate Shively's process, however: once, authors wrote from what they had within them to express but now "the book, the poem, or the article is manufactured and offered by these— these venders, just as a clown turns a summersault or plays a fresh prank— for the sake of a few pennies" (78). Shively is greatly amused by the truthfulness of this depiction. Sturm explains,

> It's the demand, the steady sale of literary work that has coarsened its quality. When a man used to give five years to the elaboration of the idea which he offered to the public, he fancied some of the real water of life sparkled in it: but these tradespeople in ink are like men who keep drinking booths at a fair. They stir up their drinks in an hour. What do they care whether they sell

nectar, or bitter beer, or ginger-pop, so that the pressing thirst of the crowd is satisfied and they get their cursed money? (78)

It is a depiction that incorporates both the publisher and the author; in this manner, Davis was able to expound on her own frustration of having constantly to produce fiction for economic reasons. It was especially galling in this instance, because she knew this novella was above the norm and had been stirring within her for a long time. It is only Shively himself who appreciates Sturm's tirade, however. He proudly pontificates:

> Yes, sir. I've known a dozen painters and authors who talked of being true to art, and meant to do some great work, and they all took to daubing pot-boilers of landscapes for the auction-shops, or scribbling skits of stories and articles for the newspapers and magazines. Pegasus is greedy for his oats, nowadays, and I can always tell when he is ready to lay his wings by and hire out to do carting by the day. No talk of Art then, but—"how much a column, Mr. Shively?" (78)

In her characterization of the publisher, Davis at last has the opportunity to renounce the pressures of production and the economic abuse she has felt for years from her publishers. There is no doubt, of course, that Mr. Shively's publications will thrive.

But it was perhaps in her depiction of Niel Goddard that Davis found her greatest relief from the old boils that had long festered but had never been allowed to burst or to heal. Niel Goddard is supported by his brother, given luxuries by Jenny, paid homage to by all of Philadelphia because he is *the* young man of promise. He has been the young man of promise for quite some time, that is true, but his potential—ah! what potential![34] Niel is like the "bloated little angel fish at the bottom [of the pond]. In front you see his wings outspread ready to fly. But it all ends with a miserable wiggle" (205). He refuses to work to support himself; he must have time to contemplate, to ponder, to shape his latest work. Very few of his works have appeared, but many are discussed. Jenny produces her columns, which Niel finds trivial and without merit, under the pain of neuralgia and worries about the "doctor's warning stories of other newspaper people who had suddenly collapsed and dropped from overwork" (200). Niel, however, will confront no such stress; he refuses to sell "whatever original power I have for mere food and clothes" (201).

In her depiction of Niel Goddard, Davis once again challenges the transcendental teachings of the supremacy of the Self; Niel "had been in the habit of making pilgrimages to Concord to sit at the feet of the Yankee Gamalile, Emerson" (206), and it is this education that has led him to believe that he is brilliant and exceptional, although he has never been put to the test. Davis does not ignore, however, Jenny's culpability in aiding Niel's self-indulgence. When Jenny first goes to the seashore and sees Audrey being badgered into paying old Pike for a fish that Audrey herself had caught, Jenny is incensed: "How can you let yourself be swindled?" she admonishes Audrey (203). And yet she fails to see that she is similarly allowing Niel to swindle her through his insistence upon his brilliance and his tricks of love; she is even willing to let him inherit the property that would have given her the financial security she needs. In Davis's opinion, men who wrote were often coddled, but women abetted the process, and it is this fact that she exposes through Jenny Derby's fate in order to warn young women who are blinded by love and the prevailing tastes of the day.

Kit Graff is certainly a more appealing male character; he is kind and caring and he truly loves Audrey. But he is like Niel in his assumption that he knows what is best for any woman better than she knows herself. Thus he insists that Audrey would be a fool to pursue her music; he assumes she would need Niel's assistance (as Niel also assumes, although Audrey has never considered the need for assistance), and that he would dupe her into performing in a theater with "tinsel, and bedaubed with paint, men reeking with liquor and tobacco flinging you bouquets" (205). Kit is certain that this fate awaits Audrey because he assumes she has no real talent. In fact, everyone assumes they can advise Audrey, and both men don "an air of ownership" when they are around her. That they are oblivious to her inner strength, to the fact that she ignores all of their advice, and that she refuses even to take their arms—a physical rejection of their profferings of protection and support—completely escapes both men; they are confident in the correctness of their assumptions because they are male and have been educated to that belief. Perhaps most representative of male "ownership" is Niel's interpretation of Audrey's talent as merely the evocation of a muse for himself; it never occurs to him that she may pursue her talent in her own way and for her own self-satisfaction. The tragedy of her story, of course, is that she abandons her talent to act as nurse (the practical muse) for Kit. Davis's narrative is not bitter or condemning in tone; she simply presents the details of these four characters' lives and their beliefs in the plot of the working woman's realm (realism) and the mystic legend of the seashore (romanticism). Ultimately, the romantic legend is defeated; only the reality of the two women's caged souls remains.

Marriage is no longer a solution, a happy ending, for Davis's fiction; it is merely part of the commonplace tragedy. This novella deserved attention in the literary periodicals, but, because it was not published in book form, it received virtually no critical comment. It has been almost equally abandoned by scholars in the last century. It deserves better.

*   *   *

In addition to writing "Berrytown," *Earthen Pitchers*, and several short stories, Davis had continued to prepare the *Andross* manuscript. After *Waiting for the Verdict*, this novel has probably received the most attention from twentieth-century critics. Tillie Olsen suggests that, while *Andross* was "the first novel of this kind" and Davis's "alive social intelligence" remained, her "power for art [was] wasted and gone."[35] If one studies Davis's sources and her fictional treatment of them, however, challenges to that assertion become apparent. An earlier, melodramatic depiction of the Whiskey Ring had been published by J. F. Hume, but as George Arthur Dunlap correctly asserts, Davis's novel "is notable for its fearless revelation of the operations of the Whiskey Ring . . . a realistic account of the deep hold that the Ring has on John Andross."[36] The characterization of Houston Laird "is one of the best portraits of the political boss that we shall find" in American literature.[37] As Gordon Milne observes in his study of the American political novel, few political novelists of the time had yet taken on "the big bogey of the corporation's rule"; Davis was one of the rare exceptions.[38] Hamlin Garland continued the tradition, eighteen years later, in *A Spoil of Office* (1892), as did Upton Sinclair in *The Jungle* (1906).[39] But as always, Davis was concerned with "the story of to-day," and this story came from the front page of the newspaper she wrote for, the *New York Daily Tribune*.

It was, as several scholars have observed, a courageous act for an individual to write about William Tweed's Whiskey Ring at the time when the ring and others like it were still in power. In fact, Tweed's conviction came only days before the first segment of her serialized novel appeared. The trials for many of his associates were as yet forthcoming. The *Tribune*'s continuing exposés on Tweed's illegal maneuverings, including his connections with the state legislatures, legal system, and President Grant's administration, played a prominent role in the overthrow of that ring.[40] The unraveling of Tweed's pervasive corruption reads like a nineteenth-century Watergate. It began in January 1870, when the *Tribune* ran several small items on various distillery frauds that had been uncovered, mostly at local New York warehouses. These small distilleries were themselves trafficking in nearly half a million dollars' worth of illicit whiskey.[41] The newspaper also recorded the strange sequence of events that subsequently raised questions about evidence and witnesses who suddenly reneged on their testimony. Several of the cases were dropped completely. The *Tribune* itself moved on to other issues, such as the new city charter proposed by William Tweed and Peter Sweeney. Persistent in its interest in these men, the *Tribune* pieced together in the next several months the connections between the city's political base and the illegal distribution of whiskey. As their evidence became more and more conclusive, the *Tribune*'s exposés moved from the editorial columns to front-page charges of corruption. It became clear that Tweed was "ravenous for the honors of the National Democratic Committee"—that is, to have control over national politics as well as local.[42] That committee's organ, *The World*, repeatedly published assaults on the *Tribune* over the next several months, but Davis's New York paper, like several others in the city, would not be silenced.

The World's rebuttals and the letters that the *Tribune* received during 1870 are a study in Americans' refusal to believe that their political leaders were engaging in corrupt practices. Even Horace Greeley, the *Tribune*'s founder and, until his death in 1872, its editor, accepted the chair of the Republican General Committee on January 5, 1871, announcing:

> I hear it asserted that we are a *Tammany* party and that we are organized in the interest of a plundering Ring! Such charges are to be answered not by words, but by deeds. If it shall at any time be proved that any member of this Committee is acting in the interest of that infamous cabal whereof Wm. M. Tweed is the embodiment, I shall move his expulsion, if no one else anticipates me in so doing. But I trust no necessity for such action will ever arise.[43]

In spite of Greeley's assertion of trust, the pervasive influence of the ring would be exposed within the year by his own managing editors at the *Tribune*.

A contested election in January of 1871 was the beginning of the end for the ring, although it would take a full year before it actually crumbled. In that January election, Horatio N. Twombly had received a majority of votes for a city position, but the party gave the position to John Carey. Twombly's protest made front-page headlines in the *Tribune* when the decision for Carey was upheld by the party at Tweed's urging. The *Tribune* doubled its efforts. In April there again seemed to be a crack in the machine, but Tweed drew together all of his resources and the April 17 headline of the *Tribune* reads: "TAMMANY JUBILANT. A Republican Judas Found." For several weeks thereafter, nothing about the ring was mentioned in the paper. However, in July, when the ring sought to disband a labor rally, a chasm opened that even Tweed could not pull together. He attempted to sacrifice the Collector, a Mr. Connelly, in hopes of saving the rest of the members of the ring, but the rallying labor force that was now adamantly anti-Tammany demanded answers. In October, the mayor of New York City was prosecuted for malfeasance, and the *Tribune* revealed that an estimated thirty million dollars of city money had been transferred to ring leaders. Most of that amount was in real estate owned by William Tweed, his wife, and his son. The ring was overthrown at the November 9 election. The next day, the *Tribune* victoriously declared the election a "People's Triumph." The corruption was linked to the highest levels in Grant's administration, and even a staunch Grant supporter such as the *Tribune* had to declare his administration a failure.

These were the bald facts out of which Davis carved her novel. Two other items, however, reveal how astutely she interpreted the inside maneuverings of the ring and translated those perceptions into fiction. In January of 1870, before the *Tribune* had connected William Tweed with the Whiskey Ring, they had published a small, seemingly unimportant item in their column on the New York legislature:

Bills Introduced

By Mr. TWEED—Amending the act relative to frauds in assessments for local improvements; authorizing the Richmond County Supervisors to issue and dispose of bonds to pay the county debt; amending the general mining and manufacturing law; to charter the Old Ladies' Retreat of Poughkeepsie; to extend the Manufacturing act; to enable the American and Foreign Bible Society to unite with the Baptist Publishing Society; to amend the act relative to the Encroachments and Obstructions of the Harbor of New-York; to enable mechanics and Laborers to adopt rules and regulations for their mutual protection; . . . to amend the charter of the Metropolitan Savings Bank of New-York; to provide for revising the Statutes of New-York.[44]

It all seemed very proper at the time, but this notice is representative of what Davis recognized as Tweed's manipulative control over every aspect of New York City's political machinery; his wisdom in interweaving his political maneuvers with seemingly charitable acts, especially those of a religious nature, had securely established him as one of New York's most generous philanthropists. In *John Andross*, Davis incorporates into her portrayal of Houston Laird this ability to manipulate not only political machines but social acceptance. Laird's characterization is juxtaposed with the honorable Civil War hero, Colonel Lattimer, who refuses to consider the evidence of corruption piling up against Laird and who thus unwittingly becomes the ring's figurehead. The colonel's bases for disbelief are precisely the philanthropic measures that Laird is so skilled at publicizing for himself.

The other source for Davis's novel is a small subtext to the ring's exposure in the pages of the *Tribune*: the fall of a Mr. Bailey, collector of the Thirty-second District, a minor figure whose function was to monitor the taxation of the distillers. But in Collector Bailey's story, Davis recognized the seeds for a study in human nature. Known as a reputable citizen, Mr. Bailey was drawn by his own financial problems into the illegalities he was supposed to conquer. The collector disappeared after embezzling 120 thousand dollars. His attempts first to cover up the embezzlement and then to regain the funds in order to rectify his original "error" become the manner in which John Andross cinched the ring's iron grip upon himself. Still, Davis knew that issues of human nature and of social pressures were more complex, and it is in these two features that *John Andross* stands out as a graphically realistic study of financial and moral corruption. If the polluted landscape of *Margret Howth* had become "thoroughly American," so too had corrupted human nature become thoroughly commonplace. In her study, Davis indicts the means by which society educates its young people to a lust for money and status while failing to educate them morally. No sentimental, panacean ending is allowed: the ring regains its force in Davis's novel, just as it would historically reshape itself and reappear in only a few years.

John Andross was first published as a serial in *Hearth and Home* and subsequently in book form by Orange Judd, the New York publishing house. In an era confronting three million unemployed workers, bread riots, and children starving in the streets (in spite of many northern women's campaigns against tenement conditions), the abuse of the public system by people like Tweed enflamed Americans' anger and frustration, but in *Andross* Davis seeks to replace anger with an understanding of the causes of individual and grand-scale corruption. Education is always prerequisite to reform.

John Andross is an especially likable young man; Dr. Clay Braddock pulled him out of the indigent life to which he was born, and John has subsequently ingratiated himself with everyone at Nittany because of his honesty and hearty good fellowship. His rise, like Silas Lapham's in Howells's novel of the next decade, is swift but less capricious, since Davis is interested in portraying how a young man like Andross becomes a pawn in the political machinery run by ruthless and powerful men.[45] But throughout John's history, Davis weaves clues of the seemingly minor erosions in his morality: while he generously uses his earnings to buy things for others, he does so excessively and often with borrowed money; Andross is also "an infidel," though, to please Braddock's mother, he attends church and sings the hymns with a singular voice; more importantly, Andross is drawn from one "caprice of theory" to another, at one moment studying "Descartes' old doctrine of naturalism" and the next tossing it aside for whatever old or new theory better "served [his] purpose."[46] Davis's opinion of a capricious reliance upon theories had been well established in previous novels and short stories and is now reinforced by the colonel's comparison of Andross with America's greatest romantics: "It's a power, sir . . . Henry Clay had it . . . and Emerson appeared to me to be a bit of sheer intellect, looking at men and women as a profitable drama; everyone of us gave him our best . . . Hawthorne was like one of his own beautiful uncanny ghosts; but Holmes was a man of men. Well, you have that same human attraction in you" (78–79). Echoing Davis's own recollections of these authors, the colonel's alignment of Andross with nonrealists supports Andross's continual dreamlike belief that all will come right, even as he slips deeper and deeper into the ring's mire.

Davis suggests that Andross's faulty education, which stemmed from his deprived childhood, represented a form of learning more readily correctable for future generations than the other kind of education—in social customs—which destroys the moral fiber of young Americans. In 1907 Henry James would briefly detail this concept in *The American Scene*, but his expatriot view was limited to what he deemed to be women's faulty education.[47] For Davis, the dangers were not those associated with gender. Andross's failings are from one form of social deviancy and another is represented in Anna Maddox, the judge's daughter. (Judges never fare well in Davis's work; Judge Maddox is typical with his "pulpy" brain and flagrant ego.) Anna is pretty, petted, and patronized; she is repeatedly defined by her "clinging-vine" attributes. Behind this facade, however, lies the Anna who has readily learned that such theatricality can give her absolute control over her male admirers. She personifies the coquette that society may claim to reject but which it in fact trains and encourages. In this education, money is equated with success and happiness. When her father's fortune, and hence her place in society, is threatened, Anna becomes the perfect dupe for the ring. At Laird's command, she seduces Andross into voting against his conscience. In contrast to Anna Maddox, Davis depicts what by then had become a standard in her fiction, what I will term "the woman of confidence": a natural woman, intelligent, plain, sensuous but never seductive, and self-confident. She prefers the country to the city, nature to artifice, honesty to theatricality. Still, Davis never allows her women of confidence to become saints; thus, Isabel Lattimer at times is hot-tempered, speaks sharply, and makes erroneous judgments. Her strength, however, is an uncompromising honesty that shields her from the allurement of men like Houston Laird.

Davis's portrayal of the ring's leader is, indeed, one of her most realistic creations. Laird is gracious, has an enviable social status, and maintains his anonymity in connection with the ring at all costs. The colonel, who represents the typical innocence of Americans with regard to political corruption, unwittingly suggests that Andross meet his Philadelphia friend "to convince you how unjust these stories about Rings are. My friend controls one of the most powerful in Philadelphia and New York, and a more estimable man I defy you to find, in every relation of life. Tender husband and father, head of Christian associations, aged workmen's homes, hospitals—I don't know what charities—" (79). The friend whom the colonel praises for his philanthropy is Houston Laird: "He delights in gathering young men about him in his office—religious clubs and so forth—and shaping their future course" (80). That is precisely what Laird does for Andross, and it almost costs the young man his life.

Davis's descriptions of the intricate machinations of Laird's ring are detailed with a remarkable precision, even considering her exposure to the events in the *Tribune*. She outlines the exact manner in which money is placed on the casks of whiskey at the distillers' warehouses; if no money is present, the whiskey is taxed. If it is present, the collector, who is supposed to regulate the taxation, pockets it and lets the barrels pass. So, too, does Davis expose the connections of the ring to newspapers, lawyers, judges, county commissioners, national political figures, and on and on. Her depiction of Julius Ware, the disreputable newspaper reporter who is under Laird's control, continues her assessment of the bias of much newspaper reporting, an examination which she began in "Life" and which reappears in several of her subsequent works and would become a staple of later naturalistic fiction. In *Andross*, however, the reporter is a willing accomplice.

Ware not only plays the ring's game but expands on it for his own profit by giving up reporting for a more lucrative profession—public ministry. This alignment of confidence men and Christianity would become an integral theme in Davis's other major novel of this decade, *A Law Unto Herself* (1878). There, too, the only person to reject the artifice of this figure is the woman of confidence.

In *Andross*, Davis returns to her naturalistic techniques in other ways as well. The ring's power is a force that traps its victims and propels them into vice and an early demise. It is the kind of force that Frank Norris was to render most graphically in *The Octopus* (1901) and *The Pit* (1903). Davis's novel stands, with the works of Norris and Theodore Dreiser, as an early representation of the American naturalists' awareness of the power of the marketplace. When Braddock tells Andross, "for God's sake, be a man. It seems to me as if you stood on the edge of the pit," he asserts that "no man [is] a thief or liar but by his own free will" (51). Andross, however, knows better:

> There are forces outside of a man nowadays—here, all around him—just as strong to compel him to ill-doing as ever there were in the wilderness or in hell. . . . For years I have been in the hold—not of a man, nor a devil, but of a corporation. . . . The purpose of this club or organization is unmixed evil. As for its power—it has money. Unlimited money. It buys and sells at will the government and interests of the city where it belongs: it controls the press, the pulpit, the courts. The best men are muzzled by it, are forced against their will to serve it . . . I'm not making melodrama out of this matter. I've been the slave of this Thing. (51–52)

Some men and women do escape the ring's control, as by mere chance Clay Braddock and Isabel Lattimer do, even though they are battered by the rippling effects of its control. Braddock himself is drawn into the peripheral arena of that world; when he escapes, he declares that it feels as if he has come out of a "befogged, impure dream" (315). The cost of escape for Braddock and Isabel, however, is the integrity of the love they once had for each other. They renew their bonds of affection at the novel's end, but when Braddock eagerly asks, "You do love me as much as before?" Isabel can only answer truthfully: "I can never say that I love you as I did, Clay" (316). Davis's readers may have wanted a romantic resolution, but her adherence to realism would not allow it.

Nor does it allow her to remedy the lives of Anna Maddox or John Andross. Anna marries Julius Ware, who professes to live a life of poverty while accepting for himself expensive gifts and luxurious housing from his followers. Only his wife, who has grown slovenly and has to teach piano to feed her children, knows what poverty is. She had been well-educated by social customs to the artifice of the coquette, but she is incapable of seeing through her own husband's artifice. She still believes Julius is a genius. Andross's blind allegiance to Anna parallels hers to Julius. He risks his own life to save her, a risk for which she is completely ungrateful. Washed ashore after rescuing Anna from near drowning, Andross for the first time sees her for what she really is; only then does he feel the desire to live. He struggles for breath, feeling that he can survive if he can bear the pain until Isabel and Braddock can reach him. Davis strikes her most naturalistic chord in the novel's concluding lines: "Could he bear it? Meanwhile the tide flowed steadily inward, but gave no answer" (324).

$$* \quad * \quad *$$

Harriet Beecher Stowe's earlier warning to Davis that she could never expect a fair review from the *Nation* proves particularly apt in the case of the magazine's treatment of *Andross*. The reviewer from Davis's old nemesis refuses to grant her the very purpose of her novel: "As an illustration of the effect on social life of the exorbitant tax on distilled liquors, it cannot be too highly praised, but it was not intended, probably, to illustrate anything of the kind."[48] Having denied her the least intelligence about her own novel, the reviewer ironically displays, in pure Colonel Lattimer fashion, a stubborn refusal to accept the pervasiveness of the ring's power. After acknowledging that *Andross* was "stronger and more real" than the other books reviewed in the column that day, he adds: "The principal characters are the 'Whiskey Thieves' . . . [who] are represented by Mrs. Davis as having held complete control a few years ago of the government of the State, as having dictated appointments, abated taxes, passed and repealed laws, murdered their enemies, and enriched their friends and themselves *ad libitum*."[49] This is, of course, precisely what the Tweed Ring had done.

The reviewer for the *Atlantic Monthly* echoed James Fields by admonishing Davis for not being cheerful, but he admits that she "writes well" and, incongruously, that she "has a very agreeable humor."[50] The reviewer apparently found the entire Whiskey Ring scandal humorous: "We may expose ourselves to the danger of being thought to be in the pay of a rich and powerful corporation—we only wish we were!—when we say that there is a chance that the power of the 'whiskey ring' is somewhat exaggerated" in *Andross*. As if upbraiding himself, he then reflects, "One should remember, however, that even in works of fiction it would be very hard to exaggerate the evil doings of Pennsylvania legislators and rings." In spite of his vacillating stance on the ring, this is the most thorough review that the novel received. The reviewer acknowledges Davis's power of description and the accuracy of her "local color." Disturbed by her depiction of Braddock as an ungainly, shy man, he prefers the characterization of Andross himself: "the acquiescence of a weak man is admirably given. . . . It is alone quite good enough to make the novel a success." Although uncomfortable with Davis's forthright tone, the reviewer somewhat snidely acknowledges the realistic portrayal of Anna Maddox: "The weak woman, Anna Maddox, is, as we have said well drawn; with a vein of malice perhaps, which, however, does not outweigh the lavish amount of praise the vine-like young woman gets from men when they write novels, and in real life. The woman who writes novels has no patience with such as she, and the authoress's scorn for the blindness of men in being so easily hoodwinked is very great." The reviewer concludes that *Andross* is "clever and interesting."

The *Harper's* review is perhaps most telling for juxtaposing Davis's realism with the preferred literary tastes of the day. It begins with comments on *Andross*: "Whatever other quality Mrs. Rebecca Harding Davis may lack as a writer, she can not be accused of being deficient in strength. In *John Andross* . . . she shows her ability to bring corporations, 'rings,' and politics into her service for working out the purpose of her story."[51] Yet the reviewer concludes: "For pleasant reading, this book contains rather too much and too deep rascality. The characters are living people, not lay figures, but are too generally not pleasant acquaintances. The story seems overburdened with material." Instead of the realistic details of Davis's novel, the reviewer asserts that he prefers the "dainty touches" of *Thorpe Regis*, a popular romance by a "lover of flowers, and the book is one to be enjoyed out-of-doors on a quiet summer day." It would be several years before these periodicals would acclaim literary realism; Davis always garnered their mixed praise, just as Stowe had predicted.

*   *   *

With the nation's centennial celebration in 1876, Davis's love of accurate history was given full voice. Such celebrations often encourage popularized versions of history, but Davis specifically wrote against the popular strain. Her meticulous research spawned articles in three major periodicals: "Old Philadelphia," a two-part serial published in *Harper's*, which, as Helen Woodward Shaeffer has observed, probably influenced S. Weir Mitchell's later novel *Hugh Wynne: Free Quaker*;[52] "Old Landmarks in Philadelphia," published in *Scribner's*; and "A Glimpse of Philadelphia in July, 1776," in *Lippincott's*. The latter periodical, of the same caliber as the *Atlantic* but less regional in scope, was edited at the time by the historian John Foster Kirk. Undoubtedly, Davis's ability to render history accurately, whether in nonfiction or fiction, attracted *Lippincott's* editor to her work. *Lippincott's* had published *Kitty's Choice* in 1874 and continued to publish Davis's novels and shorter works over the next twenty-five years. Davis made many friends among the *Lippincott's* contributors. She viewed the literary journals, and especially *Lippincott's*, as "a sort of club where we pen drivers can put on our choice apparel and meet each other with a hint of how time goes with us."[53]

The editor of the *Tribune*'s literary column wrote a long review of "Old Landmarks in Philadelphia" in the May 23 column, emphasizing Davis's "decided taste for research among the gray and cobwebbed monuments of the past, and rare skill and fidelity in recording the results."[54] "Old Philadelphia," however, is the best of the three articles. It is beautifully written, meticulously researched, laden with old photographs, and, in keeping with her own literary theory, it brings to the foreground the people rather than the city.

The first part of the serial focuses on colonial Philadelphia, beginning twenty years before Penn's arrival with the utopian vision of the Swedish king, Gustavus Adolphus, who financed a trading company in the area. His purpose was to establish a city of brotherly love with economic equity and religious freedom for all. Noting that this "first society in Philadelphia" is often overlooked, Davis details the daily lives of the Swedes who settled what is now the Southwark area of Philadelphia.[55] She describes the extreme hardships they faced, the political and personal histories of the period, their accomplishments (every child in the community was taught to read), and the discords of colonial life (the woman who renounced her husband, reclaimed her maiden name, and lived in "poverty and pride" by herself thereafter; the raucous clergyman who disrupted the community). In so doing, Davis reinforced her theory of the commonplace, making these people vibrantly real. She is also careful to name these figures from the past and to connect them to Revolutionary and present-day descendants, thus linking history with the "story of to-day." Along with William

Bradford and Benjamin Franklin, she records the histories of Margaret Mattson (a condemned witch whom Bradford released against public opinion), Jane Fenn (a noted preacher whose life deserves to be turned into "song or novel" [713]), Charles Thomson (the teacher, known for his truthfulness, who became the Secretary of the Continental Congress and an honorary member of the local Indian tribe), Charles Willing (a Philadelphia merchant), and numerous other figures. To Davis's mind, the lives of these people, not mythologized heroes, represented the true continuity of American history.

* * *

Tillie Olsen admonishes Davis for her absence when the leaders of the women's movement "sat in . . . and took over the platform to read their Women's Declaration of Rights" at the 1876 Philadelphia Centennial Exposition.[56] However, in the same letter from which Olsen selectively quotes, Davis tells Annie that the fact that she attended only one evening of the fair was "for many reasons of which lack of interest was not one." For one to gain a deeper understanding of Davis's reactions to the centennial celebration and to the women's movement further elaboration is necessary.

Sponsorship of a national celebration demanded enormous amounts of financial backing, thus a Centennial Commission was formed in 1872 to raise those funds and organize the exposition to be held in Philadelphia. The organizers' years of fund-raising, however, coincided with the Wall Street crash of 1873, which precipitated numerous bankruptcies and business failures and was followed by rampant unemployment and homelessness. Nevertheless, nearly six million dollars of private, local, state, and federal monies were devoted to the centennial celebration.[57] As Alan Trachtenberg has observed, these types of fairs in the nineteenth century "were pedagogies, teaching the prominence of machines as machines of a distinctively American progress."[58] This was especially true for the Philadelphia exposition. Although more than two hundred buildings were erected, none was so important as Machinery Hall; there, the typewriter was first displayed, along with Edison's advanced version of the telegraph and Alexander Graham Bell's addition to American technology—the telephone. One can only imagine Davis's reaction to the overall "aesthetics" of Machinery Hall. For twenty-five years she had depicted the oppressiveness of industrial capitalism's machine system on the American worker, but here, in her own hometown, was a memorial to the machine, which has been described as

> a profusion of mechanisms [that] seduced the eye: power looms, lathes, sewing machines, pumps, tool-making machines, axles, shafts, wire cables, and locomotives. . . . For sheer grandeur and sublimity, however, . . . the two most imposing structures in the Hall [were] the thirty-foot-high Corliss Double Walking-Beam Steam Engine, which powered the entire ensemble . . . and its counterpart, a 7,000-pound electrical pendulum clock which governed, to the second, twenty-six lesser "slave" clocks around the building. Unstinted but channeled power, and precisely regulated time: that combination seemed to hold the secret of progress.[59]

It is little wonder that Davis continued to write against such images of "progress" for the remainder of her life.

Equally important is the fact that, although a Women's Department was advocated by the exposition's organizers and the women were authorized to establish a separate building for their exhibits, no funds were allocated to the group. Elizabeth Duane Gillespie, chair of the Women's Department, continued her efforts in spite of this snub, and the Woman's Pavilion became a reality. However, although the pavilion included inventions and artwork by women, it was not supported by a consensus of feminist leaders. Elizabeth Cady Stanton opposed the pavilion because it ignored the challenges to the legal system that women had undertaken: "Women's most fitting contributions [to the centennial]," Stanton declared, "would have been these protests, laws, and decisions, which show her political slavery. But all this was left for rooms outside the Centennial grounds."[60] Such legal restrictions on women's lives was to be the focal point of Davis's next novel. In spite of the extraordinary efforts of some feminists to present the Declaration of Rights of Women (which the Centennial Board had refused to allow as part of the regular ceremonies) and Susan B. Anthony's courageous assertion of her right to present the document, the centennial remained a controversial issue among leading feminists and would certainly have been so for Davis.

Davis's position on women's rights is more complex, however. When she suggested to Annie that she had not attended the exposition but was certainly interested, we have a recreation of her literary stance on women's rights: interest, but from a distance. It is like the oblique preference she gives to Maria Muller's choice over *Kitty's Choice*. But no aspect of Davis's personal and professional lives carries greater irony than this stance, since she had fought against precisely this type of passivity in so many other causes. Davis explained her avoidance of organized movements to Annie: "The fact is when our sex get into corporate bodies I have an instinct that warns me off—haven't you? 'I am never less a woman than when I have been among women' as Seneca *didn't* say—."[61] Written only months after the Philadelphia exposition, Davis's statement seems a direct response to the women activists who attended the symposium. Davis abhorred organized "corporations" of any kind because she believed that even those with the best intentions tended to stifle free expression. The character of Cornelia Fleming in *A Law Unto Herself*, the next novel Davis was to publish, personifies Davis's beliefs on this count. A particularly telling clue to Davis's feelings about the movement is also discerned in her autobiography: "Before the birth of the New Woman," she asserts, "the country was not an intellectual desert, as she is apt to suppose."[62] This returns us to an awareness of Davis's resentment of what she perceived as the New Woman's corruption of history, but, more specifically, it reveals Davis's still tender sense of her own lack of formal education. Unlike Harriet Beecher Stowe, whose confrontation with Victoria Woodhill's advocacy of free love changed her attitudes about the women's movement, or Rose Terry Cooke who, in spite of her refusal to idealize women's lives, did not advocate suffrage, Davis did not oppose women's right to vote, but she did align herself with conservatism on this issue. And not opposing the vote is not the same as working for its enactment.

Feminist activists in this period had emerged out of several earlier groups that had advocated radical social changes of one kind or another. The early reformers, the subjects of and often authors of sentimental fiction, were important contributors to the rise of feminism. Although they depicted the woman's sphere as domestic because they believed that arena allowed them superior spiritual and moral domain over men, they joined the antebellum women's movement, remaining the conservative voice within it but a mainstay as well.[63] Temperance advocates also played an early role in the rise of feminism. This movement has been disparaged in the twentieth century as enlisting ultra-conservative women for a prudish cause; in reality, the seeds of feminism were strong within this activist group. They were especially concerned with recruiting working-class women and not limiting their advocates to the middle and upper classes.

Probably no group, however, was as important to the rise of nineteenth-century feminism as the women abolitionists. They acted out of a sense of moral duty, and their quiet strength gave a legitimacy to the movement that helped to draw many people to it. From this early reform group came leaders such as Sojourner Truth, Lucretia Mott, and Lydia Maria Child.

Davis adhered to the tenets of each of these three groups, although to varying extents. Though she did not consider herself a sentimentalist and, as a realist, rejected certain constraints in their philosophy, her sympathy was with the sentimentalists; and, as denoted in the analyses of several of her works, she sometimes used those fictional techniques to strengthen her own artistry. Davis's interest in temperance preceded the organization of the Women's Christian Temperance Union; she wrote several short stories and the serial "The Tembroke Legacy" to caution against the dangers of alcohol abuse. Davis most specifically adhered to the abolition movement; she not only advocated freeing the slaves, but used her fiction to argue for that cause in the pages of a major national literary periodical while the war was still in progress and the issue yet to be resolved. Thus we have Davis's alliance with all three of the preliminary movements that shaped the feminist movement of the mid- to late-nineteenth century. Yet, as her fiction, nonfiction, and correspondence show equally clearly, she could not take that final step of advocacy. To do so apparently threatened her sense of herself and her own choices: she continued to write, to have her voice as she had insisted she must when she married—that is, she advocated Maria Muller's choice in many ways; but she had taken up the reins of a workhorse, marriage and family and a sense of identity from those roles that exemplify Kitty's choice. She could prod the horse into reform, temperance, and abolition, but she could not speed it on its way to embrace feminism more fully.

Thereafter, Davis moved more and more toward a conservative position on woman's role in society. The centennial year and its events seemed to push her toward a decision; she continued to represent women of confidence and self-sufficiency, but ultimately she chose to champion the Domestic Woman, just when so many in the nation were moving on. This struggle epitomizes Davis's life: although she was a highly intelligent, creative, and productive author, she proceeded to live intellectually as well as physically within the domestic realm. She would occasionally find a political cause in the next twenty-five years that allowed her to express her liberal reform voice, but she was about to publish her last major novel of the decade—indeed, of the next two decades—which, while it realistically addresses the archaic legal restraints on married women, also reveals that this ingrained struggle was becoming her personal commonplace.

*　*　*

In the year following the centennial, Lippincott & Company published Davis's novel, *A Law Unto Herself*. Many women writers of the 1860s and 1870s were concerned with depicting the realities of married life for American women. Davis had begun her interest in this theme with her exploration of marriage-marketing in " 'In the Market,' " but the tradition of realistically depicting the marriage relationship began with the fiction of Rose Terry Cooke, and it was continued by later realists such as Sarah Orne Jewett and Edith Wharton.

In the 1870s, Cooke presented her ideas about the harsh existence of rural women's lives not only in her fiction but in her essays in the pages of *The Independent*. The breadth of Cooke's writing—moral tales, romances, and grim realism—parallels Davis's. Both writers were highly prolific and consequently have an equally broad range of quality in their writings over the duration of their careers. Undoubtedly, as Davis began to publish an occasional article in *The Independent* in the mid-1870s, she was influenced by Cooke's vision of rural women's lives. Davis extended this vision by bringing her concern for industrial "progress" to bear upon it. The influence was mutual, as Cooke would indicate in the coming years. In the early 1870s, Elizabeth Stuart Phelps, whom Davis admired, also published several articles in *The Independent* advocating new careers and rights for women, including the right to vote. These three authors—Davis, Cooke, and Phelps—often confronted similar contemporary issues, each distinctively, and yet their attitudes and artistic visions form an interesting and often representative synthesis of women writers' sociopolitical perspectives in the last quarter of the nineteenth century.

The focus of *A Law* was women's legal rights, but Davis also addressed other contemporary issues, such as the increasing interest in the occult, and she includes an excellent depiction of a séance in the opening pages of the novel. Davis realistically conveys the fashionability of this craze, unlike later writers such as John Hay (*The Bread-Winners* [1884]) or Henry Blake Fuller (*The Cliff-Dwellers* [1893]), who were themselves fascinated with the process; Davis believed that séances and other facets of the occult were simply another popular means of escaping the realities of life instead of confronting them. At the beginning of the decade she had published a study on mesmerism in *Peterson's*; in that short story, Ellen Wynn is a woman of confidence who thwarts the efforts of a confidence man to swindle a young woman out of her fortune through the use of mesmerism.[64]

A Law more fully explores the confidence man, a character type that Davis had been developing for several years. Yet there is an increasingly cynical tone that creeps into this novel. *The Nation*, still uncomfortable with explicit realism, described *A Law* as "interesting if not agreeable," but accurately noted that the "rasp of asperity characterized [Davis] more and more."[65] The reasons for this tone were both personal and professional. Davis had two children at home to care for in the midst of her writing. Charles and Nora were still small, and Richard, who was at prep school, was already showing a pronounced proclivity against academics. Two years later he would confess to his mother that he had been so unhappy during this period that he had contemplated suicide.[66] At the time of his confession, Davis recorded in her diary that Richard "told me how when he was at that wretched school he had once made up his mind to kill himself & wrote a letter beginning 'Accuse no one of this crime. I die by my own hand.' And we never knew what was in the child's mind."[67]

In addition to these personal worries, Davis's cynical tone undoubtedly evolved from her concern about the lack of change in societal attitudes during the last fifteen years of her writing career. If anything, industries and corporations were more abusive of their employees,[68] women were still treated as second-class citizens legally and socially, and the realism she had crafted over the years was still being disparaged as not "agreeable" because it was too grim—an echo of Fields's criticism of her first novel. While her personal problems of the period would abate, her professional concerns would never lessen: by the time of Hamlin Garland, Frank Norris, and Stephen Crane, Davis's early pioneering contributions to literary realism would be largely forgotten. Though she continued to write short fiction in that genre, she would find it increasingly difficult to find a publisher among the powerful New England journals. She would not find a permanent outlet for her sociopolitical commentaries until after 1889, when she became a regular contributor to *The Independent*, a period during which the New York weekly was recognized for its topical political discussions. Her association with *The Independent* lasted until her death.

In spite of Davis's cynicism, *A Law* also includes some astute observations on human nature. Her characterizations, always her strongest literary asset, are succinct and acutely revealing. Captain Swendon, for instance, has "the nervous conciliatory haste of a man long used to being snubbed," and "like every man conscious of his own inability, he asserted himself by incessant managing and meddling for his neighbors."[69] The ironic gender twist (typically such traits are reserved for a meddling woman) is of the same sort that caused the *Atlantic* to question her portrayal of Braddock as "shy" in *John Andross*. Part of Davis's insistence on realism was to deny traditional stereotyping: not all men are strong, effective, intellectual beings; some women are.

The central theme in *A Law*, as the title suggests, is the question of legal and social restrictions on women. Jane Swendon is "a law unto herself" at the beginning of the novel in the sense that she does not abide by social customs in dress, speech, or attitudes. She was not raised in upper-class society, having had to fend for herself and her father most of her life; untainted, therefore, by social regulations, she has developed her own inner strength. Yet the male characters in the novel insist that Jane is "stupid" and "dull" because she does not fit the standard criteria of femininity, and Davis exposes how, even in a woman of confidence like Jane, these evaluations wend their way into her own self-image. Thus Jane accepts this sense of herself at the same time that her daily actions counteract it.

But the legal restrictions on women's rights are even less easily challenged. When the captain learns that he is dying, he cannot bear the thought of Jane being left to her own resources; as his friend Judge Rhodes ironically asserts, Jane would be foolish enough to follow her own mind. Thus her father begins to "market" her, insisting she dress in the latest styles and enter society. He brings Mrs. Wilde, the grande dame of society, out to their home so she may educate Jane to the ways of society. Most importantly, he selects Pliny Van Ness, the Christian philanthropist, as the perfect mate for his daughter. From their first meeting, Jane is repelled by Van Ness, with good cause—he is Davis's finest depiction of a confidence-man.

Pliny Van Ness is a fully realized extension of this type of character, which she had begun developing in her short stories and had extended in the depiction of Julius Ware in *John Andross*. As Karen Halttunen has determined, the confidence-man had been a topic of American advice literature since the 1830s, as an urban stranger who seems to offer friendship to the young ruralite entering the city for the first time, or as a demagogue who professes public concerns only for personal benefit, or as the gambler who embraces capitalist speculation. In all three types, the confidence-man is an usurper of legitimate power and a social outcast.[70] Davis realized, however, that the confidence-man was no longer an outsider; he *was* the political and social power of industrialized America. Julius Ware and Pliny Van Ness are just less successful versions of the William Tweeds of the nation, and, in spite of Jane's long-standing battle against her father's plans, she is compelled by her father to marry Van Ness.

Thereafter, Davis exposes the dehumanization of married women under the nineteenth-century American legal system; Jane must now escape the home that she had struggled to buy and which has automatically become her husband's possession. Her subsequent arduous journey in search of personal freedom is painfully realistic, but it also becomes a parody of the legal maneuverings necessary for Jane to escape her husband's control. After several weeks, she believes that at last she has found refuge with her father's friends, old Glenn and his wife, in the far-off Blue Ridge mountains. But Van Ness finds her even there; and though Glenn at first orders him out of the house because of Jane's obvious antipathy to the man, he reneges and tells her she must go with Van Ness because he is her husband. Only "Glenn's wife" argues against such cruelty: "No matter if she were his wife a hundred times . . . she shall not go back if she chooses to stay" (86). In spite of "the law within her" that denies Van Ness's rights over her, Jane knows at last that she cannot deny this more powerful force: "the Law."

The novel's conclusion, involving Jane's escape from Van Ness's legal grip and her renewed attachment to Neckart, appears to deny Jane's right to control her own life. Once she is happily married to Neckart, she tells him, "I know that I made many mistakes when I was a law to myself. You are my law now, Bruce" (89). But the final lines of the novel explicitly draw this statement into question: Neckart loves her, "Yet there are times when she seems, even to him, a woman whose acquaintance he has scarcely made, and whom he can never hope to know better" (89). That is, she has remained "a law unto herself."[71] The story's ambiguity is not unlike that of *Kitty's Choice*, and although it has a theme similar to that of Rose Terry Cooke's short story, "Mrs. Flint's Married Experience," which would appear in *Harper's* in 1880 and which describes a woman who is forced to return to a slavish marriage because her parish demands it, Davis cannot boldly depict the consequences as Cooke does when she has her character die as a consequence of returning to such a life. Davis hedges, presenting neither a fully developed Cinderella plot nor a satisfying alternative. Her suggestion that Jane does remain "a law unto herself" is oblique in the same manner as her depiction of the preferability of Maria Muller's life in *Kitty's Choice*.

This hedging is representative of Davis's challenge of the "Advanced Sisterhood." Though advocating the reform of women's legal rights, Davis presents the theory of Advanced Sisterhood as entailing the danger of so many popular theories: it could become a trap for women. Jane represents true individuality because she adheres to no one else's criteria. Cornelia Fleming, the member of the Advanced Sisterhood, is a woman who sets her path toward a singular goal even though she has no talent to support that goal. She admits that her art is mediocre, but she markets her wares according to the latest European fad and surreptitiously accepts money from Judge Rhodes in order to cover her living expenses. More importantly to Davis's criteria is the fact that both women are forced at varying times to mask their sexual passion.

The issue of women's sexuality had first been broached from a realistic standpoint by Rose Terry Cooke in the late 1850s. In Cooke's short story, "Too Late," published in the *Galaxy* in 1875, she continued the theme with a depiction of a woman whose passion must be repressed. Davis had advocated realistic assertions of women's sexual passion since the beginning of her career. Indeed, as a thirty-one-year-old single woman, she had shocked the staid romantics of Concord during her 1862 visit when she had bluntly asserted that women have the same sexual desires as men.[72] Even in her depiction of Kitty Vogdes in *Kitty's Choice*, Davis reveals the burgeoning sexual feelings and their subsequent repression in this naive young woman. Kitty stands half-naked in front of her mirror, pleased with her image as she thinks of the mysterious Hugh Guinness; but as she recalls that she is engaged to another man for whom she feels no attraction, she rebels against the implied usurpation of her body through such a relationship: "Her crossed hands lay on her wide blue-veined shoulders. She almost tore the flesh from them. 'I belong to no man!' she cried."[73] It is a momentary rebellion, but startling in its violence and in Davis's awareness of the pathos and irony of the fact that either act by Kitty—the self-inflicted tearing of her flesh or marrying the older man whom she does not love—would be a defilement of a woman's body. Society offered no viable alternative between a coquette and the seemingly asexual woman. Davis ultimately can find no resolution to women's social and legal problems. Jane finds happiness through marriage, but her plaintive cry to Van Ness earlier in the novel—"It must be a comfort to give your life to any certain work. . . . It's very hard to reach middle age . . . and find one's self fit for nothing!"—still echoes at the novel's end in both her life and in Cornelia's.

The problem, of course, lies in the social restrictions on women's lives. Davis is at her best in this novel in depicting society's rampantly poor judgment. In many ways, it prefigures Edith Wharton's novels of manners, which expose the ridiculous criteria that hold together social customs: the dowager who rules over all other entrants into the social ranks by insisting upon proper "blood" rather than money; the gilded furnishings that the *nouveau riche* assume constitute good taste; and the ways in which business veils itself in Christianity as a means to increase profits. Davis was well aware that the latter issue was not the province of men only. Thus, while Pliny Van Ness personifies the confidence-man who represents himself as a philanthropic Christian, we are also given a confidence-woman in *A Law* in the figure of Charlotte Van Ness, alias Mrs. Combes's spiritual manifestation, alias Madame Trebizoff and numerous other aliases. Pliny will, like the Houston Lairds of society, always survive, and Charlotte is several times offered a livelihood outside of these schemes. But Charlotte concludes, "Respectibility is such a bore!" and remains in her chosen profession (88). The point that Davis never lets her audience forget, however, is that the social body that is so easily duped by these artificial characters is the same one that insists upon the right to regulate women's lives and to deny them any say in their own future.

The Nation's review of *A Law Unto Herself* is particularly interesting, for the American literary world then verged on the dawn of fully embracing the realism that had been developing for half a century. As usual, the *Nation*'s reviewer did not like the "unpleasant" characters in the novel:

> but there is an undercurrent of recognized aptitude and a capacity for calling a spade a spade which sets [Davis's] writing in a category far removed from French morality . . . though she shows bad taste in various ways, or perhaps because of this, she succeeds in giving a truer impression of American conditions than any writer we know except Mr. Howells, while there is a vast difference between his delicately illuminated preparations of our social absurdities and Mrs. Davis's grim and powerful etchings. Somehow she contrives to get the American atmosphere, its vague excitement, its strife of effort, its varying possibilities. Add to this a certain intensity, a veiled indignation at prosperity, and doubt of the honesty of success, and we get qualities which make Mrs. Davis's books individual and interesting if not agreeable.

It was certainly one of the most favorable reviews Davis had received from the *Nation*. The difference between Howells's delicate "preparations" and Davis's "grim and powerful etchings" is, of course, the difference between romance and realism.

*   *   *

The cynicism that infiltrated Davis's last novel of the 1870s signaled her desire for a break from her demanding artistic life. She had been writing against financial pressures and against the grain of the literary mainstream for twenty years. When Annie Fields sought at the end of the decade to reestablish their friendship by once again inviting the Davises to visit Boston, Davis was cordial: "Indeed dear Annie I should be glad to take up the dropped thread again. But a week's visit with my three young Barnegats (pirates) would be too tough a knot to tie them with, I think."[74] Davis's letter was written in August from Point Pleasant, New Jersey, the summer resort to which the Davises had been going for several years. In rejecting a visit to Boston, Rebecca's exhaustion is evident:

> Mr. Davis left us in May [on business], and since then I had been travelling through my old camping ground, the North Carolina mountains, and have just settled [in] to rest. This has been our summer home for thirteen years and it has grown into a habit for my mother, brothers, and other friends to meet us here every August.
>
> The gathering of the clan is now in progress and of course I can not go away.
>
> Mr. Davis expects to join us the middle of September.
>
> Can you not spare time for a letter? Consider it one of the talks we might have had if I had gone and let me have a glimpse of you both and your sea side home, of which I have heard pleasant things.[75]

The staccato paragraphing suggests her mental fatigue. She took a deep breath of the coastal air and stepped back from the literary battlefield for a well-deserved rest; it was to be her "Indian Summer." Though in later years she would publish alongside America's best-known realists, this self-imposed "retirement" was probably the single most important factor behind the fact that her early contributions to American literary realism were often forgotten, since the 1880s are the years traditionally designated for the "rise" of realism.

5. Across the Gulf

DAVIS'S "RETIREMENT" was relative only in terms of her usual, prolific literary output. In the 1880s she published one previously serialized novel, ten short stories, five essays, and numerous children's stories, and she shifted her journalistic writings from the *Tribune* to *The Independent*. Although Davis's writings were especially sparse in the early years of the decade, her reputation was so well established that when her eldest son Richard introduced himself to his new acquaintances at prep sechool, their typical response, as he proudly wrote his mother, was: "any relation to Davis the authoress?"[1] Richard wrote his family almost daily from school, and each time he mentioned meeting any renowned literary figure, from Dr. Holmes to Walt Whitman, the message was always the same—their regard for his mother's work. Perhaps because they were secure in their reputations, the established American romantics always more readily praised Davis's innovativeness in bridging the literary genres of romanticism and realism than did the newcomers to realism. Perhaps, too, they were receptive to Davis's style because the 1880s was a period of literary and social transitions: Whitman published his autobiographical narrative, *Specimen Days and Collect* (1882), which combined realistic details of the Civil War and romanticized reminiscences of his youth but, in its literary criticism, focused on British romantics such as Carlyle; and James Russell Lowell's *On Democracy* (1884) sought to combine Old World charm with new American ideals. At the same time, Joel Chandler Harris was drawing upon his own experiences in the South to craft his African American folklore with its authentic dialects, and Henry James published his exquisite novel of psychological realism, *The Portrait of a Lady* (1881). Like Davis and Whitman, Mark Twain explicitly bridged the two genres, publishing *The Prince and the Pauper* (1882), *Life on the Mississippi* (1883), and *Huckleberry Finn* (1884). And, as the editor of the *Atlantic* and author of *A Modern Instance* (1882) and *The Rise of Silas Lapham* (1885), William Dean Howells was in the process of securing his place at the forefront of the new

American realism, while writers such as Mary Murfree, Sarah Orne Jewett, and Harold Frederic extended Howellsian realism, as Davis had, beyond the "smiling aspects of life."

America's sociopolitical changes during the decade were equally varied. After James Garfield's brief administration and Chester Arthur's unimpressive four years in the White House, Grover Cleveland (a close friend of the Davises and Clarke's fishing partner) took charge of the presidency. The organization of the American Federation of Labor seemed to signal fresh attitudes toward and of the working class, but the Haymarket Riot of 1886 shattered the nation's sense of political stability. In conjunction with this tenuous state of affairs, Davis would return in the latter part of the decade to her uncompromising literary critique of American society.

Davis spent the summer of 1879 at the family's usual Point Pleasant retreat. The rest and companionship of her family helped restore her peace of mind, and when she returned to Philadelphia at the end of summer, she carefully guarded her health by publishing more selectively. When one publisher became too aggressive in his attempts to secure her commitment as a regular contributor, she responded: "I do not see the use of any 'definite agreement.' If I can find time I will send you a story before Dec. 5th . . . As I may not—possibly—be able to do it—(though I have no doubt I shall)—it would be safe for you not to announce the story until you had the *Ms* in hand."[2] With this wavering assurance, it is little wonder the publisher sought a concrete commitment, but the author held her ground for the present. When the editors of *Current Literature* wanted to include a profile of Davis in an upcoming issue, she thanked them but declined: "There really is nothing to be said about me—for Current Literature. I am not writing any book and do not expect to publish one soon."[3]

Davis did choose to publish a select group of short stories, however. Momentarily feeling financially secure enough to publish selectively, she produced several excellent short stories during this decade. When time was an economic pressure, there was no room for theoretical experimenting; but when Davis had time to craft her short fiction, she often included naturalistic techniques. The first of her important short stories of this period was published in May 1880 in *Scribner's Monthly*. The issue in which Davis's story, "Walhalla," appeared reflects the synthesis of romanticism and realism that prevailed at the time in the major literary periodicals: the serialization of George Washington Cable's *The Grandissimes*,[4] the conclusion of Frances Hodgson Burnett's "Louisiana," John Burroughs's serial

"Notes of a Walker," and a long study by Edmund Clarence Stedman, "Edgar Allan Poe."

"Walhalla," a moral tale for metarealists, continues Davis's disparagement of the pressures that force an artist to market his or her wares. Young Hans, who resides in a small German colony in the mountains of South Carolina, is a wood-carver whose delicate craftsmanship reveals "an undiscovered genius."[5] But the peace of the colony and of Hans's artistic imagination are shattered when Reid, a young Englishman traveling in America, propels the local artists into a competitive marketplace atmosphere by announcing that the best wood-carver in Walhalla will be hired as a panel-carver for his brother's New York firm. "Walhalla" is an American folktale in the trickster tradition, but Davis's concern is not with the stranger who enters this community; rather, she focuses upon the citizens of "Walhalla" who must suffer the consequences of their attraction to the trickster's gambits. Davis synthesizes the trickster tradition with the modern realities; thus her language in this moral tale recalls her earlier usage of the scientific principles of deterministic fiction: Reid eyes each person as a "specimen" whom he must analyze and categorize, and his interloping into this community, armed with the ideals of marketplace competition, immediately enacts an evolutionary decline in the Germans' humanity. Davis had always highlighted this "disease of money-getting" in her fiction, and her later articles for *The Independent* would continue that tradition.

In Reid's journey to Walhalla, Davis also satirizes the mythological Valhalla against the realities of such a journey: Reid's passage involves the pastoral "two weeks of climbing among the clouds, of solitary communion with Nature," but Davis's vision of communion with nature includes "unmitigated dirt, fried pork, and fleas" (48). Once in Walhalla, Reid proposes the contest among the carvers; the winner will accompany him to New York with the assurance of "high and steady wages" (50). Appropriately, the subject for their carved panel must be the Flight into Egypt, and the promise of wealth quickens the blood of these native artists: "New York? Riches? Fame? The blast of a strange trumpet, truly" (51). The community quickly embraces the spirit of competitiveness, pitting the young Swiss, Hans, against George Heller. Hans is beloved by the Germans but, though they know he is their best artist, they assume because of his easy-going manner that he "will never make a stir in the community"; the blustery George Heller, however, is noted for his ambition and his fingers that "used to be as nimble as his tongue" (51). George sees the contest as a means for personal fame as well as for recognition for the community, thereby seeming to blend the American ideals of individualism and the common good; but the townspeople, relishing their own potential glory through association, are incapable of distinguishing art from artifice and thus support George. Hans, after all, was "a stout, common-place creature . . . beside this brilliant fellow!" (52)

Hans has lived a life of quiet comfort, working only as much as necessary and always finding hours to lie in the grass and listen to the sounds of nature. He is driven to enter the carving competition, however, by his love for Christine Vogel, a single mother, whose hard life has taught her that success and money are not trifles. In the competition that ensues, Davis, ever the pragmatist, delights in satirizing the myth of the artist as an impetuous soul whose every outlandish act must be excused by the title of artist. Thus, while Hans continues his regular chores and works on his carving in the evening, George, like Niel Goddard, foregoes all other work for the sweat and frenzy of his artistic production, of which he makes sure his neighbors are aware. To ease his feverish endeavors, George also "went to Godfrey Stein's inn and drank wine and brandy, and then more brandy, and forgot to pay. Genius is apt to leave the lesser virtues in the lurch"; but Stein understands: "he's got the true artist soul," he assures himself as he shuts his empty till (54).

The only person who believes in Hans is his mother, secure in her creed that God must ensure Hans's success because his good works have earned him such rewards. It is, however, Hans's own passivity, his own dreaming-self, that destroys his chance in the competition; to lose the competition is, in fact, a kind of salvation, since the city is a place of corruption. What Hans loses, however, is much more significant—that invaluable sense of his own artistic vision. He believes that George has captured in his carving the beauty, "that inscrutable meaning," which Hans found only in nature (58). Incapable of understanding how a "paltry sot" like Heller could "compel the secret [of nature] into his work, which to him was but a holy dream" (58–59), Hans destroys his own carving, deciding it is "but a fairly cut mule" next to Heller's (59). Only after he destroys it does he realize there may have been "great hidden merit" in his seemingly commonplace carving (60). Davis recreates in this scene the artist's dilemma that she had first recorded in Hugh Wolfe's story—that attraction to the prevailing standard of Beauty that denies the value of "cruder" but more realistic works of art.

Ironically, this metarealistic short story was the last fiction Davis published in *Scribner's Monthly*. The periodical was discontinued in 1881, but its publishers continued the same policies in *Century Magazine*. Howells became a leading contributor to the *Century*, and his publications there included not only fiction but literary criticism, including an 1882 piece on his protégé, Henry James. In the remainder of that year, James published two articles in the *Century* and subsequently became another of its regular contributors. While the *Century* thus was a receptive place of publication for Howells and James, Davis would not find a place in its pages until 1895. This was due in part to her own decision to publish less in the early years of the decade when the periodical was changing formats, but it was also due to the lack of a mentor-advocate system among women writers. The major women editors of the period were relegated almost exclusively to periodicals of children's literature; in that capacity, they encouraged and published other women's writings, but there were few other such connections, male or female, available to Davis or the other women authors of this period. A survey of *Scribner's Monthly* and its continuation as *Century Magazine* for the 1880s reveals patterns not unlike those recorded during the editorial transition at the *Atlantic* in the previous decade, although the patterns are of an even greater extreme in this case. Thus, while a few women such as Davis, Constance Fenimore Woolson, and Helen Hunt Jackson published fiction or essays in the periodical during the decade, the woman writer most often published was "Mrs. Schuyler van Rensselear," who specialized in architectural essays. Once again, in the categories of fiction and essays (that is, works other than poetry), men's contributions constituted 83 percent of the published works. Although an impressive array of nineteenth-century American women authors appeared in the periodical during the eighties—Elizabeth Stuart Phelps, Celia Thaxter, Mary Mapes Dodge, Louise Chandler Moulton, Rose Terry Cooke, Julia Ward Howe, Elizabeth Stoddard, Rose Hawthorne Lathrop, "Sara Jewett," Harriet Prescott Spofford, and Annie Adams Fields—they were almost entirely relegated to the poetry columns. Yet, male authors now retained 60 percent of this category as well, with women's contributions limited to 17 percent of the fiction and essays and 40 percent of the poetry published.[6]

Josephine Donovan has documented the decline in "authentic works of women's literary realism" during the 1880s among New England "local colorists" as a result of the nation's move away from "a reverence for female activities, values and traditions."[7] Elizabeth Stuart Phelps's shift from realism occurred during this period, as did Rose Terry Cooke's criticism of the women's movement; other women authors incorporated or extended their literary techniques to accommodate the changing literary attitudes (one thinks of Sarah Orne Jewett's development of "imaginative realism"). Others continued to emphasize romantic and/or sentimental domestic themes, but that trend was specifically at odds with the literary periodicals.

The 1880s were difficult years not only for women authors; in all professions, the backlash against the feminist ideals publicly advocated during the seventies was beginning. Even careers traditionally assumed to be a woman's arena felt the brunt of the rise in conservative attitudes. Thus the policy of dismissing married women from the teaching profession, which began in the nation's capital, quickly spread geographically and to other professions as well. The idea of women having permanent careers became anathema to many Americans.[8]

Many women reacted by turning their attention to broad social issues. Davis had focused upon workers' living conditions as early as 1861, and by the late 1880s this became an important facet of the women's movement's concerns. Activists such as Jane Addams and Ellen Gates Starr worked to eradicate urban slum conditions by establishing settlement houses. One opposing response—escapist utopian ideals, such as those advocated by Edward Bellamy in his highly popular novel *Looking Backward* (1888)—had never been Davis's choice, and it would not be so now.

＊　＊　＊

The travels through the southern mountain ranges that Davis had described to Annie were published in a quasi-fictionalized, three-part travelogue for *Harper's New Monthly Magazine* from July through September of 1880. Davis had contacted the *Harper's* editors in 1878, suggesting that her experiences from "burrowing in the mountains during part of the summer" over the last several years would make a practical and informative contribution to their periodical, especially since she had "manag[ed] to get quite out of the ordinary routes of travellers."[9] The Adirondack area was then the fashionable summer resort locale, but Davis recognized that many people were now looking for new vacation spots that combined luscious scenery and economical accommodations. She proposed to draw upon her travels in "the Pennsylvania hills in Clinton & Centre counties[,] in the Southwestern part of Virginia or the higher ranges of Tennessee and North Carolina," observing that this was virgin territory for travelers as well as a new literary perspective.[10]

Although Davis had assumed she could publish the article that summer, her negotiations with *Harper's* and her writing of the long, fictionalized travelogue took nearly two years. "By-Paths in the Mountains" follows the route taken by a small group of well-to-do Americans who decide that their summer holiday should encompass more than just the usual fashionable resorts. "The average American," Davis narrates, "is afraid not to move with the crowd" (168), but the Morleys and their guests discover the new "Ca-na'an" wilderness and the strangely beautiful, quiet haunts nestled in the Maryland and Virginia mountains.

The travelogue is another example of Davis's exploration of documentary realism, and the storyline is complemented by detailed maps and landscape drawings of the mountain areas. These representations are sustained in the text by her attention to geographical details and the histories of the native people whom the Morleys meet during their travels. Meshach Browning, for instance, "was the Daniel Boone of Western Virginia. He lived to an extreme old age, and told the history of his life shortly before he died, in the rude, marrowy pioneer's vernacular. It fills a certain gap in American literature," Davis observes, "being not only a picture in detail of the savage youth through which every one of the States has passed in turn, but of a man of the woods . . . in whom the sense and the hunting instinct were as keen and strong as in a sleuth-hound" (176). In spite of these interesting asides about the state of American literature, "By-Paths" is not of the same caliber as Davis's earlier ventures into documentary realism. The fatigue and exhaustion out of which she penned this travelogue are evident. In spite of her usual lush descriptions of nature and commonplace people, the pace of "By-Paths" lags, and the laconic tone never attains the keen reflections that her readers had come to expect.

In the next year, Davis wrote only two short pieces for *Peterson's* and two children's stories for *Youth's Companion*. In July of 1881, however, she published a well-written short story in *Lippincott's Magazine* entitled "Across the Gulf,"[11] which is distinguished for its satire of a narrow-minded clergyman who believes he is a man of the world and for its acceptance of women who turn to the stage for economic survival. This latter theme was becoming a standard in Davis's fiction and was undoubtedly strengthened by the numerous acquaintances she and Clarke had made in the theater. Although Georgiana Drew and Maurice Barrymore were recognized as leading American actors (a tradition their children, Lionel, Ethel, and John, would continue) and *attending* the theater was now socially acceptable, the choice of acting as a profession was still considered morally dubious, especially for the lesser-known members of a troupe. "Across the Gulf" is also notable for its naturalistic themes, including that of the "brute" self revealed within the Reverend William Imlay when he is confronted with a life-threatening crisis. So, too, does Davis question which arena incorporates the greater elements of acting: the stage where the traveling actors perform or the social stage on which the Reverend Mr. Imlay and his society friends interact. When Imlay is befriended by the Finns, a family of actors, his two selves struggle against his admiration for what he observes as the reality of their hard-working, virtuous lives and what he, as a minister, has preached as the evils of theater life.

Davis ironically parallels Imlay's ultimate rejection of this family against his acceptance of Mr. Sperry, the socially acceptable speculator who trades in beet sugar. Society will bridge the gulf for the coarse trader who is successful but not for the industrious albeit poor stage laborers. Davis's theme of an artificial "gulf" between classes and/or races extends back to her first professional publications. In "Life in the Iron Mills," when Hugh accepts the visitors' valuation of himself, he believes "that between them there was a great gulf never to be passed." The metaphor of a "great gulf" satirizes the "social riddle" that the mill visitors and the Reverend Imlay seek to uphold; this is especially ironic in the Reverend's case, since it alludes to the scriptural passage in which Jesus asserts that the gulf between earthly life and heaven cannot be crossed by the wealthy. In the parable of Lazarus and the rich man ("between us and you there is a great gulf fixed" [Luke 16:26]), Lazarus finds comfort in heaven; the fate of the rich man, however, is to be cast into hell. It is a parable that the Reverend Imlay undoubtedly knew but his failure at the end of the story to practice these teachings ironically implies his alignment with the fate of the rich man, as he links up with Mr. Sperry for his journey "home."

After the publication of "Across the Gulf," Davis remained silent for almost a year, writing only a few children's stories and short items for *Peterson's*. Most of her time was devoted to raising her three children, two of whom were now in their exuberant teens. During this time, however, she was approached by the editors of *The Independent*. She had published occasional items in the New York weekly during the 1870s, but the editors now sought her as a regular contributor. *The Independent* had been founded in 1848 by the Congregationalists as a religious journal and had been edited by Henry Ward Beecher in the early 1860s. His successor, Theodore Tilton, however, preferred a somewhat more secular focus and had included articles on issues of the day, such as women's suffrage and the fate of the freed slaves, with contributions to the latter discussion by notable abolitionists such as Harriet Beecher Stowe and William Lloyd Garrison. In the 1880's, when the editors contacted Davis, they had synthesized the weekly's former focus into a format that encouraged both interdenominational religious articles and literary styles of the romantics and the realists (from Longfellow to Bret Harte).[12] When Davis complied in February 1882 with *The Independent*'s request for a sketch, she was careful to note that it was "altogether true. No fiction. I intended to call it Studies for Stories."[13] She received thirty-five dollars for the manuscript but for the next seven years would refuse to write more than one or two brief items for the periodical each year. It was not until 1889 that Davis became a regular contributor to *The Independent*.

At this time Davis was also contacted by Albion W. Tourgée, editor of a new Philadelphia periodical entitled *Our Continent*. Most of the journal's works of fiction were popular romances, but it aimed toward a progressive editorial stance, printing articles on Herbert Spencer, African literature, and other topical issues. Davis's first item for *Our Continent* was entitled "A Day in Tadousac";[14] the issue included poetry by Sidney Lanier and Louise Chandler Moulton, a quotation from Elizabeth Stuart Phelps, and a serial by E. P. Roe. Although the journal focused on the domestic aspects of women's lives, it was especially open to women writers and afforded Moulton and Davis's friend, Kate Field, regular columns in the periodical ("Our Society" and "Art of Adornment," respectively).

This was also the period in which the works of Philadelphia's adopted son, Walt Whitman, created a publishing sensation. In 1881, his Boston publishers, Osgood and Company, had surrendered to the censors' outcries over the new edition of *Leaves of Grass* and ceased its publication. That decision made Whitman a celebrity, and the Philadelphia printer D. McKay negotiated to pick up the project. The new edition under the Philadelphia imprint sold three thousand copies in one day. Davis certainly did not advocate censorship, but she had mixed responses to Whitman, in large part due to the overzealous claims made by his disciples. Their "popular prejudice clothed [Whitman] with abnormal qualities," she asserted, including the insistence that Whitman was "the one bard of the century . . . [and] the chief Patriot of his age."[15] Most disturbing to Davis was the reenactment of a scene she had witnessed twenty years earlier in Concord when Emerson was the reigning literary Sage: "So profound was the faith of his devotees in Whitman that they made incessant pilgrimages to his house in Camden as to a shrine, never coming away without laying gifts upon the altar" (215–16).

In recent years, selective quotations from Davis's comments on Whitman have led scholars to depict her as responding prudishly to Whitman's poetry. But her assessment was much more balanced. She did not approve of what she viewed as certain indecencies in his poetry, asserting that "Whitman simply was indecent as thousands of other men are indecent, who are coarse by nature and vulgar by breeding" (218). But she thought the claims of "demoniac possession" that were lodged against Whitman by his enemies were ridiculous and did not warrant serious response. She admonished Whitman's detractors for their extreme position just as she had his devotees: "On the other side was a large, equally unreasonable public, who believed Whitman to have been a sort of devil. They denied him any spark of divine fire" and outlandishly forced his removal from his government position and censored his poetry. "Surely," Davis insisted, "a cool posterity will acknowledge that this huge, uncouth fellow had the eye and tongue of the seer. To him, as to Dante and the oracle, it was given sometimes to be spokesman for the gods, to talk of death and life, in words not unworthy of their themes" (216–17). Davis admired the poet, but not the "boorish, awkward *poseur*" (217).

Whitman's artistic vision and especially his concern for the working class appealed to Davis, but while he "sang of the workingman as of a god" she observed that "he never did an hour's work himself if he could live by alms . . . he cursed shams, while he played the part of 'bard,' as he conceived it, in flowing hair and beard, gray clothes, broad rolling collar and huge pearl buttons, changing even his name to suit the role" (217). If she accurately captured Whitman's creation of the bard persona, she unfairly charged him with "sound[ing] the note of battle for the slave" but not fighting in the Civil War. Either she was unaware of his nursing activities during the war or she was blinded to his nontraditional form of service, but her overall disagreement was with the man, not with his work.

Davis may have been acquainted with Whitman, since their close mutual friends included some of the leading figures in Philadelphia's literary circle of the late 1880s—S. Wier Mitchell, George Boker, and the Shakespeare scholar, Horace Howard Furness—and we know that Whitman was familiar with Davis's work.[16] If they never met, they knew one another by reputation. In spite of Davis's dislike for Whitman's "vulgarity," she concluded that he was one of the "men of genius" of her era.

*   *   *

Davis also used these intervening years to continue guarding her time in order to write short stories of quality. In addition to "Walhalla" and "Across the Gulf," Davis published two other short stories in 1883 for *Lippincott's* and *Harper's*: "A Wayside Episode" and "A Silhouette," respectively.[17] "A Wayside Episode" is especially interesting for its analysis of a marriage that appears to the couple's friends to be a mismatch. At the beginning of the story, Emily and Edwin Wootton wonder themselves if this assessment of their relationship is not true. Emily's friends are disgusted that she is "dominated" by her "fussy little imbecile" husband, as they put it; but they fail to see that in great part Emily is the controlling partner (145). She knows her husband's joy at outwitting her, so she merely says the opposite of what she wants and thereby gains her way. It is the limited kind of power many women gained through the "cult of domesticity," and Davis recognized the controversial aspects of a power that relies on covert manipulation. Mrs. Penryn-Clay, the society dowager who has just returned from France, describes Emily as "one of those model, cow-like wives that one sees in a farce, but nowhere else in America" (145); however, Mr. Franciscus[18] insists that "Emily Souders set out to be eccentric,—an Advanced Female!" (146) The story forces the reader to determine whether or not Emily "is a radical," as Mr. Franciscus claims, or if she is merely reacting against her husband's obsessive fear of committing any social improprieties.

Mrs. Penryn-Clay is an extension of the dowager type that Davis had first created in *A Law*, but she also represents one of Davis's most insightful characterizations: the social doyenne whose acerbic commentaries on colleagues at once reveal her acceptance of and yet disgust with the theatricality of social manners. She reminds everyone that Edwin's grandfather was merely a grocer and that his uncle "did something in sugar which brought in their millions," but she is also uneasy when these *nouveau riche* histories are articulated by others: "I thought there was a compact among all Americans to keep up these little illusions for each other" (147). Her comment is also a slight against Mr. Franciscus, whose uncle is still a tanner in New Jersey, but Franciscus is quite secure in his new-found position as one who "echoed the opinions of society" and thus has his own realm of power, especially over people like Edwin who are ruled by ephemeral social codes (147).

Davis's delightful satire of upper-class society is preliminary to Edith Wharton's later, more fully developed studies of the same class. Davis's fiction in the following decades, especially in her novels, turns more and more toward narratives of manners. Like Wharton, Davis does not allow her characterizations to devolve into types. Thus, Edwin Wootton is bumbling in his insecurity, but he also has a greater concern for others than does his wife. Emily is self-indulgent in her charities, beginning with all-out enthusiasm and then dropping them when something else attracts her fancy. In the previous year, she had been avidly involved in charities for invalids, orphans, blind paupers, and beggars' children, but now she found the demands of these activities too much "trouble" and shut her door to them all. It is Edwin who quietly picks up the threads and continues the projects.

Still, Davis is sympathetic to Emily's sense of society as a cage, a glass box that encases "a few gold-fishes and minnows" (150). Davis had used the metaphor of society as a cage in her earliest fiction of the 1860s, and the naturalists of the next decade would widely incorporate that metaphor into their deterministic fiction. In "A Wayside Episode," Emily knows what it is to "bump against the sides" of the glass-box cage (151), and it is her awareness of the social trap in which she and her husband have secured themselves that makes her life tragic. Her contemplation of an affair with the woodsman whom they meet on their summer excursion into the wilderness is an endeavor to escape that glass box. She sees him as a man hindered by "no law, no rule of propriety . . . he could lose himself in the woods and shut the world out,—wholly out" (154). But Davis never idealizes the frontier life; she reveals the struggle between Emily's "two selves" as Emily attempts to escape one glass box only to discover that each society, of the city or of the frontier, has its own trap.

Davis had explored the idea of a person's better and "brute" self in her early naturalistic studies, and its recurrence here aligns her again with the young realists of the 1890s who would delve even further into that aspect of the human personality. Frank Norris was especially interested in this realm of psychology. His ability to render the horrifying emergence of the brute self out of the better self is most sharply detailed in *McTeague* (both in the title character's decline and in Maria's lascivious greed), and the theme recurs in *The Pit* and *The Octopus*. After the turn of the century, Jack

London studied the concept in *The Call of the Wild* (1903) as did Theodore Dreiser in his characterization of Hurstwood, Henry James in his creation of Lambert Strether, and Edith Wharton in Newland Archer, to name only a few. In Davis's study, she ironically details the woodsman's evolution into a ruthless capitalist and counters that theme with what she viewed as the progressive relationship of Emily and Edwin, whose financial decline and reformation constitutes their return to "Western" values. The Woottons remake their lives through hard work and find in that endeavor the ability to discard their social masks and rediscover their concern for one another. The conclusion of "A Wayside Episode" reflects Davis's philosophy about what constitutes a better life for women. She had consistently realized the importance of self-fulfilling work for women, but for Davis the ideal required that work be enhanced by a marriage alliance that was a partnership.[19] For Emily and Edwin Wootton that partnership is twofold: personal and economic. When the Woottons lose all of their money through Emily's father's speculations, they stave off debilitating poverty by returning to agrarian industriousness: Edward plants a seed farm and Emily raises poultry and establishes a bee colony. Their combined endeavors eventually earn them a comfortable life; ten years later they were not rich, but they were "solid." It was, in many ways, an apt description of the status of the Davises' marriage in the 1880s.

*   *   *

In 1884, Davis's mother died. Rachel Leet Harding's physical absence from her daughter's life now became a literal "cypher" that could no longer be bridged by occasional hurried visits to Washington, Pennsylvania. The old family home that had passed from Rebecca Leet Wilson to Rachel now passed to Davis, but Rachel's true legacy for her daughter was much more complex in its intangible nature. Rachel had been a product of her own time and had instilled in her eldest daughter a conservative belief that a woman's primary role in life was to be a supportive wife, but her insistence upon "industry and frugality" had served Davis well as necessary survival skills; they were the skills that the daughter in turn continued to encourage all impoverished and oppressed people to develop. More significantly, Rachel had encouraged the development of Rebecca's imagination and writing talents. She had nurtured her daughter's intellect as devoutly as she had her spirituality. Not a single word survives from Davis about her mother's death; her greatest pains were always buried within herself. And this was, undoubtedly, a magnificent sorrow in her life.

* * *

By the mid-1880s, Davis's eldest son, Richard, was beginning to embark upon his own literary career. Richard was a dashing, flamboyant young man whose fame was first gained by posing as the male figure in the renowned "Gibson Girl" portraits. His early fiction involved almost exclusively tales of adventure, such as *Soldier of Fortune* and the Gallagher series. Later in life, however, he would turn to journalistic realism in his own writings, drawn as they were from his experiences as a reporter first in the New York Bowery and later at the warfront in Cuba and during the Boer War. His companion and friendly rival in these locales was the young Stephen Crane, and it is hard to imagine that Crane did not know the work of his friend's mother. She was still publishing, both the old-guard romantics and the new-guard realists knew her work, and Crane was especially alert to the changing modes of literature during this period.

Davis was instrumental in encouraging Richard and in seeing that his early work was published. In 1885, Richard convinced his mother to pay for the publication of his first full-length work, *Adventures of My Freshman*.[20] She advised him to publish anonymously at first, as she had, so that his apprenticeship could serve him well and not discourage his later reputation.[21] Richard had begun to send articles to *The Current* and a few rudimentary poems to *Life* magazine; both periodicals paid him $2.50 for his contributions.[22] Richard's confidence grew when Mary Mapes Dodge, editor of *St. Nicholas* and one of his mother's long-standing editors, accepted a short story of his for publication. Rebecca, however, was his severest critic, even if she was also his greatest enthusiast, and she once again cautioned him about his early writings:

> except for your own disappointment—I know it would be better if you would not publish under your own name for a little while. . . . Dr. [Josiah] Holland used to say for a young man or woman to rush into print was sure ruin to their lasting fame. They either compromised their reputations by inferior work, or they made a great hit and never played up to it, afterwards, in public opinion.
>
> Now my dear old man this sounds like awfully cold comfort. But it is the wisest idea your mother has got. . . . I think you are going to take a high place

among American authors, but I do not think you are going to do it by articles like that you sent to *The Current*.[23]

Perhaps most telling in Davis's advice to her son is her own acknowledgment of the struggle she had waged for many years against Clarke's indifference to her writing.[24] She saw it extended now to their son and hoped to counter its rebuff with her own skillful encouragement:

> Understand me. I don't say, like Papa, stop writing. God forbid. I would almost as soon say stop breathing, for it is pretty much the same thing. But only to remember that you have not yet conquered your art. You are a journeyman not a master workman, so if you don't succeed, it does not count. The future is what I look to, for you.[25]

To his later regret, Richard did not follow his mother's advice to publish anonymously during his early years, but he did continue to write, and he continued throughout Rebecca's lifetime to seek her criticism of his work. Davis's comments to her son are also significant for their revelation of her own continuing sense of herself as an artist. If she was sometimes embittered by having to sell her wares to the highest bidder, she never abandoned her belief in herself as a serious artist or in writing as of primary importance to her intellectual and emotional well-being.

*   *   *

The mid-1880s also constituted Davis's reemergence from her self-stylized cocoon. Perhaps most important for her literary career was her decision to emphasize nonfiction writings. She did not abandon fiction, and some fine additions to that genre were yet to come, but she regained her literary voice in nonfiction exposés and commentaries. In the summer of 1885, she began discussions with the current editor of the *Atlantic*, Thomas Bailey Aldrich, about once again writing for that periodical. Aldrich was known for his " 'Boston-plated' traditions,"[26] and that editorial preference may have been one reason that Davis's submissions to her literary alma mater were limited. But Davis had learned her lessons well, and even if she was once again welcome in the pages of the *Atlantic*, she would never again trust her career to one periodical. In August she submitted "Some Testimony in the Case" to Aldrich, noting, "I really think it is impartial."[27] Published in the November issue, which also included serializations by Oliver

Wendell Holmes and Henry James, "Some Testimony" analyzes the relations between blacks and whites ("the Negro Problem") in the South two decades after the end of the Civil War. To Davis's mind, Northerners still held a distorted perspective: "The discussions of the negro problem in Northern and Southern reviews last winter, it is true, showed us the subject from widely different points of view. But if any Northerner, living quietly at home, surrounded only by white faces, supposes that these pictures of the great struggle of race in the South have discovered the whole of it to him, he is greatly mistaken."[28]

Though Davis had insisted to Aldrich that her account was "impartial" and reiterated that assessment in the opening of her article by describing herself as an "impartial traveler through the Southern States," she had never been impartial about the South. Having lived in a border state during the Civil War, she abhorred the South's racism and slavery systems, but she dearly loved the people and the region. In her fiction of the previous twenty-five years, she had recurringly satirized the Northerner's ignorance of the South and his sense that Southerners were almost a race apart. In her nonfiction she often sought to reeducate the Northerner at the same time that she demanded changes from the Southerner. She prophetically observes that there is a "great game" in progress in the country at this time, and its consequences "will decide the future of the negro. . . . The result of this struggle, if not a matter of life and death to either race, will certainly affect permanently [both races'] domestic relations, their commercial prosperity, and the place which the South will hereafter hold in the scale of civilized people" (602–3).

The language and tone of "Some Testimony" remains impartial. Yet the selection and structuring of the testimonials resound with Davis's antiracist beliefs concerning both blacks and Southerners in general, even though she still displays a blindness to certain aspects of the attitudes of late nineteenth-century Southerners. She allows the still-racist Southerner to condemn himself: the cotton planter in Montgomery who wants the entire black race to "be lifted *en masse* and dropped into Africa" (603); or the aged Virginian woman who still lives on her family's now-decrepit plantation and who regrets that the black man has lost his former "ennobling quality" of loyalty to his master (604); or the Mississippian who justifies the new form of "convict labor" because white Southerners now have "a mass of ignorant paupers to carry" (606). Interwoven with these long-held racist views, however, are the testimonies of white Southerners who, to a limited degree, are beginning to change their attitudes, such as the New Orleans businessman who asserts that blacks as a whole should not be judged by the present generation because he feels the race is "still weighted by the ignorance of slavery" and by a "self-conceit" encouraged by carpetbaggers. The latter group, this Southerner explains, taught blacks that they were equal to whites without benefit of education; the next generation will learn that one's place in society is earned by the quality of one's work. The businessman seems unaware of the irony of this "old dream," as Davis had termed it in "Life in the Iron Mills," but to Davis's mind, he represents those Southerners who were at least attempting to adapt to the ways of the New South. The emphasis she places upon this man's opinion suggests her own, if unwitting, alignment with much of what he asserts.

More importantly, Davis records the testimonies of numerous African Americans who *are* building new lives for themselves and who recognize the importance of education. Madame Clotilde is "a stout, neat, keen-eyed mulatto," who lives in the Gulf states and recognizes that it is the formerly rich Southern planters who cannot now recover from the shock of their loss because previously their labor had always been performed for them. Her husband points to the symbols of change in their society when he notes that the old whipping post stands not far from the college their children now attend. Yet he cannot forget that it was merely the chance of time that gave his daughters this benefit; had they been born before the war, they probably would have been taken from him and sold into another region. Davis adds: "It is impossible to see the present of the negro in its true light without the background of the past" (606). For Davis, the "story of to-day" must always be recorded from the perspective of accurate history.

In the conclusion of "Some Testimony," Davis points to what she deems a paradox of Southern culture: first, that there is a great need for skilled laborers in the South, so much so that they have sought European immigrants to fill these positions; and second, that the New Orleans Exhibition's display of the crafts of the black race demonstrated that race's desire for mastery of these trades but lack of training as well. General S. C. Armstrong, head of the Hampton Industrial School, which trained blacks in these trades, attests to their capabilities and willingness to learn. Davis questioned the priorities of blacks in their quest for an education; she noted the current emphasis on Latin and metaphysics in several black colleges, while Hampton was the only industrial school training freedmen for the trades. (Booker T. Washington's model for vocational and industrial training would not become prevalent until the turn of the century.) As a "practical" observer, Davis concludes that this is the trend that all Southerners should encourage: blacks should be trained not just in the history of ideas but in practical skills that will allow them to house and educate themselves. Ever aware of the economic and nationalistic attitudes of her readers, Davis also asserted that it was to the South's benefit to employ these skilled freedmen rather than surrendering their industries "to foreign capitalists and foreign laborers" (609).

This vision for African Americans and the nation as a whole seems limited from a twentieth-century perspective, and in many ways it is. The belief that social equality would arise from economic independence had a certain validity, as Booker T. Washington later suggested in *Up from Slavery* (1901). Davis's stance, however, like Washington's, is most conservative in its advocacy of assimilation and its devaluation of higher education for blacks. But an awareness of the economic conditions for blacks in America during the 1880s, more than fifteen years before Washington's Atlanta speech and W. E. B. DuBois's more enlightened assertions, may help us understand Davis's position. Her focal point was always Philadelphia, and in this instance it was a particularly important focus since at the time the city had the largest black population of the Northern urban centers. Yet economic opportunities in the "City of Brotherly Love" were limited; blacks, who had been afforded little opportunity for gaining the skills needed in the new industries, were also confronted with an influx of immigrants who competed with them for employment in industry. Immigration continued throughout the decade, and 1882 constituted the highest influx—800,000 immigrants had entered the Atlantic states in that year alone.[29] As in the antebellum era, most of the newcomers turned to industrial labor as an immediate means of support.

But it was not, of course, simply a matter of having skills that ensured employment in a competitive marketplace. Even well-qualified blacks were barred from many positions because of the prejudice of white employers, and labor unions did not admit blacks at the time. The League of Colored Mechanics, one of the first trade unions that attempted to promote blacks in the trades, was not formed until 1897. By the end of the decade, only one percent of Philadelphia's black population had found employment in the industries. That meant that most black males were employed as unskilled laborers at abysmally low wages, and black women were relegated to domestic service; yet even in these positions their progress was limited. White immigrants were most often given the higher-paid service positions of coachmen, butlers, and nursemaids.[30]

Because higher education was costly and remained beyond the means of most blacks, Davis's immediate concern was to raise blacks at least into positions that afforded them living wages. Nor was her position limited to race. She published several articles in *The Independent* at the end of the decade that supported the concept that people of all races needed to learn practical skills; and she had already published in 1882 a series in *Youth's Companion* on "Homely Hints for Homely Occupations" that suggested "industries which women can pursue profitably at home, those which require no long nor costly education or training." Davis was especially interested in ways in which women could "stike out a new path and create a market for wares which she only can furnish." It was an idea that she had first formulated in " 'In the Market' " (1868) as a viable economic means for the impoverished to gain the dignity of a decent living environment through work well performed. As she had observed to her publisher when she submitted the article on home occupations to *Youth's Companion*, "I think I have mentioned those [occupations] that are practicable and profitable."[31] Although Davis had advocated training in the trades for several years, she may also have been influenced by the ideas of Harriet Robinson, who, in 1881, had given the opening address at the Boston Convention of the National Woman Suffrage Association. In a subsequent publication of statistics on labor, Robinson asserted, "Skilled labor teaches something not to be found in books or in colleges. [Women mill workers'] early experiences developed their characters . . . and helped them to fight well the battle of life."[32] Washington, Robinson, and Davis were shortsighted and unwittingly conciliatory in many ways, but each acted out of a belief that he or she was aiding the oppressed.

*   *   *

In 1886 Davis published her only novel of the decade, a reprint of the serial, *Natasqua*. The reason this novel was chosen for reprint by Cassel and Company, a New York publishing firm, is unknown. It certainly was not Davis's most distinctive fiction of the period, but it was a relatively "safe" novel if the publisher wanted to avoid the controversy that would undoubtedly have ensued from the publication of a work like *Earthen Pitchers*. The bland responses to *Natasqua* did nothing to enhance Davis's reputation,[33] but they did nothing to damage it either. A "pleasant note" she received in early 1886 from a Miss Dickinson, requesting a photograph of Davis suggests her public's continuing interest in her. Davis's response, however, reveals her own reticence toward such personal exposure: "I should be very glad to send my photograph if it would give a moment's pleasure to (an) invalid who I am sure is trying to make the best of her suffering but there is no such thing to send. I have had no picture taken for nearly thirty years."[34] Her staunch belief in personal privacy had in-grained "a great aversion to seeing a portrait of myself,"[35] and she would not breach that aversion for readers or publishers. It was a trait so well known within her family circle that when Richard, now employed by Harper & Brothers publishers, wrote his mother that year that he had sent for her novel, he amusingly added, "If you don't look out I shall publish your portrait in the Weekly—."[36] One other humorous sign of Davis's con-tinuing popularity was a request from a Kentucky church group which asked Davis for a recipe, apparently to be included in a celebrity cookbook. Davis was amused, since she felt that the last thing she should be recog-nized for were her culinary skills, but she complied with a recipe for "Savoury" that she noted was favored in Cornwall.[37]

On a more significant note, Davis's reputation as a serious writer was acknowledged in a very pleasing manner by Rose Terry Cooke. Davis had long admired Cooke and, as suggested earlier, was influenced to a degree by Cooke's earlier fiction. To Davis's pleasure, Cooke now contacted her and indicated that she would soon be visiting Philadelphia and that she wished to interview Davis. Davis responded warmly, acknowledging that she had long wished to write Cooke in order to convey her admiration for a collection of Cooke's early poems, "But I never could summon courage." In spite of her busy schedule, Davis enthusiastically encouraged Cooke to visit her and Clarke: "I shall be engaged next week[.] But week after next (after Tuesday the 30th) I shall be at home. You shall have all the dates you choose, and even if they will not be enough for you to make an article, come,—not as an interviewer but a friend to discover two friends who have admired and honoured you for twenty years. Let me know on what day and train to expect you and come directly to the house and spend the night with us." No article about Davis by Cooke is extant, but at the end of the decade they would collaborate with three other women authors for an ar-ticle in the *North American Review*. Davis's hunger for the opportunity to exchange ideas with another woman writer who embraced many of the same themes and values as herself is evident in the postscript she attached to her letter: "If you have a copy of that book with you bring it and we will go over it together. Don't forget. To think I should read 'Done For' with Rose Terry herself!"[38]

＊   ＊   ＊

In the spring and early summer of 1887, Davis traveled throughout the South, gathering details for her next serial for *Harper's New Monthly Magazine*. Published in five parts between July and November 1887, "Here and There in the South" is, like "By-Paths," an example of documentary realism, but this serial signals Davis's revitalized literary artistry, an artistic energy that would carry her through the next quarter-century, until her death in 1910. If any of her work of the decade deserved to be published in book form it was this serial, far more so than *Natasqua*.

A brief study of the articles and works of fiction that were published in *Harper's* at the time of "Here and There in the South" reveals the changing literary trends in America as the end of the century neared. The July issue's lead article, a long, carefully illustrated essay on the book-printing business, was the seventh in a series on "Great American Industries" by R. R. Bowker. In the same issue, the series "Social Studies" published Richard T. Ely's discussion of "The Future of Corporations," which confirmed the accuracy of Davis's early concerns about the abuses of American industrialists. Ely asserts that "the State, which is the only possible power capable of such regulation," must institute restrictions on corporations which now control "one-fourth part of the national resources" (259). On a lighter note, during the run of "Here and There in the South," *Harper's* published William Dean Howells's nearly forgotten novel, *April Hopes*; poetry by William Wordsworth; Kate Field's "Our Summer's Outing"; and Henry James's sketch, "John S. Sargent."

"Here and There in the South" is consistent with the mood of the nonfiction articles published in *Harper's* that year, since it critiques the South of the late 1880's. The serial is beautifully written, the tone is keen and at times sharply witty, and the content recaptures Davis's astute eye for social farces and personal tragedies. The serial is accompanied by the highly detailed landscape drawings of W. H. Gibson and by W. H. Drake's beautiful and sometimes painfully realistic sketches of freed Southern blacks as they struggled to regain their dignity and to carve a place for themselves in American society. Davis's themes in this study indicate the renewed intellectual vitality she was enjoying: the evolution of Southern belles into industrious Southern women (such as Lola Pogue, who set aside her despair after the Civil War and reshaped her life through hard work and ingenuity); the next generation of young men to inherit this industriousness and who control the New South; and the great personal and cultural progress of freed blacks in that region. Davis observes, as she had in "Some Testimony," that there remains a need for more diverse industries in the South and a need for that region to take control of its own economy.

In this study, Davis's realism is at its most acute since the early 1870s. Her observations have the specificity of a literary botanist as she interweaves her story of the journey of the enthusiastic clergyman, Mr. Ely, and his skeptical wife, Mrs. Ely, with industrial statistics and observations on the emergence of the resort industry as a thriving business. Davis also records the personal histories of these new Southerners, praising their personal industriousness and condemning what idleness remains because it has led to increasingly alarming reports of drunkenness. She realistically details the various locales of the South, from thriving Atlanta to the old French Market in New Orleans, and she acknowledges not only the innovativeness of the New Orleans Exposition, which included a display of crafts by Southern blacks, but its economic impact as well.

Davis's realistic fiction, which always encompasses the commonplace lives of the people and their surroundings, integrates these histories with the Southerners' present lives. When Mr. Ely journeys into the Bayoux, for instance, he travels along the Bayou La Fourche. Its meandering current symbolizes Davis's artistic threading of history and present-day action:

> Bayou La Fourche was the first of these bright slow-moving rivers which [Mr. Ely] entered. As early as 1810, Breckinridge and Schultz, making journeys from Canada to the Gulf, noticed and wrote of the beauty of this bayou and its shores, although, as the land was then owned by French and Spanish *paysans*, it was not guarded by proper levees, and inundations occurred almost yearly. Opulent creole planters, however, soon bought up the grounds of the *petits habitants*, and the result is the immense estates which now line the shores of the upper La Fourche like a beautiful panorama. (755)

Davis cannot conceal her love of the South when she adds: "Not even a small New England farm can surpass in order and method a great sugar plantation" in the Bayoux (755).

The education Mr. Ely receives from his travels through the South is that which Davis seeks to instill in every Northerner:

He understood now that the meanings of this strange country which had perplexed him are those of age. The primeval forests in the North impress the intruder as fresh and virgin; they have no history. . . . But these great silent prairies, the giant trees decaying for centuries, the huge parasitic growths, the black scavenger-birds crossing with swift aim the low-hung sky—all these come out of a hoar antiquity. It is a land with a past. (925)

In spite of her admiration and love of the region, Davis perceives that the South remains an "ancient enchanted land, whose ghosts still dwelt therein" and that the "real world . . . shops, markets, passions, and life" remained in the North (925), to which she returned along with her fictionalized clergyman.

One other noteworthy element of "Here and There in the South" is Davis's return to a critique of the literary tastes of the day. She satirizes both Mrs. Ely, who wanders the streets of New Orleans's French Market expecting to find "Mr. Cable's creoles" (601), and Mr. Ely, who, "like most Northerners, [knew] New Orleans only through Mr. Cable's marvelous pictures" (603). But young Betty, their companion, who has seemed to be little more than a preening debutante, asserts herself against this stereotype of the Creole: "Why put us in a magazine story to amuse the world?" she demanded. "You should read Gayarré's books on Louisiana, or Picket on Alabama. They are books of dignity, monsieur. We have had our historians!" (603)

An interesting episode detailing the literature of the South reveals Davis's continuing disdain for excessive glorification of authors:

> In Mobile, the Elys are directed to the house of the most famous woman, probably, of the South—Mrs. Augusta Evans Wilson, the author of Beulah, Macaria, etc. She is held in as proud regard by the mass of Southern people as was George Eliot by the English. Her beautiful home on Spring Hill is a kind of Mecca to which her admirers make pilgrimages.
>
> "All American authors," said Mr. Ely, "should be born in Boston or the far South."
>
> "The South never neglects her gifted children," replied Colonel Mocquard, gravely, "when they are true to her." (440)

Augusta Jane Evans Wilson was a Southern sentimental novelist whose highly moralistic novels of the 1850s and 1860s had been tremendously popular, especially *St. Elmo* (1867), a novel in which the Georgia heroine, Edna Earl, epitomizes woman as spiritual and moral exemplar. It is an interesting novel to compare with Davis's novel of that year, *Waiting for the Verdict*;

but Davis's depiction here of Wilson's canonization and of the pilgrimages to her luxurious home recall, though with notably less harshness, her comments about the "wild-eyed Harvard undergraduates" who flocked to Concord to sit at the feet of Emerson and the disciples of Whitman who marched into Camden to lay gifts on the poet's altar. To Davis's mind, it was a practice that served neither the pilgrim nor the author.

While *Harper's* published the last of this study of the South, *Scribner's Magazine* was publishing another of Davis's significant short stories of this period, "Tirar y Soult."[39] *Scribner's Magazine*, founded in 1887, openly welcomed the new realism. At first, this magazine was more available to women writers than *Scribner's Monthly/Century Magazine* had been. In the first six months of *Scribner's Magazine*'s publication, women's contributions in fiction and essays equaled more than one-quarter of the items published, and included works by Octave Thanet, Sarah Orne Jewett, and Elizabeth Akers. By the end of the decade, however, that figure had rapidly declined to an even more minimal representation than in the other surveyed journals: only fourteen percent of the nonpoetry items were by women. On the poetry side, however, the journal did balance their accepted submissions: women constituted forty-five percent of published poets. In the same issue as Davis's short story, a segment of Harold Frederic's first novel, *Seth's Brother's Wife*, appeared; and at the end of the year the magazine published work by Bret Harte and again by Sarah Orne Jewett. In the following year, the periodical serialized Henry James's four-part study, *A London Life*, and in December 1889, it presented as its lead item Jacob A. Riis's "How the Other Half Lives: Studies Among the Tenements." Riis's exposé, appearing more than twenty-five years after Davis's "Life in the Iron Mills," revealed how insightful Davis's early study had been and how little had changed in America during the last half of the nineteenth century.

Scribner's Magazine thus seemed to be a suitable place of publication for Davis's fiction of the 1880s, and she selected it for the publication of this excellent short story. "Tirar y Soult" is in many ways a complementary piece to "Here and There in the South." Set in Louisiana, it is the story of the ironically named Robert Knight, a newly graduated civil engineer who was "born, bred, and trained in New England, suckled on her creeds and weaned on her doubts" (21). His first job is on M. de Fourgon's Louisiana plantation, the Lit de Fleurs, where he is to help the community drain its marshes and establish larger rice farms. "Tirar y Soult" is the study of local entrepreneurial industries that were often distorted and destroyed by the seemingly beneficial intrusion of Northern industrialists. Knight writes home to his friend, Emma Cramer, expressing his sense of being immersed into another world: "From Boston to the Bed of Flowers, from the Concord School of Philosophy to the companionship of ex-slave-holders, from Emerson to Gayarré! I expect to lose my breath mentally" (21–22). Knight may lose his mental "breath," but the cost of his actions for the Louisianians is anything but chivalric. Knight's education parallels that of Hester Manning in "A Wife's Story," detailing the near-fatal combination of Concord philosophy and capitalism's encouragement of speculation. But the story is also a critique of the old Southern ways that are no longer feasible in the modern world and that suffocate the new Southerners, as symbolized by the bog of quicksand near the plantation.

Like Hester, Knight will be rescued from his decline, which begins when he is seduced by the luxurious lifestyle of the Louisiana plantations. Although he will finally return to her, Knight initially forsakes his friend Emma, who survives by writing two-dollar columns for a Boston newspaper. Knight reevaluates the formerly dull Miss Lucretia Venn when he discovers that she is the largest landowner in the territory and has an additional ten-thousand-dollar annual income: "She was no longer only a dull, fascinating appeal to his imagination. She was a power . . . like a Building Association or a Pacific Railway" (31–32). Davis's metarealism demands a resolution that the new realists were beginning to reject. Thus, for her characters, crises thwart their blindness and allow them to see the delusions under which they have been functioning. The endings of her best works of short fiction of this period blend the closure of romanticism with the themes of realism. Davis would return periodically to this literary border for the remainder of her career.

The last work of fiction Davis published during the 1880s, "Anne," is an excellent story and also includes issues she had addressed in "The Wife's Story," although without the earlier work's forced resolution. In "Anne," Davis continues her theme of the wastefulness of letting dreams overtake one's life, even if reality is harsh.[40] The title character of this short story lives a life of order until she falls asleep and finds herself at the mercy of nature, where "great forces [are] at work, both good and evil" (225). These forces of nature are ambiguous and house strange creatures "who do not enter into the little wooden or brick boxes in which we cage ourselves" (225). Davis's rendering of this dream-state consciousness is modernistic in that it places the reader in the same position of knowledge as the dreamer; we hear snatches of conversations, see bits of scenery, but little is logically connected as Anne drifts in and out of consciousness. Ironically, Anne's dream is a very "old dream," too—in reality she is not a young, flirtatious woman who still imagines she can lure George Forbes away from his new love. She is fifty, homely, and worn from enduring years of an unhappy marriage. Like Audrey Swanson in *Earthen Pitchers*, Anne no longer has the voice of a sweet nightingale but "a discordant yawp" (227). Yet her soul refuses to accept that she is Mrs. Palmer: "I am here—Anne!" she tells herself as she reaches for the orderly work basket that holds her "account-book" (227). This item becomes a metaphor for Anne's story, for she is going to have to account to herself for her own life. Instead of confronting herself at this point, however, she goes to her room and shuts herself in to avoid her children's "hard common-sense" (228), thereby figuratively caging herself.

It is in this caged state that we learn her name is Mrs. *Nancy* Palmer.[41] This person, unlike the sweet-voiced Anne, has been widowed and has had to raise her children alone. She managed the family plantation after her husband died "with remarkable energy and success" and wisely invested the profits in Western land (228–29). But the Literary Circle and the church sociables that her children value stifle her. She longs for her youth, when "Nature had known her and talked to her" and music had had a word just for her (232). Her passions and hates had been extreme and lively, but when she thinks of love, she feels a chill grip her entire body as though Anne, the creature within her, is struggling to be freed. Davis's psychological realism in revealing this woman's split personality is chilling in its accuracy. As Nancy/Anne flees the confines of her orderly home, Davis forces the reader to question whether this woman is caged in or shut out of life in that environment. Anne decides that she must leave, that she will seek the life of "music and art and the companionship of thinkers and scholars" that she had always desired (234). She is riddled with the hot blood of her sixteen-year-old self: "It was now dawn" (234).

There is a sense in which anyone reading this short story wants Anne to emerge, but a part of us that knows Davis intends this as another in her tradition of ironic dawns, for Nancy has never been honest with herself. As she rides on the train, feeling free but unsure of where she's headed, she decides that her destination will not be Europe; she wants to avoid all the "Americans trotting about Europe" (235). Perhaps she will go to Egypt or the Nile or "Iceland . . . among the glaciers and geysers" (235). This ironic blending of the hot and cold atmospheres—the Nile and Iceland, glaciers and geysers—represents her own waffling sense of destination and, more deeply, of her very Self. Further, it represents her vacillation between her affection for Job Palmer, whom she had married and who she knew "had been a good commonplace man," and George Forbes, whom she had loved as a young woman. It was he who had called her "Anne." George was "a Seer, a Dictator of thought to the world" (235). Ironically, Anne buys a ticket to Boston.

On her journeys, both the literal and figurative ones, Anne discovers that the now-famous author, George Forbes, and his crowd are "mere hucksters of art and humanity" (238). It is Nancy who returns home, and she does so with a clear vision and with a new respect for herself and the life she has made among the Palmers. But Davis thwarts this seemingly happy ending by the ironic discovery that Nancy now lives "a quiet, luxurious, happy life being petted like a baby by all the Palmers" (242)—hardly the admirable self-sufficiency Nancy had attained before she entered that strange world of nature's forces. The story's ending evokes both the pathos of Nancy's wasted life and of Anne's lost vitality and intellectualism:

> Yet sometimes in the midst of all this comfort and sunshine a chance note of music or the sound of the restless wind will bring an expression into her eyes which her children do not understand, as if some creature unknown to them looked out of them.
> At such times Mrs. Palmer will say to herself, "Poor Anne!" as of somebody whom she once knew that is dead.
> *Is* she dead? she feebly wonders; and if she is dead here, will she ever live again? (242)

The story ends with no sense of reconciliation between the two selves. It is a keenly modern rendition of a fractured society as it is echoed in the human personality . . . "the women come and go / Talking of Michelangelo." And it is impossible not to interpret these two selves as elements of Davis's own personality, especially in terms of her earlier studies of woman's changing role in society.

∗   ∗   ∗

Davis's last publication of the decade was a collaborative nonfiction article for the *North American Review* entitled "Are Women to Blame?"[42] It had been two decades since Charles Eliot Norton had sought Davis as a contributor to the *Review*; then, she had remained loyal to the *Atlantic*. Subsequently, two substantial changes had occurred in the periodical's focus: the monthly had relocated from Boston to New York, thus, under the new editorship, the Boston Brahmins no longer dominated the magazine's pages; second, because of that physical and literal separation, the magazine moved from its more traditional editorial perspective to a concern with contemporary issues, especially those of a sociopolitical nature.

At the end of the decade, the editors of the *North American Review*, noting what seemed to be a decline in the number of congenial marriages, asked five women writers to discuss whether or not women were to blame for the state of American domestic affairs. The writers were instructed to deal with the issue "as frankly as possible" (632), and their responses are an amazing revelation of the prevalent attitudes about women and by women in late nineteenth-century America, in spite of the inroads gained by the "New Woman" movement. The contributors to the symposium were, in order of publication, Davis, Rose Terry Cooke, Marion Harland, Catherine Owen, and Amelia E. Barr. Only Davis and, to a lesser degree, Harland give balanced assessments of the domestic situation; all three other contributors insist that the decline in the state of marriages is, indeed, the fault of women because they will not accept their due place in society as subordinate to their husbands.

Rose Terry Cooke begins her essay by saying that "men also have their share of that unpleasant responsibility" if a marriage is unhappy, but she continues: "it must be allowed that women are often seriously and recklessly in fault when the marriage relation is not only unhappy, but disgraceful" (626). She lists six reasons for women's responsibility for unhappiness in their marriages: women marry from erroneous and "inexcusable motives"; they have false expectations of marriage and of their responsibilities in that relationship; the wife is typically impatient; women are too "exacting both by nature and education"; "women are inconsiderate"; and they "are almost always jealous" (626–29). But Cooke offers a remedy for this unfortunate state of the institution of marriage: if women want happy marriages they must become "Christian women" and cultivate "their womanly virtues; become patient, considerate, submissive, and gentle" (629–30).

Marion Harland was the pen name of Mary Hawes Terhune, a prolific sentimental novelist whose fiction was often set in the South during the antebellum or Civil War eras. In this essay, Harland asserts that the entire American system of marriage is founded "upon a blunder . . . [a] conventional farce" that insists women be coy and asexual before marriage and that they are "unfinished" if they do not marry (63). Yet from the moment a man and woman take their wedding vows, all the rules of the farce change, as Harland denotes by the sexually allusive, metaphoric horse race: "Courtship was the porch; Marriage is the house, and [the husband] is in possession. Wooing was the caracoling and prancing, the trial spurt in front of the grand stand before the business of the race began" (631). But the wife is most often at fault because she views marriage through "rose-colored glasses"; it is her nature, Harland confirms. For the man, "it is an acquired trick—seldom a taste" (631). Problems occur when the wife continues the farce after marriage but the husband immediately drops it. Harland admonishes women for "bewailing [their] disillusion" (632), but she astutely notes that older women encourage "Our Maiden's delusion by euphoniously senseless twaddle of joining hands for the minuet of life . . . when in our middle-aged wisdom, we know marriage to be nothing of the sort" (632). While the man has his share in the guilt by exciting expectations he has no intention of gratifying, the woman is more to blame because she allows her imagination to intensify the unhappiness of her married life. Harland concludes: "Courtship is play; marriage is work" and the sooner women learn this truth the sooner they will find happiness in "our sin-warped world" (633).

Catherine Owen, like Davis, feels that the availability of divorce makes unhappy marriages seem more prevalent in this era. Divorces are positive in that women no longer have to endure "domestic woes" as they once did, Owen asserts, but she adds that "among the wiser [women] perhaps, the endurance was silent" (634). This insistence on silently bearing "woes" is Owen's central theme. Men are, for the most part, sincere in trying to be good husbands; the problem is that they immerse themselves in their business life and forget the affection that their wives desire. "Unfortunately she can rarely hide her suffering," Owen observes, and she therefore begins to nag her husband about his lack of attention, which drives him further away. Owen concludes that the "woman's nature is to blame"; she will be better off if she learns her lesson and settles down "to accept the facts" (637). Divorce ensues because women turn to other men for flattery, and there is little hope for change, Owen laments, "while man's nature and woman's are just what they are" (637).

Amelia E. Barr was one of the most prolific writers of nineteenth-century America, producing more than seventy-five books in her lifetime. A romance and sentimental novelist, Barr was conservative in her position on women's roles in society and marriage. In her autobiography (*All the Days of My Life* [1913]), Barr stressed the injustices that take place against women, but in this earlier essay she states forthrightly that, in her opinion, women are at fault in the marriage situation because of their false expectations. "But if weak, gushing wives have much to answer for," she asserts, "perhaps superior ones have more. Who does not know these perfect women, cold and proper . . . the burning passions which send men into danger and sin are inconceivable to them" (638). Thus Barr places the blame for a man's infidelity on the woman, because "babbling women" who express their suffering drive men to the divorce court. Barr concludes that women simply must learn to have "conjugal reticence" (639).

These responses undoubtedly reflect the backlash of the decade against women's expanding public role. In comparison to the other four essays, Davis's assessment of the state of marriage in America is refreshingly modern in perspective. Not surprisingly, she begins her discussion with the assertion that the question is as old as history, surviving from Adam and Eve to the present. Nor does it matter to what race or class a couple belongs—unhappy marriages are a consequence of social training and the marketplace mentality of a society that puts a young woman "out for sale to the highest bidder" (623). Happiness between husband and wife, Davis counters, comes from "genuine love, a habit of honest thinking and acting, a little leisure in their lives, and, above all, reverence for a Power higher than themselves" (623). The question ought to be, she asserts, whether the conditions in American society today are conducive to the growth of a positive relationship: the pursuit of money corrupts every aspect of American life; in the papers and in the pulpit, young women are encouraged to make the best possible match.

Like Harland, Davis uses the horse-race metaphor for courtship: the young woman "is brought out at last like a horse upon the course. . . . Every step she takes, every triumph, is recorded in the vulgar publicity of the Society columns. . . . If she marries a rich man, she is congratulated in them as having made good running" (623). Poor young men see rich older men purchase the young women they love, and the young men learn to desire only women with large dowries. In truth, love is a rare commodity in all of this, but Davis reminds her audience that this is the way of the city; in the rural segments of American life—for the "American *per se*"— that is not the case. She asserts that there they seldom marry "without a hearty, honest throb of love" (624). To Davis's mind, if women were to blame in urban society for adhering to their training and marrying according to the marketplace ideal, men were to blame in the country because, even though they marry in honesty, they are in ever-increasing numbers succumbing to the "greed for riches . . . [that] is debasing and vulgarizing our whole life" (624). In her conclusion, Davis's optimism rises, however, and she asserts that "the vast majority of marriages in this country are happy" (626). She concludes by rewriting the original question: "How can we decide whether the credit is due to the husband or the wife?" (626)

* * *

For twenty years, Davis had been a contributing editor and integral member of the staff of the *New York Tribune*. She undoubtedly would have continued for many years to voice her opinions in the pages of the *Tribune* on topical issues and her lucid insights into American society's evolution; but Davis was a writer of integrity, as her resignation from one of the most respected and powerful newspapers in the nation proved. Whitelaw Reid had succeeded Horace Greeley as editor in 1872, and his interests in the effects of Reconstruction on the South and, like Greeley, his advocacy of blacks' suffrage, had given him and Davis a basis of common concern in the early years of his assistant editorship and subsequent control of the *Tribune*'s editorial perspective. At the end of the 1880s, however, Davis wrote a series on the abuses being perpetrated by Northern industries that were diverting the chemicals they needed for their manufacturing processes away from the South, where they were also desperately needed to treat diseased patients. It was a carefully detailed exposé, but many of these Northern industries were major advertisers in the *Tribune* and they resoundingly protested the series.[43] To Davis's amazement, she was advised to abandon the issue. This was the era in which the great city dailies such as the *Tribune* were replacing the older, established journals as the arbiters of public opinion, but with the unprecedented—and often unanticipated—surge of new papers that emerged during the 1880s, competition became the byword of the industry. Within this new, competitive atmosphere, circulation numbers became crucial, and circulation, like profits, was enhanced by advertising. Davis came face to face with the threat she had warned against throughout the 1870s and 1880s—advertisers' control over public opinion. She did not flinch. Nor did she compromise. As a political protest against this infringement upon her First Amendment rights, Davis resigned.

Her departure came unpropitiously at the moment when access to such a public arena coincided with her own ability to meet such demands: she was healthy, comparatively rested, and increasingly concerned with the socioeconomic conditions in America. *The Independent*'s earlier offer of regular-contributor status now resurfaced as a viable alternative to the *Tribune*, an alternative which, in fact, allowed her to express her concerns in a more prolific and subjective manner. She had published occasional items for *The Independent* in the early years of the decade. "Only Father" (December 1880) is notable for its assessment of wasted American lives but also for its reference to Émile Zola. In discussing Americans' fascination with the grotesque, she remarks:

> Our Irish fellow-citizens, who exult in a corpse and go to a funeral with the keen relish and for precisely the same reasons that their neighbors in the wider street read Zola or fill the theaters when a tragedy is well played, perhaps find intellectual comfort in that sort of scheduled horror. The bill of mortality is the printed program, the libretto of the real play to them. They can pore over it and make alive for themselves the *dramatis personae* of corpses.[44]

Davis suggests that instead of our fascination with how people die, with recording "bills of mortality" (obituaries) upon their physical death, we should observe "another sort of bill of mortality"—the lifelong corruption of our dreams and ambitions. We should detail when a person begins to die, especially when he sets aside his goals to provide excessive material goods for his children or squanders his meager fortune in avaricious speculation. Davis had long abandoned scientific determinism as a philosophy; she was interested in the "bill" of life, not of death.

One aspect of that focus was also revealed in her essay "Next Door" (January 1882), in which she lamented the "interminable rows of dwelling houses in Philadelphia."[45] These houses "ugly, snug, comfortable, every marble step and door-knob the precise duplicate of a thousand twin brothers," she observed, were "the delight of the political economist." Still the largest city in the nation, Philadelphia was then termed the "city of homes," a conglomeration of row-house neighborhoods linked by a massive system of street railways and cable cars which allowed 117 million passengers annually to evince the rise of the urban commuting system.[46]

Davis continued to address these social concerns when she became a regular contributor for *The Independent* at the end of the decade. In 1889, she published a dozen articles, ten of which were lead items, immediately establishing her as *The Independent*'s most prominent voice.[47] Over the summer months, her dateline altered from Philadelphia to Marion, Massachusetts, to Point Pleasant, New Jersey, as she "vacationed" with her family. But for the time she did not write out of compunction. She and Clarke were able to support their family comfortably, if not luxuriously, so that her writing remained a necessity but was not as intensely pressured as it had been in the seventies.

But another issue now faced Davis. Her sons were grown and would soon establish their own residences, and Nora at seventeen had her own social circle and interests. The woman who had consigned herself to ride the "family horse" now discovered that, in her mid-fifties and still intellectually vibrant, she was considered middle-aged and no longer the center of her children's lives. In "A World Old Story" she records a middle-aged woman's sense of alienation from her offspring. In another essay of that period, she asserted that in a society increasingly dependent upon credit, the "baby creditors" had been abandoned: the woman at home who has been forgotten by the man of business; the self-sacrificing mother who eagerly sought to give her children every advantage but who in fact taught them "her own anxiety for money, position, fashion"; and the elderly parent who receives no words of gratitude for years of care.[48] These domestic creditors, Davis suggests, are as significant as their financial counterparts, but their "accounts against us will never be sent in here." There is certainly a twinge of self-pity in the two essays, but Davis was never one to indulge herself under hardships; thus she grasped her pen with renewed energy and discovered that she had much yet to say.

Her essays of 1888–89 for *The Independent* confront five major issues: the "new religion"; charitable activism; the American national character as the nation neared the end of the century; the status of blacks in America; and the status of America's urban working women. Many of these issues had been at the heart of Davis's fiction and essays for the first thirty years of her career; all of them would continue to interest and concern her over the remaining twenty years of her life.

Her legacy of sociopolitical essays chronicles the issues of the day in late nineteenth-century America. Davis's essays on the new theological propositions that seemed to arrive on one's doorstep as regularly as the morning newspaper are especially enjoyable for their tone and style. Instead of the sometimes too ardent sentimentalism of her lesser works, she has a tongue-in-cheek, above-the-fray perspective in both of her essays on this subject that is far more devastating in its rejection of the new theologies. "The New Religious 'What Is It?' " is the best of the two; it is an analysis of Mary A. Ward's *Robert Elsmere*, the success of which, Davis notes, has made Ward, justifiably, "the organ and mouthpiece of the new sect" of Oxford disbelievers to which Ward belonged. Ward is confident, Davis observes, that her attacks on Christianity will have everlasting effects: "By the time the last ram's horn shall be blown the walls of this ancient jericho within which the good people of the world have sheltered them-selves for eighteen centuries will be leveled with the dust."[49] The confusion and fear that Ward has perpetrated among naive Christians is easily eradicated, however: "As everybody knows the only thing to be done to a frightened horse is to lead it up directly to the object which has scared it. Let us look closely, therefore, at Mrs. Ward and her vaunted 'new doctrine,' and find what cause for alarm lies in either." This supposedly new doctrine, Davis asserts, is nothing more than the old "hackneyed dogmas of the Hicksite Quakers and of other branches of the Unitarian Church in this country. . . . The lion that roars so loud is no lion, but only Snug, the joiner, whom we have known so long."

But Davis is in fact less concerned with Ward's theology than she is with her abandonment of novel writing. Throughout the essay, Davis is careful to acknowledge Ward's literary abilities: an "able novelist," Ward's strengths are "dramatic insight" into setting and characterization and a power of expression that rewards the "thoughtful reader." However, these are the traits that Ward has abandoned in her new theological zeal. Though Davis mocks Ward's rhetorical style as "charmingly feminine" because it ignores the conventions of supporting an argument, she sees that it is in fact drawn from "the unconscious lofty self-sufficiency of the Arnold clique in England." What Ward ought to do, Davis concludes, is abandon her dogma and "betake herself to her real work and give us a genuine, good novel," such as her earlier novel in which "Miss Mary Anderson was the *motif*." Thus Davis asserts that this talented woman should abandon her male-usurped vision to return to her "real work" as a novelist of women's lives.

In two essays of this period, Davis returned to the issue of how charity should be administered in America. "The Plague Spot of America" suggests the need for community action, while "At Our Gates" explores the individual's responsibilities.[50] Most wealthy Christians in America, Davis observes, extend themselves to assist with every form of disease and misery—except one: leprosy. Advocating that leprosy "be brought under the control of Christian charity and scientific skill," Davis denotes the hereditary nature of the disease and charges that it will not be eradicated until the victims are isolated and humanely nursed. She outlines the history of leprosy in America and its rampant spread in present-day Louisiana, especially in the La Fourche Bayou region. If Americans truly wished to honor the recently deceased Father Damien, she suggests, they should develop a "practical movement to relieve, isolate and nurse" the lepers in their own communities. This article was cited and quoted at length in *Littell's Living Age*, a weekly noted for reprinting the best articles from foreign periodicals and, occasionally, from American publications.

In "At Our Gates," however, Davis addressed a less dramatic but potentially pervasive situation that had surfaced in a recent and widely reported incident in Connecticut. A man who was driven by hunger to beg at a farm for a cup of coffee had been arrested, fined thirty dollars, and imprisoned for one month. These events recalled to Davis's mind a New York incident which she had reported a decade earlier in "Indiscriminate Charity." In that instance, a starving woman and child were turned away from charitable institutions during a winter's evening because they did not have the proper papers; the child froze to death. The problem, Davis asserts, was that Americans were relinquishing their responsibilities to the large charitable societies. This lifelong assertion of Davis's culminates in the essay's astute recognition that the reason Americans preferred institutions was not because they were better equipped to aid the poor but because they were such an effective means of protecting the sensibilities of the well-to-do from the realities of impoverishment.

The devastation caused by the Johnstown flood of 1889 acted as the impetus for a series of essays by Davis on American national traits; in this case, beyond the immediate causes of the flood, Davis discerned a broader issue to be addressed. In "Some Significant Facts," she asserted that the "death-trap" that had been created at Johnstown was, in fact, only a reflection of a pervasive American complacency: "The people of Johnstown, living beneath this poorly caged bell of water, 'took it for granted all was right.' "[51] That phrase becomes the refrain in Davis's essay on similar and oft-repeated tragedies. There is "a momentary spasm of popular rage. . . . But in six months the danger, the law and the penalty are all forgotten by the jolly, easy-going American, who takes it for granted all is right." But Davis abruptly shifts to the "German and Irish toughs" who absconded with the first provisions sent to aid the victims of the flood and the "Gangs of Hungarians [who] prowled over the valley, robbing and mutilating the bodies of the dead." Thereafter, the essay descends into an uncharacteristic xenophobia and concludes that immigrants must exhibit *American* manners and morals, not those of their native countries: "It is liberty, not license, that we offer our guest." During the 1880s and 1890s America witnessed a rise of extremely bitter xenophobia, and ultraconservative organizations such as the Know-Nothing Party and the American Protective Association were formed.[52] As early as 1882 the federal legislature had enacted a Chinese Exclusion Act, and these decades saw a rampant rise in racism and religious intolerance. But from a long-standing advocate of human rights, "Some Significant Facts" is a shocking descent.

Davis's other two essays on national traits, however, are of the standard we would expect from her. The first addresses the decline in the integrity of journalistic reporting, and, like so many of Davis's essays of this period, it speaks to issues still relevant a century later. Of greatest concern to Davis is journalism's willingness to probe into and publicly air every morbid aspect of a citizen's life. But, ultimately, who is to blame?—"Publishers, editors and reporters, like any other retail dealers, merely furnish the wares which the public most earnestly demand." Have we come, she asks, to the point that the commonplace individual, "bewildered with the chances which our American life affords of rising in the world, . . . fancies that notoriety is elevation and a vulgar exposure of his affairs to the public is distinction?"

This assessment leads her, in a subsequent essay, to detail "Our National Vanities." She outlines two specific vanities that are eroding the national character. The first and perhaps "most ludicrous" is the modern American's insistence on his ancestors' high birth, a complete misrepresentation of the "respectable poor folk who came here to better their condition."[53] The most ardent Americans in this endeavor, Davis insists, are New Englanders whose "sectional vanity" forces them to insist that "these heroic pioneers" were inured with graces of extraordinary merit that warranted "the veneration of the country." It is simply a myth, Davis asserts: the New England settlers "neither left religious freedom nor did they give it, to anybody but themselves, as witness the Baptists, Episcopalians and Quakers, whom they whipped at the cart's tail and the poor savages whom they shot and burned, 'the smell of whose sizzling flesh,' according to the godly Pilgrim father of Plymouth, 'went up as a sweet savor to the nostrils of the Almighty.' " The religious tolerance with which America prides itself was established, Davis notes, by the early Swedish settlers who endeavored to settle the Pennsylvania wilderness under Gustavus Adolphus's funding and by the subsequent efforts of William Penn, who accomplished that goal. The second vanity, however, reveals the danger of the first, for we still believe, Davis asserts, that individual freedom is a way of life in America; and it is—unless one's skin is red or black. She concludes the essay with a stinging indictment of American racial hypocrisy: "Our other American conceits are laughable, but there is something tragic in our vanity on our national freedom and justice, when we see that they now depend wholly on the color of a skin."

These ideas led Davis to consider the status of American blacks nearly twenty-five years after the Civil War. The two essays in which she explored this issue, however, appear to be written by two people with significantly disparate attitudes. While "What About the Northern Negro?" asserts that prejudice as a factor is not being underrated, it patronizingly insists upon assimilation and upon the recognition that blacks are naturally more capable as farmers than as tradesmen. The essay reveals an ingrained racism even in one who feels that she is enlightened and free of prejudice. On the other hand, "A Word to Colored People" is Davis at her best. The author, who believed in attempting to cross all gulfs of race and class, admonishes "white demagogs" who insist that race presents "an impassable gulf," referring to Home Missionary minister Josiah Strong's assertion in 1886 that "an almost impassable gulf" existed between America's working class and its industrial employers.[54] Davis calls upon blacks to build a sense of racial union, which she has not observed among them. The fact that she did not perceive among African Americans a "race feeling" leads her to assume that it does not exist, and yet she rises above this limited perspective and cites "an old Negress in Boston" who counsels her children in racial pride: "*It's your business to be black.*" Davis embraces the woman's idea and concludes: "There can be no nobler work for a man than that of lifting up his own despised race. If God has sent you into the world a Negro, make it your business to be black. So bear yourself that the next generation of men shall not mistake you for a white man, but wish that they too were Negroes." Davis had been a voice in the forefront of equal rights for thirty years, but her literary record remains a paradoxical symbol of "enlightened" attitudes among whites, as these two essays illustrate: at times she was sadly blinded to her own prejudice; at other times she was able to rise to her ideal of equality.

The last theme of this series of essays centers on women's status in urban America, and Davis is especially concerned with young women who envision the city as a means to enjoyment, wealth, and a good marriage. In "Shop and Country Girls," she asks, "Is there no way by which the hours of women's labor in the retail shops can be regulated?"[55] Unlike their male counterparts, women clerks did not receive overtime pay and thus were "wholly at the mercy of their employers as regards wages and time." Ironically, the power vested in the employer comes, as Davis notes, from the sheer number of young women who leave their homes in the country to seek employment in the city, a fact Theodore Dreiser would render explicitly in his turn-of-the-century novel, *Sister Carrie*. The country girl who comes to the city ends up a "poor white slave" in a department store, earning as little as $2.50 per week for fifteen-hour daily shifts. Davis gains a moment of undoubtedly satisfying retribution when she observes that the daily press is under the control of large advertisers—such as the department stores that are abusing this labor force—and, therefore, they cannot be relied upon for assistance. Her answer is ultimately to recommend that young women remain at home: "There is no hope. Don't be deluded, girls, by silly stories in the Sunday papers of 'marvelous and sudden successes of unknown girl artists,' or of their 'happy, innocent Bohemian life' in charming apartments of their own, where, unchaperoned, they give teas and 'receive brilliant men and women nightly.' " In this conclusion Davis exposes her own bitter sense that the industrial capitalists have won.

Although young women were entering the large American urban centers by the thousands each year, Davis fought against the prevailing tides. In "Low Wages for Women," she extended that fight against the popular belief that "man is in full possession of the ship Labor, steers and sails it, while poor shipwrecked woman clutches half drowning at the gunwale, trying to climb on board."[56] She herself had suggested as much in her earlier essay, but, as with her position on racial prejudice, she was often able to emerge from the conservative mainstream and present insightful alternatives to submission. Many women—especially those of the upper class—offer "sympathy for their underpaid sisters," but surely, Davis insists, this is not what the working woman needs: "Shall we stand and weep with the lines of hungry seamstresses waiting for the gingham shirts or inquire into the reason why they are there? Is there no better-paid work? Why is it not given to them?" Instead of pretending that women can change the way of the marketplace, they must realize that "Competition in every line of labor is so great that only the specialist who does one thing better than his fellows can succeed. Men recognize that fact. Women, as yet, do not." As she had in " 'In the Market,' " Davis suggests that women should study their environment and create occupations for themselves that fill an as yet unmet need. Then as now, she acknowledged, it is not a glamorous alternative, but it is a pragmatic one. Davis believed that only by following such a course

would a self-supporting woman be able to turn her back on the manufac-
turer and his abusive employment policies.

*   *   *

The decade closed with comments about Davis by two renowned literary figures who speak to the reputation she had maintained in spite of
her reduced literary output and, more importantly, acknowledge her ability to move "across the gulf" between both romanticism and realism. The
first comment came from Walt Whitman. As a rising young journalist,
Richard Harding Davis had interviewed the great American poet; after
Richard left, Whitman is reported to have remarked to his long-time
friend, Horace Traubel, "So you say that was the son of Rebecca Harding
Davis?"[57] More explicit was William Dean Howells's grudging admittance
that Davis was a writer to be reckoned with. In his "Editor's Study" column for *Harper's*, Howells remarked: "Mrs. Rebecca Harding Davis has
written stories which, if of an effect too nearly immediate, are very intense."[58] The intensity of her realism, especially in the articles she would
write for *The Independent* in the coming decade, would continue to increase, as would her demand for attention to the ills of American society.
Davis was crossing the gulf once again, with renewed vigor.

6. The Decadence of a Race

THE TRADITION IN DAVIS SCHOLARSHIP has been to assert that Davis's writings of the last two decades of her life were insignificant in terms of her own canon and in relation to American literary history.[1] Yet her renewed vigor of the late 1880s was carried forth into the next decade, and Davis's nonfiction and fiction alike offer well-written, insightful commentaries on the end of the nineteenth century, and they move into the modern period both artistically and thematically. It was not Davis's fin de siècle, and we do her and American literature a disservice by ignoring these later contributions. The themes that had concerned her for the past thirty years—stifled lives, the consequences of speculation and greed, the shameful glorification of war—became topical once again in the 1890s, as the country entered a period of increased progress coupled with high unemployment, insurrections, colonization, and military involvement in other countries.

When Davis was not traveling, she regularly published her social commentary in *The Independent* and continued writing for *Peterson's, Youth's Companion*, and *St. Nicholas*. In addition, she returned to the renowned literary journals of the day, including *Harper's, Century Magazine*, and the *North American Review*, and she expanded her forums for publication to include periodicals such as *The Living Age, The World*, and *Good Housekeeping*. More important, two leading publishing firms, Charles Scribner's Sons and Harper & Brothers, each published two full-length works by Davis in this decade. Thus, as she entered her sixties, she not only saw both of her sons establish themselves in the field of literature but returned to it herself as a commanding presence.

One of her first major works was the 1890 short story, "An Ignoble Martyr," published by *Harper's New Monthly Magazine*. This was the year that saw the publication of William James's *Principles of Psychology*[2] and Jacob A. Riis's *How the Other Half Lives*. Seemingly disparate, the themes of James's and Riis's studies were anticipated in Davis's short story through the psychological realism of her characterization of that "other half." She had chronicled the lives of the working oppressed in "Life in the Iron Mills," but her attention now focused more and more upon the stifled lives of women, as it had in the 1870s. In this fictionalized form, and in a later outspoken essay on New England's abandoned spinsters, Davis was concerned with the psychological damage suffered by women who were deprived of healthy relationships and satisfying careers. But Davis also demanded activism; these women needed to insist upon changes and to accept them when the opportunity arose.

In "An Ignoble Martyr," Priscilla (Prue) Pettit represents the failure of both society and the individual—her social education thwarts her ability to prevail against traditions, and her own reliance upon the safety of tradition forces her to deny herself the route to personal fulfillment that she desires. The people in Prue's hometown of North Leedom have taken an honest virtue and distorted it into a destructive obsession: "they had reduced the economy of their Puritan ancestors to an art so hard and cruel that it dominated them now in body and soul. To save . . . had become the highest of duties."[3] Each generation's niggardliness had increased until their lives are now stripped of all means of enjoyment: "They came at last in their fierce zeal for saving to begrudge smiles and welcomes to each other or kisses and hugs to their children" (96). This excessive frugality leaves them physically and spiritually hungry, so much so that when opportunity enters in the form of M. Rameaux, they deny their own desires for a different way of life. Rameaux, a Mississippian whose community "carried the kindness and pity of their hearts ready for constant use" (99), offers Prue a chance for a new life in his symbolically fertile homeland. But because she has rarely seen anyone courted and more rarely seen love expressed, she has insufficient courage to leave her resolute mother: "it seemed to her, the gates were opened, the kingdoms of the world were laid at her feet. Of her own will she had given them up" (108).

Prue does incorporate some of Rameaux's influence into her barren life after he leaves. She plants a few flowers, reads some novels, and even visits New Bedford, where she rallies her courage enough to step into a retail shop and touch "some crimson silk and black-plumed hats" (109). But Davis discerns no heroism in martyrdom;[4] she presents these touches of finery in an otherwise destitute life as pathetic substitutes for the full life Prue might have lived. Davis had explored this theme in several of her longer works of the 1870s, and Rose Terry Cooke had detailed a similar theme in the late 1850s; but in "Ignoble Martyr," Davis expressly presents the complicity women bear in this process, a position that Mary E. Wilkins Freeman also presented in several of her short stories, including "A Poetess." As the women of the 1890s explored new avenues of personal development, Davis presented in "An Ignoble Martyr" a warning against the bleak alternatives to such activism.

This short story also challenges a prominent theme in New England literary traditions. From *The Scarlet Letter* to "A New England Nun," that region's authors had repeatedly suggested that a prolonged courtship or chastity itself enabled "the flowering of man";[5] Davis, however, following Catherine Maria Sedgwick's early if incomplete challenges to the premise, envisioned New England provincialism as a potential arena for women's entrapment. There is no "flowering" for Prue, only a slow death upon the stifling vine of New England custom.

*   *   *

Davis had been associated with the Boston weekly *The Living Age* for some time when, in May, they reprinted portions of her essay, "The Plague Spot of America." *The Living Age* reprinted American fiction, poetry, and essays and was known for its reprints of the best fiction and articles from English periodicals such as *Blackwood's, Macmillan's*, and *The Spectator*. The weekly's motto was, "These publications of the day should from time to time be winnowed, the wheat preserved, and the chaff thrown away," and the editors had discerned that "The Plague Spot" and several short stories by Davis warranted preservation. Thus Davis took advantage of this association to tout the talents of her eldest son to Mr. Bridgeman, an editor for *The Living Age*. Bridgeman had commented positively on some of Richard's early work, for which Davis heartily thanked him: "I am glad that you like my boy's work. You would like *him*. I have never heard him say an unkind malicious thing of any human being. And I have known him a long time!"[6]

She drew on other literary contacts to encourage Richard's career as well. In April, she wrote to her old friend from Houghton, Mifflin, Horace Elisha Scudder, who had recently accepted the editorship at the *Atlantic Monthly*. "Do you remember a talk we once had about our children and our hopes for them?" she asked Scudder, who, like Davis, had published many works for children. "Now my boy has done something which gives a hint of what manner of man he is and I venture to ask you as an old friend to let the Atlantic pass judgment on it." But she cautioned Scudder that she did not want preferential treatment for Richard: " 'Be just and fear not' even a mother's disappointment, if the verdict is not favourable."[7] Scudder took her at her word and declined the manuscript. Davis had not told Richard of her efforts on his behalf, however, so he remained unaware of this rejection. He was, in fact, gaining his own way in the literary world. He had been working for the New York *Evening Sun* as a reporter for almost six months, under the tutelage of managing editor Arthur Brisbane, and in March of 1890 the Van Bibber stories began to appear; they were to make him a household name. Charles published short fiction and essays, but he never gained the recognition of his elder brother. Today, Charles's authorship is known primarily in terms of *The Adventures and Letters of Richard Harding Davis* (1917), his laudatory assessment of his brother's life.

Three Davis authors—Rebecca, Richard, and Charles—soon found themselves congenially competing for space in several literary periodicals. No tensions of competitiveness seem to have marred their relationships; instead, their letters reveal a heartfelt encouragement regarding each other's work. A few years later, when Rebecca and Richard had books published simultaneously, Richard wrote to his mother: "I am so glad to hear about the book. It seems too cosy and nice for us to be coming out together. People will buy both so as to be sure to get the right one and we will get rich and go to Europe *by land*. . . . I am so glad about it and much more interested than if it were my own."[8] He signed the letter with his usual phrase, "Your boy, Dick." Although scholars have since forgotten, the Davises were one of America's most prolific and prominent literary families at the end of the nineteenth century.

In 1891, Davis's sons encouraged her to return to longer fiction. Though *Natasqua* had been reprinted four years earlier, no significant long fiction by Davis had appeared in novel form since the 1870s. She contacted her old friend Richard Watson Gilder, who had been an assistant editor of *Scribner's Monthly* when she was a regular contributor and who now headed *Century Magazine*. "Are you for treating us to a long serial?" Davis asked Gilder. "My boys have been anxious for a long time that I should write one." Davis had the novel well under way and had an offer from another publisher, but, as she told Gilder, "I would rather see it in the Century than anywhere else."

Davis, however, felt a certain trepidation at reentering the field of novel writing. It had been more than fifteen years since she had put her mind to an endeavor of such length and, she cautiously observed, "Whether my hand has lost whatever cunning it once had, I cannot tell."[9]

She need not have worried. Her fiction of this decade has the grace of tone and style reflective of an ability to write out of artistic interest rather than financial compunction. The novel was *Kent Hampden*, an excellent story designed for adolescent readers, which draws on the factual history of Wheeling and is reminiscent of Davis's own early family life.

Other factors made *Century Magazine* a logical source for Davis's fiction, since the journal was now devoting much of its space to the new realistic fiction. In this decade the *Century* serialized Howells's *A Modern Instance* and *The Rise of Silas Lapham*, Henry James's *The Bostonians*, Jack London's *The Sea-Wolf*, and Joel Chandler Harris's "Uncle Remus" stories. The periodical also published several essays and works of fiction by established and new women realists, including Elizabeth Stuart Phelps, Mary E. Wilkins (Freeman), and Octave Thanet (Alice French). In a few years, Davis would return to its pages with her own realistic fiction, but she or Gilder, or perhaps both, decided against *Century Magazine* for *Kent Hampden*.

Instead, the novel was serialized in *Youth's Companion* and published in book form by Charles Scribner's Sons in 1892. The novel was dedicated to her brothers, Hugh Wilson Harding and Richard Harris Harding, "who have hunted over every foot of Kent's hills"; it was for them that she "inscribe[d] this little story of our old home." The Hampden family bears many resemblances to the Hardings, especially in terms of its father figure, but the story is a fictionalized retelling of early nineteenth-century life in West Virginia that includes excellent adventure and mystery sequences. The reviewer for *The Critic* especially praised Davis for her attention to "local color" and the "spirit" with which she recreated life in Wheeling at the beginning of the century.[10]

If Davis had learned anything from her self-imposed "retirement" of the 1880s, it was that she needed to balance her highly productive literary career with periods of rest and relative quiet. Thus she informed William Hayes Ward, superintending editor of *The Independent*, that she wished to take a year's leave from her regular contributions to the periodical. She held as closely to this goal as possible, considering the creative energies recently awakened in her: she published four short pieces for him in 1891. Her decision to forego journalism for a time was not made so that she might have more rest; instead, she sought time to complete several long works that she had in mind. In subsequent years, Davis produced some excellent fiction that brought her once again into the arena of contemporary experimental fiction.

Throughout this decade, Davis was also barraged with requests from editors of national dictionaries and literary collections for biographical details, interviews, and photographs. She graciously produced details of her life or referred the inquirer to previously published data. One of the most interesting mentions of Davis in a study of the period was Helen Gray Cone's study of "Woman in American Literature," which appeared in the October 1890 issue of *Century Magazine*. Cone began her study by acknowledging the negative effects of considering women's literary contributions separately from men's, which has allowed "the suave and chivalrous critic, . . . judging all 'female writers' by a special standard," to assess women's works according to a different set of criteria.[11] Thus Cone sought to produce an objective literary history of women's writings that acknowledged the "accessions of force" attained in women's literary contributions in recent years, a force which she felt was gradually increasing (921). Beginning with Anne Bradstreet, Phillis Wheatley, and Mercy Otis Warren, and moving through the nineteenth century, Cone includes Davis as one of the notable women of the mid- to late-nineteenth century, along with Catherine Maria Sedgwick, Lydia Maria Child, Harriet Beecher Stowe, Elizabeth Stuart Phelps, and others.

Such acknowledgments Davis welcomed, but she continued to refuse requests for photographs or interviews. When Charles Wells Moulton requested a portrait to illustrate a sketch of Davis's life that he was preparing, she declined both, asserting, "Nothing ever happened to me which would give point to an item. And I have a dislike to seeing anything about myself (personally) in print. But I quite appreciate your compliment."[12] While Davis's reluctance to promote herself in the literary marketplace was perhaps honorable, it was also detrimental to her lasting fame. But, as she asserted in "The Temple of Fame," honor is always preferable to fame.

What Davis did appreciate was the personal rather than the public gesture. Thus she was delighted when the renowned Philadelphia Shakespeare scholar Horace Howard Furness honored her by sending her a copy of *The Tempest*. The gift recalled to her mind the joy and the strange otherworldliness she had discovered in the bard's pages when, at age eight, she had received copies of *Julius Caesar* and *The Tempest* from her mother. "But if I had been told," she wrote Furness,

> that some time the high priest of Shakespeare for all the world would send the Tempest to me—*me*, it would have seemed much stranger and more unreal than Ariel or Caliban or any of their spiriting.

> So I won't be humble and think that you sent this to Clarke's wife or Dick's mother but to—*me*. And I'm very glad you did it.[13]

Her appreciation of Furness's thoughtful gesture echoed her response when she had heard, so many years earlier, that Nathaniel Hawthorne intended to visit her in Wheeling.

Even more delightful to Davis was her renewed association with Mary Mapes Dodge, editor of *St. Nicholas*. Davis had not published in *St. Nicholas* since the mid-1870s, in large part because *Youth's Companion* paid so much more than Dodge's periodical,[14] but perhaps also because Dodge had, for a short time in the mid-seventies, replaced Annie Fields as Davis's most intimate female correspondent. With her children grown, Davis may have felt the need for renewed contact—this time without the urgency that her strained relations with Fields had added to her earlier contact with Dodge. Thus, in the summer of 1890, Davis decided to submit a short story ("The Great Tri-Club Tennis Tournament") to *St. Nicholas*; Dodge published the story in the September issue. The following spring, Dodge invited Davis to a tea she was hosting in New York. Davis declined, but her letter reveals the pleasure she received from the offer:

> My dear Mrs. Dodge
> I cannot content myself with sending cards to show how sorry I am not to be able to go to your tea.
> How long it is since I saw or heard from you! Do you never come to this quiet corner of the earth? We live in the same old house [at] 230 South 21st Street. *Do* come. I heard you had a boy in town but I suppose he would be bored by an old woman.
> If I ever go to New York I shall find the Cordova and claim friendship with you.[15]

Yet Davis and Dodge remained in contact only sporadically over the intervening years. It was not until 1897 that they would renew their literary association and revive a friendship that extended until Dodge's death in 1905.

During this period, Davis also continued her personal activism for women in her community, and she did not hesitate to use her literary connections in these endeavors. For example, she contacted Richard Watson Gilder at the *Century* and urged him to publish two articles that had been sent to her by "a little Scotchwoman here in whom Mr. Davis and I are much interested." Davis described the unnamed woman as bright and sensitive but impoverished and struggling to provide a home for a severely retarded child. Davis asserted that the illustrated articles, "one on Barrie's country and the other on Gladstone's early life," ought to be of interest to the *Century's* readership since they were drawn by the pen of a writer who came from the "Thrums" region.[16] Davis also sought Horace Scudder's assistance. This time, Davis and a friend, Mrs. Wells,[17] were attempting to send a sick woman to the country for a much-needed rest. Davis approached Scudder with a translation that Mrs. Wells had prepared and hoped to publish in *Riverside Magazine*. Davis wittingly relied upon Scudder's senses of humor and honor: Mrs. Wells, she observed, "has an idea that you publishers have a sort of Ali-Baba cave—of which one only needs to know the pass-word to go in and pick up gold in bushel measures. I gave her the pass-word now and—*have not undeceived her*. I am sure *you* will not for the honor of the craft."[18] Mrs. Wells remained "undeceived."

*   *   *

In conjunction with her enthusiasm for returning to full-length works of fiction, Davis aggressively pursued a publisher for her second book of the period. Scribner's had recently published *Kent Hampden*, and she now proposed to them the publication of a collection of her short stories, which they enthusiastically agreed to publish.[19] Davis's collection, drawn from stories she had written over the previous twenty years, is indicative in itself of her pioneering work in the field of realism. In 1891 Hamlin Garland had published his collected study of the decaying countryside, *Main-Travelled Roads*, and Mary Wilkins Freeman had also published her short-story collection, *A New England Nun*, which presents the same images of decay but with a special focus on women's lives. The realism, nostalgia, and at times bitterness of these two authors' works deeply echo the mood of Davis's collection, *Silhouettes of American Life*.

Silhouettes is one of those forgotten "gems" in American literature. The writing is superb, the vision Davis gives us of America in the last half of the nineteenth century is invaluable, and the stories entertain as well as educate. The short stories, with one exception, had been previously published in *Scribner's, Harper's, Lippincott's*, and the *Atlantic Monthly*. Many of these stories have been discussed in previous chapters, but a few warrant special attention here. The one new entry, "The End of the Vendetta," follows a literary trend of this period of returning to the early eras of American life. Recent publications that manifested this trend included biographies of Lincoln, John Fiske's study of *The American Revolution*, Thomas Nelson Page's *The Old South*, Stephen Crane's *The Red Badge of Courage*, Moses Coit Tyler's *Literary History of the American Revolution*, and Mary Wilkins Freeman's *Giles Corey, Yeoman*, which focused on the Salem witch trials.

"Vendetta" is set in the days of Reconstruction and follows a young Northern woman, Lucy Coyt, as she journeys into the South, expecting adventures at every turn and "a very different human species" from any she has known (197). Davis delights once again in satirizing the Northerner's preconceived notions about the South and its people. Lucy Coyt believes she is an expert when it comes to analyzing human nature; after all, she "had gone to the Fairview Female Seminary, and had read Carlyle, and the Autocrat in the 'Atlantic,' and 'Beauties of German Authors' " (198). There is an element of self-mockery in this as well, since Lucy's early history closely parallels Davis's own youthful education and reading patterns. But "Vendetta" suggests that Lucy has the potential to set aside her romantic perspectives and gain a truer sense of herself and of Southerners. Lucy, however, returns to the North after accepting a marriage proposal, thus ending "her experiment" in the South, and the people she tried to "educate" return to their own "usual quiet routine of life" (217). The final mood is one of enveloping stasis in which Davis questions the effectiveness of Northern influences on the long-held traditions of the South. Prior to writing "Vendetta," Davis had vacationed in Warm Springs, Virginia, during the summer of 1892, and her observations of the region left her with the disquieting realization that, although Reconstruction had ended officially in 1876, little had changed on either side.

One of the most interesting stories in the collection, both in terms of its artistry and its place in American literary history, is "The Yares of Black Mountain," subtitled "A True Story." Originally published in *Lippincott's* in 1875, this story chronicles the integrity of an impoverished mountain family that had tried to remain neutral during the war but, in the end, had paid dearly in lives and memories. The realistic detailing of the mountain life and the abject poverty of the Yares' existence is graphically rendered, but the story is most interesting for Davis's attention to the vernacular of the mountain people and to the role that women played in the Underground Railroad during the war. In addition, Davis satirizes the new breed of political writer, in the person of Miss Cook, who converses with a few people for five or ten minutes, assuming that they, and now she, have the "facts" about this region. Miss Cook visits the jail-house at the foot of the mountains where, as she records it, men "are actually secured in iron cages like wild beasts! I shall use that fact effectively in my book on the 'Causes of the Decadence of the South': one chapter shall be given to 'The Social and Moral Condition of North Carolina' " (251). When a local woman protests that Miss Cook will need her entire vacation to gather materials for such a project, the political essayist responds with haughty patronization: "Why, child, I have them all now—got them this morning. Oh, I can evolve the whole state of society from half a dozen items. I have the faculty of generalizing, you see" (252).

Davis juxtaposes Miss Cook's surface reporting with the reality of the existence and "terrible history" of the Yares (259). The sons who had tried to remain neutral during the war are forced into hiding in order to avoid being drafted into the Union army, but Jonathan Yare is badly wounded. Although their home is occupied by Union soldiers, their sister, Nancy, manages to sneak away at intervals to build a hut in which John is protected from the bitter cold of the winter nights while he recovers from his wounds. She cuts down logs, builds a six-by-ten-foot hut, floors it, and covers it with brush. When the hut is discovered by the soldiers, however, she is jailed and threatened with imprisonment in the Salisbury prisoner-of-war camp or hanging if she refuses to reveal her brother's whereabouts. Nancy remains silent; she and her four brothers are saved only by their tenacity and Lee's surrender two weeks later. All that remains of value in the Yares' lives is their serene if impoverished existence in the mountains and the knowledge that the family is together again.

Davis's story, which was innovative in theme as well as in its attention to North Carolinian vernacular, had influenced several writers of the seventies. Mary Noailles Murfree published at that time a series of stories on the Cumberland Mountain region under the pseudonym of Charles Egbert Craddock; one of these early stories had appeared in the same issue of *Lippincott's* as "Yares," and a subsequent story, "The Dancin' Party at Harrison's Cove," is indebted to Davis's "Yares" in its assimilation of several themes and scenes from the Davis work.[20] Helen Woodward Shaeffer's early biography of Davis more explicitly acknowledges the importance of "The Yares" in American literary history. "Yares" also influenced Murfree's *In the Tennessee Mountains* (1884), and Shaeffer recounts the ongoing discussion of the 1940s, when she was completing her biography of Davis, as to whether Murfree or Constance Fenimore Woolson "was first in presenting a picture of the North Carolina mountaineers"; in fact, Shaeffer notes, Murfree's "Dancin' Party" and Woolson's "Crowder's Cove: A Story of the

War" both appeared after Davis's story was published in *Lippincott's*. In "Yares," Shaeffer confirms, "Mrs. Davis shows her realistic writing at its best."[21]

Davis is also in top form in "Marcia," another short story collected in *Silhouettes*; it had first appeared in *Harper's* in 1876.[22] In this short story, Davis exposes the limited opportunities that existed for women in the major American periodicals, but she is especially concerned with the prevalence, in contemporary writing, of young authors who refuse to learn their craft. Davis had expressed similar ideas in her essay "Shop and Country Girls" (1889), wherein she observed that often a young rural woman "painted a few plates or had a few months' instruction in crayon drawing, and is looked upon as a genius by her family and neighbors. She comes to town. She fails. 'Art is a drug,' she tells her fellow artist, as they sit in their bare attic making pathetic little sketches in their bedaubed apron."[23] Marcia's writings are sentimental; she tells the established woman writer who acts as narrator of the story that she "had vowed herself to literature . . . resolved to assist in the Progress of humanity" (270). At this juncture in her professional life, Davis reflected current literary trends by moving away from an appreciation of sentimental literature; here, she no longer synthesizes her realism with that perspective nor does she praise those who continue in that mode.

Marcia Barr thinks she needs only to be educated in the ways of Philadelphia publishing, but the narrator notes that the young woman's manuscripts are crude at best: her "spelling was atrocious, the errors of grammar in every line beyond remedy. The lowest pupil in our public schools would have detected her ignorance on the first page" (273). Had this been the sum total of Marcia's talent, the narrator would have sent her away as she had so many other young would-be writers. But, in spite of the crudity of Marcia's writing, the elder woman notes a potential for developing realism in the young woman's style: "there was no trace of imitation"; instead of repeating the locales of the popular fiction, Marcia writes about her home— about what she knows (273). The narrator detects the potential for originality, *if* the young writer is willing to learn her craft, willing to labor for two or three years in order to hone her talents. But Marcia has accepted the "popular belief in the wings of genius, which can carry it over hard work. . . . Work was for commonplace talent, not for those whose veins were full of the divine ichor" (274). Thus Marcia's "fate," not unlike Hugh Wolfe's, is especially tragic because she had the talent necessary for her art. Instead, she struggles to survive in the city and finally is jailed after she succumbs to theft in order to survive. Her persistent lover from home comes to her assistance, but that "salvation" is tragic. Life as Mrs. Biron (certainly an intentionally ironic name) will be little different for Marcia than her residency in the city jail. At the story's conclusion, Marcia knows that she has sold her talent—her entire future—and now must substitute for it this marriage that she abhors. When Marcia asks that her work be destroyed and departs in silence, it is because she knows, at last, this excruciating truth.

Silhouettes was both a critical and popular success. It was reviewed widely and repeatedly praised for its "strong, clear impressions" of American life.[24] *The Independent's* reviewer was laudatory in his comments, as would be expected from a publication for which Davis was a regular contributor. But the reviewer also captures the two most significant aspects of Davis's fiction that had made her a lasting figure in American literature for almost three decades: the stories are "strikingly original, and they are all thoroughly and truthfully American."[25] One of the best reviews came, surprisingly, from Davis's old nemesis, *The Nation*. Although the reviewer began with typically lukewarm praise (the sketches are "worth the reading"), he took exception only with "A Wayside Episode" (a woman-centered story), and concluded: "Among the rest, where there is such an even range of excellence, it would be hard to pick."[26] It was impressive praise from the usually reticent *Nation*. *Silhouettes* went into three editions, and Richard wrote his mother after the third edition appeared in 1893, "These *young* writers are working me to the wall."[27]

*   *   *

In 1893, Davis's thirty-two-year association with *Peterson's Magazine* ended—with neither a breach nor a celebration but with a farewell "grumble." *Peterson's* had begun the decade with Davis at the top of its list of notable contributors, and she had published four items during the nineties before ending her career with the magazine. In January 1893, the editors began a new series and retitled the periodical *The New Peterson Magazine*. Several authors new to the magazine appeared in its pages at this time, including Julian Hawthorne, Joseph Kirkland, Agnes Repplier, Thomas Wentworth Higginson, and Octave Thanet. In the first issue of the *New Peterson's*, the editors began a section entitled "By the Fireside," devoted to their better-known authors' contributions.

The new magazine's first issue became Davis's last, since the Davises had finally reached a financial stage wherein she could forego the higher payments made by *Peterson's* and concentrate on writing only those books and articles that interested her. Davis's final essay for the magazine, "A Grumble," was printed in the "Fireside" section. In the essay, she lamented the lack of American individuality at the end of the nineteenth century: no single footstep can be heard, only "the measured tramp of clubs, committees, guilds, and congresses, both day and night."[28] No longer is there time to sit "By the fireside" and have discussions with old friends (a rather ironic lament, since Davis's life had afforded her scant time for such endeavors). You can neither hate nor love the new breed of American, she asserts, using scientific metaphors: "They are molecules in the mass which moves against capital or labor, which lifts the lower classes by university extension lectures or college settlements or Browning clubs. They will not allow you to creep along your own shady path, either—they make a molecule of you too; you must be an atom of a committee or an organization, or you are naught" (103). She returns to the fears of her first major literary publication when she worries that "we shall all be stifled" by the mass consensus and discipline of modern existence (104). Although she admits her "protest is as vain as is the chirp of the sandpiper against the incoming tides of the ocean," she recalls an ancient parish priest, Reverend Walker, whose personal concern and charitable activism had earned him the nickname of "The Wonderful" (104). He had survived a grueling life by reserving for himself one hour of solitude every day; today, Davis asserts, "he would rush to a club or convention when his soul needed repairs" (104). It is true, she admits, that there is useful work in the modern world; but her final words for *Peterson's* acknowledges her sense of loss: "we have no more Wonderful Walkers" (104).

Her farewell was made easier by the fact that it cost her no personal alienation from old friends, as had occurred so often in the past when she separated with a long-term publisher. Charles Peterson, her long-time friend and editor, had died in 1887. She simply passed the baton without remorse to the next generation of *New Peterson's* authors. That next generation included her second son, Charles, whose fiction appeared in the February issue, and younger metarealists such as Harriet Prescott Spofford and Mary Wilkins Freeman. Indeed, an interesting aspect of the canonization of American literature was visible in *New Peterson's* during late 1896 and early 1897, when the editors ran a five-part series entitled "Pioneers of American Literature." Those pioneers, according to the series' authors, were Irving, Cooper, Hawthorne, Emerson, and Poe. *Peterson's* own loyal pioneer realist was not included nor was any other woman writer. However, if Davis had closed the door on this phase of her literary career, she was about to reopen it to full-length works of fiction. She had no intention of relinquishing her artistic voice.

*   *   *

While Davis allowed her next two novels to develop in her mind, she returned to her regular contributions for *The Independent* and wrote several other pieces for major periodicals over the next two years. In 1894, however, when it seemed that everyone in the family was basking in the luxury of fame and well-being,[29] a frightening event occurred that caused Davis to set aside her own writing for a period of time. Charles then held a government post in Italy, Nora was in Florence visiting her brother, and Clarke, who had taken over the editorship of the Philadelphia *Public Ledger* the previous year when William V. McKean had retired, was engrossed in the work that would occupy him until his death. Richard, who at age thirty was consulting with his employers at Harper's about the possibility of resigning that post for an opportunity to do more traveling, was suddenly stricken with another of his recurring attacks of sciatica; this time, however, it resulted in a far more serious bout with severe depression, and Richard returned to his family home to be nursed by his mother.

Davis had suffered her own mental travails when she was in her early thirties, and she understood the devastating realities of depression in a way that friends and family could not. Richard had been ordered to bed for a month because of the sciatica, but the emotional disturbance that befell him lasted for more than ten months.[30] It is little wonder that Davis's letters of the period are rife with apologies for failure to attend to her mail. A typical letter reads, "Your letter with many others have been neglected because of serious illness in my family. I hope that you will believe that no discourtesy was intended by the delay."[31]

At the beginning of summer, difficulties also began to arise in Davis's long-term, friendly association with *The Independent*. She had not had to barter with Dr. Ward over payments until H. S. Chandler, the publisher, interceded. The tension is evident in a brief letter Dr. Ward sent to Davis in June: "My dear Madam: I am very sorry to say that I am not now allowed by our publishing department to pay $100 for a story of 3,500 or 4,000 words, such as yours have been. I wish I might do it."[32] On Ward's copy of the letter, there is a handwritten note in the upper right-hand corner: "Copy shown to H.S.C. who said 'That is all right, sir.' " Chandler wished to limit payment to fifty dollars, or one-half of what Davis was accustomed to receiving, and on at least one occasion she was forced to quibble over whether they would pay her twenty-five or thirty dollars for a short article. This occurred at a time when Davis received, on an average, between forty and one hundred dollars for her articles, depending on length. Not surprisingly, she balked, and Ward himself was obviously dismayed at Chandler's tactics. The era of the genteel publisher was nearly over. A revealing letter from Chandler to Susan Hayes Ward, a staff member of *The Independent* who also had argued on Davis's behalf, suggests the publisher's attitude toward literature and authors:

> My dear Miss Ward:
>   A story is a story and business is business. The idea that writers for newspapers and magazines are not supposed to do business in a business way, it seems to me, ought to be exploded. The only way to treat with R. H. D. or with any other writer is from a business standpoint. If they write for money they enter the business arena and they must treat and be treated accordingly.[33]

The tension grew between Davis and her editor. She became reluctant to write for *The Independent* and returned to the specificity of conditions that she usually reserved for new places of publication:

> Dear Sir
>   I did not understand that I was to send you a story. When you asked me for one, I declined to write it, for the very low price paid by the Independent and asked you if you were willing to pay more, to write to me.
>   I received no answer of any kind.
>   I am very busy at other work but if you have counted on my help I will try and send you a short story by Saturday Dec. 14. The price to be $50 *paid on receipt of Ms*. If this will suit you please write by return mail.[34]

The friendship between Davis and Ward was eventually restored, but, ironically, Chandler's concern for proper business methods seemed to operate only in one direction: Davis often had to write *The Independent*'s business manager to remind him that she had not received payment. In September she informed Ward that the manager had not responded "by money nor apology. How blessed the next world will be—where we shall have no use—let us hope, for money or business managers!"[35] She continued to raise the issue of payment before each submission now, insisting that for longer stories she receive full compensation:

Dear Dr. Ward   Sept 20
    I have a Thanksgiving story in my mind—do you want it when it is on
paper for the Independent? The price will be $100.
    I write to you now because you often have asked me for stories so near to
Thanksgiving or Christmas that I could do justice neither to you nor myself.
Please let me hear from you soon.[36]

When, in spite of this letter, Ward waited until early November to request
a Thanksgiving story, Davis responded with a delightfully cryptic note:
"Dear Dr. Ward— I will try. But you *are* an unconscionable man!"[37] She
continued to write for *The Independent* during the remainder of her life—
and she continued to name her price before submitting an item.

              *   *   *

    In addition to writing several topical essays for *The World* during this
period,[38] Davis wrote fiction and essays for the *Congregationalist*, a Boston
weekly. Harriet Prescott Spofford also contributed to the periodical in the
mid-nineties, and Frances E. Willard found in its pages a platform for her
temperance petition. Alice Morse Earle, a nineteenth-century chronicler of
early American women's lives, also began to publish short articles on the
New England Puritans in the *Congregationalist* during this decade. The
weekly was conservative and opposed to women's suffrage; and while it
advocated women's higher education, its essays on that theme, such as
"The College Girl—Her Present Need, Her Future Possibility," by Mary
M. Adams of Wisconsin University, unwittingly reflected the limited inroads women had made in higher education to date. Adams propounds the
"clear and untrammeled right" of young women to a college education and
the "healthful and . . . stimulating" atmosphere of college life, but she concludes that women should have a curriculum distinguished from men's
course of study by its emphasis upon the "true woman" theme.[39] Davis's
work for the *Congregationalist* similarly focused on topical themes, such as
marriage, charity, and blacks' roles in society, but her presentations were
often didactic in style and conservative in their conclusions. That conservatism, always quivering beneath the surface of Davis's less distinguished
writings, would emerge periodically in her final years, as it had throughout
her life.
    In February of 1895, however, Davis returned to the pages of *Century
Magazine* with one of her finest essays. That periodical's attention to the
new realistic fiction and to social consciousness in its essays had attracted

such authors as Joel Chandler Harris, Mary E. Wilkins (Freeman), Elizabeth Stuart Phelps, Octave Thanet, and John Hay. Hamlin Garland published "A Spring Romance" in *Century Magazine* early in the decade, and Mark Twain's *Pudd'nhead Wilson* was serialized the year before Davis's article appeared. Kate Chopin was also beginning to appear in the magazine's pages; she published a few short stories and one poem during the decade. In the following years, Frank Norris found the magazine receptive to his reporting of the Spanish-American War, and Annie Fields published several articles of literary criticism in the pages of the *Century* at the end of the decade. Although the distribution of male authors' works in the *Century* compared to that of female authors remained relatively unchanged from the previous decade, the magazine, instead of relying upon a few women contributors, had expanded its number of female authors significantly.

Davis had last published in the journal in the early 1880s, when it was still *Scribner's Monthly*. Her return was marked by the startling aggressiveness and outspoken realism with which she presented a theme she had been developing over the last two decades: how society perpetuates women's wasted intellectual and emotional lives. It is in this essay, "In the Gray Cabins of New England," that Davis's theme is fully realized.[40] Many New England women writers, including Phelps, Stowe, and later, Jewett, praised the matriarchal isolation of rural New England; but Davis, extending Rose Terry Cooke's lead, recognized that the region was not a utopia. The realities of a desperate impoverishment and sense of abandonment, to Davis's mind, only led women to personal and spiritual deprivation.

In her inimitable spirit of questioning outdated "orthodox formulas," Davis begins her essay by challenging the long-held belief that the greatest intellectual energy in America was to be found in "the gray cabins of New England" (620). True as this idea may have been one hundred or even fifty years earlier, it is, she insists, an arguable assertion in the mid-1890s. While this assertion continues Davis's lifelong rejection of the primacy of Boston literary modes, she had learned over the years to temper her attacks through initial acknowledgment of the values of Boston-centered literature as well. Thus she notes that "nobody who is not made imbecile by prejudice" would deny that Boston, Concord, and a select few other New England cities constitute the most influential literary centers in America. She is also aware that the pattern of questioning the validity of this concentration of influence (which she had begun in the early 1860s) was now the vogue. Momentarily, Davis takes the side of the Boston literati and confirms that they do occasionally acknowledge outsiders' work, and she praises them for their genuine intellectual pursuit of contemporary literature, which they strive for instead of responding only to the classics.

The problem with their widely praised perspective, Davis asserts, is that they have failed to recognize their own region's intellectual decline, and, with this turn in the essay, Davis documents that process of decline. Ten years earlier, she notes, she had visited one of these lonely districts in the very "soul of New England" that are supposed to be harboring the next generation of Hawthornes and Emersons. What she found, however, echoes Hamlin Garland's Border stories: there were only "dull-eyed old men and lean old women"; the young people had gone west or south. Yet even more important was the fact that the remaining New Englanders, who had been well educated, now preferred "the most sensational fiction in a circulating library" and never touched the cover of the best of contemporary fiction (620–21). When the young men left, the vitality of intellectualism went with them. The most pathetic residue of this abandonment were the unmarried women: "These people have not enough food for their bodies, or occupation for their minds. The niggardly economy forced upon their forefathers by the barren soil . . . is honored as the chief of virtues" (621).

This "barren soil" metaphor symbolizes the women both spiritually and sexually. The New Englander's "plain living," Davis asserts, has not "lifted him into high thinking. He is stingy of love, of friendship, of emotion" (621). She had fictionalized the pathos of this tradition of abject economy in "An Ignoble Martyr" and in her characterization of Emma Cramer in "Tirar y Soult," but in "Gray Cabins" Davis pursues the theme more broadly. The enshrinement of the Puritan faith and temperament, she discerns, has led to increasing numbers of divorces but it has carried a greater price: the New Englander has lost "the secret" of God's election and thinks only of "milk-cans or potatoes," and the "most hopeless feature in his case is absolute complacency" (62). He has remained since the days of Emerson's reign so assured of himself as "the highest type of man" that, though the soul beneath may be "true and generous," his inherited "iron armor of self-control" will not let it surface. Activism and passion, of the intellect and of the emotions, has been completely stifled.

The lively activities of the New England cities cloud that area's recognition of its own declining country counterpart, Davis asserts. The New England city dweller mistakenly identifies "the eventless drama" of the country dwellers' lives as picturesque and fails to perceive that it is "the symptom of the decadence of a race" (622). The children, having never been educated in the English language and grammar, still speak "with an Irish brogue or a Canadian patois." The community as a whole is no longer interested in religion since they have found spiritualism, faith cures, or theosophy. Davis's ever-present demand for activism comes in her deeply sardonic comparison of the New Englanders' present spiritual condition with that of their forefathers: "Really the whipping of Quakers and the hanging of witches argued a better spiritual condition than this apathy. When Cotton Mather declared that 'the smell of the roasting flesh of the savages was a sweet savor in the nostrils of the Almighty,' he had at least a live faith in—something" (622).

But one segment of the population has the most urgent need for change, Davis avers: the unattached women who, though well educated, have no important work:

> they have sensitive instincts, strong affections, and the capacity to do high work in the world. But from the sheer force of a single circumstance,—the majority of their sex in certain States,—they have neither husbands nor children, and there is no occupation for them but household drudgery. Nervous prostration is an almost universal ailment among them, following, as it always does, long self-repression. (622)

Wealthy New England women have the power to remove themselves, to live in the region's prosperous cities and to "find an outlet for their strength, if not in marriage, in active work, charitable or literary or social" (622). With revealing modernity and in a significant shift from her own traditional stance of lauding the rural over the urban, Davis adamantly rejects the proposition that contact with the outside world, as it were, is in any way a detriment to these urban women: "Friction with the world has kept them healthy in thought" while their country-bound sisters "for want of work and that friction are overtaken by neurosis, or driven to spiritualism, to Buddhism, or to opium" (622).

While Davis admonishes New Englanders for their ignorance of this situation, she also demands that these village women share in the responsibility for their wasted lives. Though there are many new opportunities for women in turn-of-the-century America, they refuse to leave the security of their homes. Education simply becomes part of the burden: "The intellectual training of these women only makes their cramped existence more intolerable. . . . Education [the New Englander] believes to be the royal road to civilization. But to what does it lead in these villages—in fact, not in theory?" (622) It unfits the woman for village life and allows her no outlet for her intellect. Following the same vein, Davis strongly rejects a sentimental perspective of New England women's lives, observing that "Miss Jewett, Miss Wilkins, and Mrs. Slosson . . . have written the petty tragedy of [these women's] lives with a power which has held the whole country attentive" (623); unfortunately, she asserts, these stories are so powerful that the spectator has forgotten there is no need for these lives to be petty or tragic:

> These genre artists show us the tender, heroic spirit in a famishing woman which makes her boil her last egg for a neighbor nearer starvation than herself. But if the heroic spirit be there, why should it not have a nobler outlet than the boiling of an egg? With the whole big, seething world around us full of God's highest work to do, one grows a little impatient of human souls who make a life-drama out of their hair pictures or muddied kitchen floors. (623)

Women who have become little more than silent "human machines" should not be praised for what is, in part, self-repression.

What these women do need is our attention, Davis contends. New England villages are not just "*materiel*" for the artist or author, but a problem of wasted human life and force" (623). Davis demands that New Englanders, known for their generosity with "the freedman, the Indians, the lepers in India, and Nihilists in Siberian mines," do not forget "these starved, coffined lives at home" (623). Do not bathe them in sympathy, she instructs. Give them "practical help": remunerative work at home, and, if that is not available, help them emigrate to the West or South or Middle States, just as their brothers have. Second, once they have found work, encourage them to marry. Davis's insistence that women as well as men needed sexually active lives scandalized some of her "puritanical readers,"[41] much as, in 1862, she had shocked her New England hosts in Boston and Concord by asserting that women's sexual needs were as strong as men's. Still, in "Gray Cabins," Davis emphasizes that the best means of assistance is employment: "Nothing need be done for them after that. Through wholesome work and intercourse with healthy-minded people they will soon find again what they have now entirely lost—their proper relations to their brother-man and to God" (623). At the time of the publication of "Gray Cabins," a young Edith Wharton was beginning to publish her poetry and short stories in many of the same periodicals as Davis. This essay, Davis's next two novels, and several of her earlier short stories, as noted earlier, are precursors to Edith Wharton's distinctive literary themes and style. In the next decade, Wharton would begin to publish her excellent novels of New England that continued the tradition of depicting women's wasted lives.

One amusing response to "Gray Cabins" came from Frances E. Willard, the leader of the temperance movement and president of the Women's Christian Temperance Union, who was, like Davis, a contributor to the *Congregationalist*. Willard, however, was more conservative than Davis in her approach to the realms of women's lives. In a conversation, she reportedly asked Davis if New England women's involvement in the temperance movement, which Willard deemed a spiritual movement, did not constitute sufficient activism for ladies. Davis is reported to have simply "smiled in silence."[42]

*   *   *

The 1890s are often defined by the rise of the leisure class in America, which was most prominently signaled by the increase in European travel by Americans. In Philadelphia during this decade, however, the emergence of numerous and varied clubs—sports clubs, religious societies, the Association of Working Women's Societies—reflected the social stratification and group consciousness that was part of the leisure-class world,[43] that society which Davis had commented upon in "A Grumble." It was this underside of the leisure-class nineties that Davis would explore in her fiction and essays of the decade. But she, too, participated in the mobilization of Americans when she traveled to Europe during the summer of 1895.[44]

In spite of a three-decade career in the literary arts, Davis could not afford such a luxury on her own. It was her son, Richard—who became a symbol of the era as the male figure in the Gibson Girl portraits—who funded his mother's vacation from his royalties from *The Rulers of the Mediterranean*.[45] Nora, a distinguished young woman of nineteen who often visited New York and had already traveled in Italy while her brother Charles was residing there, accompanied her mother to Europe. Clarke preferred Grover Cleveland's invitation to do some serious fishing in Marion, Massachusetts.[46] The Davis family had moved its summer home from Point Pleasant to Marion after the summer of 1892, when Clarke had first visited the Massachusetts area with Cleveland and fallen in love with the region. No record remains of Davis's specific travels in Europe, but her final novel of the decade draws heavily upon these locales and critiques the blind nationalism so many traveling Americans projected onto their European experiences.

Whether Richard could actually afford his magnanimous gesture of funding his mother and sister's trip was another question. In the following year, Davis discovered that her son's flamboyant lifestyle was paralleled by his fiscal irresponsibility, and she severely admonished him. Richard had intended to visit his brother Charles in Florence, but Davis insisted that he postpone his plans until he straightened out his finances. As Richard explained to Charles, "she got it fixed in her mind that I must pay off those bills first and . . . that if I went abroad I could not finish my South American stories in time to get the money necessary to pay for them."[47] Clarke at first sided with Richard, who at thirty-one was surprisingly acquiescent to his parents' control, but Davis prevailed. For a writer who had spent her life scrimping and manipulating payment for her work so that it arrived in time to pay the monthly bills and who had often found it necessary to forego her own serious writing in order to produce the quantities of fiction necessary to the family's survival, slack fiscal policies were intolerable at any age, and she would not countenance it in a son who had received the benefits of her own sacrifices.

*   *   *

With her commentaries continuing to appear in *The Independent* and her return to the pages of the major literary journals, Davis was reaffirmed as a renowned and sought-after author. The unexpected consequences of this, however, were that she was once again confronted with the economics of literature. On the morning of October 17, 1895, she picked up the latest issue of *The Critic*, a literary magazine edited by Jeannette and Joseph Gilder that was especially interesting to Davis for its insightful reviews and openness to innovative works, including the early writings of Whitman and Joel Chandler Harris. But on this morning, Davis was astonished to discover an advertisement for a children's magazine, *Frank Leslie's Pleasant Hours for Boys and Girls*, which announced that Davis was a contributor to their first issue. Upon investigation, Davis learned that a story she had written many years earlier had already been reprinted in the first issue of *Pleasant Hours*. She quickly wrote the Gilders a letter disclaiming association with the Frank Leslie Company and detailing the events of publication, concluding, "The matter is, of course, of no real interest to the general public, but still I think I should feel more comfortable if you would say for me that I never have written and never expect to write a line for the Frank Leslie publications."[48]

Frank Leslie (the pseudonym of Henry Carter) was an English emigrant who began his career as an engraver and became a publisher of several American illustrated journals; the most widely known was *Frank Leslie's Popular Monthly*. Davis had been a prolific writer of children's stories for the highly reputable *St. Nicholas* and *Youth's Companion* magazines, but she had no desire to extend this aspect of her writing, especially for a publisher who used such tactics. Although the tone of Davis's letter had downplayed the apparently unscrupulous nature of Leslie's use of her fiction, the Gilders published her letter under the heading of "Editorial Ethics." Frank Lee Farnell, editor of *Pleasant Hours*, promptly responded, denying any wrongdoing on the magazine's part. He purported that the inclusion of Davis's manuscript was a last-minute decision that was made because there had been insufficient time to commission a new story. A search of the magazine's inventory had led the editorial staff to Davis's story, which was deemed "appropriate and worthy of reproduction." The story was, Farnell observed, the property of *Pleasant Hours*; it had been purchased at an earlier date from "a publishing firm in Boston." Thus the editors felt "no hesitancy" in reprinting the story. He concluded: "Had Mrs. Davis known that it is a common practice among leading publishers who issue more than one periodical to reprint in one of them matter that has previously appeared in another, she would not, I feel sure, have written as she did, although she was certainly justified in letting the public know that the story did not represent her latest work."[49] All previous reprints of Davis's fiction in other journals or in collections had been published with her explicit permission and with appropriate compensation. Farnell admitted that the success of the first issue in which Davis's story appeared had made the magazine "well known" and that the editorial offices were now "overrun with submitted manuscripts." That the Leslie Company had legitimately purchased another publisher's copyrights did little to appease Davis's sense of misappropriation—not only of her work but of her name, which had helped *Pleasant Hours* establish itself as a reputable children's magazine.

*   *   *

Davis's last two novels, *Doctor Warrick's Daughters* (1896) and *Frances Waldeaux* (1897), are well written and often modern in theme and style. Both focus on the wealthy upper class, or those who yearn to enter that class, and both novels were published by Harper & Brothers. *Doctor*

Warrick's Daughters earned Davis a flat twenty-five-hundred-dollar serial-rights fee and fifteen percent of the retail price of each novel sold; for *Frances Waldeaux*, a shorter novel, Davis was paid seven hundred dollars and the same percentage on copies sold.[50] At the beginning of the decade, she had dedicated her short story collection, *Silhouettes of American Life*, to her eldest son, Richard; now, *Warrick* was dedicated to Charles, and *Waldeaux* to her daughter, Nora, with the inscription: "A Remembrancer of BRITTANY for the Best Fellow-Traveller in the World," recalling their excursion two years earlier to England, which was the locale for most of the novel's action.

Doctor Warrick's Daughters is an astute critique of recent changes in American society: "Even as early as '65, Luxborough [Pennsylvania] was called a city by the contractors who had recently pushed in and built mills."[51] She notes that the builders immediately took control of the business segment of the community by electing themselves to the mayorship and city council. They tried, too, to influence the architectural tastes of the burgeoning city with their homes, mere imitations, Davis notes, of all other styles with interior decors that reeked "of gilt and plush and vases of alabaster" (1). But the descendents of the town's founding families refused to be influenced. They ignored the contractors as they had the rest of the world. While Davis continued to abhor the consequences of seeming progress, she also delightfully captures in *Warrick* that small-town self-satisfaction in the community's belief that they constitute "the final result of the creation" (1). Luxborougheans refuse to lower themselves to participate in trade; thus they "wrapped [their] poverty about [them] as a royal garment and smiled down patronage on the world" (2). New England was not the only region to pride itself on its past while its future slipped away. But the second generation declension, so lamented in New England, is also evident here; this generation is less willing than their parents to ignore the ways of the newcomers and thus has lately converted their ancestors from Swedish peasants and Penn's mechanics into Scotch and English noblemen (recalling a theme Davis had explored in her essay, "Our National Vanities"). Old Luxborough asserts its own sense of privilege "most strenuously in the Monthly Whist Club (established A.D. 1767)" (2). No mill owners were allowed admittance, to their barely hidden chagrin.

In this atmosphere, Davis creates the tensions of two worlds that clash socially and economically and are represented through the maturing of Dr. Warrick's two daughters: Anne, the social climber who, as a child, liked to pose in the barn window for passersby, pretending to be "Liberty" or a bride; and Mildred, self-effacing, homely, and so completely acquiescent that no one had ever heard her express an opinion of her own. Davis readdresses in this novel several themes that she had begun in earlier works. Her characterization of the doctor, for instance, presents a wonderful study of the type of individual she had begun to identify in her early fiction of the 1860s: the good-hearted but completely unreliable "provider" who erroneously believes he has a genius for a particular trade. Dr. Warrick believes his innate "genius" will lead him to discover the germ for cholera, though he is not a scientist and much prefers to read novels than sit in his expensively furnished laboratory. This dreamer, professing all the while to be terribly overworked and burdened by his need to support his daughters, is in fact incapable of supporting anyone, including himself. The financial crisis into which he allows the family to drift precipitates the social and developmental crises that Anne and Mildred must face as they attempt to support their father, assuage his ego, and maintain their honor and dignity in the face of social Old Luxborough. The novel details the moral decline of a local society that represents America at large—"the decadence of a race," as Davis had termed it in "Gray Cabins," that is governed by greed. Only Mildred finds fulfillment and an inner strength to resist the influences of money; Anne discards her passionate love for John Soulé in order to marry a wealthy but repugnant man, David Plunkett.

Although Davis now more explicitly rejected sentimentalism than she had in the past, she also recognized that sentimentalism was not an exclusively female tradition. Thus in this novel she critiques the literary "*poseurs*" of the age "who could take and hold the centre of the stage" with their melodramatic, ultrasentimental prose and verse. John Soulé's essays, published in the *Picayune* (where Davis herself published several articles), are purely sentimental melodramas, resembling the excess of Emmeline Grangerford's poetic creations in Twain's *Huckleberry Finn*; but Anne, deeming herself an astute literary critic, insists that John's work constitutes great poetry. The poems are, Davis notes with wry sarcasm, highly publishable. Davis's own prose in this novel has a newness of style that prefigures the early works of twentieth-century modernists. When Anne experiences her first emotional awakening, "She could not breathe . . . She saw, far off in the bay, a white sail flicker up out of the mist and slowly disappear" (128). For Anne, that brief flickering of the sail symbolizes her own fleeting happiness, captured in the dream-like world of the gulf state bayoux but snuffed out by her submission to the impulse toward greed. Her wealthy spouse, determined as a youth to write great poetry, also forfeits that desire to the power of money. On rare occasions, David "felt the strength that was in him to do wider work in the world; strength that could never be used . . . that struggle in the soul, that choking pant of unspent power" (300). It was, to Davis's mind, the tragedy of contemporary American life.

One ironic aspect of the publication of *Doctor Warrick's Daughters* was that the last pages of the hardbound edition included four pages of advertisements for the novels of William Dean Howells. Though Davis preceded Howells both in the creation of realistic fiction and in the theory of the commonplace by more than twenty years, it is his reputation that remains intact today, while Davis's is relatively forgotten. As James C. Austin has noted concerning *Warrick*, "The revolutionary character of Mrs. Davis's writing was no longer noticeable or objectionable. She had anticipated the taste of the nineties and subsequent decades."[52] In her own day, *Warrick* was widely reviewed and highly praised. The exception, oddly enough, was *The Independent*, whose reviewer was offended by Davis's realism and by the novel's lack of retributive punishment for immoral characters. However, the *Nation*'s reviewer once again expressed nothing but hosannas for her novel:

> 'Dr. Warrick's Daughters' is good reading, for its excellent workmanship were there no other reason. It is a pleasure to miss the crudities of the average novel. . . . [*Warrick*] is full of interest, depicting with practised touch life in an old Pennsylvania town . . . The Gray and the Blue, differentiated with the skill of a minute observer, shimmer through the fabric of her story, and even so blend, light and dark, the weaknesses and virtues of her many characters. The sermon of the book, breathed not preached, is against the great god Mammon, who is made very repulsive, while yet his worshippers are seen to be sometimes men of like passions with ourselves.[53]

Although Harriet Beecher Stowe died the year that *Warrick* was published, one might delight to imagine her amazement at such praise from what she viewed as an old cigar-smoking male bastion!

*   *   *

If numerous earlier texts by Davis call to mind the novels of Henry James and Edith Wharton, *Frances Waldeaux* explicitly does so, especially in its awareness of Americans' attitudes toward their European experiences. In the figure of James Perry, a minor character who is an assistant editor of a literary magazine, Davis satirizes the American who travels to

Europe only to criticize the Old World for not being American. Perry, so full of himself and his assistant editorship, scoffs at the history of the ancient buildings, preferring "a clean, new American church."[54] While he professes to be concerned only with the issues of the day—"the negro problem, or Tammany, or the Sugar Trust"—his rejection of history reflects his ignorance of its importance in relation to contemporary events.

Frances Waldeaux is not a heroine either, for this novel is keenly realistic. She is a woman whose wasted life is a result of pretension and excessive self-sacrifice for her child. For years she has posed as a wealthy widow so that her pompous son might pursue an active social life and commit himself to study at Princeton. In fact, Frances Waldeaux has scrimped all her life to provide for George because her husband had been a speculator and had left them completely impoverished upon his death. Frances's earnings come chiefly from her satiric writings for a less-than-reputable periodical. If Frances is merely a poseur, she has ingrained in herself all the values of the upper class. She is without sympathy for lower class women who try to better themselves but succumb to a life of decadence. This type of woman is represented in Frances's mind by the now-deceased Pauline Felix, and when George unwittingly marries Pauline's daughter, Lisa, Frances cannot forgive the daughter for her mother's sins. Frances is so driven by her controlling love for her son and by her rejection of any sign of taint from his wife that she attempts to murder Lisa. Frances is not punished, but Lisa dies after giving birth to a son. Frances has to live with her crime, but she believes that her newly found faith in God will help her live with the knowledge that "I have it in me still to be worse than a murderer" (204).

Davis's characterization of this woman is so well developed that, while we detest her act, it is impossible not to champion her independence. In her fifties, Frances refuses to be supported by others, "If I live to be seventy, or a hundred, I shall be the same Frances Waldeaux. . . . Even out in that other world I shall not be only a mother. I shall be me. *Me!*" (202, 204). Although Frances's characterization is not autobiographical, this statement resounds with Davis's own self-image. She used the exact phrasing—". . . me. *Me!*"—at least twice when her work was acknowledged by other literary figures whom she admired, most notably Nathaniel Hawthorne and Horace Howard Furness. If she had ended the 1880s with concern over the diminishing role of motherhood in her adult children's lives, she had subsequently grasped the opportunities that newly found freedom afforded her and proudly acknowledged that in "that other world" she had earned a place of recognition.

Ironically, several reviewers interpreted Frances's turning to God as complete salvation. Chicago's *Living Church* reviewer, for instance, praised the novel and declared that it was absolutely "absorbing" and that the characterizations and situations reverberated with "a real vitality."[55] More perceptive as to the novel's ending is the reviewer for *The Critic*: "The concession of a good ending, however, is not made by the author to the reader, but by Providence to Frances Waldeaux's intensity, which is so great that it imposes the fulfillment of her desires even upon the universal order of things. The story of her later life is conceived with power and told with directness." The reviewer is less comfortable with, and yet compelled to admire, the modernity of Davis's prose style:

> If one were to complain of anything in the book, it would be of its excess of lucidity. The style is concise to the point of dryness. We are told only the things which are directly pertinent to the tale, and the result is a certain lack of atmosphere. The characters stand out with the crystalline brilliancy of figures seen through an expanse of plate-glass, and in admiring their clearness we forget now and then that the reader's task is that of sympathy.[56]

If *Warrick* ironically included advertisements for Howells's work, a similar irony is notable in this review of *Waldeaux*: directly preceding it is a review of Honoré de Balzac's *Juana and Other Stories* in which the reviewer discusses Balzac's continual "remodelling" of the theme of the revolt of the oppressed class. The reviewer notes that "Zola has attempted the same subject—far less successfully—in 'La Terre,' for in Balzac we have realism drawn from actual experience."[57] As closely aligned as these reviews are, critics of the time failed to recognize the correlations between Davis's work and that of the French realists, just as many of them failed to remember her pioneering work of the 1860s and 1870s. Only at her death would the comparison be made, and then the chronology would be reversed, identifying Davis's work as "Zolaesque."

*   *   *

At age sixty-six, with two novels recently completed and critically acclaimed, Davis decided to return to children's literature and journalism, both of which were less demanding but profitable forms of writing for her since financial demands never completely abandoned her. She also took this opportunity to renew her acquaintance with Mary Mapes Dodge: "It *is* I—," she wrote Dodge in June of 1897, "still in the flesh—although so many years have passed since I have heard from you." Davis wanted to write a story for boys and inquired as to Dodge's interest in the piece for *St. Nicholas*. She enclosed a copy of *Kent Hampden* "to show you what kind of a story-teller for boys I am. I could not do better than 'Kent.' "[58] She insisted that Dodge make the decision herself and not allow an assistant to determine its worth. She closed her letter with reminiscences of their pleasant association "in the old time." No record remains of Dodge's response to this unidentified manuscript, but the overture from Davis acted as stimulus for their renewed interest in each other as literary associates and friends.

*   *   *

For the remainder of the decade, Davis devoted herself to journalism. Though she wrote for *Harper's* and the *North American Review* during this time, she continued to find her greatest freedom of expression in the pages of *The Independent*, in spite of her financial differences with Chandler. When she decided to return to *The Independent* on a regular basis, she wrote William Hayes Ward, as adamant about the timeliness of her work as she had been as a young novelist in 1861, "It is a long time since I sent you any comments on the world and its ways. So I hope you will welcome this little paper. It is something which I thought somebody ought to say *now*."[59] She knew that while she had traveled to Europe and worked on her novels *The Independent* had maintained its reputation for aggressive commentary on social, economic, and political issues. In these last years before the turn of the century, she was joined in the pages of *The Independent* by socially conscious writers such as Booker T. Washington, president of the Tuskegee Institute; the great Russian realist, Leo Tolstoy, who submitted essays on "The Czar's Peace Conference" and a "Letter to the Russian Liberals"; Henry James; Agnes Repplier; Paul Lawrence Dunbar; and W. E. B. DuBois, who had recently joined the faculty of Atlanta University.

At the end of the previous decade, Davis had collaboratively addressed the issue of women and marriage; in this decade, she was again asked to join a select group of notable women to address the question of "The Enlargement of Woman's Sphere," as the headlines to *The Independent's* series of comments termed it. Subtitled "Views of Distinguished Progressive Women," the series includes essays by Julia Ward Howe, Frances E. Willard, Lucy Stone, Susan Hayes Ward, the Reverend Phoebe Hanaford, and nearly a dozen other women. Each approached the question of woman's sphere from her area of expertise: Howe wrote on "Women in Politics," Grace Dodge concentrated on the New York Association of Working Girls' advances, and Davis discussed "Women in Literature."

In addition to the significance of the collaborative element of the series, Davis's essay is also important in terms of understanding her own assessment of American literature at the end of the nineteenth century and, especially, the position women held in that field. She begins with a direct assertion: "There can surely be little doubt that women will occupy a much wider space in American literature during the next thirty years than they have done hitherto."[60] This will be true, Davis asserts, for several reasons, including the fact that increased population will compel greater numbers of women to earn their own living and that literature is a reputable field in which "you can, if you choose, find the best of good company," while other women will seek the "crown" of fame and notoriety. In the final reason Davis lists, however, she defines her sense of herself as an artist: there are a few women, she asserts, who will write "because there is in them a message to be given, and they cannot die until they have spoken it" (1). For whatever reason women enter the field, there will be sufficient numbers who will satisfy their own needs and help the world at the same time through their artistic expressions.

While it is difficult to define what new fields of literature will emerge for women, Davis asserts, genres such as the memoir, the journal, and the autobiography have been greatly overlooked by the American author. On the other hand, there is one facet of literature which she hopes all writers will avoid: the Great American Novel. No canvas would be large enough to do it justice, to capture the various "phases of our national life" or the complexities of groups such as "the red man; the Mafian and Molly Maguire brethren; and the Chicago millionaire!" (2). It is preferable to present "Genre pictures of individual characters in our national drama, each with his own scene and framing" (2); and this is the realm that women authors have already conquered through their natural perception for detail, their concern for the individual, and their powers of dramatic representation.

Not only does Davis suggest that the "distinctively American portraits and landscapes are the work of woman" in our literary history, but she records their achievements, naming those whom she signifies as the major American realists in terms of "genre pictures":

> Marion Harland preserved for us the old Virginia plantation with its men and women. Miss Murfree has made the mountaineer of Tennessee as immortal as his mountains. Mary Dean painted pictures of rural New York with a touch as fine and strong as Meissonier's own. Mrs. Catherwood and Mary Halleck Foote have sketched picturesque poses of the Western man. Miss Woolson on her larger canvas inserts marvelous portraits of gentle lazy, shrewd Southern women, and while Elizabeth Phelps draws the educated Puritan woman from the life, Sara Jewett and Miss Wilkins give us pictures of the race in its decadence, the New England villager, hungry in soul and body, with a fidelity equal to any other photographs of dying men. (2)

In this succinct summary, Davis canonizes the contributions of late-nineteenth-century American women writers and defines realism itself as "genre pictures," that is, as a literary perspective that incorporates a distinctive style but moves us away from the question of what *is* realism to an enlightened sense in which we should be asking how realism *functions*, how it apportions discourse. It would be almost three-quarters of a century before the contributions of these women whom Davis acknowledges as the instigators of this style of realism would once again be remembered and so accurately assessed.

*   *   *

Davis's themes in the pages of *The Independent* during the 1890s ranged from the effects of money on morality, to the ongoing question of equality for blacks, to the swindling of the government by ex-soldiers who falsified injuries and service in order to claim pensions while the country was struggling to survive economic depressions; on the other hand, her xenophobic position on immigration is also continued, most notably in "Achill." Several articles from this period deserve special attention.

"The Work Before Us," published in January 1899, is a strong indictment of English and American colonization practices.[61] Commenting on Lord Kitchener's ongoing attempts to Anglicize the Sudanese, Davis asserts the need for each race to retain its own culture and customs. She foresaw the backlash of such Anglicized "education" that has become prevalent in the Third World today, where the English-educated nationals are "no longer at ease" in their old society and never fully accepted into the new.[62] "The plain fact," Davis asserts, at the end of the nineteenth century, is that this plan of Kitchener's "has its root in the complacent self-conceit of the English race" that is shared by Americans: "We are always right; hence all other races must be more or less wrong" (178). Our language, customs, and dress become the criteria for measuring other races; that we presume they are inferior represents a "monstrous content with ourselves" (178). Davis recognizes in this arrogance our own loss as well, since it "blinds us, too, to the possibilities in other races, and unfits us to deal with them intelligently" (178). All of her life Davis had challenged the distorted sense of progress in America, and she raises that challenge again in this new context: "Is civilization after all a matter of railways or even the ballot box?" (179). Relying upon American history, Davis reminds her readers that we chose a policy similar to Kitchener's with our own Native American peoples and have the ever-present record of that failure before us. Public men must be held accountable for their motives, Davis concludes. Are they concerned about their nation or the next election? Is their worship of God or money?

In three other articles for *The Independent* during the 1890s, Davis confronted the tension-filled issue of racism in America at the end of the nineteenth century. In 1892, she published an essay entitled "Alien Brothers," in which she observed that "Every philanthropist and politician has now a pet theory or scheme to hurl at the poor struggling [Negro]."[63] While these advisers are well meaning, their arguments are flawed, Davis asserts, because they continue to view blacks as a type rather than as individuals. In acknowledging the social and educational differences among blacks, she argues that they must cross those gulfs and embrace each other if the race is to advance: "Despite the centuries of savagery and slavery through which they have passed, no race has preserved more noble qualities. Why should they be ashamed of each other?" (7). If the decency of this argument is not sufficient, Davis counters, "A more ignoble reason is that it is the surest and quickest way to win that respect and recognition from the white race which they weakly crave. Douglass, Bruce, Tanner, and Durham have achieved success by *being black*. They were satisfied to be the exponents and representatives of the Negro race" (7). Because of the accomplishments of these men, there is "a sufficiently large class of educated, refined and often wealthy colored people in our cities to form a society among themselves and to exercise an elevating influence upon their less lucky brethren" (7).

Davis continues this theme at the end of the century in two essays, "Two Points of View" and "Two Methods With the Negro." The first is her reaction to the opposing views of W. E. B. DuBois and Booker T. Washington; as in the past, Davis conservatively preferred Washington's stance. She agrees with DuBois that the oppression of his race has been and continues to be extraordinary: "The prejudice against the Negro in the Northern States has been as unjust and cruel in its effects as was slavery. We opened our schools and universities to him, and when he was ready and eager to earn his living we barred every way before him except those which led to the kitchen and the barber-shop."[64] However, she abhors the tone of despair and lack of hope in his vision, especially as a vehicle for change. The other point of view, she observes, had recently been submitted by the Committee of the General Negro Conference at Hampton; the committee's perspective "is alive with energy and hope and common sense," all of the traits which Davis had admired throughout her life. Davis asserts that this group of blacks has no concerns for the opinions of whites; instead they are building their own communal infrastructure to raise their people out of poverty and hardship.

As always, there is an underlying conservatism to Davis's position on blacks in American society, although she believed she was presenting a radically liberal stance. Thus she cannot forego reminding DuBois and his followers that, while their charges of prejudice are true, "it is to the white man he owes his freedom, his right to vote, the chance of education" (2). She insists that, as strong as prejudice remains, "it is weakening every day. In 1847 it was an offense punishable by law in the South to teach a Negro to read. In 1897 every district has its school or college for black pupils" (2). She discusses amalgamation, but adds, "The Negro should remember, however, that his progress depends, not on his affiliation, political, mercantile or social, with the whites, but on the development of his own people. The time that he spends . . . in denouncing them or upbraiding them, is only so much time wasted" (2). For all of her good intentions, her view remains the perspective of one who was an "outsider."

In the following year, Davis returned to the issue, admonishing the American public for attending so assiduously to the "noise of the 'Maine' " (the U.S. battleship that was sunk in February of 1898, thereby precipitating the Spanish-American War) and ignoring the Negro Conference at Tuskegee and the "plans of these earnest black leaders."[65] Her position was that "a war with Spain is an affair of months, while the progress of this people will concern us for all time. I know of no more important or dramatic action in contemporary history than the slow upgrowth of this nation within the American nation" (1). In that statement, we have the

strength and the weakness of Davis's lifelong position: an honorable concern for the well-being and fair treatment of all races, and yet an unwitting
reconstitution of separation, revealed in her rhetoric of "this nation within
the American nation." Although she insists she wants blacks to be her
"neighbor and friend," she fails to understand the depth of prejudice that
remained in the country and in herself. In one respect, however, she truthfully captured the extraordinary differences between experiences with slavery and the younger generation's fortunate lack of such experience. It
would be easy to brush aside her assertion in "Two Methods"—"I came
from a slave State, and the evils that I saw in slavery made me an Abolitionist before these excitable young men probably were born"—as the pon-
tificating of an elderly woman who feels herself at odds with the youth of
America. However, the almost inconceivable changes that Davis had confronted in her lifetime are revealed in her son's assertion that it was "mo-
mentous" actually to view enslaved people when he traveled in Morocco.[66]
Perhaps no two generations were as distinguishable as those of pre– and
post–Civil War Americans.

In her most notable essay from these last years of the century, "The
Mean Face of War," Davis finds herself, thirty years after her first challenge
to the romanticization of war, faced with that issue once again. Disturbed
by the American policy of policing the Philippines and recognizing that
the present generation had only been exposed to stories about war rather
than its realities, she begins her essay by outlining the ways in which wars
are made heroic through the intentional use of romantic symbolism: the
heroic Mars doing battle for his country, or the noble Christian doing
God's work.[67] But she commands her readers to look this "god" in the face
and see its true ugliness. In challenging the chivalric view of war that was
being perpetuated in the pages of newspapers and in political speeches,
Davis insists that genuine history be recorded, not this falsified brand. She
recalls living in a border state during the Civil War days of her youth and
demands that Americans envision the reality of that experience, not its romanticized history-book version. Certainly, Davis acknowledges, there
was truth in the "countless paeans" to the heroism of soldiers in the North
and South, "But I never yet have heard a word of the other side of the
history of that great campaign, which is equally true, of the debilitating
effect upon most men in mind and morals of years in camp, and the habits
acquired of idleness, of drunkenness and of immorality" (1933). In her seventieth year, Davis would center her autobiography on her desire to record

that genuine history of the Civil War period and the harsh realities of its effects upon the American people and the country.

Her sense of the political manipulation of public sentiment for building an American war machine in "The Mean Face of War" still carries reverberations for the late twentieth century. Politicians are trying "to induce the American people to make war its regular business," Davis asserts (1933). The people are told we must increase the size of the army and glorify military service and its economic rewards; the persuaders especially include the "talk of glory and heroism and the service of the country," and it is a sure-fire means to entice "gallant immature boys" (1933). But Davis exposes the fact that the motives behind these speeches were not so heroic: "What is really intended, of course, is the establishment of a uniformed guard to police the Philippine Islands in the interests of certain trusts" (1933). Davis concludes her essay with a challenge to Americans to confront the "ugly, mean features" of war before committing themselves to such policies. The implications of these policies remain with us in the twentieth century, of course. As journalist Katherine Ellison recently noted, "the erratic and confused U.S. drift—for reasons at once racist, greedy and idealistic—into an imperial role" in the Philippines remains a noteworthy chronicle.[68] Davis, at the moment of crisis, recognized that "racist, greedy and idealistic" drift and attempted to reveal its insidiousness to the American public.

*   *   *

As Davis entered the last years of her life, her voice of social consciousness rang as clearly and as truly as it had when she began her critique of American society and literary styles in the comparatively innocent era of antebellum America. When the publisher Paul Reynolds now approached her with his unwittingly ironic offer to republish some of her novels in England, Davis could decline the once-longed-for opportunity. Secure in her reputation and desirous of continuing her commitment to social commentary, she refused his offer with the simple statement, "I have no book which I wish to republish in London now."[69]

Another ironic episode of this period centered on an offer from Albert Bigelow Paine, a dramatist[70] and novelist as well as an editor. He had greatly admired *Kent Hampden* and indicated that if Davis were preparing another novel for children he would be interested in publishing it. She did not want to extend herself at this time to write a full-length work for children, but she did suggest that since she had already written about boys' adventures in *Kent Hampden* she would like to prepare a collection of "short stories for girls—all written of the same village—if you choose. Something like Mrs. Deland's 'Old Chester Tales.' The same town and the same families—."[71] Margaret (Margaretta) Wade Campbell Deland, born in Pennsylvania, also used her native region as the setting for many of her novels and short stories. *Old Chester Tales* had appeared in 1898; the collection centers on the lives of the citizens of Old Chester, which was modeled on Deland's hometown of Manchester. Davis's proposition suggested that her collection of stories for girls would repeat the historical realism and depth of characterization that had made *Kent Hampden* a success, but whether Paine was not interested in stories about girls or for whatever reason, he did not respond to Davis's suggestion. Today Paine's own best-remembered works are his three-volume biography of Mark Twain and his collection of Twain's correspondence, both of which appeared shortly after Davis's death. One can only imagine how different Davis's own literary fate might have been if such immediate attention to preserving her works and thoughts had occurred.

7. The Coming of the Night

THE NEW CENTURY'S FIRST DECADE would be Davis's last. Though her health declined and she sometimes relished a nostalgic perspective on the past, she remained intellectually vibrant until her death. During this final decade, she published her autobiography, more than a dozen short stories, and nearly forty topical articles that carried forth her strong voice of social protest. She published her fiction and nonfiction in the major periodicals of the era, including *Harper's, Scribner's* and *Century Magazine*, and she became a frequent contributor to the *Saturday Evening Post*, beginning in 1902. Although the new century was certainly the foothold for American naturalists such as Jack London, Stephen Crane, Theodore Dreiser, Edith Wharton, and Frank Norris, it was also a period in which historical romances, such as Mary Johnston's *To Have and To Hold*, or adventure-romances, including those by Richard Harding Davis (such as *Ransom Folly* and *Captain Macklin*), were highly popular. Davis herself continued to bridge numerous genres and styles that in this decade included topical realism, reminiscent histories, autobiography, and even a brief period of strained conservatism. But she ended the period with the dynamic writing that her readers had come to expect.

As the decade opened, Davis began publishing segments of her historical and personal reminiscences which would eventually be collected and shaped into her autobiography. The first of these segments appeared in *Harper's* in February 1900. "Under the Old Code" is a study of the Big Spring cotton plantation country where Davis had spent several of her early childhood years.[1] Though reminiscent in tone, the story is realistic in theme. Davis recalled the paradox of the gulf state region, "the mixed magnificence and squalor of the life on the plantations" (68). If Southern life at times seemed bucolic, Davis most readily remembered those early years as an "uneasy dream" in which the "washing of reputations clean by blood was going on perpetually" (71); perhaps more disturbing was the unwillingness of neighbors to interfere in these familial vendettas: "nothing in their code could have been more underbred than interference," she sardonically recalls. Davis also rendered the depths of meaning in the local dialect, rooted as it was in the concept of honor indigenous to an agrarian society. The expression signifying a person who lacked character, for instance, was that he couldn't "raise cotton"; as Davis notes, that was "a most venial fault of character" in a member of a plantation society (77–78).

Perhaps nothing so clearly signifies the link between the metarealists and the new realists and naturalists as a survey of the contributors to the issue of *Harper's* in which "Under the Old Code" appeared. In one issue, we have not only Davis's story but the serialization of Stephen Crane's *Whilomville Stories* and an essay entitled, "The Railroad and The People: A New Educational Policy Now Operating in the West," by Theodore Dreiser, who, in a few short months, would publish his seminal naturalistic novel, *Sister Carrie*. There was no decline of the early realists that left a vacuum out of which the "rise of realism" developed. It was a *continuing* process in which the new realists built upon the literary foundations of the earlier metarealists.

In November, Davis published in *Scribner's Magazine* the second excerpt from her forthcoming autobiography. "A Little Gossip" focuses on Davis's visit to Boston and Concord after the publication of "Life in the Iron Mills" and was later reshaped into the second chapter of her autobiography, "Boston in the Sixties." Although this was Davis's last item for *Scribner's*, Richard became almost as regular a contributor in its pages during this decade as his mother had once been, and Charles also subsequently published several short stories in the magazine.[2]

In early 1901 Davis also published her final work of fiction for *Century Magazine*, entitled "An English Passion Play." The story contrasts the prevalence of a theatrical religious attitude in many American churches with genuine religious devotion, and it satirizes Americans' egotistical attitudes toward English peasants. This story was directly preceded in the periodical by Hamlin Garland's serialization of "Her Mountain Lovers," and the issue also included a short story by William Dean Howells entitled "At Third Hand: A Psychological Inquiry." Not only was Davis still a prominent figure during this period, but her status at the time is reinforced by the numerous requests from critics and historians for information about her to be included in studies of contemporary American literature.

Davis's writings for *The Independent* during the first years of the new century evidence her continuing attention to realism that raises the social consciousness of American audiences. In October, she published a short article entitled "Two American Boys," in which she continued to defend Booker T. Washington ("No leader among us, of any rank or color, has proved himself more effective, more sane, or more just") and admonished "Society, the spirit of American Civilization, as we love to call it," for putting blacks and native Americans "outside the gate" of that alleged civilization.[3] Davis never relented in her efforts to keep the realities of racial oppression before the American public so they could not be forgotten. In several other articles of this period, Davis drew attention to the abuse of native Americans. In "A Quiet Hour," she favorably compares Johnny Wilson, a Delaware Indian, with renowned American moral leaders such as John Woolman. "There is a kingly line in every nation," Davis asserts, "of finer strain of blood than Guelph or Stuart, tho it flows sometimes through the veins of tradesmen, or ditchers, or negro slaves. We, too, have our royal family, and these men [like Johnny Wilson] were of it."[4] This emphasis recalled a major facet of her lifelong concern for the recording of genuine history.

She continued this theme in other directions as well; in "On the Jersey Coast,"[5] Davis called attention to the need for an accurate history of New Jersey. But the essay also raises a theme that would increase in importance for Davis in these last years of her life—the need to come "nearer to the Unseen," not only as individuals but as a nation, now under the everworsening influence of greed, militarization, and political corruption. In this essay, as in her fiction, Davis maintains her democratic principles; she is particularly dubious of the "elect" attitude of various churches or sects and praises only the Unitarians because, she argues, they alone accepted even the most commonplace worshipper under their roof. The response to "On the Jersey Coast" was so enthusiastic that the editors of *The Independent* urged Davis to continue her analysis. Thus, in December she published "An Unwritten History" of the Delaware Bay area, focusing on the early inhabitants who peopled the area before the Puritans and Quakers.[6] In this historical essay, Davis records the story of Captain Cornelis Mey, who built the first mud fort at what is now Camden (and for whom Cape May is named), and she acknowledges the Native American tribes that had hunted and fished for centuries in this area. As she had in her centennial histories of Philadelphia, Davis again notes the influence of King Gustavus and Queen Christina in supporting the settlers' desire for freedom of worship. If, Davis notes, these early settlers in what is now Delaware and Pennsylvania "had landed on a beach of New England their names now would be familiar to us in song and story" (3083).

Davis's literary purpose remained what it always had been—to compel the reader to action. Thus she encourages her audience "to study for themselves the traditions" of the Jersey coast or Delaware or any of the other numerous areas rich with early American history (3082). She concludes that "great chapters" about these colonies remain to be written and suggests studies of the dramatic historical past of Newcastle or of the Native Americans who sought to maintain a peaceful community against the settlers' attempts to have convicts sent into their region in order to alleviate the more established areas' difficulties with handling social outcasts. She also includes, in the tradition of her earlier historical articles, brief histories of the commonplace folk, such as Lady Armegot, the "wolf-woman" who appalled the Swedes with her devolutionary personal habits, choosing to live in isolation and drunkenness; and she details significant aspects of the settlers' daily life, such as the tremendous value they placed on the three printed books they had managed to accumulate in their first sixty years. Davis sought to encourage her readers' interest in pursuing the history of this area, but she did so with an adamant restriction in the concluding lines that had served as her own guide: "I do not ask for a historical fiction about these forgotten folk, but the truth set forth in order" (3085).

Davis's other notable essay of these early years of the twentieth century appeared in *The Independent* on February 4, 1901. Several years earlier, Davis had questioned the tactics of Britain's renowned Lord Kitchener, and in this essay she again challenges "Lord Kitchener's Methods."[7] A perceptive analyst of the paradoxes of human sympathies, she applauds the British citizenry's recent outcry over the slaughter of albatrosses by English sportsmen; but where, she asks, is an equal outrage over Lord Kitchener's orders to starve the Boer soldiers because the British army had been unable to conquer them militarily? Why is the silence continuing when it is reported by English women living in the region that numerous local women had been "out-raged" by English soldiers and that children as well as soldiers had been left to starve? It is an ironic policy at best, Davis observes, since the purpose Lord Kitchener espouses is "to make the citizens of these conquered republics loyal subjects to the King" (328). The hatred of other brutally conquered peoples—Munster Fenians, Hindus, even American Southerners—ought to have taught both England and America that such policies are disastrous. Davis explicitly quotes proposed actions from Kitchener's South African policy reports that include his reasons for such actions. These rationalizations, Davis asserts, should never be tolerated by a nation that prides itself on being an advocate of fair play and a defender of the oppressed. The effects of Kitchener's policies are self-evident, she asserts; but what will be the long-term effect of the English people's equally propitiatory silence?

* * *

On June 24, 1901, Davis celebrated her seventieth birthday. Richard was by this time transforming himself from a very famous New York man-about-town, who had reaped a great deal of attention through his modeling and adventure romances, into a bona-fide reporter. In 1899 Richard had married Cecil Clark, a daughter of the wealthy Chicago Clarks. He was also beginning to gain a more honored reputation because of his reports on the Cuban and Puerto Rican conflicts; these reports and his efforts in Africa would eventually make him the best-known reporter of his era. He had always valued his mother's stern literary criticism of his work, and for her birthday he penned a tribute to her contributions to American literature and to the welfare of all manner of commonplace people:

> From the day you struck the first blow for labor, in "The Iron Mills" on to the editorials in *The Tribune, The Youth's Companion* and *The Independent*, with all the good the novels, the stories brought to people, you were always year after year making the ways straighter, lifting up people, making them happier and better. No woman ever did better for her time than you and no shrieking suffragette will ever understand the influence you wielded, greater than hundreds of thousands of women's votes.[8]

Davis was deeply gratified by Richard's praise (and undoubtedly agreed with his assessment of suffragists), but she was by no means through with her literary and social crusades. In the last major piece of fiction she published, she depicts a seventy-year-old narrator confronting his own mortality, through which he determines, "I must go to work at once for the time here is short!"[9] It was a credo that Davis applied to her own life.

For the next three years, she wrote for *The Independent* a series of articles that confronted some of the most pressing issues of the day. In "An Unlighted Lamp," she acknowledges the growing power of advertising in a manner similar to our own present-day concerns for the rise of that medium's influence.[10] The changes in advertising policies, she noted, serve as the most "significant index to the condition of a people," and she voiced concern about the theatrical implications of churches that advertised the musical pieces and organist for Sunday's service while failing to mention the topic of the sermon (1903–04). Davis pinpointed a phenomenon that was, in fact, the culmination of a long process of disintegration in many church services from an act of faith to an act of social posturing. In the 1850s, with the rise in popularity of etiquette manuals, no aspect of American life was without its code of conduct. Proper church etiquette now became a topic of discussion: how one entered and exited the church or sat during prayers became a theatrical performance in genteel repose rather than an unconscious aspect of piety.[11] By the turn of the century, advertising had replaced etiquette books as the model of theatricality and, as Davis feared, as the twentieth century unfolded, advertising would only increase its power over every aspect of American "beliefs."

Davis's essay on the aftermath of President McKinley's assassination also bears a special pertinence for a late twentieth-century audience that has also lived through several presidential assassinations.[12] In Davis's lifetime, three American presidents were murdered, and she concludes that these acts are the result of a "mad longing for notoriety which has become a national disease"; American public's complicity in such acts is seen in its insatiable hunger for newspaper sensationalism that feeds the desire for notoriety (2513).

Additional articles of the period by Davis exposed other American paradoxes. (Upton Sinclair was also becoming a frequent contributor to *The Independent* and would soon draw together his ideas on these same paradoxes in his exposé, *The Jungle*.) On the one hand, Davis observed, Americans were a generous and caring community; on the other, they revealed a brute nature that caused them to respond as they recently had with the "ludicrous . . . spasm which convulsed the country" when President Roosevelt invited Booker T. Washington to dine at the White House. In this instance, although the article as a whole reiterates Davis's usual DuBois-versus-Washington stance, her defense of Washington's right to be so honored ran decidedly against the stream of conservatism. Davis's outrage at the public's response captures the irrational nature of prejudice:

> Your white American will sit calmly every day while a negro shaves him, rubs his face and hair, touches his eyes and lips with his black fingers; or he will eat bread kneaded by other black fingers, or meat which they have seasoned and cooked; he will put his child into the arms of a black nurse; he will come, in a word, into the closest personal contact with the ignorant and often unclean low class of negro, and yet, when Mr. Roosevelt asks one of the foremost Americans, a gentleman by instinct and habit, to sit down near him and be helped to the same mutton and potatoes he shrieks with dismay the Republic

is in peril! Unimaginable horrors will follow this recognition of the fact that a man with a dark skin is a leader in thought or a gentleman in instinct and habit.[13]

Nor does Davis withhold condemnation of the South in this instance either: "The most absurd explanation of this action [by the American public] was given by certain Southern editors who gravely assured us that as soon as the negro was admitted to the table of the white, general miscegenation would follow!"(338) In her seventies, as ever, she retained a keen eye for hypocrisy, regardless of on which side of the Mason-Dixon line it occurred.

Responding to recent articles on the concentration of wealth in America, Davis published an essay on "The Disease of Money-Getting"[14] and several articles that focused on what she perceived to be causes of a rampant moral decay in America. Several times during these final years, Davis reiterated in her correspondence her longstanding position on the dangers of speculation, telling her sons how thankful she was that they had "nothing to do with stocks" and observing that "New York seems like a huge gambling pit,"[15]—an attitude complementary to that of Frank Norris in his 1903 novel, *The Pit*. In another essay, "Country Girls in Town," Davis continued her assault on Americans' moral decline by focusing upon young urban women who work in the large department stores. Reminiscent of Davis's essays and fiction of the 1870s and of Dreiser's *Sister Carrie*, this article associates the highly public work of these young women with their similarly public lifestyles which Davis abhorred. They come to the city with little talent and large dreams of success, Davis observes, but they end up like some "live creature lost on a bog, slowly sucked down, inch by inch, to the black death below."[16] In an article that has been described as "one of her most incisive,"[17] Davis also attacked yellow journalism, especially that which pandered to the taste for lurid details about real-life murders.[18] The symptoms of decay exposed in this latter essay are, of course, mere extensions of the increasingly irrational desire for notoriety—everyone's "fifteen minutes" of fame, as Andy Warhol defined it in the last half of the century.

Perhaps the quest for notoriety was in part so distasteful to Davis because she had known so many extraordinary people in her lifetime who deserved national recognition but whose lives remained blank pages in the national record. In January of 1903, when she learned of the death of her dear friend Jessie Benton Frémont, whom she had known since the early 1860s, she sought to rectify that obscurity in her own tribute to a woman whose life deserved remembering. Davis asserts in her *Independent* article that during the Civil War Jessie Benton Frémont had been "the most conspicuous and probably the most influential woman in the country."[19] Although Frémont "belonged to a time when a woman valued her personal reserve and privacy as her chief prerogative," she had been privately educated to the degree that "[i]n her knowledge of history and of politics few men of her time equaled her" (238). Thus it was that her personality, "so potent, so magnetic and compelling a force," shaped her husband's career along the political lines to which they both adhered (238). Frémont was an advocate of the under-recognized, whether they be the freed slave or the impoverished shop girl, "an obscure genius like Bret Harte whom she . . . helped to permanent comfort and to honor" or "some grizzled hunter, like Kit Carson, in whom she discovered the knight and gentleman" (239). Although Frémont endured many hardships during her life, the only tragedy of her existence, Davis asserts, is that "[h]er name has almost died out of public remembrance; the regiment who bore it into the war are disbanded long ago. . . . The Republic which her husband enriched left her to die unrewarded and poor"; her memory, however, is cherished by those "for whom she widened life . . . in this world" (239). Davis could not have known the irony of her tribute to Frémont—that "public remembrance" would be equally fickle for her, in spite of her much more direct influence for half a century.

* * *

Davis's work schedule in these last years of her life was little different from what it had been for the last forty; even during summer "vacations" at Marion, she continued to write. In the summer of 1903, for instance, when the extended family (which now often included Cecil's parents) gathered in Massachusetts, Davis not only entertained her eldest son's new in-laws and participated in many activities with her family, but also salvaged time to submit one article for publication and wrote or began outlining the three short stories and two essays that she would publish in the fall.

That summer, however, was especially memorable to Davis for personal rather than professional reasons. With Nora living at home and Charles close at hand, she had uninterrupted contact with her two youngest children. But Richard's life-style and his recent marriage kept him away from his family home for months at a time, and Davis felt deeply the separation from her eldest child. This summer, however, Cecil and Richard spent with the Davises in Marion, and Richard began each morning with a visit to his parents' cottage. Cecil and Richard were having a home built at Mount Kisco, New York, and the progress of "Crossroads Farm" was a daily topic of conversation and entertainment. When Davis returned to Philadelphia in the fall, her sense of losing the routine of being a family again was pervasive, as she explained to Richard: "Here we are in the old library and breakfast over. There seemed an awful blank in the world as I sat down just now, and I said to Dad 'Its Dick—he must come *this* morning.' " She recalls the wonderful drives they had taken together, but then forces herself to turn to the future, "Well we'll have lots of drives at the Crossroads. You'll call at our cottage every morning and I'm going to train the peacocks to run before the trap and I'll be just like Juno."[20]

It was not, however, an enthusiasm for the future that she was always able to maintain. Perhaps in response to what she viewed as depressing changes in America's national purpose and moral fabric, Davis began to publish several uncharacteristic commentaries that revealed a sudden conversion to narrow-minded conservatism regarding young women and religious training.[21] Facets of conservatism had always been a part of Davis's position on women's rights, but for forty years she had argued for a woman's right to a full life, one that included work outside the home. She would return to that stance, but at seventy-two Davis momentarily rebelled against what she interpreted as an implosion of moral decay in the nation. In one of her best stories of the period, "An Old Time Christmas," she reflects upon the changes she has encountered in her lifetime: "The world that we lived in when I was a child would seem silent and empty to this generation. There were no railways in it, no automobiles or trolleys, no telegraphs, not one anxious whisper about Trusts or Labor Unions."[22] Instead of collapsing under the weight of these changes, Davis made a conscious effort to find a catharsis for her fears about the future. Her solution was to write about her own past experiences as a means of preserving her memories and the values that shaped them.

Published in 1904, Davis's autobiography, *Bits of Gossip*, serves as the best source for our knowledge of her early years. But it is much more. It is one person's perspective on the great historical and literary movements of the age. As always, Davis diverts the attention from herself and focuses upon the vibrant era of her youth in which the literary transition from antebellum romanticism to the realism of the Civil War helped to shape the nation's sense of itself. *Bits* captures the spirit of an era in a manner that no history book could achieve. There was a flurry of similar personal reminiscences being published at the time, including Theodore Roosevelt's *The Strenuous Life* (1900) and William Dean Howells's *Literary Friends and Acquaintances* (1900),[23] and for several years Annie Fields had been publishing her personal studies of the people she had known through her unofficial but influential association with the *Atlantic Monthly*. The rather facile title of Davis's autobiography is immediately belied by the moving epigraph that identifies her purpose:

> It always has seemed to me that each human being, before going out into the silence, should leave behind him, not the story of his own life, but of the time in which he lived,—as he saw it,—its creed, its purpose, its queer habits, and the work which it did or left undone in the world.
>
> Taken singly, these accounts might be weak and trivial, but together, they would make history live and breathe.

In this study of her era, Davis presents history as a living, ongoing force. Her sense of the link between human beings as the greatest force of all is given full voice as her culminating thesis of what constituted "accurate history."

In conjunction with this thesis, Davis's autobiography is especially interesting in that its narrative structure supports its contextual commentary. In the opening chapter, Davis recalls her early years and then sets those memories against the succeeding chapters' record of the time in which she grew up. A child raised then, she observes, was like an acorn in a forest, one of "a thousand seedlings massed and tended in a hothouse" (6). But then, too, the Revolutionary and Indian wars were "close and real"; living relatives had been the enactors of these historical events. One childhood anecdote expresses her early understanding that words could only fleetingly represent the imaginative life that she had felt a need, even then, to express:

> In each room [of the Harding home] was a huge fire of bituminous coal. The black soot hung and swayed in the great chimneys like a mass of sable mosses, and, beneath, yellow and red and purple flames leaped up from an inky base of coal to reach them, while on this base, black and shining as jet, was a gray lettering that incessantly formed itself almost into words and then crumbled away. You knew that the words, if you could read them, would tell you the secret of your life, and you would watch them late into the night, until you fell asleep and woke to watch again. But the words always crumbled away before you could read them.
>
> These flames and gray ashes have burned always in my memory, and made

the wood-fires, of which poets talk so much, seem thin and meaningless to me. (8–9)

This memory is a recognition of Davis's own "muse": the very real elements of her environment—the bituminous coal and the ashes and the ever-present soot—that would lead to her pioneering work in shaping American literary realism and naturalism as techniques for reform.

The second chapter of Davis's autobiography, "Boston in the Sixties," relates her mid-nineteenth-century meeting with the Boston luminaries of American literature; this segment of *Bits* warrants a close study by Americanists for the insightful personal glimpses it gives us of these renowned literary figures. Subsequent chapters express the need for a changed perspective of early American history: colonial New England's history, Davis contends, has come to be viewed as the official American history. She notes that the contributions of the Scotch-Irish settlers in Pennsylvania and West Virginia are yet to be recognized, and she satirizes the primacy given to the first New Englanders: "It was no doubt a very poetic, picturesque thing to land on Plymouth Rock; but surely it was a stupid thing to stay there!" (90) She also analyzes the changes in the country from before the Civil War to the beginning of the twentieth century in terms of community attitudes and habits, and educational and religious practices.

After the opening chapter, however, Davis is not nostalgic about the past and recognizes both its limitations and strengths. If work rules modern Americans, she points out, prosperity has paradoxically "softened" them. The well-to-do person of the early twentieth century is much more willing to assist his neighbor than was his grandfather, whose life's project was "to save his own soul" (106). If the American businessman has no time for his own soul, as evidenced by the empty churches in every metropolis, hospitals have been built for the care of others and have been well funded by these businessmen. Even if an ironic concern for money underlies the teachings of "brotherly love," these teachings nevertheless are promoted, she confirms.

Most compelling, however, is Davis's firsthand record of the Civil War. Living in a border state as she did, and in a town that had been confiscated for military maneuvers by Generals W. S. Rosecrans and John Frémont, she conveys the facts as she knew them in a manner that history books or even other realistic novels (such as *The Red Badge of Courage*) do not achieve: "The histories which we have of the great tragedy give no idea of the general wretchedness, the squalid misery, which entered into every individual life given up to the war" (116). That "general wretchedness" is the image of war that pervades the chapter:

> Even on the border, your farm was a waste, all your horses or cows were seized by one army or the other, or your shop or manufactory was closed, your trade ruined. You had no money; you drank coffee made of roasted parsnips for breakfast, and ate only potatoes for dinner. Your nearest kinsfolk and friends passed you on the street silent and scowling; if you said what you thought you were liable to be dragged to the county jail and left there for months. The subject of the war was never broached in your home, where opinions differed; but, one morning, the boys were missing. No one said a word, but one gray head was bent, and the happy light died out of the old eyes and never came to them again. Below all the squalor and discomfort was the agony of suspense or the certainty of death. But the parsnip coffee and the empty purse certainly did give a sting to the great overwhelming misery, like gnats tormenting a wounded man. (116–17)

Davis admits that these details are not what her children's generation wants to hear, any more than it wants to know about whole regiments formed out of prison inmates who "raged like wild beasts through the mountains of the Border States" (123). The atrocities they committed are described by Davis with unrelenting honesty. She points out that men who volunteered were not necessarily patriotic; they often sought profit from the war. Others, forced to serve, thereby rationalized their pilfering or worse deeds. Continuing her themes from "The Mean Face of War," Davis asserts that young people "have come to look upon war as a kind of benefi cent deity"; they need to know "that some of her influences debase and befoul a people" (124–25).

Davis's autobiography is a gold mine of personal glimpses of other famous people of the period: Horace Greeley of the *Tribune*; Frances Harper, the black lecturer and abolitionist; Elizabeth Peabody, a complex character who amazed and frustrated Davis; Charles Sumner; John Greenleaf Whittier; Henry Ward Beecher; Eliza Randolph Turner and Lucretia Mott, the Quaker abolitionists; and the group that Davis never abandoned: the numerous commonplace and often forgotten women who struggled to survive on their writings for pulp magazines during the period. She studies also the political leaders of her time, such as Henry Clay and James G. Blaine (a distant cousin of Davis). But Davis concludes her study with an analysis of several literary figures, beginning with a defense of Edgar Allan Poe.

Davis notes that she never had the opportunity to meet Poe when he lived in Philadelphia, but they had several mutual friends, including Susan Archer Talley (Weiss), a friend with whom Poe corresponded for years, and Charles Peterson, who had known Poe when Peterson served as editor of *Graham's Magazine*. These friends "always spoke of 'Edgar' affection- ately, as a loveable, nervous man, who, like too many men of that day, drank hard, and fell in and out of love easily" (211). In admonishing Poe's detractors who "asserted that even as a boy he was 'a moral monster,' " she observes that these people most often had never met Poe. The source of Poe's defamation, of course, was R. W. Griswold, whom Poe had the mis- fortune to consider a friend. Charles Peterson had told Davis that "Gris- wold frequently boasted to Mr. Peterson that he 'had a rod in pickle for that fellow' " (212–13). Poe's fate at the hands of Griswold is well known and has been essentially rectified, Davis observes, and Poe should now be appreciated for his literary contributions instead of as a grotesque human being.

Davis's assessment of Walt Whitman as recorded in *Bits* has been de- tailed, but earlier in the decade Davis had included an amusing episode about the poet in an article for the *Congregationalist*. "On the Uplands" is a tribute to George W. Childs, whom Davis knew as publisher of the *Ledger* and whose philanthrophy, she asserts, shaped charity into "a fine art."[24] In identifying Childs's varied methods of philanthrophy, Davis re- calls the following episode:

> The poet, Walt Whitman, was for years one of [Childs's] constant bedes- men. The story has been told before of how he offered Whitman a regular salary one fall if he would ride on all the horse-cars in the city, find out how many of the drivers had overcoats for the winter and report to him, so that he might provide for the needy.
> Whitman was once asked if this story were true.
> "Yes," he said, "I did not refuse the job. It wasn't hard work. He paid me a good salary, and then I had the satisfaction of knowing that I was helping Childs out of his difficulties." (854)

Davis also acknowledges the numerous editors of the period whom she had known, such as Charles Peterson, Dr. Josiah Holland, and Daniel S. Ford. But, while she appreciates the American public's refusal to honor women only for their titles or for whom they marry, she laments that the American public has not seen fit to champion a "woman author or clever reformer." She names several Southern women who deserve to be "fixed stars" in the American record: Nelly Custis, Theodosia Burr, Dolley Madison,

Sally Ward, and others. Northern women have the same traits as these Southern women but "with the addition in most cases of some intellectual force" (224). In this category she places Jessie Benton Frémont and Frances Willard, and includes the details of their lives that qualify them such honors. Davis's final note is worthy of her lifelong tribute to the commonplace person: she knew many of America's "greats," but she concludes that the nameless stay with us just as much as the famous. So many could have been great, she reflects, given the chance.

The most rewarding aspect of Davis's autobiography for a contemporary audience is her skill as a storyteller. Her anecdotal histories render the facts about her past with wit, irony, and pathos. Years later, when Richard was trying to impress his in-laws, he wrote home to his mother: "I am now proudly relating incidents of my family's history to the Clark's [sic] at dinner time and much impressing them with both my ancestors and my knowledge of the time in which they lived. All clipped from your 'History.' "[25] The reviewer of *The Nation*, however, was less pleased with Davis's account of the past.[26] Not surprisingly, he takes umbrage with most of her criticisms of the North, though he readily affirms those of the South. In this two-column review, nearly half of the space is devoted to refuting Davis's opinion of John Brown. Davis had erred in her dates, referring to Brown's death as having occurred in October instead of December; the reviewer uses this fact to insist that the whole account is fabrication. It is the fullness of her perspective that seems most to trouble this reviewer. He takes special exception to her comments on the use of prisoners by both sides in the Civil War; perhaps this occurred in the South, he piously intones, but certainly not in the North. The reviewer also charges that Davis portrays all abolitionists with "a general character for eccentricity" (505); in fact, she adamantly refused to make these historical figures into one-sided heroes. So, too, does her depiction of General Frémont arouse the reviewer's ire. Davis had realistically portrayed the leader, praising his abolitionist endeavors but admitting, though he had been a lifelong friend of hers, that Frémont had no true sympathies for the enslaved—it was slavery itself that he abhorred; the reviewer, however, insists that she had made Frémont into "a hero" (505). The most interesting facet of *The Nation*'s review is that Davis's nearly forty-page discussion of "Boston in the Sixties" receives only passing mention. Ironically, the reviewer's entire commentary on this chapter is: "Among the Concord circle she speaks most warmly of Hawthorne" (505), a statement which allows him to avoid those about whom she did not speak so warmly!

Helen Woodward Shaeffer, Davis's first if unpublished biographer, recognized the spirit of Davis's autobiography: "One puts aside *Bits of Gossip* with a sigh, and wishes that he could have known Rebecca Harding Davis herself even as she knew these men and women whom she has made to live and breathe in this volume." Like most readers, Shaeffer wishes for more definitiveness in Davis's record—dates, "various facts," and so forth. "Yet," she concludes, "this more spiritual impression is the one she purposely chose to leave with us: . . . her spirit actually seems to move in the work . . . leavened with a keen sense of humor and a great measure of commonsense."[27]

Even more to the point is a two-page review of *Bits* written by Percy F. Bicknell for *The Dial*. Bicknell begins his review by placing it in the context of Henry David Thoreau's precept, "We do not learn much from learned books, but from true, sincere, human books, from frank and honest biographies,"[28] and he asserts that Davis's book qualifies for that designation:

> A frank and human and at the same time most entertaining book of the honest . . . autobiographical kind is [*Bits*], a piece of writing whose only serious fault is that it is not longer. Mrs. Davis is best known, at least to older readers, by her story of 'Life in the Iron Mills,' one of the earliest, and perhaps the most powerfully written, of the many stories of laboring-class life in America. (303)

Bicknell carefully reviews each section of the autobiography, noting the breadth of the American vision Davis displays and acknowledging that she "views her fellow countrymen and women with no provincial narrowness of vision, and comments on their sectional peculiarities with the large tolerance and understanding of one to whom fulness of years and wealth of experience have brought kindliness as well as wisdom" (303). Unlike *The Nation*'s reviewer, Bicknell recognizes Davis's ability to "see both sides of the perplexing question" of slavery that resulted in the Civil War, "a far less comfortable frame of mind, as she truly remarks, than that of the thorough-going partisan" (303). Her impartiality, he concludes, allows her to render a "delightfully honest and not too reverential treatment" of the great Boston-Concord romantics. He appreciates that the transcendentalists are "all handled, not roughly, but certainly without gloves" and that her perceptions are "almost always shrewd . . . however much the reader may at times feel inclined to dissent" (303). Bicknell's concluding analysis of *Bits* identifies Davis's style as metarealism; if she can appreciate "the romantic in character and situation," he asserts, it is because "she has so firm a hold on reality and so keen a scent for sham and humbug" (304).

∗   ∗   ∗

The enthusiastic public reception of Davis's autobiography was pleasing to all of the Davises, but it was quickly forgotten when, two months later, on December 14, the family's serenity was shattered by Clarke's death. His health had been declining for the past year, and he had recently been homebound with attacks of angina pectoris.[29] As Charles recalled, his father's death was the first taste of tragedy that he, Nora, and Richard had encountered. For Nora and Charles, it was only the beginning of their losses: in the next dozen years, they would lose their mother and their elder brother, who died only six years after Rebecca. The shock of loss in Clarke's case came in part because he had always been such an active man— for fifteen years the editor of the Philadelphia *Public Ledger* and a participant in local and national politics. His death brought personal tributes from judges, military leaders, doctors, and professors as well as from his long-time associates, such as Secretary of State John Hay and President Grover Cleveland. Cleveland wrote: "In the death of Mr. Davis the press has lost a fearless advocate of civil righteousness, his country has lost a high example of good citizenship, and his city has lost a watchful guardian of her best interests" (quoted in Shaeffer, 331–32).

For Davis, who was at his bedside when he died, the loss was devastating. They had been married for more than forty years; it had been, she asserted at the time, a good marriage. The funeral was held at the Davis home; an Episcopal service was performed by Dr. Floyd Tomkins, and in a personal gesture that Davis valued most, their longtime friend, W. C. Richardson, assisted the minister in the prayer service. The body was cremated; Clarke was buried next to his parents in a Baptist cemetery in the Roxborough section of Philadelphia (Shaeffer 332). Clarke's will left everything to "my dearly beloved wife, Rebecca Harding Davis, absolutely, and as if it had been hers from the beginning of the world" (quoted in Shaeffer 332). Clarke's comments are a tribute to their mutual love; on the practical side, however, Clarke's estate was worth only four thousand dollars and that was almost entirely in the form of personal belongings.[30] The Davises had always lived at the edge of their means, and that Davis wanted to continue her writings did not mitigate her financial need to do so.

Compounding matters, Davis's own health began to decline shortly after Clarke's death. She wrote to her cousin, Clara Wilson Baird:

> I am glad that you wrote to me. I know you appreciated Clarke and love him. Who could help loving him? As you wrote to me "Nobody ever knew him do a selfish thing."
>
> I was glad too to have a loving word from you after our long silence. We are too near the shore of the great river to forget our deep affection of the past.
>
> I cannot write to you at length for my eyes are giving me much trouble and I am only allowed to use them a short time each day.[31]

Davis signed her letter "Cuddie," the family nickname that Clarke had also used for her throughout their married life.

Though Davis only briefly mentions her eyesight problems to Clara, her eyes had been troubling her off and on for some time. In an earlier letter to Richard, she had also attempted to downplay the seriousness of her difficulties, but her handwriting, as the last words of the letter angle downward off the page, reveals more than her words could cover.[32] Yet she did not despair. After a five-month period of silence following Clarke's death, she began again. Seventeen articles appear in *The Independent,* *Youth's Companion,* and *St. Nicholas* during her remaining years, as well as two major pieces of fiction, one each in *Century Magazine* and *Scribner's Magazine.* They were not easy years; her letters to Richard during the period reflect the vast gap left in one's life when a beloved spouse is lost: "I've been sometimes so awfully alone—I oughtn't to feel that way. It is wicked. I have you & Charley & Noll— And God has come so close since I was left alone just like my Father—that is the way He seems now—No creeds nor theories—Just our *Father*." Davis's sense of loss was sustained by her return to a deep and abiding faith; she concluded her letter with the kind of affirmation that filled her final writings: "Oh I know now in whom I have believed!"[33]

And yet, Davis did not lose her keen voice of social protest. By the end of 1905 she was again writing essays for *The Independent* that challenged the American "caste system" which determined household workers to be "lower" than a mill worker: "There is no nation in the world in which caste is more important than in ours, altho we profess to have no such thing. Every village has its grades of social demarkation, laid on absolutely baseless lines."[34] Reminiscent of her position in "Life in the Iron Mills," she admonished the public to wake up to the plight of domestic workers:

"A little kindness and sympathy, a recognition of the human soul in every man or woman who comes near us, will send strange heavenly airs blowing through the darkest places in the world. We form clubs to carry help to prisons and to slums. What if each of us went alone with it every day down into her kitchen?" (675) This was a theme that Davis had approached earlier, especially in the 1870s and 1880s, in her essays on home industries. In 1903 Charlotte Perkins Gilman had published her polemical study, *The Home: Its Work and Influence*, which, when compared with Davis's position, affords us a fascinating study in the differences between the utopian-activist and the realist-activist, between an advocate for organizing the household on a model of manufactory efficiency and an advocate for individual management that retains the shell of the domestic-servant system within a context of advancement.

Even in her more traditional holiday literature, Davis continued to challenge contemporary policies that she deemed injurious to public welfare. In "Jane Murray's Thanksgiving," one of her better holiday tales, her challenges to modern educational "innovations" speak to late-twentieth-century readers as well. Jane Murray was an underpaid but caring teacher who instilled in her pupils "a hungry desire to learn."[35] But new pedagogical methods devalue Mrs. Murray's insistence that her pupils know both when and why historical figures lived. As the new head mistress explains, the latest pedagogical methods prepare students to pass standard exams: "The girls must have no more of such fancy training; they must go thru the regular textbooks to make ready for the college exams" (1268).

The theme of what constitutes a proper education, especially for women, runs throughout Davis's writings during this decade, as she extended and refined the attitudes toward education that she had brought to bear upon her work since the end of the Civil War. In 1899 she had published in the *North American Review* an article on the subject, in which she asserted that not every student should receive the same education but, rather, each according to his or her ability. The American educational system has a preconceived notion of what a student must "pass" to be educated that is predicated upon a "secret reason," Davis asserts.[36] That secret is the belief in the American Dream, the myth that "Every child must be prepared for any possible position . . . because he may some day be Senator or President" or First Lady (614). While this dream has sometimes been at the heart of America's greatness, it also is "at the bottom of our discontent, of our vulgar pretension, of our intolerable rudeness, and of the false values which we are apt to place upon the things of life" (614). If we do not view education as something to be assimilated into our "everyday work," Davis concludes, it becomes a curse rather than an asset. Davis had also made this assertion in her tribute to Jessie Benton Frémont when she claimed that Frémont's private education gave her "certain advantages over our college bred women . . . because it was, to a degree, private and special. Whether she chose to be linguist, historian, or *litterateur*, there were skillful teachers to train her mind in the direction natural to its powers."

This argument, of course, ignores the limitations on women at the time not only in terms of educational opportunities but a woman's ability to pursue a career in whatever course of study she had chosen. It is notable, however, that Davis includes "*litterateur*" in her list of options, since the educational process she praises in Frémont's experience is decidedly like her own, and in her old age, as in her youth, she defensively portrayed it as better than the college education of which she had been deprived. It is interesting to note, too, that in advocating Frémont's private education over college training Davis asserts that "only the women in this country who received that individual training . . . have produced any original work which has been held worthy of preservation." It is a personally revealing statement of significance, especially in terms of the conclusion to "Jane Murray's Thanksgiving." When the elderly Mrs. Murray is forced to retire, she loses all sense of her own identity, bound as it was to her occupation. Though "Jane Murray's Thanksgiving" has the happy resolution requisite in all of Davis's later holiday fiction, it is resolved realistically. No change is made in the new educational policies. Instead, Jane finds fulfillment by working with patients at a local rest home, reading to them and giving them "some knowledge of books and of the help and comfort to be gained from them" (1270). It is what Jane had sought—to have "my own work in the world again to do" (1270). Certainly there is an element of Davis's own voice in this assertion.

There is also another, ironic parallel between the gifted but under-appreciated educator and Davis, for whom the financial haggling with *The Independent* never ceased. When she notified Dr. Ward that she had this Thanksgiving story for him which she thought he would appreciate for the "new idea in it," she also indicated that the price would be one hundred dollars. Susan Hayes Ward passed Davis's letter on to Chandler with the note, "What do you say, Mr. Chandler? She gives us the strongest stories we have."[37] But Chandler held his ground; he would not pay one hundred dollars for a short story. Davis was disappointed, but she compromised for an undisclosed amount because, as she told Dr. Ward, she had written the story "with a view to 'Independent' readers—who are not just the same as 'Harpers' or the 'Century.' "[38]

Davis was willing to compromise financially, but she refused to do so in terms of her abiding interest in the commonplace. One essay that she wrote for *The Independent* at mid-decade discusses the importance of the American family "because it is so commonplace."[39] Even the changes in family life, especially parent-child separations, are part of the new commonplace, she acknowledges; but more important to Davis than such shifting trends was the continuing oppression of many American citizens. The editor of *The Independent* had been impressed with a new anthology, edited by Hamilton Holt, that recorded the histories of sixteen commonplace workers in their own words. Ward asked Davis to review the collection and prefaced her review with the following editorial comment: "Since we are very directly interested in 'The Life Stories of Undistinguished Americans,' we have given the book for review, not to one of our regular critics, but to Mrs. Davis, an author in whose independence of judgment our readers will have confidence."[40]

Davis admired Holt's collection because he had "struck an absolutely untrodden path in the field of literature" (962). By allowing these "commonplace folk who jostle us on the streets" to speak for themselves, she observes, Holt presents to the reader "the inevitable stratum of tragedy or comedy which is hidden in all of the ordinary lives around us" (962). The collection's value lies in that "unmistakable flavor of truth" that comes from the likelihood that the story of the Scotch farmer or the black laborer or the Italian "boot-black" is repeated every day by tens of thousands of other street people. In this review, Davis abandons her earlier xenophobia and extends her review to question why it is that not one of the immigrants whose stories are told include a statement of gratitude to their new-found homeland. We open the doors wide to let them enter, she notes, but "Was there anything lacking in the gift?" Her juxtaposition of the freed slave and the immigrant, with each life of struggle reviewed in detail, places her question in the context of the limited scope of America's open-door policy; its greatest limitation is that it fails to include a consciousness of further responsibility. This American "experiment" began with the Revolution, Davis reminds her audience, yet we seem never to have learned the necessity of completing the process. Similarly, Davis's first decade as an author had led her to write *Waiting for the Verdict*, in which she asked the American public what they intended to do to educate and assimilate the slaves now that they had been freed. So much had changed—and so little.

*   *   *

In 1906, Richard gifted his mother and sister with their second trip to Europe. Nora had been ill off and on over the past several months, and Richard felt the excursion would be a healthy change for her; he undoubtedly wanted his mother to have some time away from work as well. Mother and daughter departed in May and spent most of their time in England and Italy; three to four weeks were devoted to Rome.

Because one episode from this European jaunt was noted in Gerald Langford's biography of Richard, subsequent scholars have paid special attention to it. On the cruise to England, Davis wrote a letter to Richard that detailed Nora's experiences one evening when she had joined in the singing in the ship's salon:

> The woman who was managing—there always is one—came to Nora & said "Won't you play for us?" "Thank you I don't play" Noll said. "Then you sing?" "No I don't sing." "Perhaps you recite?" "I can't recite." "Oh then you will tell a story." "No I can't tell stories." "And yet," said the woman turning to the listening room, "and yet she is Richard Harding Davis's sister!" Then everyone talked & said how they had read every word you wrote.[41]

Langford asserts that this incident represents Nora's "instability" and Davis's cruel partiality for her eldest son.[42] Regrettably, many critics have repeated this interpretation. But Langford failed to include the subsequent sentences of Davis's letter that put the episode into context: "Noll came down laughing at them. But I saw she was very much pleased."[43] Nora perceived the audacity of the "managing woman" as keenly as her mother had and obviously displayed an equally well-developed sense of humor about it. If there was anything Nora would not do, it was "market" herself for the entertainment of strangers. Nor was Nora the recluse she has been made out to be. Davis's letters of this period repeatedly remark on her daughter's social activities—she is dining in a party of four that includes William Jennings Bryant or she is spending the week with friends in Baltimore, where, according to her mother, she was to meet "a lot of 'scientific gents' " and had been invited "to brighten the situation."[44] Davis was as decidedly proud of Nora as she was of her sons.

*   *   *

Davis had been back in the States only a few months when she was once again confronted with the death of a loved one. Her brother, Hugh Wilson Harding, died on December 12, 1906. Davis had certainly grieved over the loss of her other two brothers earlier in her life, but "Wilse" had always been her kindred spirit, and his death, only two years after Clarke's, was a staggering blow. Wilse, a bachelor, had remained an integral part of Davis's life since her marriage, and he had been a loving uncle to her children. He had long ago left the confines of Wheeling, and since the early 1870s had been a professor of physics and mathematics at Lehigh University in Bethlehem, Pennsylvania. Richard and Charles had boarded with their Uncle Wilse during their tenures as students at Lehigh; and he had frequently summered at Point Pleasant and Marion with the Davises. Wilse's funeral was held in Washington, Pennsylvania, and Davis, at age seventy-five, made her final journey to her birthplace in order to attend her brother's funeral. She inscribed his tombstone with the notation, "The Pure in Heart Shall See God," reflecting the love and faith she had borne for her brother since their early childhood.[45]

As always, Davis bore her grief by turning her attention to her writing and to her family. Her letters to Richard are full of events of the day: the Thaw trial and corrupt government officials in Philadelphia,[46] a justice who recently resigned his seat on the bench, "the massacre of women and children in our last battle over which Roosevelt is so triumphant," and the prospects of a coal strike in April.[47] But her letters also contain an increasing sense of her impending mortality. She often closes her letters to Richard with comments such as "God Bless you Dick. If I only could tell you what you have brought into my life" or "how happy you [have] made me in my old age. How glad I am for your strength and your kindness to people who need help."[48] Most often, the letters are signed with the cryptic signature, "Your old Mother" and on at least one occasion, "From old Mother *and* chum."[49] But her abiding humor tempers the awareness of her limited future. She assured Richard on one occasion that, where she was concerned, he could "look back and say 'I left nothing undone'!" Lest she seem too sentimental, however, Davis adds this delightful restriction: "Of course you did begrudge me the oatmeal, but let that go!"[50]

Richard was traveling a great deal at this time as a reporter for *Collier's*. At one point, Davis suggested that when Richard had a moment he should go to a select garden spot in Oxford that she had grown to love when she was in England because deer would come up near the fence and graze while she sat, hour after hour, in thoughtful repose. Richard, however, currently had little time for contemplative repose. In 1907 *Collier's* sent him to cover the tense situation in the Belgian Congo, where atrocities against the native people had been reported. Ever aware of behind-the-scenes political machinations, Davis cautioned her son, "Be awful careful of facts about the Congo matter. It's a burning subject here now since Americans have gone into the Rubber trade."[51] Davis's letters to Richard and the advice she includes in them, reveal as much about her own philosophy and abiding concern for the downtrodden, wherever they were, as they do about Richard's activities. She praises Richard's attempts to help the poor through his writings whether "at the Congo or the Cubans or the Boers—I do thank God for the help you and Charley have given to the under-dogs in this life."[52]

Charles's contributions to American literature reveal how closely he carried forth his mother's ideals of personal responsibilities for aiding the oppressed and of debunking American myths. In Richard's case, however, his published accounts reveal a concern that often is at odds with his personal motives. His letters to his siblings are typically stories of his successful one-upmanship over some famous person. The surviving correspondence with his mother, however, is a graphic complement to his journalistic accounts of his experiences in Cuba, Japan, and the Congo. With her he knew that he could engage in lengthy discussions of the events and their causes, his frustrations at political maneuverings, and the realities of covering a war front. But the subtext to his letters also reveals a self-indulgent attitude. His reflections during his coverage of the Boer War, for instance, expose a surprisingly romantic sense of war and especially of its leaders, certainly an attitude that was in opposition to his mother's. From South Africa, Richard declared: "war as these people do it bores one to destruction. They are terribly dull souls. They cannot give an order intelligently. The real test of a soldier is the way he gives an order. I heard a Colonel with eight ribbons for eight campaigns scold a private for five minutes because he did not see a signal flag, and no one else could. It is not becoming that a Colonel should scold for five minutes."[53]

A month later, when Richard was confronted with the consequences of war, he captured in his own writing some of his mother's spirit and talent for depicting the gruesome realities of war. He writes Davis after seeing a column of twenty-two hundred men returning from battle: the soldiers "are yellow with fever, their teeth protruding and the skin drawn tight over their skeletons" (271). He reports to his mother that he and Winston Churchill "cried for an hour" over the gallantry of these ruined men whose appearance "was a most cruel assault upon one's feelings" (271–72). Ultimately, however, Richard's concern was not for the oppressed or their cause; his ability to enhance his career and to profit personally is at the heart of his decisions. Less than two weeks after his viewing of the battered column, he writes: "Sometimes they fight all day using seven or eight regiments and kill a terrible lot of fine soldiers and capture forty Boer farmers and two women. It is not the kind of war I care to report. 'Nor mean to!' I cannot make a book out of what little I've seen but I will come out about even" (277). This was the attitude toward war that Davis had resisted all her life, but she was blinded by her devotion to her son and she continued to praise his "noble" concern for the oppressed.

Though frustrated with her declining health at this time, Davis maintained a close vigil on the Congo events. Her letters to Richard suggest her own longing for the strength to be at the center of the fray: "I'm such a nervous idiot now. But I am so thankful *you* did it. All the time you have been working at this thing I thought of the words 'the voice of one crying in the wilderness—Make Straight the way of the Lord.' I always knew that when you took up some big cause you would do your best work. Here it is."[54] Davis had often been concerned about Richard's seemingly frivolous novel writing; in this effort she correctly perceived a distinct change in his writing style that would garner his greatest critical attention. Charley sent her copies of Richard's New York newspaper articles, which she proudly distributed to friends. She often wrote to Richard to let him know of the effects of his efforts. One letter in particular touchingly reveals Davis's fragile sense of life in her seventy-sixth year:

Isn't it strange to think that you, over here, can strike a big blow for thousands of negroes—who never heard of you and never will. That you can save them from torture and death!

Such a strange world! And God behind it! Sometimes I wonder we stay sane with the awful mystery of it all. But then one remembers that "the world is full—*full* of the *goodness* of God." These birds here, hopping round singing and doing their bit of work seem to be nearer the truth than we are, don't they?

But if Christ had not told us something of the mystery, what could we have done?

Forgive me; these things come so close to me lately.[55]

Davis was pleased when Richard collected his writings about the Congo and prepared them in book form. "It is the biggest stroke for the right you ever made," she commends him.[56] But because she was experiencing increased difficulties with her eyesight, she had to desist from writing as frequently. This statement praising Richard's acting "for the right" is Davis's final comment signifying her belief that Richard had accepted the literary legacy that she and Clarke had bequeathed their children.

∗   ∗   ∗

In the spring, Davis's oculist decided that an operation on her weakest eye could be postponed until fall. Davis's eye problems were in remission to the degree that by mid-summer she was able to write fairly regularly for *The Independent*. One of the best of this period's articles was "One Woman's Question," published in July of 1907. Spending several months out of the country during the previous year, Davis asserted, had allowed her to gain a fresh view of America on her return, a perspective "to which the governing American seems to be blind."[57] She uses a metaphor of the farmer's highly trained eye, which can detect in clumps of earth the condition of his fields, then extends the metaphor to "the diseases that are gaining ground in the country, just as the sour earth and fungus indicate the ailments of the worn-out farmer" (132).

Extracting ten examples from recent newspaper accounts, Davis describes this "fungus" in graphic detail: the young woman who uses her tragic experiences to get her picture in the newspaper; the popularity of fiction of "the flimsiest character"; advertising billboards along railway tracks that block the beauty of the scenery in order to sell tobacco and whiskey and about which, more importantly, no one complains; horrifying crimes that become dull by their frequency. Ironically, she notes, major crimes and exposed corruptions gain much public attention and officials rush to remedy them, but small instances of vulgarity and dishonesty, as described in several of her examples, "are the symptoms of a creeping paralysis which threatens us almost unnoticed" (1933). This time Davis does not offer faith as a panacea; in the best tradition of her demands for public activism, she concludes by challenging the reader in the style she had first used in "Life in the Iron Mills"—by turning to the individual with a direct and penetrating question that demands personal activism as a response: "What is its cure?" (133)

As the year drew to a close, Richard was especially attentive to his mother, realizing that this was the time to say what too often is left unsaid. Thus he wrote frequently, praising her work with a sincerity that acknowledges an appreciation and understanding of his mother's achievements. One Easter, when he sent luscious flowers to her and Nora, he received a letter of thanks that reveals how important Davis's faith had become to her:

> Just sixty years ago I went to the communion for the first time in Easter—and then Dad cared so much for it. And just now at church hundreds of people were crowding to the altar . . . and I remember that this was but one little church in the town and that there were thousands of towns in the country, and that all over the world they were rejoicing because He rose from the dead—and—we're trying to live like Him. Not doing it maybe. But the trying is something—for us, isn't it? Forgive me dear. But I feel as if I *had* to tell somebody. The thing concerned the whole world.[58]

She thought often, too, of the old days. She wrote her son, "I have a good deal of time now when I can't read or write—just shut my eyes and think and I find myself jogging back on the old track—the old home days. And of you . . . Daddy wrote to me once 'Our son is a grand noble gentleman.' And you were."[59]

Davis and her eldest son were not without the typical petty disputes or misunderstandings that plague any parent-child relationship, but even those were rapidly smoothed over during these last years. In the summer of 1908, one such spat concerned what Davis felt to be frivolous writing on Richard's part and her subsequent concern that she had overstepped the boundaries of criticism. The difficulty was settled by Richard's insistence that she had every right to question his work. He concluded his letter with a tribute acknowledging his literary indebtedness to his mother: "There is no one else to whom I would rather talk than to you on that subject. You taught me all I know, and, what you think is every thing to me! I need not tell you that." But he was also aware that he was not the same type of writer as she: "Only, you must not expect what is not there. Next time I am going to write a serious story, but, this time it is a light-hearted adventure of two lads and back of it a serious situation. I count on you to understand that part even should it go by the rest of the world."[60]

It was becoming apparent to Davis and her children that she could not live for many more years. The children responded with personal support and loving tributes. Davis herself, ever the pragmatist in her daily life, began to put her life in order. In order that she and her husband and subsequently her children could be buried together, she had Clarke's ashes moved to the Leverington Cemetery, which was adjacent to the Roxborough Baptist Cemetery where Clarke had been interred at his death. She also met with her attorney, Roland Morris, to prepare her will.[61] Davis was scrupulous in her endeavor to divide her legacy equally between her children. The family house in Philadelphia was willed to Nora, giving her the lifetime security of a home so that she might be free from the necessity of worrying about the means to live comfortably after her mother's death, and thereby continuing the Blaine and Harding women's tradition of willing property to a female heir. Richard and Charles were given all the bonds and stocks to share equally. Wilse Harding had left some property to Rebecca upon his death, and it, along with the Washington home she had inherited from her mother and the property (three houses and twenty-five acres of land) at Point Pleasant that she and Clarke had accumulated during their marriage, were left to her children to be divided equally. Thus Davis could enter her last years with the assurance that her children would inherit her belongings with a sense of their mother's love and concern for their well-being. For Charles and Richard, the financial aspect of her legacy could make little difference in their well-established life-styles. For Nora, however, it was a legacy of independence.

*   *   *

Davis herself was continuing to write essays for *The Independent* whenever her eyesight allowed, but two of her last publications were short stories for major literary periodicals of the period, *Century Magazine* and *Scribner's Magazine.* "An Old-Time Love Story" was published in the *Century's* 1908 Christmas issue along with works by Jacob A. Riis, Andrew Carnegie, and Harriet Monroe (spokesperson for the "new poetry" of the period). Davis's well-written story is another in her series of historically based studies of the lives of the earliest settlers of the New World. The *Scribner's* story, "The Coming of Night," was a far more significant work, however: it champions an active life for the elderly. The widowed Professor Paull is a contributing member of his family until an acquaintance, Mrs. Cross, convinces him that he is a burden to his son and daughter-in-law, and he places himself in the rest home Mrs. Cross owns. Mrs. Cross's motives actually have nothing to do with the professor; he simply enabled her to leave "her mark" on society through what she views as socially progressive institutions. That the professor's children rescue him verifies his value in their lives. The story richly confirms Davis's own beliefs: at home again, the professor realizes that the world is "only a big friendly home, and the world beyond death, which he had feared so much, just another, more friendly and more real."[62]

The most noteworthy criticism of Davis's final contribution to a major periodical (she published three other minor pieces before her death) came from Richard. In London at the time that this issue of the American periodical appeared, he scoured the city for a copy, finding one finally in Chelsea. He praised the story with keen insight: "The youth of it, and the way you take the best of the older method, and the best of the new, is wonderful. Howells, Warner, Mitchell Aldrich always seemed to me to linger too long over their sentences, then dragged. But you tell the story as though you were twenty five, and had just finished Life in the Iron Mills."[63] The point is accurate; her characterizations were as finely drawn as ever.

*   *   *

Davis's health failed intermittently in the remaining eighteen months of her life. In April of 1909 she was proud to report to Richard that she had been able to walk into the smoking room of her home and even to receive visitors. She published her last two articles that fall in *St. Nicholas*, and her unwavering spirit is revealed in another letter written that year to her eldest son. Her home had been burglarized, but she passes quickly over that and asserts: "Don't you ever think that I am tramping beside you in your walks? *I am*. My knees and eyes will be new some day and then what walks I'll take! Your old Mother who loves you."[64] Richard thoughtfully reciprocated by describing one of his walks, "a spree in the woods," as he called it. Finding there a flower that seemed the first of the season, he informed his mother that he had christened it "the Rebecca Harding Davis Flower" and promised to remember her literary advice, "dear mother and dear critic."[65] Through the year, he continued to send her proof pages of his work whenever possible and listened carefully to her comments. As late as September 1909 he forwarded to her copies of stories that he was revising.[66]

Early the next year, Davis suffered a minor stroke, but by that summer she was able to take her annual vacation. Appropriately, she traveled to the New Jersey coast that had been the locale for some of her finest fiction and which had always held for her a spiritual sustenance in a manner that no other area ever had. Later in the summer, she visited several friends in Philadelphia and Connecticut and then went to Richard's home in Mount Kisco, New York. There she became ill and was unable to return to Philadelphia as she had wished. She died at Crossroads Farm on September 29, 1910. The cause of death was noted as oedema of the lungs brought on by heart disease.[67]

After Davis's death, Charles painted a memorable portrait of his mother's last months. After Clarke's death, he recalls, she had maintained the family home in Philadelphia with attention to preserving the atmosphere that had made it the "Centre of the Universe" for her children as well, but she relished the serenity and beauty of summer visits to Crossroads Farm and always tried to preserve her time there as a true vacation, enjoying it as a brief respite from writing. On her final visit, Charles notes, she radiated an inner peacefulness: "her faith was implicit and infinite . . . Through these last long summer days she sat on the terrace surrounded by the flowers and the sunshine that she so loved. Little children came to play at her knee, and old friends travelled from afar to pay her court."[68] In her last years, a friend commented on "what a beautiful life" Davis had had and, as she told Richard, "it is true. A beautiful happy life."[69] Her "summer days" had come at last.

Davis had wanted to die in her own home, but her health had been too precarious to have her moved from Mount Kisco. However, Richard had her body returned to Philadelphia for a private funeral service. As with Clarke's funeral, Davis's was held in the family home at South Twenty-first Street, and Dr. Floyd Tomkins once again performed the service.[70] Davis was cremated and buried with Clarke in the grave at Leverington Cemetery. Clarke had always joked that he spent half of his life being the husband of Rebecca Harding Davis and the other half as the father of the equally well-known Richard.[71] But he garnered the last bit of renown. Their joint tombstone simply reads, "L. CLARKE, DAVIS, 1834–1904" and below that, "AND HIS WIFE"![72]

This was not the only irony of Davis's passing. *The Independent*, for whom she had been a regular contributor for nearly two decades, made no mention of her death. Her own city's major newspaper, the *Philadelphia Inquirer*, for which Clarke had been an editor for several years, noted her death only as part of a two-column, alphabetical listing in which she was identified simply as the "widow of L. Clarke Davis." No mention of her fifty-year literary career was included. No comparable number of tributes filled the pages of literary journals as they had in newspapers after Clarke's death. The most notable tribute, that of the *New York Times*, contained its own irony. Recalling "Life in the Iron Mills" as one of America's classic depictions of "the grinding life of the working people," the obituary writer recalled the national attention it had attracted: "many thought the author must be a man. The stern but artistic realism of the picture she put alive upon paper, suggested a man, and a man of power not unlike Zola's."[73] The irony, of course, is that Davis's pioneering fiction had preceded that of the great French naturalist by several years. But the commemorator was correct when he described Davis's writing as containing a power that awakened literary consciousness across the nation. It was a power she retained for her fifty-year literary career, bequeathing her vision to generations of readers and especially to the next generation of realists.

Perhaps the most astute personal tribute to Davis's intellectual vitality and energetic confrontation with life came from Richard several years after his mother's death. Gravely ill himself, Richard reminisced with Charles about their youth together in Philadelphia, and he found sustenance in rereading the enormous body of correspondence between himself and his parents, most of which had been directed to his mother. "I know why we were such a happy family," he confided to Charles. "It was because we were always, all of us, of the same age."[74]

But the most noteworthy tribute, and the one which Davis herself would have appreciated most, came the month after Davis's death from her longtime friend, Elizabeth Stuart Phelps (Ward).[75] In an essay for *Century Magazine* entitled, "Stories That Stay," Phelps asserted, "A short story is, or should be, a work of art, and this is the closest sense of that elastic word. It has long been my conviction that more art, so to speak, is required for the making of a good short story than for the making of a long one; that the creative qualities needed for this kind of literary effort are so peculiar to the case as to demand standards of their own."[76] Those standards that signify the "elements of permanence" are notable in four words: "originality, humanity, force, and finish" (123).

Of the half-dozen stories that Phelps personally selects as worthy of permanence because, in her opinion, they incorporate those four elements,

"Life in the Iron Mills" is not only included but given special status by Phelps's acknowledgment of her "sense of personal indebtedness" to its author. Phelps accurately assesses the strengths and weaknesses of Davis's short story, again noting her artistic indebtedness to her friend:

> That story was a distinct crisis for one young writer at the point where the intellect and the moral nature meet. It was never possible after reading it to ignore. One could never say again that one did not understand. The claims of toil and suffering upon ease had assumed a new form. For me they assumed a force which perhaps it is not too much to say, has never let me go. (120)

For a writer who had devoted her life to presenting the world's injustices with the specific hope that her words would inculcate a sense of responsibility in her readers, this was the perfect tribute. If she had sought to tell other women's lives, her own had a telling effect not only on "one young writer" but on a nation.

Notes

Letters from and to Rebecca Harding Davis (RHD) are designated with an "L." Permission to quote from the following sources is gratefully acknowledged:

BC		Overbury Collection, Barnard College Library
BE	-G:	James Fraser Gluck Collection;
BE	-M:	Charles Wells Moulton Collection;
		Buffalo and Erie County Public Library
BPL		Boston Public Library, by courtesy of the Trustees
CHS		Connecticut Historical Society
CU	-G:	General Manuscripts Collection;
	-H:	Harper Bros. Papers;
	-R:	Paul R. Reynolds Papers;
	-W:	Theodore F. Wolfe Papers;
		Rare Book and Manuscript Library, Columbia University
DU		St. James Episcopal Church Papers, Duke University
HH		The Huntington Library, San Marino, California
HHU		The Houghton Library, Harvard University
JHU		James R. Gilmore Collection (MS. 37), Special Collections, Milton S. Eisenhower Library, The Johns Hopkins University
NYPL	-A:	Alfred W. Anthony Collection;
	-B:	Henry W. and Albert A. Berg Collection;
	-C:	William Conant Church Papers;
	-CC:	Century Company Records;
	-H:	Josiah Gilbert Holland Papers;
		Rare Book and Manuscripts Div., New York Public Library, Astor, Lenox and Tilden Foundations
PML		The Pierpont Morgan Library, New York (MA 1950)
PU	-D:	Donald and Robert M. Dodge Collection of Mary Mapes Dodge;
	-M:	Mary Mapes Dodge, *St. Nicholas* Correspondence;
	-W:	Wilkinson Collection of Mary Mapes Dodge;
		Princeton University Library

UI   Special Collections and Manuscripts, University of Iowa

UP   Horace Howard Furness Memorial Library, Special Collections, Van Pelt Library, University of Pennsylvania

UV   Richard Harding Davis Collection (#6109), Clifton Waller Barrett Library, Manuscripts Div., Special Collections Dept., University of Virginia Library

WVU   Archibald W. Campbell Papers, West Virginia and Regional History Collection, West Virginia University Libraries

Introduction

1. Thomas H. Johnson, ed., *The Letters of Emily Dickinson*, 3 vols. (Cambridge, MA: Belknap, 1958), 2: 372–73.

2. Quoted in Donald Weber's "Introduction" to Perry Miller's *Jonathan Edwards* (Amherst: University of Massachusetts Press, 1981), xix.

3. *New York Daily Tribune*, Jul. 13, 1870, p. 6.

4. Sharon M. Harris, "RHD: A Continuing Misattribution," *Legacy* 45 (Dec. 1988): 33–34.

5. See section II, below, for a discussion of RHD's theoretical stance.

6. Edwin H. Cady, "Preface," *The Road to Realism: The Early Years 1837–1885 of William Dean Howells* (Syracuse, NY: Syracuse University Press, 1965), vii.

7. Gerald Langford, *The Richard Harding Davis Years: A Biography of a Mother and Son* (New York: Holt, Rinehart and Winston, 1961), 9–10.

8. Tillie Olsen, "Bibliographic Interpretation," in *"Life in the Iron Mills" and Other Stories* (Old Westbury, NY: Feminist Press, 1985), 157.

9. Judith Fetterley, "Introduction," *Provisions: A Reader from 19th Century American Women* (Bloomington: Indiana University Press, 1985), 7.

10. See Jane Tompkins's "Introduction," *Sensational Designs: The Cultural Work of American Fiction, 1790–1860* (New York: Oxford University Press, 1985).

11. Lawrence Buell becomes entrapped in such terminology in *New England Literary Culture: From Revolution to Renaissance* (New York: Cambridge University Press, 1986). Early in his discussion of the transition from romanticism to realism, he acknowledges that "local color" is often a limiting label; yet he tends to reserve that term for women writers and later in the text contrasts Thoreau's "regionalism" with "local colorists" and asserts that the latter have a "liableness to syrupiness" (331).

12. Josephine Donovan, *New England Local Color Literature: A Woman's Tradition* (New York: Frederick Ungar, 1983), 2. Surveys such as Donovan's and Nina Baym's *Woman's Fiction* (Ithaca, NY: Cornell University Press, 1978) now need to be integrated with studies of individual writers in order to gain a less regionalized perspective on women's contributions to the rise of realism.

13. Alan Trachtenberg, *The Incorporation of America: Culture and Society in the Gilded Age* (New York: Hill & Wang, 1985), 182.

14. See Eric Sundquist, "Introduction," *American Realism: New Essays* (Baltimore: Johns Hopkins University Press, 1982), and Joan Lidoff, "Another Sleeping Beauty: Narcissism in *The House of Mirth*," ibid., 238–58. Sundquist acknowledges, "The problem lies in part in the central difficulty of describing the program of a group of writers who virtually had no program but rather responded eclectically, and with increasing imaginative urgency, to the startling acceleration into being of a complex industrial society following the Civil War," but he focuses on "*the* decade of literary realism in America," the 1890s (viii, vii). My assertion extends Sundquist's acknowledgment back to the early realists of antebellum and Civil War America.

15. Sundquist, p. 10.

16. The term is Buell's; see his chapter 12 for a discussion of regional prose and the literature of place.

17. Sarah Orne Jewett's "imaginative realism" is more closely aligned with transcendentalism in its precept that excessive realism deters the flights of imagination that spur the artist to dream (see Donovan, 102–3). This insistence on transcending reality, especially into a kind of dream state, is at odds with RHD's theory (see chapters 1 and 2, below).

18. Langford, p. 15.

19. See John Irving's comments on his own artistry in "Compassion in the Novel," *New York Times Book Review* (Aug. 2, 1987), p. 24.

20. Van Wyck Brooks, *The Times of Melville and Whitman* (New York: E. P. Dutton, 1947), 240–41.

21. See, for instance, *A New Home—Who'll Follow?* (1839; reprint, ed. Sandra A. Zagarell, New Brunswick, NJ: Rutgers University Press, 1990).

22. William Dean Howells, *Criticism and Fiction*, ed. Clara Marburg Kirk and Rudolph Kirk (1891; reprint, New York: New York University Press, 1959); "strange beauty" is the term applied to the Korl Woman in "Life."

23. Hamlin Garland, *Crumbling Idols*, ed. Jane Johnson (1894; reprint, Cambridge, MA: Belknap, 1960); see chap 1, "Provincialism."

24. Ibid., 39. In spite of Zola's insistence upon scientific objectivism, he often presented moral guideposts for the reader. For instance, in *L'Assomoir* (1876; reprint, New York: Penguin, 1970), when the drunken Coupeau kisses Gervais, Zola blatantly directs the reader's attention to the moral of the scene: "the smacking kiss they gave each other full on the mouth amidst the filth of her trade was a sort of first step downwards in their slow descent into squalor" (87). These guideposts continue until the end of the novel, when Zola again ensures the reader's understanding of the causes of Gervais's decline by remarking on her slow death: "People mentioned the cold and the heat," the narrator observes, "but the truth was that she died of poverty, from the filth and exhaustion of her wasted life" (388). So, too, does Zola occasionally employ sentimentalism; this is most apparent in his depiction of Lalie. The abusive reality of "good" Lalie's life is depicted in horrifyingly realistic details; yet the author cannot refrain from inserting: "She was dying of having, at her age, the mind and spirit of a real mother in a frame too delicate and small to contain such an all-embracing maternity. . . . Yes, quite naked, the bleeding, agonising nakedness of a martyr. . . . From head to foot she was one black

bruise. Oh, what a massacre of the innocents—those brutal male paws crushing a sweet little thing, what an abomination to see such weakness staggering under such a cross!" Both of these passages are examples of the authorial control upon which Zola also, if paradoxically, insisted.

25. See Garland, *Idols*, chap. 9, "Impressionism"; subsequent references to *Idols* are in the text.

26. "Life in the Iron Mills," *Atlantic Monthly* 7 (Apr. 1861): 431; subsequent references are in the text.

27. Of course, few realists were able to maintain that ideal themselves, and recent studies have challenged authorial representations of the ideal (see Sundquist's *American Realism*, and June Howard's *Form and History in American Literary Naturalism* [Chapel Hill: University of North Carolina Press, 1985]).

28. For a discussion of RHD's term "Western," see chapter 2.

29. For an alternative perspective, see Margaret M. Culley's "Vain Dreams: The Dream Convention in Some Nineteenth-Century American Women's Fiction," *Frontiers* 1.3 (1976): 94–102.

30. Buell, p. 63.

31. L, to James Fields, October 25, 1862 (UV).

32. L, August 17, [1861] (UV).

33. See Buell, p. 167.

34. For a succinct discussion of the Brahmin historians, see Buell, pp. 40–45, 200–209.

35. *Legacy* 4 (Fall 1987): 59–60. I am especially in agreement with Martin in her concern for Buell's exclusion of Cathy Davidson's and Jane Tompkins's scholarship in this area.

36. To consider this as any real advantage for Louisa May Alcott stretches the concept of advantage; few American authors with such a renowned literary heritage were subjected to such early poverty and economic struggles.

37. See Buell, pp. 376–92; subsequent references to *New England Literary Culture* are in the text.

38. Baym, pp. 36–37.

39. Fetterley, *Provisions*, p. 10.

40. Sundquist, p. vii.

41. Nathaniel Hawthorne, "Preface," *The House of the Seven Gables: A Romance* (Boston: Ticknor, Reed, and Fields, 1851), iii.

Chapter One: "Life in the Iron Mills"

1. The stone house had been built in the eighteenth century by David Bradford, who had gained national attention during the Whiskey Rebellion of 1794. I am indebted to Helen Woodward Shaeffer's unpublished dissertation, "RHD: Pioneer Realist" (University of Pennsylvania, 1947), for many details about RHD's early life, quoted by permission of the Special Collections Department, Van Pelt Library, University of Pennsylvania. Although I disagree on several points of interpretation, Shaeffer's early biographical work, which was completed when many of

RHD's friends and family acquaintances were still living, gives us invaluable facts and personal testimonies.

2. RHD, *Bits of Gossip* (New York: Houghton Mifflin, 1904), p. 1; subsequent references are in the text.

3. Harriet Preble was an "aunt" through distant family marriages that also distantly linked RHD to Joel Barlow.

4. RHD, *Bits*, p. 30.

5. No list of books read by RHD and Wilse remains to clarify whether or not they read the early French and German realists; we may surmise that they studied the German philosopher, Johann Gottlieb Fichte (1762–1814), since *Margret Howth* is a direct attack on Fichte's philosophy.

6. Quoted in Shaeffer, pp. 35–36. Sherrard Clemens was a Virginia statesman whose political commentaries appeared often in local newspapers, where his activities were also widely reported. RHD probably knew Clemens through her father.

7. The *Intelligencer* went through several name changes in the 1850s and 1860s, including *Daily Intelligencer* and *Wheeling Daily Intelligencer*. Archibald Campbell edited the paper before and during the Civil War, and Edward Everett and Horace Greeley were among his correspondents.

8. One of RHD's existing letters to Campbell reveals an ardent concern that he understand certain actions of hers at a public gathering, suggesting she may have formed some attachment to him; however, as she told Annie, if she had really cared about him, she would never have mentioned him in her letters. This self-imposed dictum was obeyed when she became involved with Clarke; Annie was a regular correspondent at the time but had no inkling of his existence in RHD's life until shortly before the wedding.

9. RHD published anonymously in the *Intelligencer*, thus those works are lost to us (see note 12).

10. L, to Campbell, January 30, 1859.

11. Ibid.

12. Printed anonymously; with caution, I am attributing this to RHD because a letter to Campbell details the enclosure as an article for his women readers. "Women and Politics" is the only such item to appear in the paper around the time of her letter.

13. L, November 16, 1861 (UV).

14. Although Rebecca Harding did not become "Davis" until her marriage in 1862, I am using that designation here because it is the name with which her work is identified.

15. Langford, p. 15; Olsen, p. 83.

16. *Harvest of Change: American Literature 1865–1914* (Englewood Cliffs, NJ: Prentice-Hall, 1967), 53.

17. *Norton Anthology of Literature by Women: The Tradition in English* (New York: Norton, 1985), 903.

18. "Lost and Found," *Ms.* 2 (Apr. 1974): 117.

19. "Assailant Landscapes and the Man of Feeling: RHD's 'Life in the Iron Mills,'" *Journal of American Culture* 3.3 (1980): 488.

20. *Sarah Orne Jewett* (New York: Frederick Ungar, 1980), 2.

21. *Local Color*, p. 33.

22. A shorter version of the following discussion appeared as "RHD: From Romanticism to Realism," *American Literary Realism* 21.2 (1989); reprinted by permission of McFarland & Company, Inc., Publishers, Jefferson, NC.

23. Conron identifies "three overlaying points of view" in "Life" but does so in terms of the "assailant landscapes." Further, Conron fails to recognize RHD's naturalistic techniques and often her irony; an awareness of the narrative structure helps clarify what he terms her "ambiguities of judgment."

24. What appears to be a fair copy of "Life" is part of the Huntington Library collections (MS. FK 1170).

25. See Catherine Clinton, *The Other Civil War* (New York: Hill & Wang, 1984), for a discussion of immigration into industrial areas during the nineteenth century.

26. From a March 1905 letter to Fred D. Warren, editor of the socialist newspaper, *Appeal to Reason* (quoted in Ronald Gottesman, "Introduction," *The Jungle* [New York: Penguin, 1985], xvii–xiv).

27. Annette Kolodny, *The Lay of the Land* (Chapel Hill: University of North Carolina Press, 1975), 135; see also Conron, note 23 above.

28. *Bits*, p. 36.

29. Clinton, pp. 22–25.

30. As Tillie Olsen has observed, this depiction of the workers' lives directly counters the paradisiacal view of cotton mills popularized in the 1840s by publications such as the *Lowell Offering* (165). Edited by a factory worker, Harriet Farley, the *Lowell Offering* (later the *New England Offering*) included contributions by other women mill workers, but the Lowell Company funded the project only so long as its content was acceptable to them. When the Lowell Female Labor Reform Association was formed in 1845, the owners withdrew their financial support.

31. Trachtenberg, "Experiments in Another Country: Stephen Crane's City Sketches," in Sundquist, p. 143; and Trachtenberg, *The Incorporation of America*, p. 148.

32. See Donovan's discussion of Harriet Beecher Stowe and other women writers' early use of the vernacular in *Local Color*, and Buell's discussion of oratorical styles in chap. 6 of *New England Literary Culture*.

33. For depictions of the corrupted reporter, see Harold Frederic's *The Market-Place* (1899), Robert Herrick's *The Web of Life* (1900), and Frank Norris's *The Pit* (1903).

34. *The Incorporation of America*, p. 52; chap. 2 of Trachtenberg's study discusses the impact of mechanization on American society and the discomfort that writers such as Twain and Whitman felt in saluting the new technology.

35. Josephine Donovan also identifies Charlotte A. Fillebrown Jerauld as an "anti-industrialist," although Jerauld adhered to a rural-utopian vision (*Local Color*, pp. 33–34).

36. Donald Pizer notes in *Realism and Naturalism in Nineteenth-Century American Literature* (rev.; Carbondale: Southern Illinois University Press, 1984) that Zola's experimental method can be "explained [by] the use of such 'scientific' elements in literature as the force of heredity and environment" (97).

37. Henry James also employed this technique, although more ambiguously, in his early novels. In *The Europeans* (1878; reprint, New York: Penguin, 1964), for instance, the affectation of tossing about French phrases is a central aspect of his characterization of the Europeanized cousins who visit Boston. On the way to meet her American cousins, the self-important young Baroness Munster surveys the objects of the countryside, and "she pronounced them *affreux*. Her brother remarked that it was apparently a country in which the foreground was inferior to the *plans recules*" (62).

38. "The Wife's Story," *Atlantic Monthly* 14 (Jul. 1864): 1–19.

39. Pizer, p. 34; subsequent references are in the text.

40. "Literary Contexts of 'Life in the Iron Mills,' " *American Literature* 49 (1977): 70–85; in general, however, I view "Life" in a quite different context from Hesford's anti-realism reading.

41. See Tompkins, pp. 148–50, and Buell, pp. 166–90.

42. Kenelm Burridge, *New Heaven, New Earth* (New York: Schocken, 1969), quoted in Tompkins, p. 221.

43. "Success and Failure of RHD," *Midcontinent American Studies Journal* 3.1 (1962): 45.

44. The movement away from Calvinism had been growing since the early nineteenth century and extends back in literary history to Charles Brockden Brown's *Wieland* (1798). For opposing perspectives on the "feminization" of religion at the time, see Donovan's "Introduction" to *Local Color* and Ann Douglas's *The Feminization of American Culture* (New York: Avon, 1977); for a discussion of New England authors' difficulties in addressing this issue, see part 3 of Buell's *New England Literary Culture*, pp. 191–280.

45. "Indiscriminate Charity," *New York Daily Tribune*, Jan. 2, 1877.

46. Quoted in Charles Belmont Davis, *Adventures and Letters of Richard Harding Davis* (New York: Charles Scribner's Sons, 1917), 17.

47. "Maggie: A Girl of the Streets," *The Portable Stephen Crane*, ed. Joseph Katz (New York: Penguin, 1969), 1.

48. Houston A. Baker, Jr., *Modernism and the Harlem Renaissance* (Chicago: University of Chicago Press, 1987), 57.

49. Quoted in C. B. Davis, *Adventures*, p. 40.

50. L, January 26, 1861 (UV).

51. Ibid. The Feminist Press edition of "Life" uses the subtitle, "or the Korl Woman," undoubtedly in the spirit of RHD's comments; however, the 1861 publication was not subtitled.

52. L, March 13, [1861] (UV).

53. For a discussion of Hawthorne's influence on the "major" American realists, see Richard H. Brodhead's "Hawthorne Among the Realists," in Sundquist, pp. 25–41.

54. Undated L, (HHU). RHD indicated in her autobiography that she had included a copy of "Life" with her letter to Hawthorne. The letter quoted contains no salutation, but its contents, place of origin, and ascertained date suggest it is the note she sent to Hawthorne.

55. *Bits*, pp. 20, 29.

56. L, [March 18, 1892] (UP). In her autobiography, RHD humorously commented on her carefully monitored reading as a child: "Honest old Timothy Flint, in his 'Account of the United States,' published at that time, boasts that 'the immense number of fifteen hundred newspapers and periodicals are now published in this country.' Of these I only remember two, the 'United States Gazette' and the 'Gentleman's Monthly Magazine,' which was always expurgated for my use by pinning certain pages together" (5).

57. *Bits*, p. 31.

Chapter Two: After "Life": A Savage Necessity

1. RHD lamented the mythic and heroic status that war had attained; as an abolitionist, she supported the Northern cause, but even then it was "a savage necessity" (L, to Annie Fields, May 18, c. 1865 [UV]). Toward the end of her life, she was still adamant on this issue and felt that attitudes toward war tended to be gender-specific; see, for instance, RHD, "The Mean Face of War," *The Independent* 51 (Jul. 20, 1899): 1931–33, and "War as the Woman Sees It," *Saturday Evening Post* 176 (Jun. 11, 1904): 8–9.

2. *Daily Intelligencer*, Jan. 1, 1861, p. 1; *Daily Intelligencer*, Jan. 7, 1861, p. 2.

3. *Daily Intelligencer*, May 13, 1861, p. 1.

4. L, to James Fields, August 17, [1861] (UV).

5. Shaeffer, p. 37.

6. Quoted in Shaeffer, p. 36.

7. L, from Wheeling, April 11, 1861 (UV).

8. *Bits*, p. 29.

9. Clinton, p. 172.

10. HH, MS. FI 1165.

11. James T. Fields, *Yesterdays with Authors* (1871; reprint, New York: AMS, 1970).

12. Ibid.

13. Ibid. RHD's concern in *Howth* was to challenge Fichte's transcendental idealism.

14. Ibid.

15. Nina Baym (*Woman's Fiction*) and Josephine Donovan (*Local Color*) have asserted that women writers of this era "had a powerful ally" in their (male) publishers (Baym, 23), and in many respects this is true. Yet the control that Fields wielded over the content of RHD's fiction suggests the less-than-ideal nature of the publisher's alliance.

16. *Margret Howth: A Story of To-Day* (1862; reprint, Upper Saddle River, NJ: Gregg, 1970), 6. Subsequent references are in the text.

17. *Modernism and the Harlem Renaissance*, p. 110n.

18. For instance, see Louise Duus, "Neither Saint Nor Sinner: Women in Late Nineteenth Century Fiction," *American Literary Realism* 7 (Summer 1974): 276–78; Austin, pp. 45–48; Olsen, pp. 91–96.

19. L, August 17, [1861] (UV).

20. L, August 9, [1861] (UV).

21. L, July 30, [1861] (UV).

22. L, to Fields, August 17, [1861] (UV).

23. L, August 9, [1861] (UV).

24. L, August 17, [1861] (UV).

25. L, to Fields, September 17, [1861] (UV).

26. L, August 17, [1861] (UV).

27. L, November 26, 1861 (UV).

28. Ibid. Both Langford and Olsen assert that Knowles is based on RHD's school-years' acquaintance with Dr. F. Julius LeMoyne, the famous abolitionist whom she discusses in *Bits*; this remains problematic since Dr. Knowles resurfaces in "The Harmonists" (1866) as an advocate of the Rappists, a nineteenth-century utopian society in Pennsylvania. Thus Knowles is best defined as representative of extremist philosophies that purport reform but do so only through denigration of sexual unions. This was certainly not RHD's opinion of abolitionists or specifically of LeMoyne.

29. L, to Fields, November 16, 1861 (UV).

30. Tompkins, *Sensational Designs*, p. 128.

31. The rampant difficulties of revising by mail sometimes led to humorous situations, especially since RHD was adamant about her facts. In December, Fields had noted that it was not geographically possible to have the Wabash so close to her mill town; RHD regretted the error and suggested he substitute a train for the river that "crawled moodily" across the landscape. However, she continued, if it cannot be changed, "never mind. Western people ought to be used to having cities laid out in swamps for them by Eastern speculators by this time" (undated L, to James Fields, [UV]).

32. See L, to Fields, August 9, [1861] (UV). As usual, RHD told Fields to alter the name "if you choose," but it remained as she had written.

33. See note 11 above.

34. L, from RHD, November 16, 1861 (UV).

35. Undated L, to Fields (UV).

36. "The Murder in the Glen Ross," *Peterson's* 40 (Nov.–Dec. 1861): 346–55, 438–46; in this story, RHD repeatedly uses upturned faces and organic writing metaphors, much in the manner that Michael Fried has described, in conjunction with Stephen Crane's writing, in *Realism, Writing, Disfiguration—on Thomas Eakins and Stephen Crane* (Chicago: University of Chicago Press, 1987).

37. Ann Sophia Stephens (1810–86) was a prolific writer of historical novels and author of the first dime novel, *Indian Wife of the White Hunter* (1860), which sold more than 300,000 copies. She also published comic novels under the pseudonym "Jonathan Slick." Like Davis and Benedict, she had a life-long career in the pages of *Peterson's*.

38. It was Fields who originally recommended that RHD publish anonymously because a work such as "A Story of To-Day" might create untoward attention for a single woman; she agreed, "although I don't think the public will wonder to any alarming extent—" (L, August 17, [1861] [UV]). By the time the story was published in book form, she asserted a "repugnance . . . to seeing my name in print" (undated L, [UV]). In part, this was prepublication jitters, but in January

she reasserted her position to Fields, "Always remember first and last and all the time that my grand petition is when Margret is out to keep my name out of the papers" (L, January 16, [1862] [UV]). Her family had at first cautioned her against the use of her name in publication, and Clarke may have suggested the same. In the fall of 1862 she wrote Fields, " 'Will you put my name in as contributor?' In my most emphatic tones I write *NO*. My best friends and advisers hearing of Mr. Fields wild proposition say—Not yet if ever," and she humorously signs her letter, "Yours—*forever* / The Author of Margret Howth" (undated L, probably September 1862, [UV]). She continued to embrace the banner of anonymity until years after her marriage when Clarke encouraged her to allow her name to appear as "Mrs. R. H. Davis." However, during and after the 1870s, when she focused on women's stories, she changed her by-line to "Rebecca Harding Davis."

39. "Editor's Table," *Peterson's* 47 (Apr. 1865): 312.

40. L, to Fields, November 26, 1861 (UV).

41. Undated L (UV).

42. Ibid.

43. L, January 6, [1862] (UV).

44. Ibid.

45. L, February 20, 1862 (UV).

46. That RHD's refusal could have affected her reviews is well supported by recent studies of pressures brought to bear upon reviewers in antebellum and Civil War America; see Jane Tompkins's *Sensational Designs* (chap. 1); Buell's *New England Literary Culture* (on "major" authors); and Nina Baym's *Novels, Readers, and Reviewers* (Ithaca: Cornell University Press, 1984).

47. *Continental Monthly* 2 (Aug. 1862): 239–40; *Continental Monthly* 2 (Sep. 1862): 366–68.

48. *Continental Monthly* 2 (Nov. 1862): 637.

49. *Continental Monthly* 1 (April 1862): 467. Subsequent references are in the text.

50. Olsen, p. 97.

51. "John Lamar," *Atlantic Monthly* 9 (Apr. 1862): 411. Subsequent references are in the text.

52. Shaeffer, pp. 20–21 (from oral testimony).

53. Quoted in *Bits*, p. 171.

54. *Bits*, p. 163.

55. Frémont's enthusiasm often caused him more harm than good; Lincoln had removed him from command in Missouri when he decreed slaves of all Confederates in the state to be free. However, political pressure was brought to bear upon Lincoln by Frémont's supporters, and he was given the command of the West Virginia region.

56. *Bits*, p. 188. Subsequent references are in the text.

57. L, to Annie Fields, dated only June 15, probably 1863 (UV).

58. Undated L, probably late 1863 or 1864 (UV).

59. Frederick Douglass, *My Bondage and My Freedom*, ed. Philip S. Foner (New York: Dover, 1969), 269–70. See Eric J. Sundquist's essay, "Slavery, Revolution, and the American Renaissance" (in *The American Renaissance Reconsidered*,

ed. Walter Benn Michaels and Donald E. Pease [Baltimore: Johns Hopkins University Press, 1985], 1–33), to which I am indebted for its discussion of the positions of Stowe, Delany, and Douglass on slave rebellions.

60. Louisa May Alcott's *Hospital Sketches* are much more realistic than "The Brothers." One of the best Civil War short stories is Elizabeth Stuart Phelps Ward's "The Comrades," but it was not published until 1911.

61. Undated L, to James Fields, probably April 1862 (UV).

62. Ibid.

63. The Reverend Dr. Cyrus Dickson may have been the minister who had publicly praised *Howth*; Davis had requested a copy of the sermon from Fields several months earlier.

64. L, May 14, [1862] (UV).

65. Ibid.

66. L, May 27, [1862] (UV).

67. William Charvat, *The Profession of Authorship in America, 1800–1870*, ed. Matthew J. Bruccoli ([Columbus]: Ohio State University Press, 1968), 311–13.

68. Ibid.

69. Warren S. Tryon and William Charvat, eds., *The Cost Books of Ticknor and Fields and Their Predecessors, 1832–1858* (New York: Bibliographical Society of America, 1949).

70. *Gail Hamilton's Life in Letters*, ed. H. Augusta Dodge, 2 vols. (Boston: Lee & Shepard, 1901), 2: 624.

71. L, to Fields, May 27, [1862] (UV).

72. L, May 8, [1862] (UV).

73. For discussions of Annie Adams Fields see Donovan, *Local Color*, pp. 38–49, and Donovan, *Sarah Orne Jewett* (New York: Frederick Ungar, 1980).

74. *Bits*, p. 30. Subsequent references are in the text.

75. *Life in Letters of William Dean Howells*, ed. Mildred Howells, 2 vols. (1928; reprint, New York: Russell & Russell, 1955), 1: 30.

76. *Gail Hamilton's Life in Letters*, 1: 340–41.

77. RHD was one of a growing list of women writers whom Hawthorne *excluded* from his reference to "scribbling women." See chap. 6 of *Bits* for RHD's own quite different discussion of "scribbling women."

78. *Bits*, p. 43. Another incident that also disturbed RHD was Emerson's "perception of character," especially in terms of the recently deceased Henry David Thoreau. After expressing his wish that RHD had met Thoreau, he added, "Henry often reminded me of an animal in human form. He had the eye of a bird, the scent of a dog, the most acute, delicate intelligence—but no soul. No, Henry could not have had a human soul" (*Bits* 44). If he intended it as a compliment to Thoreau, RHD did not understand it as such. Years later, she commented to Annie Fields that she always thought of her Boston trip when she saw a picture of Emerson: "Emerson in that unhomelike library of his with the pines shivering outside and that blanched wife and her ghostly eyes—are the most vivid recollections" (L, March 12, [1863?] [UV]).

79. L, dated only August 10, probably 1865 (UV).

80. This, of course, is the well-known concluding line to Emerson's essay, "Nature" (emphasis added).

81. *Life in Letters of William Dean Howells*, 1: 37.

82. L, July 10, [1862], from Baltimore (UV).

83. Ibid.

84. L, March 12, [1863?] (UV).

85. L, August 28, [1862] (UV). In the hustle of her professional and personal commitments, RHD often let correspondences slip. Years later, Kate Field, apparently unfamiliar with the pressures of Davis's life, admonished her friend for claiming to be busy; in fact, RHD had lost Fields's address and had to send her response through Annie.

86. Sophia's L to Annie Fields, May 3, 1863 (BPL).

87. Ibid.

88. L, April 25, 1866 (BPL).

89. L, July 10, [1862], from Baltimore (UV).

90. Ibid.

91. Ibid.

92. L, August 4, [1862] (HH; they date it August 21).

93. Ibid.

94. L, August 28, [1862] (HH).

95. Ibid.

96. L, to the Fieldses, August 4, [1862] (HH).

97. L, July 10, [1862], from Baltimore (UV).

98. L, October 25, 1862, from Wheeling (UV).

99. "David Gaunt," *Atlantic Monthly* 10 (Sep.–Oct. 1862): 257–71, 403–21; subsequent references are in the text. What appears to be a fair copy of "Gaunt" is part of the RHD holdings at The Huntington Library.

100. *Bits*, p. 226. Subsequent references are in the text.

101. *Bits*, pp. 110–11.

102. In the *Red Badge of Courage*, this is Crane's term for the individual soldier's eradication of self and identification with the collective cause: "He had grown to regard himself merely as a part of a vast blue demonstration."

103. *Bits*, p. 126; subsequent references are in the text.

104. L, August 28, [1862] (UV).

105. L, August 22, [1862] (BC). Nichols won this round: "Papaws" was the spelling used in publication. However, in 1871, when RHD published a short story in *Youth's Companion*, her preferred spelling was used: "The Paw-Paw Hunt."

106. L, to Fields, "Wheeling July 30, [1862]" (UV).

107. L, October 25, 1862 (UV).

108. *The Profession of Authorship*, pp. 312–13.

109. L, to Kate Field, dated only "February 3rd" (BPL). Shaeffer dates it 1877.

110. L, September 4, [1862] (UV).

111. Quoted in *Yesterdays with Authors*, p. 158. In this 1871 recollection of the exchange with Dickens, Fields does not credit RHD with authorship of "Blind Tom"; he simply notes that it was "an article, that was soon to appear in the Atlantic Monthly" (158).

112. Quoted in James C. Austin, *Fields of the Atlantic Monthly: Letters to the Editor 1861–1870* (San Marino, CA: Huntington Library, 1953), 380. The term "idiot-savant" was the clinical term of the period (although it did not actually receive general attention from the medical profession until 1877). Today we recognize these symptoms under the term "autistic-savant," a personality disorder in which only a minute percentage of the retarded autistic-savants have extraordinary talents. In 1988, the concept was popularized in film by Dustin Hoffman's portrayal in *Rain Man*.

113. "Blind Tom," *Atlantic Monthly* 10 (Nov. 1862): 585.

114. L, to Fields, December 6, 1862 (UV).

115. L, October 20, [1862] (UV).

116. Ibid.

117. L, to Fields, November 3, [1862] (UV).

118. L, December 6, 1862 (UV).

119. *Wheeling Daily Intelligencer*, Jan. 11, 1859, p. 3.

120. Ibid.

121. L, February 18, [1863] (UV).

122. Quoted in Clinton, p. 61; the evangelical *Advocate* was "one of the most widely read of the age."

123. Clinton, pp. 59–60.

124. That Charlotte is intended to highlight God's mercy and man's hypocrisy is evident in a note RHD sent to Annie thanking her for intervening with James in getting the story published. She insists that her observations of life are becoming "more *practical*" and adds: "That reminds me of a touching little incident that if it were in a novel would be called unnatural—there is a man here under sentence of death for a most cold-blooded murder—a vile hardened wretch raised on the skirts [?] with neither father nor mother to stand near him in the dock. His whole life has been a singularly lonely vicious one. The day after he was sentenced a wild ringdove came in the cell window and has remained there ever since—uncaged, close by him. The wretch clings to it as if it were a real God sent messenger—as it is" (L, December 6, 1862 [UV]).

125. "The Promise of Dawn: A Christmas Story," *Atlantic Monthly* 11 (Jan. 1863): 19; subsequent references are in the text.

Chapter Three: Other Women's Stories

1. L, January 10, [1863] (UV).

2. L, dated only "Monday evening," probably late January 1863 (UV).

3. L, February 18, [1863] (UV).

4. See note 2 above.

5. Undated L, to Annie Fields, probably late January 1863 (UV).

6. L, April 21, [1863] (UV). Benjamin Franklin Butler was a general in the Union army. He had been military governor of New Orleans in 1862, but because of the harshness of his command, he was removed. In 1864, he would command the forces that sought to seize Fort Fisher in North Carolina, an expedition that

failed, once again costing Butler his command. A radical Republican, he is perhaps best known today for spearheading the impeachment proceedings against President Andrew Johnson.

7. Austin, "Success," p. 45.

8. "Paul Blecker," *Atlantic Monthly* 12 (Jul. 1863): 69. Subsequent references are in the text.

9. Phelps, "At Bay," *Harper's New Monthly* 34 (May 1867): 780. RHD used the same title for a short story in *Peterson's* in October 1867, perhaps to return the honor.

10. L from RHD's woman friend is undated; L to Annie Fields is dated only January 10, [1863?] (UV).

11. L, to Annie Fields, May 1, [1863] (UV).

12. Ibid.

13. L, to Annie Fields, May 1, [1863] (UV).

14. L, to Annie Fields, June 3, [1863] (UV).

15. L, to Annie Fields, September 29, [1863] (UV).

16. L, dated only "Tuesday," probably late 1863 (UV).

17. See note 18 below.

18. L, dated only July 1, probably late 1860s (UV). Since her late-1863 illness was RHD's only near-death experience, it seems likely from this comment that Mitchell was her physician at the time.

19. "Mademoiselle Joan," *Atlantic Monthly* 58 (Sep. 1886): 328. The narrator is male, one more instance of RHD's use of a distancing technique when the issues were autobiographical.

20. Ibid.

21. See note 16 above.

22. L, to Annie Fields, February 25, [1864] (UV).

23. Undated L, to Annie Fields, probably late 1863 (UV).

24. L, to Annie Fields, December 23, [1863], from Wheeling (UV).

25. Ibid.

26. Olsen, pp. 121–27; Margaret M. Culley, "Vain Dreams: The Dream Convention in Some Nineteenth-Century American Women's Fiction," *Frontiers* 1.3 (1976): 94–102. Culley depicts RHD as forlorn over her pregnancy and despondent because her "hopes of a serious career as a writer [were] slipping away" (101). If RHD did fear a decline, it was unfounded. Within two years she would write her most significant novel, *Waiting for the Verdict*, and she would continue to consider herself a serious writer until her death in 1910.

27. L, March 25, [1864?] (UV).

28. L, dated only "Monday"; references to Richard's age and items appearing in the *Atlantic* suggest that the letter was written after "The Wife's Story" was published.

29. *Bits*, p. 37.

30. Mark Seltzer, "*The Princess Casamassima*: Realism and the Fantasy of Surveillance," in Sundquist, pp. 95–118. Seltzer is careful to note that it is "James's attempts to disaffiliate himself from the realist and naturalist 'group,' and from the politics that their method implies, that I am emphasizing here" (118n).

31. "The Wife's Story" (*Atlantic Monthly* 14 [Jul. 1864]: 26–31), in *"Life in the Iron Mills" and Other Stories*, pp. 177–78. Subsequent references are in the text.

32. Myra Jehlen, *American Incarnation* (Cambridge, MA: Harvard University Press, 1986), 93–94.

33. Carlyle to Emerson on the publication of *Essays*: "I have to object still, that we find you a Speaker, indeed, but as it were a *Soliloquizer* on the eternal mountain-tops only, in vast solitudes where men and their affairs lie all hushed in a very dim remoteness; and only *the man* and the stars and the earth are visible" (quoted in Jehlen, p. 120). As Jehlen observes, there is an "implicit difficulty in [Emerson's] identity of man and nature . . . that the unlimited power of the Emersonian individual to fulfill all the possibilities in nature may preclude his creating new possibilities and changing nature" (125). While there are, of course, arguments both for and against this assessment of Emerson, it clearly reflects what RHD questioned in his philosophy.

34. RHD again explores this theme in her short story "Marcia," *Harper's New Monthly* 53 (Nov. 1876): 925–28. (See chap. 6 for a discussion of "Marcia.")

35. Émile Zola, "The Experimental Novel," in *Documents of Modern Literary Realism*, ed. George J. Becker (Princeton, NJ: Princeton University Press, 1963), 176.

36. See Buell, pp. 359ff.

37. L, to Annie Fields, May 17, [1864] (UV).

38. Ibid.

39. Undated L, to Annie Fields (UV).

40. Ibid.

41. L, May 17, [1864] (UV).

42. For details of wartime Philadelphia and the 1864 Central Fair, see Russell F. Weigley, "The Border-City in Civil War, 1854–1865," in *Philadelphia: A 300-Year History*, ed. Russell F. Weigley (New York: Norton, 1982), 363–416.

43. L, to Annie Fields, June 15, [1864] (NYPL-B). I have been unable to identify this woman further.

44. L, July 27, [1864] (UV).

45. Quoted in Shaeffer, p. 205.

46. Ibid.

47. L, dated only "March 19" (HHU).

48. See below for Harriet Beecher Stowe's letter to RHD on this topic. In 1865 the Henry Jameses, Senior and Junior, became reviewers for *The Nation*, and Henry James, Jr.'s hostility toward sentimentalists, realists, and women writers in general (with the notable exception of Edith Wharton) is repeatedly commented on by women writers of the era (see note 111 below). It is unfortunate that RHD did not become a contributor to *The Nation* since she had much in common with its editorial perspective, including a concern for "the laboring class of the South," the education of freed slaves, and later the exposure of the corrupt Tweed Ring (see chap. 4).

49. L, August 28, [1862] (UV).

50. L, July 27, [1864] (UV); "Debby's Debut," *Atlantic Monthly* 12 (Aug. 1863): 160–82.

51. L, [February 14], possibly 1863 or 1864 (UV).

52. L, March 30, [1866] (UV).

53. Ibid.

54. The phrase, "the inevitability of male dominion" is Donovan's; see *Local Color*, p. 82. See chap. 7, below, for Phelps's final tribute to RHD.

55. L, November 8, possibly 1864 (UV).

56. "A Half-Life and Half a Life," *Atlantic Monthly* 13 (Feb. 1864): 157–82.

57. Undated L, to Annie Fields, ascertained date of October 20, 1863 (HH); L to Annie Fields, [February 14,] probably 1863 or 1864 (UV).

58. L, to Annie Fields, [February 14], probably 1863 or 1864 (UV).

59. Fetterley, *Provisions*, p. 120.

60. L, December 6, 1862 (UV).

61. Ibid.

62. Kirkland, *A New Home—Who'll Follow?*, chap. 44.

63. Undated L (UV).

64. Ibid.

65. L, to Annie Fields, May 6, [1863] (UV).

66. L, May 11, [1863] (UV).

67. L, to Annie Fields, dated "Phila. May—I don't know what—Friday" (UV).

68. C. B. Davis, pp. 5–6.

69. Undated L, to Annie Fields from Point Pleasant, probably summer of 1864 (UV).

70. Ibid.

71. L, to Annie Fields, August 10, probably 1865 (UV).

72. For a discussion of RHD's influence on later New Jersey writers, see Shaeffer, pp. 201–3.

73. Buell notes that this is a technique used by John Neal as well (296).

74. L, April 20, [1865] (UV).

75. L, to Annie Fields, May 18, probably 1865 (UV).

76. "Out of the Sea," *Atlantic Monthly* 15 (May 1865): 533; subsequent references are in the text.

77. Undated L, to Annie Fields, probably late 1864 (UV).

78. L, March 2, [1865] (UV).

79. *Atlantic Tales: A Collection of Stories From the Atlantic Monthly* (Boston: Ticknor and Fields, 1865).

80. L, to Annie Fields, March 2, [1865] (UV).

81. Ibid.

82. L, to Annie Fields, dated only "July" (UV).

83. Quoted in Shaeffer, p. 117.

84. Ibid.

85. L, August 10, [1865] (UV).

86. The latter explanation seems most plausible, since RHD again details Ellen Carroll's story in *Bits* (130–34).

87. L, September 17, [1865] (UV).

88. Ibid. Stowe extended her pro-women's rights arguments in 1869 in a series

of *Hearth and Home* articles. For a discussion of Stowe's abandonment of a feminist perspective, see chap. 4 of Donovan's *Local Color* and her essay, "Harriet Beecher Stowe's Feminism," *American Transcendental Quarterly*, no. 48–49 (Summer 1982).

89. L, to Annie Fields, September 17, [1865] (UV).

90. Both of Clarke's brothers died in the Civil War; one sister survived.

91. L, to Annie Fields, dated only "Sunday evening," probably February 1866 (UV).

92. L, March 30, [1866] (UV).

93. Ibid.

94. Undated L (UV).

95. Tillie Olsen erroneously identifies Stephen Holmes from *Howth* as the character who is recreated in "The Harmonists."

96. "The Harmonists," *Atlantic Monthly* 17 (May 1866): 529. Subsequent references are in the text.

97. Other items in that issue included poems by Longfellow, Lowell, and Whittier; excerpts from Hawthorne's notebooks; Stowe's continuing "Chimney Corner" column; and Howells's "Question of Monuments."

98. L, to Annie Fields, October 26, [1866?] (UV).

99. Ibid. It is amusing to note that Emerson's portrait has been replaced by that of Dante! The "Annie" referred to in this letter was the German-trained nurse the Davises had hired to assist RHD with the care of the baby.

100. L, to Clara "Callie" Wilson Baird, November 30, [1866]; quoted in Shaeffer, p. 102.

101. Ibid.

102. L, to F. P. Church, June 4, 1866 (NYPL-C).

103. The payment for *Waiting* is cited in Langford, p. 49.

104. L, to William and F. P. Church, November 1, [1866] (NYPL-C).

105. L, June 4, [1867] (NYPL-C).

106. Ibid.

107. *Waiting for the Verdict* (1867; reprint, Upper Saddle River, NJ: Gregg, 1968), 309–10. Subsequent references are in the text.

108. RHD had followed DeForest's career for some years; in the early 1860s she had written to Annie Fields about a story appearing in the *Atlantic* that she felt was "marvelously well done—especially in the Deforest style—wasn't it? Several persons won't be persuaded that it is not all true . . ." (undated L, perhaps late 1863 [UV]).

109. *Nation*, Nov. 21, 1867, p. 410.

110. L from Stowe, January 13, [1869?] (UV).

111. Dodge's L to James, August 12, 1864, *Gail Hamilton's Life in Letters*, 1: 433. On the other hand, Louisa May Alcott had a personally demeaning experience with James. In January 1865, when she was well known for *Hospital Sketches*, she met the Henry Jameses in Boston. While James Senior treated her appreciatively, she noted, "Henry Jr. wrote a note of 'Moods' for the 'North American,' and was very friendly. Being a literary youth he gave me advice, as if he had been eighty and I a girl"; she was thirty-one at the time—he was twenty-two (Ednah D. Cheney, *Louisa May Alcott* [1889; reprint, New York: Chelsea House, 1980], 165).

112. "Literature of the Day," *Lippincott's* 1 (Jan. 1868): 118.

113. L, May 10, n.y. (UI; transcript Duke).

114. Charvat, *Profession of Authorship*, pp. 300–301.

115. *Bits*, p. 125.

116. *Bits*, p. 123.

117. *Bits*, p. 136.

118. L, to James Fields, November 26, n.y. (UV).

119. *Gail Hamilton's Life in Letters*, 1: 606–7.

120. Ibid.

121. L, to Annie Fields, March 1, [1867] (UV); written prior to RHD's breach with the *Atlantic*.

122. Ibid.

123. *Life and Letters of William Dean Howells*, 1: 124.

124. L, March 1, [1867] (UV).

125. L, to Annie Fields, July 1, probably 1868 (UV).

126. *Dallas Galbraith* (Philadelphia: Lippincott, 1868), 5. Subsequent references are in the text.

127. *The National Baptist* and the *Philadelphia Evening Bulletin*, respectively.

128. *Nation*, Oct. 22, 1868, p. 331.

129. Quoted in Alfred Habegger's *Gender, Fantasy, and Realism in American Literature* (New York: Columbia University Press, 1982), 263.

130. Ibid.

131. *Nation*, p. 330.

132. *Nation*, p. 331.

133. Quoted in *Lippincott's* 2 (Nov. 1868): 3.

134. *Local Color*, pp. 27–28.

135. This series ran in the *Atlantic* from November 1868 through March 1869.

136. " 'In the Market,' " *Peterson's* 53 (Jan. 1868): 49. Subsequent references are in the text.

137. "Boheme," as one who is free and easy; a bohemian.

138. The issue of an overabundance of women seeking teaching positions is another astute insight by RHD, much like her attention to immigration trends, manufacturing practices, and the realities of war—that is, she "reads" America's, and especially women's, economic situation with a clear vision. Following the Civil War, teaching had been a viable and reputable career for many young women, and some women were able to move into administrative positions within the educational system. But since teaching constituted one of the few acceptable careers for women, schools were soon turning out far more women than the number of positions available. It has been estimated that, by mid-century, in Massachusetts alone one woman in every five taught school at some point during her life. Even in the early period of women entering that profession, they were paid only about 60 percent of what male teachers received, and by mid-century, when teaching had become a "woman's career," salaries decreased. See Clinton, pp. 121–46.

139. L from Stowe, January 31 [1869].

140. "Men's Rights," *Putnam's Magazine* 3 (Feb. 1869): 212–24; subsequent references are in the text.

141. Mary Kelley, *Private Women, Public Stage* (New York: Oxford, 1984).

142. *Bits*, p. 30.

143. RHD scholarship has traditionally suggested 1869 as the year she began her association with the *Tribune*; however, correspondence between RHD and John Russell Young, her first editor at the *Tribune*, indicates that Young began pursuing RHD as a contributor as early as 1866. On New Year's Day 1867 she agreed to open discussions on this possibility; several items by her appeared from mid-1867 through 1868. In the following year, she became a regular contributor to the newspaper. (John Russell Young Papers, Library of Congress.)

144. L, to Annie Fields, September 9, probably pre-1868 (UV).

Chapter Four: Women of Confidence and Confidence-Men

1. L, January 13, 1870 (HH).

2. Ibid.

3. L. Clarke Davis, "A Moderne Lettre de Cachet, *Atlantic Monthly* 21 (May 1868): 602.

4. L, to "My dear Sir," probably RHD's friend, the poet Paul Hamilton Hayne, May 10, [1869?] (UI).

5. Ibid.

6. *Peterson's* 57 (Jun. 1870): 472. RHD's anonymity was maintained as usual, but to such an extent that Peterson referred to the author of this novel in the generic masculine.

7. Ibid.

8. "Put Out of the Way," *Peterson's* 57 (May 1870): 440; subsequent references will appear in the text.

9. "Two Women," *Galaxy Magazine* 9 (Jun. 1870): 802; subsequent references will appear in the text.

10. Quoted in L, to Annie Fields, July 19, [1870] (UV).

11. L, May 13 [23?], 1872 (UV).

12. L, September 11, [1870] (UV).

13. *New York Daily Tribune*, Jan. 3, 1870, p. 1.

14. *Nation*, Jul. 1, 1886, p. 14; this and subsequent reviews appeared after the book form of *Natasqua* was published.

15. *The Independent* 38 (Jun. 3, 1886): 12.

16. *Bits*, p. 221.

17. *Putnam's Magazine* (May 1870): 617.

18. Ibid.

19. *Putnam's*, pp. 618–19.

20. L, to Annie Fields, December 22, [1870] (UV).

21. L, October 28, [1873] (PU-D).

22. L, April 15, [1874] (HHU).

23. Ibid.

24. *Scribner's Monthly* (Nov. 1873).

25. Quoted in Hart, *Companion*, p. 737.

26. As noted below, similar trends also occurred in other major literary journals of the period, challenging the assumption that women writers dominated the pages of American periodicals and thus limited male contributors' opportunities for publication.

27. Rossiter Johnson, ed., *Little Classics: Childhood*, vol. 10 (Boston: Houghton Mifflin, 1875).

28. In previous years, RHD had rendered her unfavorable verdict on "this Ouida school and style." It was, she concluded, "wearisome" and encouraged imitative writings such as "Joaquim Miller's noisy effort," which she had just read and felt "little prepared by the English critiques for this hodge-podge of Alexander Smith, Byron, and Swinburne" (L, to Annie Fields, dated only "September 16" [UV]).

29. This story was reprinted in RHD's short-story collection, *Silhouettes of American Life* (New York: Charles Scribner's Sons, 1892; reprint New York: Garrett, 1968); for scholars' convenience, the Garrett Press edition is cited in the text hereafter.

30. *Kitty's Choice: A Story of Berrytown, and Other Stories* (Philadelphia: Lippincott, 1876), 4; subsequent references are in the text. The other stories in the collection were "The Balacchi Brothers," a continuation of RHD's defense of theater people, focusing this time on attitudes toward male participants; and "Leonard Heath's Fortune."

31. Quoted in *National Cyclopedia of American Biography* (New York: James T. White & Co., 1924), 8:177. This is not unlike RHD's praise of Hawthorne: "He belonged to no tribe" (see chap. 2).

32. I do not think too close a link should be drawn between Jenny Derby and Louisa May Alcott, but RHD had followed Alcott's life through its travails and successes for more than fifteen years; she may have drawn on that knowledge to shape certain aspects of her character's life.

33. "Earthen Pitchers," *Scribner's Monthly* 7 (Nov. 1873–Apr. 1874): 75. Subsequent references are in the text.

34. This had been RHD's opinion of Bronson Alcott when she met him in 1862. At that time, he had not yet published any of his accumulated folios, and RHD described him as a "vague, would-be prophet" whose lack of example did not hinder his reputation (*Bits* 43). Emerson had told RHD that he once asked Alcott " 'what he would do when he came to the gate, and St. Peter demanded his ticket. "What have you to show to justify your right to live?" I said. "Where is your book, your picture? You have done nothing in the world." "No," he said, "but somewhere on a hill up there will be Plato and Paul and Socrates talking, and they will say: 'Send Alcott over here, we want him with us.' " 'And,' said Emerson, gravely shaking his head, 'he was right! Alcott was right' " (*Bits* 37).

35. Olsen, p. 146.

36. George Arthur Dunlap, *The City in the American Novel—1789–1900* (New York: Russell & Russell, 1962), 155–56.

37. Ibid.

38. Gordon Milne, *The American Political Novel* (Norman: University of Oklahoma Press, 1966), 30.

39. Henry James asserted in 1898 that the American business tycoon had been avoided as a subject by American novelists; his vision of the tycoon, however, was "an epic hero, seamed all over with the wounds of the market and the dangers of the field, launched into action and passion by the immensity and complexity of the general struggle . . . driven above all by the extraordinary, the unique relation in which he for the most part stands to the life of his lawful, his immitigable womankind" (quoted in Warner Berthoff, *The Ferment of Realism* [Cambridge: Cambridge University Press, 1965], 36). James was familiar with RHD's fiction, of course; but his vision, as detailed here, is of the business tycoon as heroic. RHD had a quite different vision.

40. Several major newspapers were also involved in this process of exposure. I focus upon the *Tribune*'s process since it was the one in which RHD was involved.

41. *New York Daily Tribune*, Jan. 21, 1870, p. 3.

42. Ibid.

43. Quoted in the *Tribune*, Jan. 6, 1871, p. 4. RHD was not an admirer of Greeley, although she was wise enough to couch her criticism in a seemingly balanced assessment. She had first met him as a young girl, when he was at his height of fame: "Every man in the town took the New York 'Tribune' and accepted it as gospel, and Horace Greeley was believed to write the whole of it, down to the death notices" (*Bits* 181). Years later, as a member of the *Tribune*'s editorial staff, she knew how many people contributed to its publication and felt no awe for Greeley's "absurd and childish doings," though she suggested that, undoubtedly, "great and sincere was the soul beneath them" (182–83).

44. *New York Daily Tribune*, Jan. 19, 1870, p. 1.

45. *The Rise of Silas Lapham* was published by Ticknor and Company in 1885. It is interesting to note that in a review of Howells's novel, the reviewer asserts that Howells is "on the point of discovering the secret of the best novelists," suggesting he has not quite attained that level; nor is Howells considered a full-fledged realist at this time since he remains "unabashed by the difficulties and dangers which beset the realistic writer" (*Lippincott's* 36 [Oct. 1885]: 421–22). Though today *Lapham* is still typically discussed as the first "major" text in the "rise of realism," a return of scholarly attention to the opinions of the day not only challenges that assumption but reveals that writers of realism were well established as a point of reference against which *Lapham* could be compared. Indeed, the review ends with a wish to see Howells expand his talents in that direction.

46. *John Andross* (New York: Orange Judd, 1874), 27; subsequent references are in the text. This novel had been serialized in *Hearth and Home* (Dec. 13, 1873–May 2, 1874) before publication in book form.

47. *The American Scene* (Bloomington: Indiana University Press, 1968), 342–52.

48. *Nation*, May 21, 1874, pp. 336–37.

49. Ibid.

50. *Atlantic Monthly* 34 (Jul. 1874): 115.

51. *Harper's New Monthly* 49 (Jul. 1874): 290.

52. Shaeffer, pp. 240–41.

53. Letter to "My dear sir," probably RHD's friend, Paul Hamilton Hayne, May 10, [1869?] (UI).

54. *New York Daily Tribune*, May 23, 1876, p. 6.

55. "Old Philadelphia," *Harper's New Monthly* 52 (Apr.–May 1876): 709; subsequent references are in the text.

56. *Life in the Iron Mills and Other Stories*, pp. 146–47.

57. For a discussion of the fund raising, and the benefits and difficulties to the City of Philadelphia as a consequence of housing the centennial, see Dorothy Gondos Beers's essay, "The Centennial City 1865–1876," in Weigley, pp. 460–70.

58. *The Incorporation of America*, p. 41.

59. Ibid.; Trachtenberg is, of course, concerned with the ironies of this image of progress, as his discussion in the following pages, and indeed in his entire study, indicates.

60. Quoted in Clinton, p. 184.

61. L, November 6, [1876] (UV).

62. *Bits*, p. 101.

63. My discussion of these preliminary movements is informed by Clinton's chapter on "Organization and Resistance"; *Feminism: The Essential Historical Documents*, ed. Miriam Schneir (New York: Vintage, 1972); and Keith Melder's *Beginnings of Sisterhood* (New York: Schocken, 1977).

64. "Mesmerism vs. Common Sense," *Peterson's* 80 (Jul. 1881): 52–57.

65. Quoted in Olsen, p. 148.

66. Quoted in Langford, p. 64. Langford suggests this was probably just boyish posturing; though, after the fact, Richard's language may seem dramatic, I see no reason to doubt the sincerity of his feelings at the time.

67. Ibid.

68. RHD saw this at first-hand. In Philadelphia from the late 1860s through the 1870s, the Republicans controlled the city's highly corrupt political system. It was not until 1887 that the Gas Ring, controlled by Philadelphia's most powerful political boss, "King" James McManes, was dissolved. (McManes may have been a source, in addition to William Tweed, for RHD's character study of the political boss in *John Andross*.)

69. *A Law Unto Herself* (Philadelphia: Lippincott, 1878), 3; subsequent references are in the body of the text. *Law* had been serialized in *Lippincott's Magazine* 2 (Jul.–Dec. 1877): 39–49, 167–82, 292–308, 464–78, 614–28, 719–31.

70. Karen Halttunen, *Confidence Men and Painted Women* (New Haven, CT: Yale University Press, 1982), 1–32.

71. This is the same term that Hawthorne used to define Pearl Prynne's sense of herself in the chapter entitled "The Leech and His Patient": Pearl is "like a creature that had nothing in common with a bygone and buried generation. . . . It was as if she had been made afresh, out of new elements, and must perforce be permitted to live her own life, and be a law unto herself, without her eccentricities being reckoned to her for a crime." In the conclusion of *The Scarlet Letter*, however, Pearl escapes the confines of the Puritan community, goes to Europe, and marries a wealthy man. RHD's character simulates this requisite closure of the romance, but with significant differences that challenge the romance perspective.

72. Langford, p. 28.

73. *Kitty's Choice*, p. 35.

74. L, August 13, [1879?] (UV).

75. Ibid.

Chapter Five: Across the Gulf

1. Quoted in Langford, p. 70.

2. L, dated only "Oct. 19" (NYPL-A).

3. L, dated only "September sixth"; I designate it as from this period because there was no other time, until the last years of her life, when RHD was not working on a novel. The handwriting of the letter also supports the 1880s date.

4. RHD briefly critiques Cable's novel in her 1887 study, "Here and There in the South" (see below). In 1884 Richard also published a parody of Cable's style in *Life*.

5. "Walhalla," *Scribner's Monthly* 20 (May 1880): 139–45; reprinted in *Silhouettes*, pp. 46–66.

6. In arriving at these statistics, I have excluded the accounts of the "Battles and Leaders of the Civil War" that ran from late 1884 for several years, since these accounts of the war would historically be almost exclusively by male contributors. The journal ran from 25 to 30 such accounts per issue during the mid-1880s, and only rarely was a woman's account printed. Had I included this segment of the periodical in my statistics of non-poetic works, the domination of the category by male authors would have been much higher than the recorded 83 percent.

7. Donovan, *Local Color*, p. 5.

8. See Clinton, chap. 7, "Pathbreaking and Backlash."

9. L, March 20, 1878 (PML).

10. Ibid.

11. "Across the Gulf," *Lippincott's Magazine* 27 (Jul. 1881): 59–71; reprinted in *Silhouettes*, pp. 111–44; subsequent references from the latter are in the text.

12. Hart, p. 404.

13. L, February 22, 1882 (NYPL-A).

14. "A Day in Tadousac," *Our Continent* 1 (Feb. 15, 1882), 6–7.

15. *Bits*, pp. 214–15; subsequent references are in the text.

16. See Whitman's comments at the end of this chapter.

17. Subsequent references from "A Wayside Episode" (*Lippincott's Magazine* 31 [Feb. 1883]: 179–90) in *Silhouettes*, pp. 145–71, are in the text.

18. Mr. Franciscus is called "Miss Fanny," traditionally a homosexual rubric, by the younger people in their social circle. It is the only place in RHD's fiction in which such sexual preferences are suggested, although the fact that so many of her female characters use "male" nicknames raises gender issues far beyond the scope of this study.

19. See the discussion below of "Are Women to Blame?" for RHD's nonfiction comments on marriage as a partnership.

20. Langford, p. 77.

21. Langford, p. 86. One ironic aspect of these years of Richard's apprentice-ship was his association with the Bethlehem Steel magnate, William W. Thurston. He summered in Cuba with the Thurstons and gained entrance into upper-class society through their acquaintance. Considering RHD's lifelong antipathy toward capitalists, her silence about this association indicates an extraordinary maternal reticence, trusting that Richard's upbringing would serve him best. The irony is deepened when we realize that the Cuban trip was instigated because of Thurston's interest in the *iron mines* in Santiago de Cuba.

22. Ibid.

23. Quoted in C. B. Davis, pp. 33–34.

24. In a memorial statement published after Clarke's death, a friend asserted that Clarke "had only contempt" for the school of realism (quoted in Langford, p. 58). Clarke was probably referring to naturalists such as Zola and Dreiser, but his preferences always leaned toward romance literature.

25. Quoted in C. B. Davis, pp. 34–35.

26. Hart, p. 18.

27. L, August 20, [1885] (BE-G).

28. "Some Testimony in the Case," *Atlantic Monthly* 56 (Nov. 1885): 602; sub-sequent references are in the text. A handwritten version of this article survives (BE-G).

29. Clinton, p. 112.

30. Weigley, *Philadelphia*, p. 492.

31. L, to Daniel Ford, editor of *Youth's Companion*, dated only "Dec. 19" (NYPL-A).

32. The text is the fourteenth annual report of the Massachusetts Bureau of Statistics of Labor (1883), quoted in *Feminism: The Essential Historical Writings*, ed. Miriam Schneir (New York: Vintage, 1972), 57.

33. See chap. 4 for a discussion of the critical reviews of *Natasqua*.

34. L, dated February 8, 1886 (NYPL-A). One wonders, of course, if this was *the* Miss Dickinson, who died in May of 1886. Unfortunately, the original letter requesting RHD's photograph has not survived. Dickinson certainly knew RHD's work (see chap. 1), which often appeared in the same periodicals as those of Dick-inson's friend, Thomas Wentworth Higginson. Josiah Holland and Helen Hunt Jackson were known by both women, too; but no further identification of "Miss Dickinson" is possible.

35. L, to Harper & Brothers, dated only "Oct. 2" (PML).

36. Undated L, c. 1886 (UV).

37. L, dated only "March fourth" (Duke).

38. Fragment of L to Cooke (CHS).

39. "Tirar y Soult," *Scribner's Monthly* 2 (Nov. 1887): 563–72, reprinted in *Sil-houettes*, pp. 21–45; subsequent references to the latter are in the text.

40. "Anne," in *Life in the Iron Mills and Other Stories*, pp. 224–42; subsequent references are in the text.

41. "Anne" is, of course, a derivative of "Nancy"; but RHD uses the nickname to suggest the split personality.

42. "Are Women to Blame?" *North American Review* 148 (May 1889): 622–42; subsequent references are in the text.

43. Shaeffer, pp. 271ff.

44. *The Independent*, Dec. 30, 1880, p. 1.

45. *The Independent*, Jan. 5, 1882, pp. 26–27.

46. For a study of the rise of public transportation in Philadelphia, see Nathaniel Burt and Wallace E. Davies's essay, "The Iron Age 1876–1905," in Weigley, pp. 471–523.

47. RHD's fiction for *The Independent* was always minor in quality; her significant contributions were her sociopolitical commentaries.

48. "Our Creditors," *The Independent* 41, Jan. 3, 1889, p. 1.

49. *The Independent*, Feb. 28, 1889, p. 1.

50. "The Plague Spot of America," *The Independent*, Jul. 4, 1889, p. 1; "At Our Gates," *The Independent*, April 11, 1889, p. 3.

51. "Some Significant Facts," *The Independent*, June 13, 1889, p. 1.

52. Clinton, pp. 116–19.

53. *The Independent*, Nov. 21, 1889, p. 1.

54. Quoted in Trachtenberg, p. 78.

55. *The Independent*, Aug. 15, 1889, p. 1.

56. *The Independent*, Nov. 8, 1888, p. 1.

57. Quoted in Langford, pp. 91–92.

58. William Dean Howells, *Editor's Study*, ed. James W. Simpson (Troy, NY: Whitston, 1983), 66.

Chapter Six: The Decadence of a Race

1. See, for instance, Langford and Olsen; a notable earlier exception was Shaeffer, RHD's earliest biographer.

2. William James's classic study presented the development of psychological knowledge in America to this time. RHD had used the term "psychologist" as early as 1861 in "Life" and had composed works of psychological realism over the subsequent three decades; she was keenly perceptive about issues of human motivation and free will.

3. Subsequent references to "An Ignoble Martyr" (*Harper's New Monthly* 80 [Mar. 1890]: 604–10) in *Silhouettes*, pp. 92–110, are in the text.

4. It was only in her early sentimental fiction for *Peterson's* that RHD suggested a value to martyrdom and then with limitations. In "One of Life's Martyrs" (*Peterson's* 54 [Oct. 1868]: 282–90), for instance, John Lennox's life was devoted to the care of others and thus he is depicted as having a worthwhile purpose in his otherwise tragic martyrdom.

5. The term is Thoreau's. I am indebted to Buell's discussion of this motif, pp. 345–46. While *The Scarlet Letter* is, as Buell suggests, an anachronism in some ways in the tradition, I intentionally include it to suggest that even within distinctive approaches the theme is pervasive.

6. L, March 10, probably 1890 (BC).

7. L, dated only "April 27" (HHU).

8. Undated L, on Harper & Brothers' letterhead (UV), probably 1892, when RHD published *Silhouettes* and Richard published *Van Bibber and Other Stories*.

9. L, dated on August 5, from Point Pleasant (NYPL-CC).

10. *The Critic*, Feb. 4, 1893, p. 61.

11. Helen Gray Cone, "Woman in American Literature," *Century Magazine* (Oct. 1890): 921; subsequent references are in the text.

12. L, March 15, probably 1890 (BE).

13. L, March 18, 1892 (UP).

14. At one point after the publication of *Kent Hampden*, RHD observed that Ford had offered her "a huge price" for a boy's story for *Youth's Companion* (L, dated only "Jan. 15th" [PU-M]).

15. L, April 2, 1891 (PU-D).

16. L, dated only "Feb. 19" (NYPL-CC).

17. I have been unable to identify this woman further.

18. L, dated only "April 18" (HHU).

19. Subsequent references from the Garrett Press edition are in the text.

20. See Richard Cary, *Mary N. Murfree* (TUSAS 121. New York: Twayne, 1967), 21–22.

21. Shaeffer, pp. 307–8.

22. "Marcia" has recently been reprinted in *Legacy* (Sp 1987), with an introduction by Jean Pfaelzer. Pfaelzer accurately notes that in this story RHD "challenges the rationalization that the family promises women a refuge from economic and worldly tensions" (4). However, Pfaelzer asserts that "Marcia" is a sentimental story; I would argue that *Marcia's* writings are sentimental, not Davis's. Other comments of this decade suggest RHD's move away from sentimentalism at this juncture in her professional life, as detailed below.

23. *The Independent*, Aug. 15, 1889, p. 1.

24. *The Critic*, Feb. 4, 1893, p. 61.

25. *The Independent*, Nov. 3, 1892, p. 23.

26. *The Nation*, Oct. 6, 1892, p. 262.

27. Undated L, [1893] (UV).

28. "A Grumble," *Peterson's* 103 (Jan. 1863): 103; subsequent references are in the text.

29. The exception, of course, is always Nora. RHD refused to "market" her daughter, but she had so long advocated the need for young women to learn a trade for their own self-sufficiency that one can only wonder if Nora was thus educated; no record is extant. She apparently chose not to turn to writing as a vocation, as every other member of her family had. Perhaps this in itself was her act of independence.

30. Langford, pp. 148–49. Langford attempts to downplay Richard's depression, but it was a chronic ailment that plagued him throughout his adult life.

31. L, March 28, 1894 (HH).

32. L, June 16, 1894 (BC).

33. Undated L (BC).

34. L, dated only "Dec 6" (BC).

35. L, September 15, [1894], from Marion, MA (BC).

36. L, dated only "Sept 20" (BC).

37. L, November 3 (BC).

38. RHD's correspondence with her editor at *The World*, Mr. Moffatt, is housed at the Huntington Library.

39. *The Congregationalist*, Apr. 12, 1894, p. 524.

40. Subsequent references to "In the Gray Cabins of New England" (*Century Magazine* 49 [Feb. 1895]: 620–23) are in the text.

41. Langford, p. 163.

42. Downey, p. 309.

43. Burt and Davies, pp. 520–23; see also Larzer Ziff, *The American 1890s* (New York: Viking, 1966).

44. Shaeffer dates RHD's vacation in Europe as the summer of 1891; however, I agree with Langford that the correct date is 1895.

45. Langford, p. 149. Tillie Olsen has depicted RHD as a reclusive, humbled writer in her later years, asserting that from the mid-1870s until her death RHD "went almost nowhere" (146–47). In fact, RHD had a wide circle of friends in Philadelphia with whom she socialized, many of whom were in the literary field; and, in addition to the family summers at Point Pleasant, New Jersey, and Marion, Massachusetts, RHD traveled to North Carolina in 1874 and Alabama in 1884 to gather materials for her writing, as well as vacationing in Warm Springs, Virginia— all prior to her trip to Europe in 1895. She also visited Richard in New York City several times during the decade. RHD led an active and full life until her health failed in her final years.

46. RHD and Richard were less enamored of Cleveland than Clarke. RHD was vocal in her criticisms of Cleveland's policies; in "The Death of John Payne" (*The Independent* 50 [Jul. 28, 1898]: 241–49), for instance, one character discusses the tremendous burden of the national debt upon American citizens due to "Cleveland's loans."

47. Quoted in Langford, p. 161.

48. *The Critic*, Oct. 26, 1895, p. 271.

49. *The Critic*, Nov. 2, 1895, p. 285.

50. Rates for comparable works of the period are difficult to ascertain, but it is interesting to compare these rates with Edith Wharton's publication of *The House of Mirth* a few years later. For *Mirth*, Wharton received a flat fee of five thousand dollars and a royalty of fifteen percent of the list price; by the time Wharton published *The Age of Innocence* in 1920, she received eighteen thousand dollars for serial rights alone (R. W. B. Lewis, *Edith Wharton* [New York: Fromm, 1975]).

51. *Doctor Warrick's Daughters* (New York: Harper and Brothers, 1896), 1; subsequent references are in the text.

52. Austin, "Success," pp. 47–48; however, Austin echoes the typical—and, as I have asserted throughout, to my mind, erroneous—claim that RHD "had made her compromise with the sixties, and although she continued to write about as well as she began, she did not progress." If RHD is judged even as having maintained the stature of her writing of the sixties, her reputation will be secure, although much will be lost by ignoring her later work.

53. *Nation*, Jun. 11, 1896, p. 459.

54. *Frances Waldeaux* (New York: Harper and Brothers, 1897), 71; subsequent references are in the text.

55. Review quoted on recto of title page to *Waldeaux*.

56. *The Critic*, Apr. 10, 1897, p. 251.

57. Ibid.

58. L, June 17, [1897] (PU-D).

59. L, dated only "August 16" from Warm Springs (BC).

60. "Women in Literature," *The Independent* 43 (May 7, 1891): 1; subsequent references are in the text.

61. Subsequent references to "The Work Before Us" (*The Independent* 51 [Jan. 19, 1899]: 177–79) are in the text.

62. The phrase is taken from Nigerian author Chinua Achebe's 1960 novel of that title and theme.

63. "Alien Brothers," *The Independent* 44 (Jul. 7, 1892): 7; subsequent references are in the text.

64. "Two Points of View," *The Independent* 49 (Sep. 9, 1897): 2; subsequent references are in the text.

65. "Two Methods With the Negro," *The Independent* 50 (Mar. 31, 1898): 1; subsequent references are in the text.

66. Quoted in Langford, p. 135.

67. Subsequent references to "The Mean Face of War" (*The Independent* 51 [Jul. 20, 1899]: 1931–33) are in the text.

68. Ellison's remarks are part of her review of Stanley Karnow's seminal study of the history of American involvement in the Philippines, *In Our Image* (New York: Random House, 1989); Ellison's review appeared in the *Philadelphia Inquirer*, May 7, 1989, pp. 1G, 4G.

69. Undated L (CU).

70. Paine is probably best remembered today for his play, *The Great White Way* (1901), which became the popular designation for New York City's theater district.

71. L, dated only "January 8th"; handwriting suggests late 1890s (HH).

Chapter Seven: The Coming of the Night

1. Subsequent references to "Under the Old Code" (*Harper's New Monthly* 100 [Feb. 1900]: 401–12), from the reprint in *Bits*, pp. 65–83, are in the text.

2. RHD's final pre-publication of a segment of her autobiography was "The Old Black Teapot," *The Independent* 55 (Apr. 30, 1903): 1029–31.

3. "Two American Boys," *The Independent* 52 (Oct. 4, 1900): 2375.

4. *The Independent*, May 30, 1901, p. 1231.

5. "On the Jersey Coast," *The Independent* 52 (Nov. 15, 1900): 2731–33.

6. "An Unwritten History," *The Independent* 52 (Dec. 27, 1900): 3082–85; subsequent references are in the text.

7. "Lord Kitchener's Methods," *The Independent* 53 (Feb. 7, 1901): 326–28; subsequent references are in the text.

8. C. B. Davis, *Adventures*, p. 293.

9. "The Coming of the Night," *Scribner's Monthly* 45 (Jan. 1909): 68.

10. "An Unlighted Lamp," *The Independent* 53 (Aug. 15, 1901): 1903–08; subsequent references are in the text. Most notable among contemporary studies of this phenomena is Rachel Bowlby's *Just Looking* (New York: Methuen, 1985).

11. Halttunen, p. 165. Halttunen's entire chapter on "Parlor Theatricals" (153–90) and their pervasiveness in all aspects of American life is especially pertinent to latter-day consequences such as RHD predicts.

12. "Is It All for Nothing?" *The Independent* 53 (Oct. 14, 1901): 2513–14; subsequent references are in the text.

13. "The 'Black North,' " *The Independent* 54 (Feb. 6, 1902): 338; subsequent references are in the text.

14. *The Independent*, Jun. 19, 1902, pp. 1457–60.

15. Undated L, probably 1907 (UV).

16. "Country Girls in Town," *The Independent* 54 (Jul. 17, 1902): 1691.

17. Langford, p. 231.

18. "What Does It Mean?" *The Independent* 54 (Aug. 21, 1902): 2011–13.

19. "In Remembrance," *The Independent* 55 (Jan. 29, 1903): 238; subsequent references are in the text.

20. L, from Philadelphia, September 1903; quoted in C. B. Davis, *Adventures*, pp. 295–96.

21. For instance, see "Lost," *The Independent* 55 (Jun. 25, 1903): 1504–07; and "The Woman's Word About It," *The Independent* 55 (Dec. 3, 1903): 2848–52.

22. "An Old-Time Christmas," *The Independent* 55 (Dec. 24, 1903): 3031.

23. As Lawrence Buell has observed, this form of documentary realism, which blends a collage of memories with "yarn spinning," extends, in some degree, back to Stowe's *Old Town Folks* (294–95).

24. *Congregationalist* 87 (Jun. 1902): 854; subsequent references are in the text.

25. L, August 1909 (UV).

26. *Nation*, Dec. 22, 1904, pp. 505–6; subsequent references are in the text.

27. Shaeffer, p. 330.

28. "Some Human Reminiscences," *The Dial*, Nov. 16, 1904, p. 303; subsequent references are in the text.

29. Shaeffer, p. 331; subsequent references to Shaeffer's book are in the text.

30. Langford, p. 246.

31. Quoted in Shaeffer, p. 333.

32. See L, dated only "Friday," possibly 1904 (UV).

33. Undated L (UV). The Davises used nicknames as signs of affection; in addition to the private names that Rebecca and Clarke had for each other, the children were "Hardy" (Richard), "Gus" (Charles), and "Noll" (Nora).

34. "The Recovery of Family Life," *The Independent* 59 (Sep. 21, 1905): 674; subsequent references are in the text.

35. "Jane Murray's Thanksgiving," *The Independent* 59 (Nov. 30, 1905): 1268; subsequent references are in the text.

36. "The Curse in Education," *North American Review* 168 (May 1899): 614; subsequent references are in the text.

37. L, June 11, [1905] (BC).

38. L, June 18, [1905] (BC).

39. "An American Family," *The Independent* (March 15, 1906).

40. "Undistinguished Americans," *The Independent* 60 (Apr. 16, 1906): 962; subsequent references are in the text.

41. L, dated only "May 1st" (UV).

42. Langford, p. 251.

43. Quoted in Shaeffer, pp. 331–32.

44. Undated Ls (UV).

45. I am indebted to Shaeffer's biography for the details of Hugh Wilson Harding's life (334).

46. L, postmarked March 21, 1907 (UV).

47. L, dated only "March 23" (UV).

48. See, for instance, note 31 above and L dated only "Sunday the 14th" (UV).

49. The latter concludes an undated L to Richard (UV).

50. Undated L, (UV).

51. L, February 18, [1907] (UV).

52. Undated L, to Richard in London (UV).

53. Quoted in C. B. Davis, *Adventures*, p. 270; subsequent references to quotations from this source are in the text.

54. Undated L, (UV).

55. L, dated only "Monday" (UV).

56. Ibid.

57. "One Woman's Question," *The Independent* 63 (Jul. 18, 1907): 132; subsequent references are in the text.

58. L, dated only "Sunday" (UV).

59. Undated L, to Richard (UV).

60. L, from Richard, July 9, [1908] (UV).

61. The details of RHD's business actions during this year are drawn from Shaeffer's study (341–42).

62. "The Coming of the Night," p. 68.

63. L, from Richard, January 14, 1909 (UV).

64. L, dated only "Monday" (UV).

65. L, from Richard, April 6, 1909 (UV).

66. Ls, from Richard, September 14, 15, 25, and 26, 1909 (UV).

67. RHD's estate totaled $50,000. The enormous difference between her personal worth and Clarke's was due in part to the property she had inherited from her mother and eldest brother, but it is also a testament to her careful management of money after Clarke's death.

68. *Adventures*, p. 344.

69. Undated L, probably 1907 (UV).

70. Shaeffer, p. 343.

71. Langford, pp. 246–47.

72. This became the family plot. Richard was buried there in 1916, as was Charles ten years later. A fourth, unmarked grave is part of the grouping, but no record remains to identify the person who is buried there. It would be painfully

ironic if it were Nora; however, since she married one year after her mother's death, she was, hopefully, buried with her husband and with a more suitable inscription than her mother received.

73. Quoted in Olsen, p. 153.

74. Quoted in C. B. Davis, *Adventures*, p. 312.

75. In a letter dated February 12, [1906?], to William Hayes Ward, RHD commented, "Why do you never come to Philadelphia? I know your son and daughter-in-law—Mrs. Phelps-Ward so well that I should know you" (BC).

76. *Century Magazine* n.s. 59 (Nov. 1910): 118; subsequent references are in the text.

Index

New York Female Reform Society, 100
New York Times, 307
Nichols, George, 66, 74, 96, 104, 320n
Norris, Frank, 6, 8, 10, 11, 30, 42, 44, 47, 70,
    152, 188, 197, 214, 258, 278, 284; *Mc-
    Teague*, 11, 30, 47, 214; *The Octopus*, 188,
    214; *The Pit*, 44, 70, 188, 214, 284
North American Review, 87, 117, 222, 229–30,
    242, 270, 295
Norton, Charles Eliot, 87, 117, 229
"Notes of a Walker." *See* Burroughs, John
Novels, Readers, and Reviewers. See Baym,
    Nina

O'Brien, Fitz James, 125
The Octopus. See Norris, Frank
Ohio River, 21, 78
Old Chester Tales. See Deland, Margaret
    Wade Campbell
The Old South. See Page, Thomas Nelson
Old Town Folks. See Stowe, Harriet Beecher
Olsen, Tillie, 2, 3, 4, 27, 76, 109, 182, 192,
    314n, 333n, 335n
On Democracy. See Lowell, James Russell
Orange Judd, Publishers, 185
Osgood and Company, Publishers, 211
"Ouida." *See* Ramée, Louise de la
Our Continent, 211
"Our Summer's Outing." *See* Field, Kate
"The Over-Soul." *See* Emerson, Ralph
    Waldo
Owen, Catherine, 231

Page, Thomas Nelson, 250; *The Old South*,
    250
Paine, Albert Bigelow, 276–77, 336n; *The
    Great White Way*, 336n
Parker, Theodore, 99
Parkman, Francis, 15
Parthenia. See Lee, Eliza B.
Peabody, Elizabeth, 89, 128, 289
The Pearl of Orr's Island. See Stowe, Harriet
    Beecher
Peirce, Melusina Fay, 143–44
Penn, William, 154, 168, 191, 238–39, 265
Pennsylvania Hospital for the Insane, 154
Peterson, Charles J., 72, 106, 254, 290
Peterson's Magazine, 71–73, 99, 122, 125–26,
    131, 139, 143, 152, 154, 156, 165, 167, 197,

209, 210, 242, 253–55, 333n. *See also New
    Peterson Magazine*
Pfaelzer, Jean, 3, 334n
Phelps (Ward), Elizabeth Stuart, 5, 7, 8, 10,
    42, 83, 94, 105–6, 118, 162, 164, 168, 196,
    207, 211, 246, 247, 258, 272, 307–8, 319n,
    339n; "At Bay," 105–6, 118; "The Com-
    rades," 318n; "Stories That Stay," 307–8
Philadelphia Centennial Exposition, 192–94
Philadelphia Evening Bulletin, 326n
Philadelphia Inquirer, 153, 307
Philadelphia Press, 142–43
The Philippines, 15, 275–76. *See also* Davis,
    "The Mean Face of War"
Phillips, Wendell, 79
"A Physician's Problems." *See* Elam, Dr.
The Picayune, 266
The Pit. See Norris, Frank
Pizer, Donald, 1, 47; *Realism and Natural-
    ism in Nineteenth-century American Lit-
    erature*, 1
Poe, Edgar Allan, 125, 155, 205, 254, 289–90
"A Poetess." *See* Freeman, Mary Wilkins
Point Pleasant, New Jersey. *See* Davis, resi-
    dences of
Poirier, Richard, 18
The Portrait of a Lady. See James, Henry, Jr.
Preble, Harriet, 23
Presbyterian Quarterly, 121
Prescott, Harriet Elizabeth. *See* Spofford,
    Harriet E. Prescott
Prescott, William Hickling, 15
The Prince and the Pauper. See Twain, Mark
The Princess Cassamassima. See James,
    Henry, Jr.
Principles of Psychology. See James, William
Pro Aris et Focis, 2–3, 4
Public Ledger, 255, 290, 293
Pudd'nhead Wilson. See Twain, Mark
"The Pursuit of Knowledge Under Difficul-
    ties." *See* Dodge, Mary Abigail
Putnam's, Publishers, 138
Putnam's Magazine, 139, 147–48, 152, 164–65

"Question of Monuments." *See* Howells,
    William Dean
Quinn, Arthur H., 9

"The Railroad and the People." *See* Dreiser,
    Theodore

This book has been set in Linotron Galliard. Galliard was designed for Mergenthaler in 1978 by Matthew Carter. Galliard retains many of the features of a sixteenth century typeface cut by Robert Granjon but has some modifications which gives it a more contemporary look.

Printed on acid-free paper.